Better Homes and Gardens®

Grill It!

SECRETS TO DELICIOUS FLAME-KISSED FOOD

WILEY
John Wiley & Sons, Inc.

This book is printed on acid-free paper. ♾

Published by John Wiley & Sons, Inc.,
Hoboken, New Jersey.

Published simultaneously in Canada.

Library of Congress Cataloging-in-Publication Data is available upon request.

ISBN 978-0-470-93277-3 (pbk); ISBN 978-0-470-94689-3 (ebk); ISBN 978-0-470-94690-9 (ebk); ISBN 978-0-470-94691-6 (ebk)

Printed in the United States of America

10 9 8 7 6 5 4 3 2 1

Meredith Corporation

Gayle Goodson Butler
Senior Vice President, Editor in Chief
Better Homes and Gardens® Magazine

Better Homes and Gardens® Grill It!

Editor: Jan Miller

Project Editor: Tricia Laning, Waterbury Publications, Inc.

Contributing Editor: Lisa Kingsley, Waterbury Publications, Inc.

Contributing Copy Editors: Terri Fredrickson, Gretchen Kauffman, Margaret Smith

Better Homes and Gardens Test Kitchen Director: Lynn Blanchard

Better Homes and Gardens Test Kitchen Home Economists: Elizabeth Burt, R. D.; Juliana Hale; Maryellyn Krantz; Jill Moberly; Colleen Weeden; Lori Wilson

Contributing Photographers: Jason Donnelly, Scott Little, Blaine Moats, Kritsada Panichgul

Contributing Food Stylists: Susan Draught, Jennifer Peterson, Janet Pittman, Charles Worthington, Main Dish Media, LLC —Sue Hoss, John Meyer, Lisa Siebenbrodt, Cinda Shambaugh

Prop Stylists: Carol Linnan,Sue Mitchell

Special Interest Media

Executive Food Editor: Jennifer Darling

Editorial Director: Gregory H. Kayko

John Wiley & Sons, Inc.

Publisher: Natalie Chapman

Associate Publisher: Jessica Goodman

Executive Editor: Anne Ficklen

Editor: Charleen Barila

Production Director: Diana Cisek

Production Manager: Michael Olivo

Senior Production Editor: Amy Zarkos

Manufacturing Manager: Tom Hyland

Design Director: Ken Carlson, Waterbury Publications, Inc.

Associate Design Director: Doug Samuelson, Waterbury Publications, Inc.

Production Assistants: Kim Hopkins, Mindy Samuelson, Waterbury Publications, Inc.

Better Homes and Gardens Test Kitchen

Our seal assures you that every recipe in *Grill It!* has been tested in the Better Homes and Gardens® Test Kitchen. This means that each recipe is practical and reliable and meets our high standards of taste appeal. We guarantee your satisfaction with this book for as long as you own it.

Contents

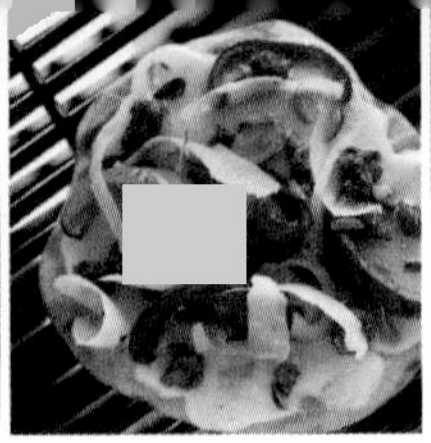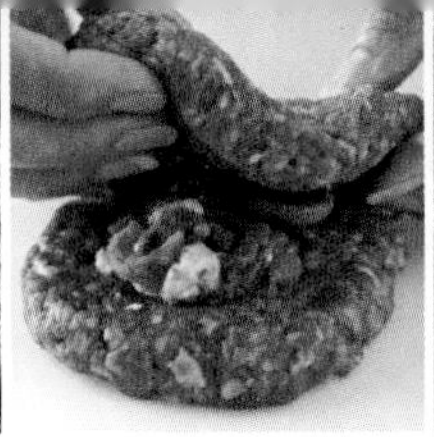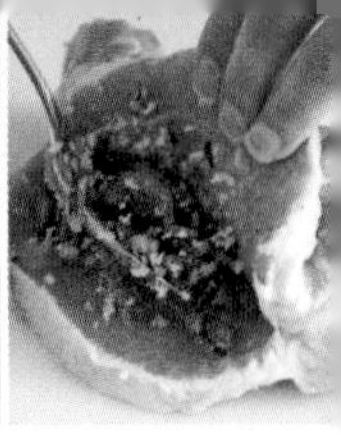

GET READY TO GET GRILLING.

THERE IS SOMETHING BOTH PRIMAL AND MAGICAL ABOUT THE EFFECT FIRE HAS ON FOOD—AND ON THOSE WHO GRILL, BARBECUE, AND SMOKE THEIR WAY TO culinary bliss. Holding a piece of meat over an open fire may have been the very first method of transforming food from raw to cooked—but this caveman-era technique hasn't lost its appeal in the modern world. In fact, it's only been made better through the use of new tools and equipment, flavoring methods, and access to a world of fresh and fabulous ingredients.

That's what *Grill It!* is all about—helping you coax the most flavor from the flame. The Grilling Basics section in the front of the book lays out everything you need to know to get started, including an examination of the types of grills, smokers, fuel, and tools available, how to control the heat, cooking methods, and safety—a necessity, of course, when you're playing with fire.

The recipes range from the traditional flavors of Kansas City, Memphis, Texas, and the Carolinas to American classics such as Spicy Buffalo Chicken Salad, Best-Ever Grilled Burgers, and Grilled Vegetable Pizzas to global flavors that include Indian-Spiced Leg of Lamb and Ginger-Lemongrass Chicken with Cilantro Rice Noodles. The Mix It Up! feature provides ingredient swap-outs that allow you to customize your sauce, sandwich, or steak just to your liking.

While *Grill It!* offers flavors of the highest caliber, it's also a look-and-cook book. Special sections at the beginning of each chapter help you identify the different cuts of meat, how to form a perfect patty, or how to cut up a whole chicken. The recipes also feature step-by-step instructions and photos to help you get the very best results from your grill, as well as gorgeous photographs of the finished food.

Whether you're a neophyte or a pitmaster, *Grill It!* will spark your enthusiasm for cooking with fire—and keep it burning.

HOLDING A PIECE OF MEAT OVER AN OPEN FIRE MAY HAVE BEEN THE VERY FIRST METHOD OF TRANSFORMING FOOD FROM RAW TO COOKED—BUT THIS CAVEMAN-ERA TECHNIQUE HASN'T LOST ITS APPEAL IN THE MODERN WORLD.

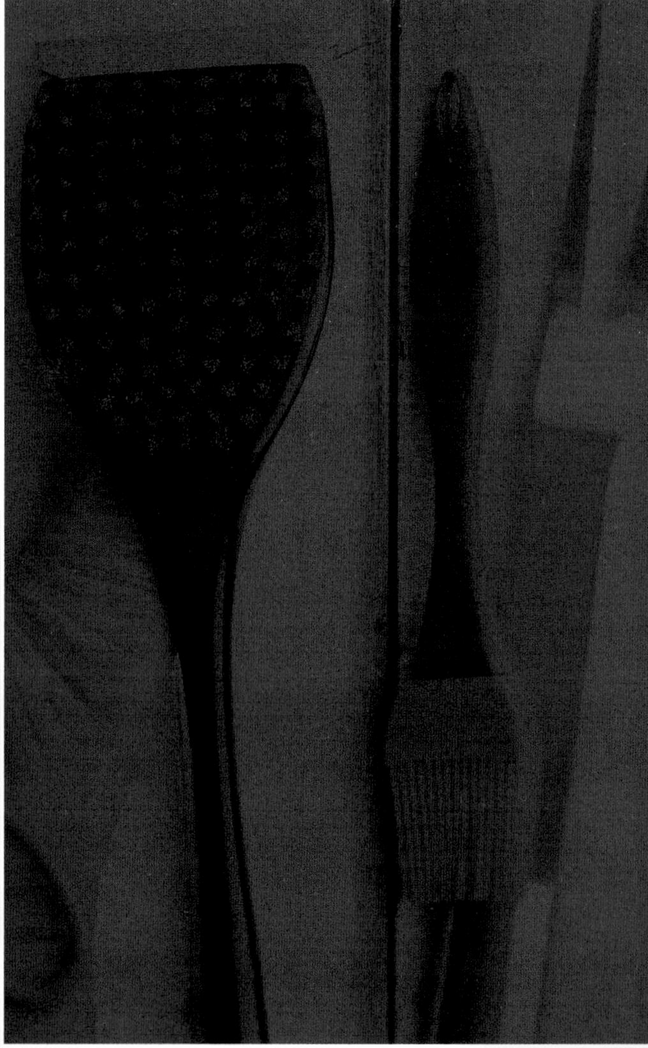

Grilling Basics

BEFORE YOU GET ALL FIRED UP, LEARN ALL YOU NEED TO KNOW. THIS PRIMER WILL GIVE YOU CONFIDENCE AND GEAR YOU UP FOR GRILLING LIKE A PRO.

Grill Types

AS FLAME-COOKING FEVER SPREADS THROUGH THE COUNTRY, GRILL MANUFACTURERS SCURRY TO PERFECT THEIR PRODUCTS.TAKE A LOOK AT THE MOST POPULAR TYPES OF GRILLS AND DECIDE WHICH IS BETTER FOR YOU.

KETTLE GRILLS

Fueled by charcoal, these grills have a round or square box construction with a charcoal grate that holds the coals on the bottom and a grill rack above. Most models feature vents on the bottom and the lid to control temperature.

Kettle grills are the most common, featuring deep-rounded bowls and lids ideal for barbecuing and smoking. The grill temperature is controlled by manipulating vents on the top and bottom. For a portable option, consider a hibachi. Originally from Japan, this grill consists of a small rectangular or oval firebox with one or two grill racks. Use it for direct-cooking small cuts of meat.

ADVANTAGES In addition to being more affordable than gas grills, kettle grills provide the primal pleasures of real flame cooking and imbue grilled foods with the highly desirable smoky charcoal flavor that gas-fired grills do not match.

DISADVANTAGES Using charcoal and lighter fluid is less environmentally friendly than gas. Kettle grills require longer start-up times, are often prohibited in multiple family housing units, and tend to wear out out more quickly than gas grills.

GAS GRILLS

A convenient alternative to charcoal, gas grills are fueled by propane tanks or a natural gas hookup. They have a metal box lined with tube-shape liquid-propane burners on the bottom. The burners are topped by a heating surface of metal bars, lava rocks, or ceramic briquettes that disperse heat from the burners throughout the grill. The smoky aroma and flavor of grilling is generated as drippings from food fall onto the bars or stones.

ADVANTAGES Gas grills are more convenient to use and reach high temperatures in a hurry. Their relative ease of operation allows grilling beginners to become successsful grillers more rapidly, and they may be the safer choice for those who grill in small spaces or around small children.

DISADVANTAGES Using a gas grill requires connection, disconnection, and transportation of fuel canisters. Models that utilize lava rock systems may cause flare-ups. Although some hybrid models combine the advantages of gas and wood or charcoal, gas-only grills do not provide the char-grilled flavor that kettle grills do.

SMOKERS

Smoking is essentially low-heat, slow barbecuing, which can be achieved on either a charcoal or gas grill. If you're serious about smoking, consider buying a smoker. The most common type is the vertical water smoker, which is easy to use, compact, and affordably priced. These cylindrical-shape vessels stand 2½ to 3½ feet high and are about 18 inches in diameter. The heat source is at the base of the vessel, where coals are fueled by charcoal, gas, or electricity. Wood chips or chunks are placed on the coals to enhance desirable smoky flavor. Above the heat source is a water pan, which provides moisture to the smoking process. Above the water pan are usually two levels of grill racks for food.

ADVANTAGES The use of a true smoker is essential to the art of real barbeque, for no other method of grilling is capable of producing the low, even, and indirect heat and intense wood-smoke-infused taste of a smoker.

DISADVANTAGES Because true smoking requires long periods of heat, fueling the unit with charcoal and natural wood can be expensive. Maintaining the strict temperature controls needed for smoking can be difficult for beginners and requires practice.

Grill Tip!

PROTECT YOUR GRILL FROM INCLEMENT WEATHER AND KEEP THE UNIT SPARKLY CLEAN AND READY TO USE BY INVESTING IN AN INEXPENSIVE GRILL COVER . PUT IT TO USE AS SOON AS THE GRILL HAS COOLED.

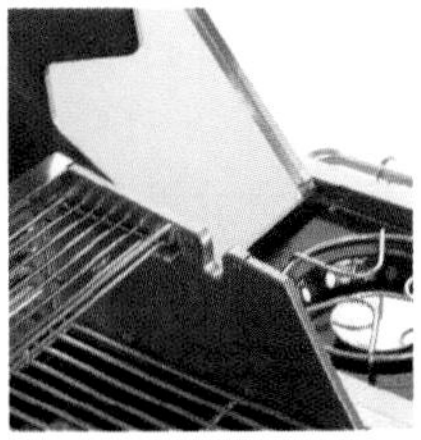

When choosing a gas grill to fit your outdoor cooking style, look for such essential features as a reliable, easy-to read thermometer; quick-start ignition; and sturdy, easy-to-clean grill grates—one of which is elevated.

Classic kettle-style grills allow heat control from two sets of vents—one at the base of the kettle and one on the lid.

The vertical-style smoker is outfitted with a bottom fuel center, where charcoal burns, as well as an easy-open side door for adding chunks or chips of natural wood. Both the bottom section and the lid of this unit have manual heat controls.

Gas Grill

ONCE YOU DECIDE THAT A GAS GRILL IS RIGHT FOR YOU, DIG IN TO DELICIOUSNESS BY LEARNING HOW TO USE YOUR GRILL SAFELY, EFFICIENTLY, AND FLAVORFULLY.

SET UP

When you're ready to get grilling, the first step is to make sure you have enough propane. Check the fuel gauge, if you have one. If you don't, just tap on the tank and listen closely. If the tank is full, rapping on the tank makes a thumping sound. If it is empty, it echoes. By tapping from the top of the canister to the bottom, you can tell whether there is enough fuel to grill your dinner.

To light the grill, lift the lid, turn the starter burner to high, and press the ignition switch once or twice. When you see flames beneath the grates, set the other burners to high, close the lid, and preheat the grill to the desired temperature. Allow 15 to 20 minutes for the grill to preheat.

Preheat the grill on high to burn off excess residue. If a lower grilling temperature is desired, reduce the heat by adjusting the burner output.

GET COOKING

To grill over direct heat, set burners on medium-high until the grill temperature reaches 400°F. If the foods you have chosen to grill do not require the surface area of all burners, shut off burners under the area you do not need and only grill over the lit burner. For foods that require indirect-heat grilling, preheat grill to high and turn off one or two burners; grill food directly over the unlit burners, leaving the other burner on high. Adjust grill temperature to 350°F.

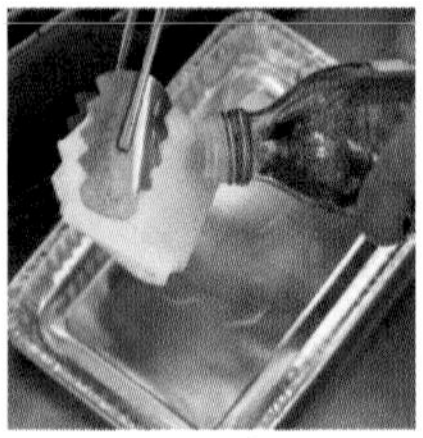

To prevent foods from sticking, apply vegetable oil to a folded paper towel clasped in tongs. Rub oiled towel over hot grill grates before placing foods on the grill.

Grill Tip!

CHECK GAS FITTINGS FOR LEAKS EVERY TIME YOU CONNECT OR DISCONNECT THE FITTINGS. TO DO SO, APPLY A BIT OF SOAPY WATER TO THE FITTINGS—IF THE MIXTURE BUBBLES, IT HAS A LEAK. TIGHTEN FITTINGS AND APPLY SOAPY WATER AGAIN TO MAKE SURE THE FITTING IS TIGHT.

FLARE-UPS To prevent flare-ups or fires, empty the grill grease catch or drip pan after each grilling session. Trimming excess fat from meats before placing them on the grill will eliminate the most combustible material from flaring. To extinguish small flare-ups, keep a water-filled spray bottle nearby—a quick spray of water will usually control the flame. If this does not help, remove foods from the grill and allow the fat to burn off completely before returning food to the grates.

CLEAN UP

Clean grill grates thoroughly before and after each use. Clean grates help prevent foods from sticking and ensure that each dinner is done to perfection. Grates clean most easily when they are hot, so preheat the grill to high before vigorously scrubbing grates with an iron-bristle brush. Scrape large bits of burned food away with a sturdy metal spatula. Once you finish cooking, scrub the grill with the brush before turning off the heat.

INSTALLING A PROPANE TANK, STEP-BY-STEP

1. To remove propane tank, turn off gas supply by turning uppermost valve screw clockwise. Then, using a clockwise motion, remove the hex nut connector.

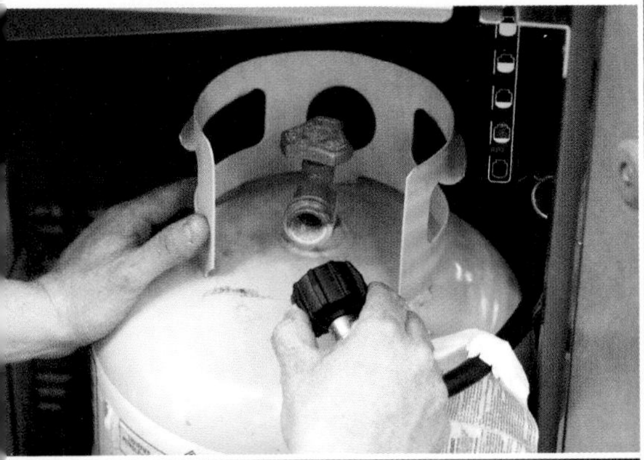

2. To reconnect a new propane canister, place the tank in position, with the valve line facing the gas line. Reconnect the hex nut using a counterclockwise motion.

To grill juicy meats, always turn meats with tongs rather than a fork. Fork piercing releases delicous juices and moisture.

3. Restore propane flow to the grill by turning the top valve screw counter-clockwise.

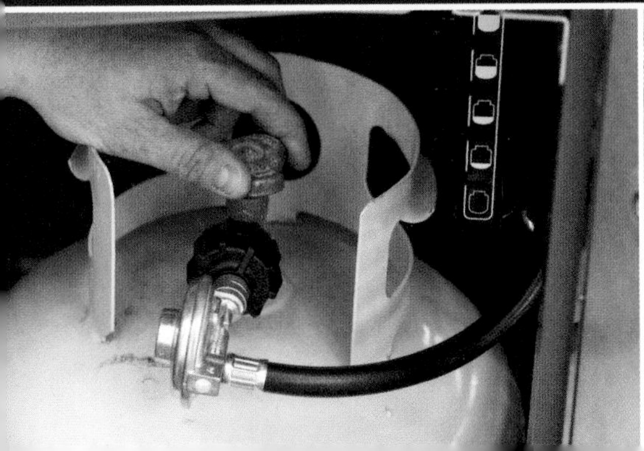

4. To light a gas grill, open the grill lid, then turn the unit's lighter knob to high.

5. Next press the ignition button. Look for a flame to determine whether ignition was successful before turning on other burners.

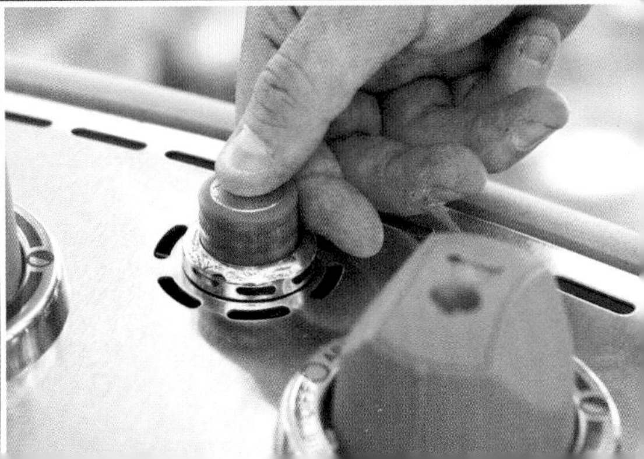

Kettle Grill

GET READY FOR YOUR TRIP TO FLAVOR CITY. LEARN HOW TO SUCCESSFULLY BUILD AND LIGHT A SIZZLEWORTHY CHARCOAL FIRE ON YOUR KETTLE GRILL.

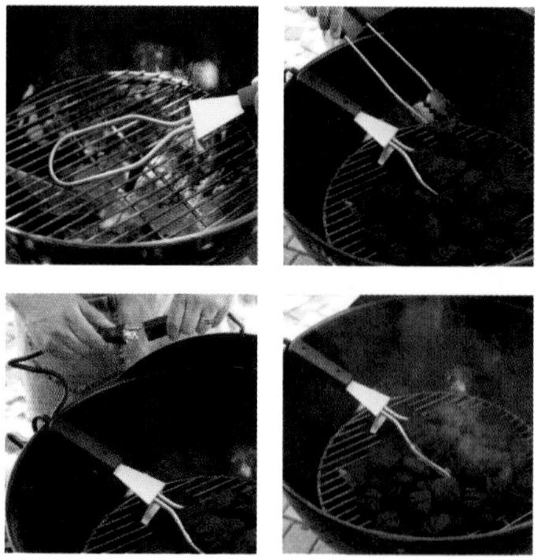

To use an environmentally friendly electric starter, place the starter on the grates, pile charcoal briquettes over the starter, plug the starter in, and wait until the starter fires up your coals.

FIRE STARTERS

Starting a gas grill is as simple as turning a knob. Charcoal grills are a bit tricky. Although ease and convenience are nice, some foods just taste better cooked in a charcoal grill. A variety of aids make the process easy.

INSTANT-LIGHT CHARCOAL These briquettes light easily, with fire cooking temperature in as little as 10 minutes. Unlike lighter fluid, which burns off relatively fast, instant-light charcoal is soaked with a petroleum product that releases fumes throughout much of the cooking process. Charcoal added during the cooking process will impart a bitter flavor to the food, and many consumers detect a chemical taste in foods cooked over instant charcoal. The product burns more quickly than regular charcoal, often necessitating refills, and, because of its convenience, instant charcoal is the most expensive charcoal product.

LIGHTER FLUID Fluid is dispersed onto the coals and allowed to soak in for a minute or two before lighting. The fluid burns off long before you begin cooking, but many communities have outlawed its use because of pollutants. Although little residue is left when coals have been properly preheated, many grillers are opposed to grilling foods over petroleum products.

PARAFFIN STARTER This environmentally safe, smokeless, nontoxic product for igniting fire is easy to use. Simply place two or three cubes of paraffin under a mound of charcoal or in the bottom of a chimney starter before lighting.

ELECTRIC STARTER This metal coil heating device is placed first, then charcoal briquettes are layered on top of it. It is plugged in and left to heat up and ignite the coals within minutes. Once the coals begin glowing, unplug the starter, carefully remove it, and place it in a safe area to cool. Although efficient and relatively inexpensive, electric starters lack the portability of using grills away from home electrical outlets.

CHIMNEY STARTER This is the preferred choice for serious grillers. This method uses a cylindrical steel pipe with vents in the bottom, a grate in the middle, and a heatproof handle. Charcoal or wood chunks are placed on the grate, and crumpled newspapers or paraffin starters are placed in the bottom of the cylinder. The chimney is then set on the bottom grate of the grill, and the newspaper or paraffin starter is lit with a long match or lighter. The cylindrical shape ensures coals light quickly and evenly. Once the coals are ready, lift the chimney and pour the coals directly onto the grill.

Grill Tip!

AS A GENERAL RULE, PLAN TO USE ABOUT 30 BRIQUETTES TO COOK ONE POUND OF MEAT. A 5-POUND BAG OF BRIQUETTES CONTAINS ABOUT 80 BRIQUETTES.

USING A CHIMNEY STARTER, STEP-BY-STEP

1. Crumple old newspapers and place in the bottom of the chimney beneath its grate.

2. Pile charcoal briquettes in the chimney cylinder.

6. Carefully pour the hot coals onto the grill.

3. Touch a match or lighter flame to the paper. Soon the briquettes will blaze.

4. Let the briquettes heat for 15 to 20 minutes.

5. Coals are ready when they are covered with a light layer of ash.

Fuel the Fire

BEFORE YOU FIRE UP YOUR GRILL, CHOOSE THE FUEL THAT SUITS YOUR STYLE.

CHARCOAL

Each of the three types of charcoal possesses distinct qualities.

NATURAL BRIQUETTES Made from pulverized lump charcoal held together with natural starches without the off-flavors generated by some composite briquettes.

COMPOSITION BRIQUETTES Made from burned wood and scraps, coal dust, camphor, and paraffin or petroleum binders. Use a quality brand; inexpensive brands contain excessive fillers that give food an unpleasant taste and leave heavy ashes.

CHARWOOD OR LUMP CHARCOAL Formed from hardwoods such as maple, oak, and hickory, which are burned down at very high temperatures. The fuel choice of chefs and professional grillers, lump charcoal lights more quickly and burns cleaner and hotter than briquettes. It is additive- and petroleum-free and retains some natural flavor. Primary drawbacks include occasional sparking, limited availability, and a higher cost than alternatives.

WOOD The first fuel used by man, natural wood continues to be the best at delivering intense heat, a long burn, and producing great smoky flavor. Natural woods, such as hickory, oak, and fruit-tree wood, are available in chips and chunks.

Grill Tip!

WHEN CHARCOAL GRILLING, BE PATIENT. BE SURE TO ALLOW ENOUGH TIME—GENERALLY 20 TO 30 MINUTES—TO BRING THE FIRE TO ITS PERFECT COOKING TEMPERATURE. COALS ARE READY WHEN THEY'RE COVERED WITH A LIGHT LAYER OF ASH.

Control the Heat

WITH THE HELP OF THIS SHORT COURSE IN HEAT MANAGEMENT, YOU'LL TEND THE FIRE LIKE A PRO—IN NO TIME AT ALL.

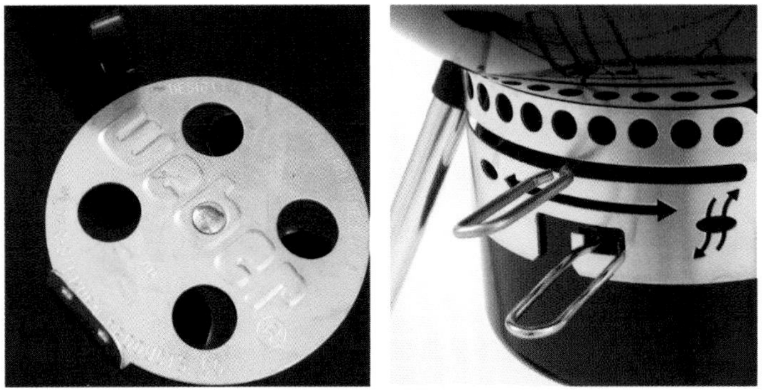

Vents on both the top and the bottom of your kettle grill will help you fine-tune grilling temperatures. To elevate grilling temperature, open the vents to allow more oxygen into the fire. To cool the temperature, close them. Practice, making several small vent adjustments instead of large ones, until you feel the command that you will have over your fire.

Whether you cook directly or indirectly, it is important to monitor the grill temperature to obtain perfect doneness. Gas grills offer simplicity with built-in thermometers and temperature gauges to adjust the heat. When using charcoal, manage grill heat using these methods:

ADJUST COALS Spread the coals farther apart to lower the heat. Or gently tap the coals with long-handled tongs to remove loose ash and pile them closer together to make the fire more intense.

ADJUST VENTS Adjust the flow of oxygen inside the grill by opening and closing the air vents: open to increase heat, or partially closed to decrease temperature.

ADJUST RACK HEIGHT Some grills have adjustable grill racks. Use low levels to sear food and high levels for slow cooking. For medium heat, place the grate about 4 inches from the fire.

HAND CHECK

Coals are ready for grilling when they are covered with gray ash. To check the temperature of coals, use a built-in or separate flat grill thermometer. Or use the method many chefs use: Carefully place the palm of your hand 2 to 3 inches above the grill rack and count the number of seconds you can hold it in that position.

TIME	THERMOMETER	TEMPERATURE
2 seconds	400°F to 450°F	Hot (high)
3 seconds	375°F to 400°F	Medium-high
4 seconds	350°F to 375°F	Medium
5 seconds	325°F to 350°F	Medium-low
6 seconds	300°F to 325°F	Low

Grill or Barbecue?

ALTHOUGH THEY'RE USED INTERCHANGEABLY, THERE IS A DISTINCT DIFFERENCE BETWEEN THE TWO COOKING METHODS.

GRILLING VS. BARBECUING

GRILLING is a means of cooking food over direct heat for a short period of time. Fire up your charcoal or gas grill and place the food on the grill rack above the coals or heat source. Because cooking time is relatively brief, grilling is best suited to thin or small pieces of food such as steaks, burgers, chicken breasts, fish fillets, and vegetables. Intense heat sears the outside of the food, sealing in juices and giving it the delicious caramelized flavor only grilling can achieve. Large cuts of meat and poultry are grilled using the indirect method. Typically the fuel used is charcoal or gas, and the temperatures climb higher than those reached when barbecuing.

BARBECUING is a slow cooking method over a low, smoldering wood fire, using indirect heat for long periods of time. Low heat enables the food to cook evenly throughout and is well suited to large roasts, whole chickens, and turkeys. Cuts such as brisket and ribs also benefit from low heat and long cooking, which breaks down connective tissue. The term "barbecue" is also used to describe a backyard party at which grilled foods are served.

Hot Tip

FOR INDIRECT COOKING, PLACE A DRIP PAN UNDER THE FOOD TO CATCH DRIPPINGS THAT CAN CAUSE FLARE-UPS. ADD HOT WATER (OR APPLE JUICE OR BEER FOR ADDED FLAVOR) TO THE PAN TO KEEP THE DRIPPINGS FROM BURNING.

DIRECT VS. INDIRECT GRILLING

DIRECT GRILLING is the method of placing food on the grill rack directly over the heat source, either with or without the lid closed (check manufacturer's directions). This method is suggested for tender, thin, or smaller quick-cooking (under 30 minutes) foods such as burgers, steaks, chops, chicken pieces, and vegetables. For even cooking, turn foods only once during grilling time.

To set up a two-burner gas grill for direct grilling, set one burner on high for searing, and one burner on medium for finishing grilling. To set up a three- or four-burner gas grill, set one burner on high and one or two burners on medium. Leave off the remaining burner.

INDIRECT GRILLING positions the food on the grill rack away from or to the side of the heat source with the grill cover closed. Similar to roasting in an oven, heat inside the grill reflects off the lid and other interior surfaces, cooking the food from all sides and eliminating the need to turn the food. This low, slow grilling method is ideal for large foods that take longer to cook, allowing them to cook through without burning.

To set up a two-burner gas grill for indirect grilling, set one burner on high and cook the food over the unlit burner. For a three-burner grill, turn on the front and rear or outside burners and cook the food in the center. For a four-burner, turn on the outside burners.

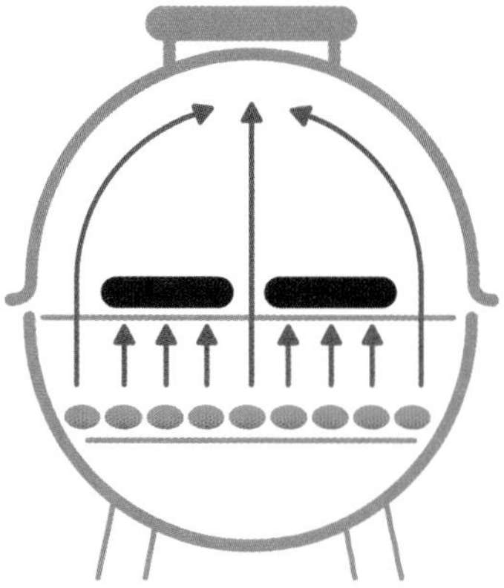

In the direct grilling method, food is placed on the grill rack directly over the heat source—whether that's charcoal or the burner in a gas grill.

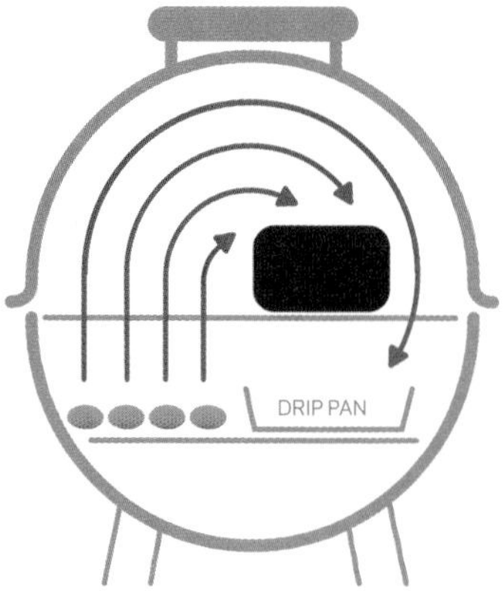

In the indirect grilling method, food is positioned adjacent to the heat source. In the same way an oven roasts, heat reflects off the interior surfaces and cooks the food from all sides.

DIRECT GRILLING METHOD

To set up a charcoal grill for the direct grilling method, spread the hot coals evenly over the bottom of the charcoal grate. Wherever the food is placed on the cooking grate, it will be directly above the heat source.

INDIRECT GRILLING METHOD

The most common way to set up a charcoal grill for indirect grilling is to set the coals to the side next to a drip pan over which to place food. You can also set up a ring of fire and place the food in the center. The reverse is the bull's-eye, which creates a small area of direct heat with a perimeter of indirect heat.

Essential Tools

CHOOSE THE RIGHT TOOL FOR THE PURPOSE. THIS MAXIM IS AS TRUE FOR GRILLING AS IT IS FOR CARPENTRY.

ESSENTIALS

SPATULA For turning food, spatulas are available in a variety of styles from basic to special purpose (e.g., fish spatula). Choose one with a long, sturdy handle and a stainless-steel blade.

FORK Ideal for moving roasts and large items. Avoid piercing deeply, especially during cooking, to not waste delicious juices.

HEAT-RESISTANT GLOVES or long grill mitts. Protect hands and forearms from hot utensils and the grill. Choose mitts that are heavy, well insulated, and flame-retardant.

CHIMNEY STARTER The preferred choice for serious grillers. This method uses a cylindrical steel pipe with vents in the bottom, a grate in the middle, and a heatproof handle.

BASTING BRUSH Used for oiling grill racks and basting foods. Choose long-handled brushes with natural bristles. For better sauce retention, try heat-resistant silcone brushes.

THERMOMETER Available in several styles, a good thermometer ensures food is cooked properly (see page 52, "Thermometer Test").

GRILL BRUSH Essential for cleaning grill racks. Look for rustproof varieties, which are better for outdoor use.

TONGS Perfect for moving and turning without piercing foods, spring-hinged, long-handled styles are best.

DISPOSABLE FOIL DRIP PANS Easy to use and clean, these pans are used for indirect grilling and holding wood chips.

SPATULA

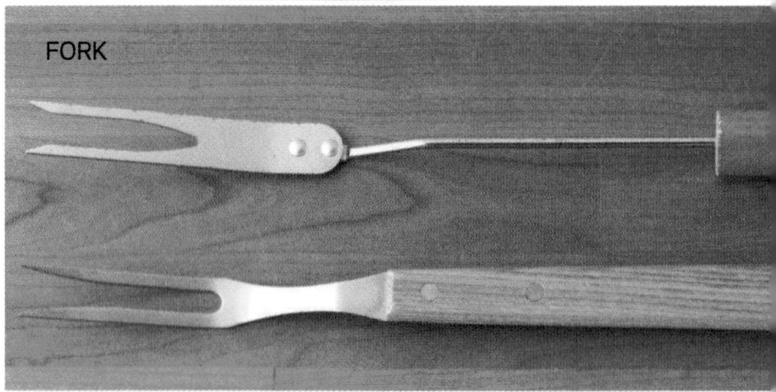
FORK

HEAT-RESISTANT MITTS

CHIMNEY STARTER

BASTING BRUSHES

THERMOMETER

GRILL-CLEANING BRUSH

DISPOSABLE FOIL DRIP PANS

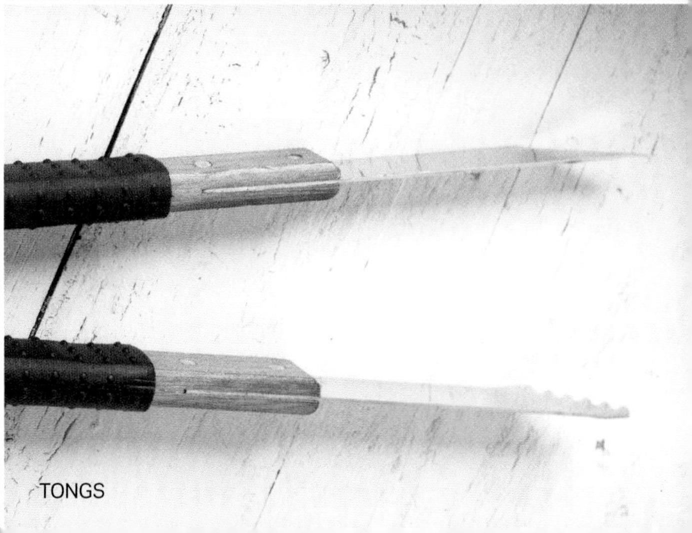
TONGS

Extra Gadgets

NOW THAT YOU'RE ON THE ROAD TO GRILLING GREATNESS, EXPAND YOUR REPERTOIRE BY ADDING A FEW NEW TOOLS TO YOUR BELT.

GRILL WOK Stir-fry your favorite foods without heating up the kitchen! Perforated bases allow smoky flavors to enhance stir-fried foods. Choose a heavy-duty wok with an extra-long handle.

GRILL BASKETS Available in a variety of shapes and sizes, some baskets feature two grates hinged together (for grilling fish, hot dogs, vegetables, and other small items that require turning). Some are basket shaped, with small openings that prevent food from falling through the grill rack.

RIB RACK These racks, which resemble a file holder, hold up to five racks of ribs vertically, taking up less space on your grill.

SKEWERS Available in both metal and bamboo, skewers are the tool to use when creating kabobs. To avoid burning, soak bamboo skewers in water for 30 minutes before grilling.

GRILL GRID A stainless-steel grill grid provides a safe perch for foods likely to fall through the grate, such as shellfish, garlic, and cubed meats.

RACK LIFTER Use this handy tool to safely grab the grill rack and move it aside, to add charcoal, or as a serving platter.

ROTISSERIE Electric motor-turned rotisseries slowly spin foods over indirect heat. Rotating bastes meat with melting fat, resulting in perfectly charred outsides and moist, tender insides. Rotisserie grilling is best for whole poultry and cylindrical roasts such as pork loins and boneless beef rib roasts.

GRILL WOK

HINGED GRILL RACK

RIB RACK

SKEWERS

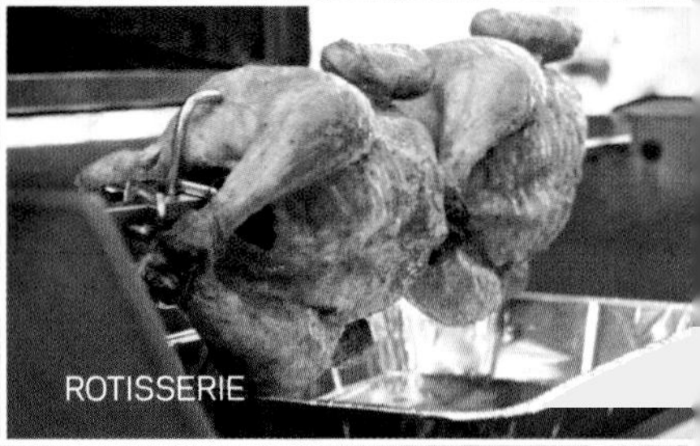
ROTISSERIE

GRILL BASKET

GRILL GRID

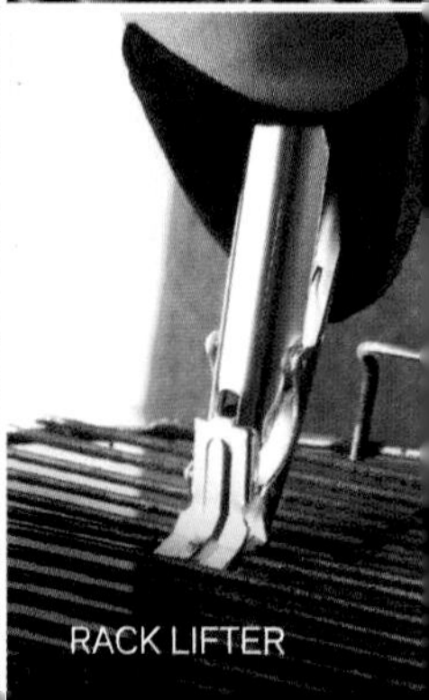
RACK LIFTER

Grill Safety

LET'S FACE IT—FIRE IS FIRE AND IT BURNS. PROTECT YOURSELF AND YOUR GRILLING COMPANIONS BY CAREFULLY FOLLOWING THESE IMPORTANT SAFETY TIPS.

GRILL SAFETY

- Read and follow the manufacturer's instructions on how to safely light and operate your gas or charcoal grill.
- Position your grill in a well-ventilated area at least 10 feet away from trees, houses, and any combustible materials. Make sure the ground surface is level and stable. Once the grill is lit, don't move it.
- Keep children and pets a safe distance away from hot grills.
- Avoid wearing loose or highly flammable clothing.
- Use heat-resistant mitts and long-handled tools.

- Never add lighter fluid to an already-lit fire.
- Keep a fire extinguisher nearby for emergencies. Do not pour water on a grease fire.
- Close lids and vents on a charcoal grill or turn off gas to extinguish flare-ups. Do not use water.
- After grilling, cover charcoal grill with the lid, close all vents, and allow coals to cool completely before cleaning or putting away your grill. For a gas grill, turn off all burners and the gas source.
- Always store propane tanks outdoors, never in a garage or enclosed space.

FOOD SAFETY

- Store raw meat, poultry, and fish separately in plastic bags and place on a tray to avoid dripping any juices onto other foods.
- Defrost meat, poultry, and fish in the refrigerator.
- Wash hands thoroughly before beginning any food preparation and after handling fresh meat, poultry, or fish.
- Remove excess fat and/or marinade from food to reduce the occurrence of flare-ups.
- Keep raw foods away from cooked foods to avoid cross-contamination.
- Use clean plates and utensils with cooked food. Do not use the same plate and utensils that you used to handle raw foods.
- Sanitize cutting boards by washing with hot, soapy water, then with a solution of 2 teaspoons of household bleach and 1 quart of warm water. Rinse thoroughly with warm water.
- When basting, brush sauces and marinades on cooked food surfaces only. With cooked food, do not reuse leftover marinades or use a brush previously used on raw meat, poultry, or fish.
- For marinades that have been in contact with raw meat or poultry, bring to a vigorous boil for at least 1 minute before using as a baste or sauce.
- Grill foods to safe temperatures as outlined on pages 25 to 29.
- Use moderate grill heat to avoid charring meats, poultry, and fish.
- Keep hot foods hot and cold foods cold. Do not allow any cooked food to sit at room temperature for more than 2 hours.

DIRECT-GRILLING VEGETABLES

To precook vegetables, bring a small amount of water to boiling in a saucepan; add desired vegetables and simmer, covered, for the time specified in the chart; drain well. For a charcoal grill, place vegetables on rack directly over medium coals. Grill, uncovered, for the time given below or until crisp-tender, turning occasionally. (For a gas grill, preheat grill. Reduce heat to medium. Place vegetables on grill rack directly over heat. Cover the grill.) Monitor the grilling closely so vegetables don't char.

Vegetable	Preparation	Precooking Time	Approximate Direct-Grilling Time
Asparagus	Snap off and discard tough bases of stems.	Do not precook.	7 to 10 minutes
Baby carrots, fresh	Cut off carrot tops. Wash and peel carrots.	3 to 5 minutes	3 to 5 minutes
Corn on the cob	Place corn with husks and silks intact in bowl or pan. Cover with water. Soak 1 hour; drain.	Do not precook.	25 to 30 minutes
Eggplant	Cut off top and blossom ends. Cut eggplant crosswise into 1-inch slices.	Do not precook.	8 minutes
Fennel	Snip off feathery leaves. Cut off stems.	10 minutes; then cut into 6 to 8 wedges	8 minutes
Mushrooms, portobello	Remove stems and scrape out gills. Grill; turn halfway through grilling.	Do not precook.	10 to 12 minutes
New potatoes	Halve potatoes.	10 minutes or until almost tender	10 to 12 minutes
Onions, white, yellow, or red	Peel and cut into 1-inch crosswise slices. Grill; turn halfway through grilling.	Do not precook.	10 minutes
Potatoes, baking	Scrub potatoes; prick with a fork. Wrap individually in a double thickness of foil.	Do not precook.	1 to 1½ hours
Sweet peppers	Remove stems. Halve peppers lengthwise. Remove seeds and membranes. Cut into 1-inch-wide strips.	Do not precook.	8 to 10 minutes
Tomatoes	Remove cores; cut in half crosswise.	Do not precook.	5 minutes
Zucchini or yellow summer squash	Wash; cut off ends. Quarter lengthwise.	Do not precook.	5 to 6 minutes

DIRECT-GRILLING FRUIT

Select fruit that's ripe and firm. Watch carefully while grilling and turn it occasionally. To check color and doneness of the fruit, slide a thin spatula under the fruit and lift it slightly—it should be golden brown. The following chart is a guideline; grilling times for fruit will depend upon ripeness.

Fruit	Thickness/Size	Grilling Temperature	Approximate Direct-Grilling Time*	Doneness
Apples	½-inch slices	Medium	4 to 6 minutes	Golden brown
Apricots, pitted	halves	Medium	6 to 8 minutes	Golden brown
Bananas	halved lengthwise	Medium	4 to 6 minutes	Golden brown
Peaches or nectarines, pitted	halves	Medium	6 to 8 minutes	Golden brown
Pineapple, peeled and cored	½-inch slices or 1-inch wedges	Medium	7 to 10 minutes	Golden brown
Plums, pitted	halves	Medium	4 to 5 minutes	Heated through
Pears, cored	halves	Medium	6 to 8 minutes	Golden
Strawberries, stemmed and skewered	whole	Medium	4 to 5 minutes	Heated through

*All cooking times are based on fruits removed directly from refrigerator.

INDIRECT-GRILLING POULTRY

For a charcoal grill, arrange medium-hot coals around a drip pan. Test for medium heat above drip pan (see page 17). Place poultry on grill rack over drip pan (if whole, place breast side up and do not stuff). Cover; grill for the time given below or until poultry is no longer pink (180°F for most cuts, 170°F for breast meat), adding more charcoal as necessary. If desired, place whole birds on a rack in a roasting pan and omit the drip pan. (For a gas grill, preheat grill. Reduce heat to medium. Adjust heat for indirect cooking [see pages 18–19].) Test for doneness using a meat or instant-read thermometer. For whole birds, insert meat thermometer into center of the inside thigh muscle, away from bone. (Poultry sizes vary; use times as a general guide.)

Type of Bird	Weight	Grilling Temperature	Approximate Indirect-Grilling Time*	Doneness
CHICKEN				
Chicken breast half, skinned and boned	4 to 5 ounces	Medium	15 to 18 minutes	170°F
Chicken, broiler-fryer, half	1½ to 1¾ pounds	Medium	1 to 1¼ hours	180°F
Chicken, broiler-fryer, quarters	12 to 14 ounces each	Medium	50 to 60 minutes	180°F
Chicken thigh, skinned and boned	4 to 5 ounces	Medium	15 to 18 minutes	180°F
Chicken, whole	2½ to 3 pounds 3½ to 4 pounds 4½ to 5 pounds	Medium Medium Medium	1 to 1¼ hours 1¼ to 1¾ hours 1¾ to 2 hours	180°F 180°F 180°F
Meaty chicken pieces (breast halves, thighs, and drumsticks)	2½ to 3 pounds total	Medium	50 to 60 minutes	180°F
GAME				
Cornish game hen, halved lengthwise	10 to 12 ounces each	Medium	40 to 50 minutes	180°F
Cornish game hen, whole	1¼ to 1½ pounds	Medium	50 to 60 minutes	180°F
Pheasant, quartered	8 to 12 ounces each	Medium	50 to 60 minutes	180°F
Pheasant, whole	2 to 3 pounds	Medium	1 to 1½ hours	180°F
Quail, semiboneless	3 to 4 ounces	Medium	15 to 20 minutes	180°F
Squab	12 to 16 ounces	Medium	¾ to 1 hour	180°F
TURKEY				
Turkey breast, half	2 to 2½ pounds	Medium	1¼ to 2 hours	170°F
Turkey breast tenderloin	8 to 10 ounces (¾ to 1-inch thick)	Medium	25 to 30 minutes	170°F
Turkey breast tenderloin steak	4 to 6 ounces	Medium	15 to 18 minutes	170°F
Turkey breast, whole	4 to 6 pounds 6 to 8 pounds	Medium	1¾ to 2¼ hours 2½ to 3½ hours	170°F 170°F
Turkey drumstick	½ to 1 pound	Medium	¾ to 1¼ hours	180°F
Turkey thigh	1 to 1½ pounds	Medium	50 to 60 minutes	180°F
Turkey, whole	6 to 8 pounds 8 to 12 pounds 12 to 16 pounds	Medium	1¾ to 2¼ hours 2½ to 3½ hours 3 to 4 hours	180°F 180°F 180°F

*All cooking times are based on poultry removed directly from refrigerator.

DIRECT-GRILLING POULTRY

If desired, remove skin from poultry. For a charcoal grill, place poultry on grill rack, bones up, directly over medium coals (see page 19). Grill, uncovered, for time given below or until the proper temperature is reached and meat is no longer pink, turning once halfway through grilling. (For a gas grill, preheat grill. Reduce heat to medium. Place poultry on grill rack, bones down, over heat. Cover and grill.) Test for doneness using a meat thermometer (use an instant-read thermometer to test thinner pieces). Thermometer should register 180°F for dark meat, 170°F for breast meat. If desired, during last 5 to 10 minutes of grilling brush often with a sauce.

Type of Bird	Weight	Grilling Temperature	Approximate Direct-Grilling Time*	Done-ness
CHICKEN				
Chicken breast half, skinned and boned	4 to 5 ounces	Medium	12 to 15 minutes	170°F
Chicken, broiler-fryer, half or quarters	1½- to 1¾-pound half or 12- to 14-ounce quarters	Medium	40 to 50 minutes	180°F
Chicken thigh, skinned and boned	4 to 5 ounces	Medium	12 to 15 minutes	180°F
Meaty chicken pieces (breast halves, thighs, and drumsticks)	2½ to 3 pounds total	Medium	35 to 45 minutes	180°F
TURKEY				
Turkey breast tenderloin	8 to 10 ounces (¾ to 1 inch thick)	Medium	16 to 20 minutes	170°F

*All cooking times are based on poultry removed directly from refrigerator.

INDIRECT-GRILLING MEAT

For a charcoal grill, arrange medium-hot coals around a drip pan. Test for medium heat above drip pan, unless chart says otherwise. Place meat, fat side up, on grill rack over drip pan. Cover and grill for the time given below or to desired temperature, adding more charcoal to maintain heat as necessary. (For a gas grill, preheat grill. Reduce heat to medium. Adjust heat for indirect cooking [see pages 16–17].) To test for doneness, insert a meat thermometer, using an instant-read thermometer to test thinner pieces. Thermometer should register temperature listed under Final Grilling Temperature. Remove meat from grill. For large cuts, such as roasts, cover with foil and let stand 15 minutes before slicing. Meat temperature will rise 10°F during the time it stands. For thin cuts, such as steaks, cover and let stand 5 minutes.

Cut	Thickness/Weight	Approximate Indirect-Grilling Time*	Final Grilling Temperature (when to remove from grill)
BEEF			
Boneless top sirloin steak	1 inch 1 inch 1½ inches 1½ inches	22 to 26 minutes 26 to 30 minutes 32 to 36 minutes 36 to 40 minutes	145°F medium rare 160°F medium 145°F medium rare 160°F medium
Boneless tri-tip roast (bottom sirloin)	1½ to 2 pounds 1½ to 2 pounds	35 to 40 minutes 40 to 45 minutes	135°F (145°F medium rare after standing) 150°F (160°F medium after standing)
Flank steak	1¼ to 1¾ pounds	23 to 28 minutes	160°F medium
Rib roast (chine bone removed) (medium-low heat)	4 to 6 pounds 4 to 6 pounds	2 to 2¾ hours 2½ to 3¼ hours	135°F (145°F medium rare after standing) 150°F (160°F medium after standing)
Ribeye roast (medium-low heat)	4 to 6 pounds 4 to 6 pounds	1¼ to 1¾ hours 1½ to 2¼ hours	135°F (145°F medium rare after standing) 150°F (160°F medium after standing)
Steak (porterhouse, rib, ribeye, shoulder top blade [flat-iron], T-bone, tenderloin, top loin [strip])	1 inch 1 inch 1½ inches 1½ inches	16 to 20 minutes 20 to 24 minutes 22 to 25 minutes 25 to 28 minutes	145°F medium rare 160°F medium 145°F medium rare 160°F medium
Tenderloin roast (medium-high heat)	2 to 3 pounds 4 to 5 pounds	¾ to 1 hour 1 to 1¼ hours	135°F (145°F medium rare after standing) 135°F (145°F medium rare after standing)

*All cooking times are based on meat removed directly from refrigerator.

INDIRECT-GRILLING MEAT *(continued)*

Cut	Thickness/Weight	Approximate Indirect-Grilling Time*	Final Grilling Temperature (when to remove from grill)
GROUND MEAT			
Patties (beef, lamb, pork, or veal)	½ inch ¾ inch	15 to 18 minutes 20 to 24 minutes	160°F medium 160°F medium
LAMB			
Boneless leg roast (medium-low heat)	3 to 4 pounds 3 to 4 pounds 4 to 6 pounds 4 to 6 pounds	1½ to 2¼ hours 1¾ to 2½ hours 1¾ to 2½ hours 2 to 2¾ hours	135°F (145°F medium rare after standing) 150°F (160°F medium after standing) 135°F (145°F medium rare after standing) 150°F (160°F medium after standing)
Boneless sirloin roast (medium-low heat)	1½ to 2 pounds 1½ to 2 pounds	1 to 1¼ hours 1¼ to 1½ hours	135°F (145°F medium rare after standing) 150°F (160°F medium after standing)
Chop (loin or rib)	1 inch 1 inch	16 to 18 minutes 18 to 20 minutes	145°F medium rare 160°F medium
Leg of lamb (with bone) (medium-low heat)	5 to 7 pounds 5 to 7 pounds	1¾ to 2¼ hours 2¼ to 2¾ hours	135°F (145°F medium rare after standing) 150°F (160°F medium after standing)
PORK			
Boneless top loin roast (medium-low heat)	2 to 3 pounds (single loin) 3 to 5 pounds (double loin, tied)	1 to 1½ hours 1½ to 2¼ hours	150°F (160°F medium after standing) 150°F (160°F medium after standing)
Chop (boneless top loin)	¾ to 1 inch 1¼ to 1½ inches	20 to 24 minutes 30 to 35 minutes	160°F medium 160°F medium
Chop (loin or rib)	¾ to 1 inch 1¼ to 1½ inches	22 to 25 minutes 35 to 40 minutes	160°F medium 160°F medium
Country-style ribs		1½ to 2 hours	Tender
Ham, cooked (boneless) (medium-low heat)	3 to 5 pounds 6 to 8 pounds	1¼ to 2 hours 2 to 2¾ hours	140°F 140°F
Ham steak, cooked (medium-high heat)	1 inch	20 to 24 minutes	140°F
Loin back ribs or spareribs		1½ to 1¾ hours	Tender
Loin center rib roast (backbone loosened) (medium-low heat)	3 to 4 pounds 4 to 6 pounds	1¼ to 2 hours 2 to 2¾ hours	150°F (160°F medium after standing) 150°F (160°F medium after standing)
Sausages, uncooked (bratwurst, Polish, or Italian sausage links)	about 4 per pound	20 to 30 minutes	160°F medium
Smoked shoulder, picnic (with bone), cooked (medium-low heat)	4 to 6 pounds	1½ to 2¼ hours	140°F heated through
Tenderloin (medium-high heat)	¾ to 1 pound	30 to 35 minutes	155°F (160°F medium after standing)
VEAL			
Chop (loin or rib)	1 inch	19 to 23 minutes	160°F medium

*All cooking times are based on meat removed directly from refrigerator.

DIRECT-GRILLING MEAT

For a charcoal grill, place meat on grill rack directly over medium coals (see pages 16–17). Grill, uncovered, for the time given below or to desired doneness, turning once halfway through grilling. (For a gas grill, preheat grill. Reduce heat to medium. Place meat on grill rack over heat. Cover the grill.) Test for doneness using a meat thermometer. For steaks, cover and let stand for 5 minutes.

Cut	Thickness/ Weight	Grilling Temperature	Approximate Direct-Grilling Time*	Doneness
BEEF				
Boneless steak (top loin [strip], ribeye, shoulder top blade [flat-iron], shoulder petite tenders, shoulder center [ranch], chuck eye, tenderloin)	1 inch 1 inch 1½ inches 1½ inches	Medium Medium Medium Medium	10 to 12 minutes 12 to 15 minutes 15 to 19 minutes 18 to 23 minutes	145°F medium rare 160°F medium 145°F medium rare 160°F medium
Boneless top sirloin steak	1 inch 1 inch 1½ inches 1½ inches	Medium Medium Medium Medium	14 to 18 minutes 18 to 22 minutes 20 to 24 minutes 24 to 28 minutes	145°F medium rare 160°F medium 145°F medium rare 160°F medium
Boneless tri-tip steak (bottom sirloin)	¾ inch ¾ inch 1 inch 1 inch	Medium Medium Medium Medium	9 to 11 minutes 11 to 13 minutes 13 to 15 minutes 15 to 17 minutes	145°F medium rare 160°F medium 145°F medium rare 160°F medium
Flank steak	1¼ to 1¾ pounds	Medium	17 to 21 minutes	160°F medium
Steak with bone (porterhouse, T-bone, rib)	1 inch 1 inch 1½ inches 1½ inches	Medium Medium Medium Medium	10 to 13 minutes 12 to 15 minutes 18 to 21 minutes 22 to 25 minutes	145°F medium rare 160°F medium 145°F medium rare 160°F medium
GROUND MEAT				
Patties (beef, lamb, pork, or veal)	½ inch ¾ inch	Medium Medium	10 to 13 minutes 14 to 18 minutes	160°F medium 160°F medium
LAMB				
Chop (loin or rib)	1 inch 1 inch	Medium Medium	12 to 14 minutes 15 to 17 minutes	145°F medium rare 160°F medium
Chop (sirloin)	¾ to 1 inch	Medium	14 to 17 minutes	160°F medium
MISCELLANEOUS				
Kabobs (beef or lamb)	1-inch cubes	Medium	8 to 12 minutes	160°F medium
Kabobs (pork or veal)	1-inch cubes	Medium	10 to 14 minutes	160°F medium
Sausages, cooked (frankfurters, smoked bratwurst, etc.)		Medium	3 to 7 minutes	Heated through
PORK				
Chop (boneless top loin)	¾ to 1 inch 1¼ to 1½ inches	Medium Medium	7 to 9 minutes 14 to 18 minutes	160°F medium 160°F medium
Chop with bone (loin or rib)	¾ to 1 inch 1¼ to 1½ inches	Medium Medium	11 to 13 minutes 16 to 20 minutes	160°F medium 160°F medium
VEAL				
Chop (loin or rib)	1 inch	Medium	12 to 15 minutes	160°F medium

*All cooking times are based on meat removed directly from refrigerator.

DIRECT-GRILLING FISH AND SEAFOOD

Thaw fish or seafood, if frozen. Rinse fish or seafood; pat dry. Place fish fillets in a well-greased grill basket. For fish steaks and whole fish, grease the grill rack. Thread scallops or shrimp on skewers, leaving a ¼-inch space between pieces. For a charcoal grill, place fish on the grill rack directly over medium coals (see pages 16–17). Grill, uncovered, for the time given below or until fish begins to flake when tested with a fork (seafood should look opaque), turning once halfway through grilling. (For a gas grill, preheat grill. Reduce heat to medium. Place fish on grill rack over heat. Cover the grill.) If desired, brush with melted butter or margarine after turning.

Form of Fish	Thickness, Weight, or Size	Grilling Temperature	Approximate Direct-Grilling Time*	Doneness
Dressed whole fish	½ to 1½ pounds	Medium	6 to 9 minutes per 8 ounces	Flakes
Fillets, steaks, cubes (for kabobs)	½ to 1 inch thick	Medium	4 to 6 minutes per ½-inch thickness	Flakes
Lobster tails	6 ounces 8 ounces	Medium Medium	10 to 12 minutes 12 to 15 minutes	Opaque Opaque
Sea scallops (for kabobs)	12 to 15 per pound	Medium	5 to 8 minutes	Opaque
Shrimp (for kabobs)	20 per pound 12 to 15 per pound	Medium Medium	5 to 8 minutes 7 to 9 minutes	Opaque Opaque

*All cooking times are based on fish or seafood removed directly from refrigerator.

INDIRECT-GRILLING FISH AND SEAFOOD

Thaw fish or seafood, if frozen. Rinse fish or seafood; pat dry. Place fish fillets in a well-greased grill basket. For fish steaks and whole fish, grease the grill rack. Thread scallops or shrimp on skewers, leaving a ¼-inch space between pieces. For a charcoal grill, arrange medium-hot coals around drip pan. Test for medium heat above the pan (see pages 16–17). Place fish on grill rack over drip pan. Cover and grill for the time given below or until fish begins to flake when tested with a fork (seafood should look opaque), turning once halfway through grilling if desired. (For a gas grill, preheat grill. Reduce heat to medium. Adjust heat for indirect cooking [see pages 16–17].) If desired, brush with melted butter or margarine halfway through grilling.

Form of Fish	Thickness, Weight, or Size	Grilling Temperature	Approximate Indirect-Grilling Time*	Doneness
Dressed whole fish	½ to 1½ pounds	Medium	15 to 20 minutes per 8 ounces	Flakes
Fillets, steaks, cubes (for kabobs)	½ to 1 inch thick	Medium	7 to 9 minutes per ½-inch thickness	Flakes
Sea scallops (for kabobs)	12 to 15 per pound	Medium	11 to 14 minutes	Opaque
Shrimp (for kabobs)	20 per pound 12 to 15 per pound	Medium Medium	8 to 10 minutes 9 to 11 minutes	Opaque Opaque

*All cooking times are based on fish or seafood removed directly from refrigerator.

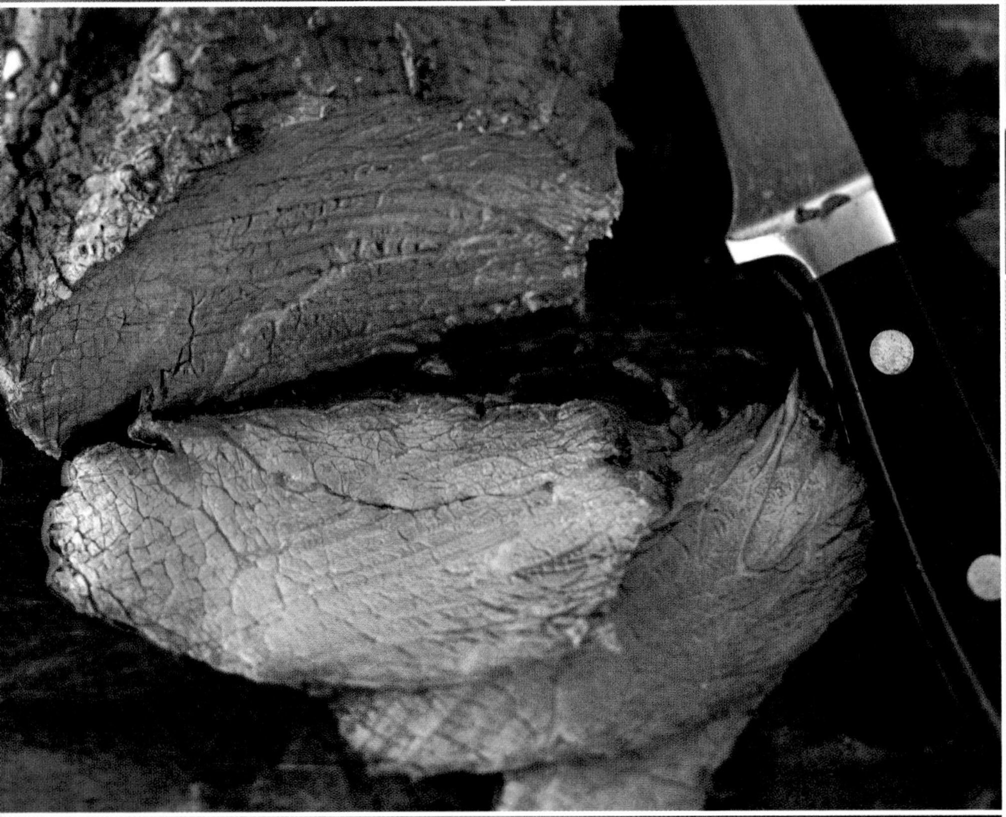

Sauces, Marinades, Rubs, Salsas, & Brines

DABS, DRIZZLES, AND DUNKINGS—ALL DESIGNED TO CATAPULT THE MOST PLAIN-JANE MEATS TO SPECTACULAR GRILLED HEIGHTS.

Sauces

THESE SENSATIONAL SAUCES HAVE YOU COVERED—TRY ONE OR TRY THEM ALL.

Kansas City Barbecue Sauce

MAKES: 1⅓ CUPS (ABOUT TEN 2-TABLESPOON SERVINGS)

- ½ cup finely chopped onion (1 medium)
- 2 cloves garlic, minced
- 1 tablespoon olive oil or vegetable oil
- ¾ cup apple juice
- ½ of a 6-ounce can tomato paste (⅓ cup)
- ¼ cup cider vinegar
- 2 tablespoons packed brown sugar
- 2 tablespoons molasses
- 1 tablespoon paprika
- 1 tablespoon prepared horseradish
- 1 tablespoon Worcestershire sauce
- 1 teaspoon salt
- ½ teaspoon black pepper

1 In a medium saucepan cook onion and garlic in hot oil over medium heat until onion is tender. Stir in apple juice, tomato paste, vinegar, brown sugar, molasses, paprika, horseradish, Worcestershire sauce, salt, and pepper. Bring to boiling; reduce heat. Simmer, uncovered, about 30 minutes or until sauce reaches desired consistency, stirring occasionally.

2 Brush sauce over beef, pork, or poultry during the last 10 minutes of grilling. If desired, reheat and serve additional sauce on the side.

Chipotle-Honey Marinade and Sauce

MAKES: 1½ CUPS (TWELVE 2-TABLESPOON SERVINGS)

- 1 pound roma tomatoes, halved and seeds removed
- Vegetable oil
- ¼ cup canned chipotle peppers in adobo sauce, undrained
- 2 tablespoons snipped fresh oregano
- 6 cloves garlic, minced
- ¾ cup honey
- ¼ cup molasses
- ¼ cup cider vinegar
- 1 tablespoon toasted sesame oil
- 1½ teaspoons ground cumin
- 1 teaspoon salt
- Fresh oregano leaves (optional)

1 Place tomato halves, cut sides down, on a lightly oiled broiler pan. Broil 3 to 4 inches from the heat for 4 to 5 minutes or until skins are charred. Cool until easy to handle. Peel and discard skins.

2 Place undrained chipotle peppers in a food processor or blender. Cover and process until smooth. Add tomatoes, oregano, and garlic. Cover and process until smooth. In a large bowl, stir together pureed tomato mixture, honey, molasses, vinegar, sesame oil, cumin, and salt. Use as a marinade and/or serve as a sauce on the side with grilled beef, pork, or poultry. If desired, garnish with fresh oregano leaves.

Espresso Barbecue Sauce

MAKES: ABOUT 2½ CUPS (ABOUT TWENTY 2-TABLESPOON SERVINGS)

- 1½ cups barbecue sauce
- 1 cup water
- ¼ cup packed brown sugar
- 2 tablespoons instant espresso coffee powder or instant coffee crystals

1 In a medium saucepan combine barbecue sauce, the water, brown sugar, and coffee powder. Bring to boiling, stirring to dissolve brown sugar; reduce heat. Simmer, uncovered, about 20 minutes or until slightly thickened.

2 Brush sauce over beef, pork, or poultry during the last 10 minutes of grilling. If desired, reheat and serve additional sauce on the side.

Soda Jerk BBQ Sauce

MAKES: 2¾ CUPS (TWENTY-TWO 2-TABLESPOON SERVINGS)

1 cup chopped onions (2 medium)
6 cloves garlic, minced
2 tablespoons butter
1 15-ounce can tomato sauce
1 12-ounce can cola, Dr Pepper soft drink, or root beer
3 tablespoons vinegar
2 tablespoons packed brown sugar
2 teaspoons Jamaican jerk seasoning

1 In a medium saucepan cook onions and garlic in hot butter over medium heat about 5 minutes or until onions are tender. Stir in tomato sauce, cola, vinegar, brown sugar, and jerk seasoning. Bring to boiling; reduce heat. Simmer, uncovered, about 1 hour or until mixture is reduced to 2¾ cups, stirring occasionally.

2 Brush sauce over beef, pork, or poultry during the last 10 minutes of grilling. If desired, reheat and serve additional sauce on the side.

Thai Peanut Sauce

MAKES: 1 CUP (EIGHT 2-TABLESPOON SERVINGS)

¾ cup reduced-sodium chicken broth or beef broth
2 tablespoons sliced green onion (1)
1 clove garlic, minced
1 tablespoon reduced-sodium soy sauce
½ teaspoon finely shredded lemon peel
1 tablespoon lemon juice
1 to 1½ teaspoons chili powder
½ teaspoon packed brown sugar
⅓ cup peanut butter
1 tablespoon grated fresh ginger or ¾ teaspoon ground ginger
Unsweetened coconut milk (optional)
Cayenne pepper (optional)

1 In a small saucepan bring broth to boiling; reduce heat. Add green onion and garlic. Cover and simmer about 2 minutes or until onion is tender. Stir in soy sauce, lemon peel, lemon juice, chili powder, and brown sugar.

2 Return to boiling; reduce heat. Simmer, uncovered, for 5 minutes, stirring frequently. Add peanut butter and ginger. Cook and stir just until heated through. If necessary, thin with a little coconut milk. Cool to room temperature. If desired, season to taste with cayenne pepper. Serve with grilled pork, chicken, shrimp, or vegetables.

Greek Dipping Sauce

MAKES: ¾ CUP (TWELVE 2-TABLESPOON SERVINGS)

½ cup olive oil
1 tablespoon finely shredded lemon peel
¼ cup lemon juice
2 tablespoons snipped fresh oregano
2 cloves garlic, minced
¼ teaspoon freshly ground black pepper

1 In a medium bowl whisk together oil, lemon peel, and lemon juice. Stir in oregano, garlic, and pepper. Let stand at room temperature for 20 minutes to allow flavors to blend. (Or cover and chill for 2 to 12 hours. Let stand at room temperature for 30 minutes before serving.) Serve with shrimp or fish.

DOUBLE-DUTY
MARINADES MAY BE USED AS DRIZZLING SAUCES AS WELL. TO TRANSFORM MARINADE TO SAUCE, REMOVE MEAT FROM MARINADE, TRANSFER LIQUID TO A SAUCEPAN, AND BOIL FOR 30 MINUTES OVER MEDIUM-HIGH HEAT.

PREPARING BASIC SAUCE, STEP-BY-STEP

1. Begin by finely chopping aromatic ingredients, such as onion, garlic, and ginger. Sautéed, these foods form a flavorful foundation for sauce.

2. Add tomato sauce to the cooked onion mixture and stir well. Bring the sauce to a boil then reduce to low heat.

3. Simmer sauce over low heat, stirring frequently to reduce volume, thicken consistency, and intensify flavor. When sauce is as thick as you like it, treat yourself to a taste, adding salt only if needed.

Sweet-Hot Barbecue Sauce

MAKES: ABOUT 2 CUPS (ABOUT SIXTEEN 2-TABLESPOON SERVINGS)

- 1¼ cups water
- 1 6-ounce can tomato paste
- ½ cup mild-flavor molasses
- ½ cup dark-color corn syrup
- ¼ cup vinegar
- ¼ cup honey
- 1 tablespoon whiskey or bourbon (optional)
- 1 tablespoon Worcestershire sauce
- 2 teaspoons paprika
- 1 teaspoon garlic salt
- 1 teaspoon liquid smoke
- 1 teaspoon bottled hot pepper sauce
- ½ teaspoon chili powder
- ¼ to ½ teaspoon cayenne pepper
- ¼ teaspoon onion powder

1 In a medium saucepan stir together the water, tomato paste, molasses, corn syrup, vinegar, honey, whiskey (if desired), Worcestershire sauce, paprika, garlic salt, liquid smoke, hot pepper sauce, chili powder, cayenne pepper, and onion powder. Bring to boiling; reduce heat. Simmer, uncovered, about 45 minutes or until sauce reaches desired consistency, stirring occasionally.

2 Brush sauce over beef, pork, or poultry during the last 10 minutes of grilling. If desired, reheat and serve additional sauce on the side.

Plum-Good Barbecue Sauce

MAKES: ABOUT 2¼ CUPS (ABOUT EIGHTEEN 2-TABLESPOON SERVINGS)

- ½ cup chopped onion (1 medium)
- 1 tablespoon butter
- 1 15-ounce can whole, unpitted purple plums, undrained
- 1 6-ounce can frozen lemonade concentrate, thawed
- ¼ cup ketchup
- 2 tablespoons soy sauce
- 2 teaspoons yellow mustard
- 1 teaspoon ground ginger
- 1 teaspoon Worcestershire sauce

1 In a medium saucepan cook onion in hot butter over medium heat about 5 minutes or until tender. Meanwhile, drain plums, reserving liquid. Remove pits from plums; discard pits. In a blender or food processor, combine plums and reserved liquid. Cover and blend until smooth.

2 Transfer pureed plums, lemonade concentrate, ketchup, soy sauce, mustard, ginger, and Worcestershire sauce to saucepan. Bring to boiling; reduce heat. Simmer, uncovered, for 10 to 15 minutes or until sauce reaches desired consistency, stirring occasionally.

3 Brush sauce over beef, pork, or poultry during the last 5 minutes of grilling. If desired, reheat and serve additional sauce on the side.

Hot Plum Sauce

MAKES: 2 CUPS (SIXTEEN 2-TABLESPOON SERVINGS)

- 1 15- or 16-ounce can whole, unpitted purple plums, undrained
- 2 tablespoons hoisin sauce
- 1 tablespoon frozen orange juice concentrate
- 1 tablespoon soy sauce
- 1 teaspoon grated fresh ginger
- ¼ teaspoon black pepper
- ¼ teaspoon cayenne pepper
- 2 teaspoons sesame seeds, toasted (optional)

1 Drain plums, reserving liquid. Remove pits from plums; discard pits. In a food processor or blender combine plums, the reserved liquid, hoisin sauce, orange juice concentrate, soy sauce, ginger, black pepper, and cayenne pepper. Cover and process until nearly smooth.

2 Transfer plum mixture to a small saucepan. Bring to boiling; reduce heat. Simmer, uncovered, about 15 minutes or until slightly thickened, stirring occasionally.

3 If desired, garnish with toasted sesame seeds. Serve with grilled pork or poultry.

Cherry-Ancho Barbecue Sauce

MAKES: ABOUT 2½ CUPS (ABOUT TWENTY 2-TABLESPOON SERVINGS)

- 1¼ cups cider vinegar
- ¾ cup ketchup
- ¾ cup chopped red onion (1 large)
- ¾ cup dried tart cherries
- ⅓ cup honey
- 2 dried ancho chile peppers, stemmed, seeded, and cut up (see Hot Tip, page 45)
- 2 cloves garlic, slivered
- ¾ teaspoon ground coriander
- ⅛ teaspoon ground cloves

1 In a large saucepan combine vinegar, ketchup, onion, dried cherries, honey, chile peppers, garlic, coriander, and cloves. Bring to boiling; reduce heat. Simmer, uncovered, about 20 minutes or until dried cherries and chile peppers are softened and mixture is slightly thickened. Cool slightly. Transfer mixture to a blender or food processor. Cover and blend until nearly smooth.

2 Brush sauce over pork or poultry during the last 5 minutes of grilling. If desired, reheat and serve additional sauce on the side.

Cajun Beer Sauce

MAKES: ABOUT 1 CUP (EIGHT 2-TABLESPOON SERVINGS)

- ¼ cup chopped onion
- ¼ cup chopped red sweet pepper
- 1 tablespoon vegetable oil
- ½ cup beer
- ½ cup cold water
- 1 tablespoon cornstarch
- 1 tablespoon Cajun seasoning
- ¼ teaspoon salt

1 In a small saucepan cook onion and sweet pepper in hot oil over medium heat about 4 minutes or until tender. In a small bowl stir together beer, the water, cornstarch, Cajun seasoning, and salt. Add to onion mixture. Cook and stir until thickened and bubbly. Cook and stir for 2 minutes more. Serve with grilled beef or lamb.

FOR SERIOUS SLATHERING, BRUSH HAND-CRAFTED SAUCES, THICKLY AND EVENLY, ON GRILLED MEATS USING A COTTON MOP BASTER.

Marinades

THESE SUPER SOAKERS TENDERIZE AND BOOST FLAVORS OF GRILL-BOUND MEATS.

Asian Marinade

MAKES: ABOUT 1½ CUPS MARINADE (ENOUGH FOR 1¼ POUNDS MEAT)

- ½ cup beef broth
- ⅓ cup bottled hoisin sauce
- ¼ cup reduced-sodium soy sauce
- ¼ cup sliced green onions (2)
- 3 tablespoons dry sherry, apple juice, orange juice, or pineapple juice
- 1 tablespoon sugar
- 1 teaspoon grated fresh ginger
- 4 cloves garlic, minced

1 In a small bowl stir together beef broth, hoisin sauce, soy sauce, green onions, sherry, sugar, ginger, and garlic.

2 To use, pour marinade over beef or pork in a resealable plastic bag set in a shallow dish; seal bag. Turn to coat meat. Marinate in the refrigerator for 4 to 24 hours, turning bag occasionally. Drain meat, discarding marinade. Grill as directed (see pages 26 to 28).

Korean-Style Marinade

MAKES: ABOUT ⅔ CUP MARINADE (ENOUGH FOR 1½ POUNDS OF MEAT, POULTRY, OR FISH)

- ¼ cup finely chopped green onions (2)
- ¼ cup soy sauce
- 2 tablespoons packed brown sugar
- 1 tablespoon toasted sesame oil
- 1 tablespoon grated fresh ginger
- 2 large cloves garlic, minced

1 In a small bowl stir together green onions, soy sauce, brown sugar, sesame oil, ginger, and garlic.

2 To use, pour marinade over beef, pork, poultry, or fish in a resealable plastic bag set in a shallow dish; seal bag. Turn to coat meat, poultry, or fish. Marinate in the refrigerator for 6 to 24 hours, turning bag occasionally. Drain meat, poultry, or fish, discarding marinade. Grill as directed (see pages 25 to 29).

Five-Spice Marinade

MAKES: ABOUT ½ CUP MARINADE (ENOUGH FOR 1 POUND OF PORK, POULTRY, OR FISH)

- ¼ cup bottled salsa
- 2 tablespoons soy sauce
- 2 tablespoons bottled oyster sauce
- 1 tablespoon sugar
- 1 teaspoon five-spice powder
- ¼ teaspoon cayenne pepper

1 In a small bowl stir together salsa, soy sauce, oyster sauce, sugar, five-spice powder, and cayenne pepper.

2 To use, pour marinade over pork, poultry, or fish in a resealable plastic bag set in a shallow dish; seal bag. Turn to coat pork, poultry, or fish. Marinate in the refrigerator for 2 to 4 hours, turning bag occasionally. Drain meat, poultry, or fish, reserving marinade. Grill as directed (see pages 25 to 29) brushing pork, poultry, or fish with reserved marinade halfway through grilling. Discard remaining marinade.

Teriyaki-Ginger Marinade

MAKES: ABOUT ¼ CUP (ENOUGH FOR 1 POUND OF MEAT, POULTRY, OR FISH)

- 2 tablespoons teriyaki sauce
- 4 teaspoons toasted sesame oil
- 1 teaspoon sugar
- 1 teaspoon grated fresh ginger or ¼ teaspoon ground ginger
- 2 cloves garlic, minced

1 In a small bowl stir together teriyaki sauce, sesame oil, sugar, ginger, and garlic.

2 To use, pour marinade over beef, pork, poultry, or fish in a resealable plastic bag set in a shallow dish; seal bag. Turn to coat meat, poultry, or fish. Marinate in the refrigerator for 30 minutes, turning bag occasionally. Drain meat, poultry, or fish, discarding marinade. Grill as directed (see pages 25 to 29).

Ale-Citrus Marinade

MAKES: ABOUT ¾ CUP (ENOUGH FOR 1 POUND OF MEAT, FISH, OR SEAFOOD)

- ½ cup amber ale or other desired ale
- ½ teaspoon finely shredded lime peel
- ¼ cup lime juice
- 2 tablespoons snipped fresh cilantro
- 1 small fresh jalapeño chile pepper, seeded and finely chopped (see Hot Tip, page 45)
- 1 clove garlic, minced
- ¼ teaspoon ground cumin
- ⅛ teaspoon cayenne pepper

1 In a small bowl stir together ale, lime peel, lime juice, cilantro, jalapeño pepper, garlic, cumin, and cayenne pepper.

2 To use, pour marinade over beef, pork, fish, or seafood in a resealable plastic bag set in a shallow dish; seal bag. Turn to coat meat, fish, or seafood. Marinate in the refrigerator for 30 to 60 minutes, turning bag occasionally. Drain meat, fish, or seafood, discarding marinade. Grill as directed (see pages 25 to 29).

Spice Marinade

MAKES: ABOUT ½ CUP (ENOUGH FOR 1 POUND OF MEAT)

- ¼ cup lime juice
- 2 tablespoons chili powder
- 1 tablespoon olive oil
- 1 clove garlic, minced
- 1½ teaspoons ground cumin
- 1½ teaspoons ground cinnamon
- ½ teaspoon bottled hot pepper sauce
- ¼ teaspoon salt

1 In a small bowl stir together lime juice, chili powder, oil, garlic, cumin, cinnamon, hot pepper sauce, and salt.

2 To use, pour marinade over beef, pork, poultry, or fish in a resealable plastic bag set in a shallow dish; seal bag. Turn to coat meat, poultry, or fish. Marinate in the refrigerator for 4 to 24 hours, turning bag occasionally. Drain meat, discarding marinade. Grill as directed (see pages 25 to 29).

Stout-Caraway Marinade

MAKES: ABOUT 2 CUPS (ENOUGH FOR 1¾ POUNDS OF MEAT OR POULTRY)

- 1 12-ounce bottle stout
- ½ cup chopped onion (1 medium)
- ¼ cup honey mustard
- 3 cloves garlic, minced
- 1 teaspoon caraway seeds

1 In a small bowl stir together stout, onion, honey mustard, garlic, and caraway seeds.

2 To use, pour marinade over beef, pork, lamb, or poultry in a resealable plastic bag set in a shallow dish; seal bag. Turn to coat meat or poultry. Marinate in the refrigerator for 6 to 24 hours, turning bag occasionally. Drain meat or poultry, reserving marinade. Grill as directed (see pages 25 to 28).

3 Meanwhile, in a small saucepan bring reserved marinade to boiling; reduce heat. Simmer, uncovered, about 15 minutes or until marinade is reduced by about half. Brush meat frequently with reduced marinade during the last 10 minutes of grilling. Discard remaining marinade.

HOW LONG IS LONG ENOUGH? CHICKEN, PORK, AND TOUGH CUTS OF BEEF BENEFIT FROM 4 TO 12 HOURS' MARINATION. FOR SMALL, ALREADY TENDER CUTS OF LAMB OR BEEF, 2 TO 4 HOURS WILL DO. BATHE FISH AND SHELLFISH FOR ONLY 30 MINUTES.

PREPARING BASIC MARINADE, STEP-BY-STEP

1. Combine marinade ingredients in a small nonmetal bowl. If using citrus peel, grate peel extra finely to allow zesty flavor to permeate the marinade.

2. Pat fish, poultry, pork, or beef dry with paper towels and place in a large nonmetal pan or in a resealable plastic bag. Avoid metal containers because they may impart an unpleasant metallic taste to marinated foods.

3. Pour marinade over meat or fish. Spread marinade evenly over top surfaces, then turn meat over to coat all sides. Cover tightly, then refrigerate, turning food once or twice while marinating.

Coconut Milk Marinade

MAKES: ABOUT 1⅓ CUPS MARINADE (ENOUGH FOR 3 POUNDS OF MEAT OR POULTRY)

- 1 cup unsweetened coconut milk
- ⅓ cup finely chopped onion (1 small)
- 2 teaspoons dry mustard
- 1½ teaspoons ground coriander
- ½ teaspoon salt
- ½ teaspoon ground turmeric
- ½ teaspoon ground cumin
- 1 clove garlic, minced

1 In a small bowl stir together coconut milk, onion, dry mustard, coriander, salt, turmeric, cumin, and garlic.

2 To use, pour marinade over beef, lamb, or poultry in a resealable plastic bag set in a shallow dish; seal bag. Turn to coat meat or poultry. Marinate in the refrigerator for 4 to 24 hours, turning bag occasionally. Drain meat or poultry, reserving marinade. Grill as directed (see pages 25 to 28), brushing meat or poultry with reserved marinade halfway through grilling. Discard remaining marinade.

Lemongrass Marinade

MAKES: ABOUT ½ CUP (ENOUGH FOR ¾ POUND OF PORK, POULTRY, OR FISH)

- 2 tablespoons lime juice
- 1 tablespoon olive oil
- ¼ cup finely chopped shallots (2 medium)
- 1 teaspoon chili powder
- 1 teaspoon curry powder
- 1 teaspoon lemongrass, finely chopped
- ¼ teaspoon black pepper

1 In a small bowl stir together lime juice, oil, shallots, chili powder, curry powder, lemongrass, and pepper.

2 To use, pour marinade over pork, poultry, or fish in a resealable plastic bag set in a shallow dish; seal bag. Turn to coat pork, poultry, or fish. Marinate in the refrigerator for 1 to 4 hours, turning bag occasionally. Drain pork, poultry, or fish, discarding marinade. Grill as directed (see pages 25 to 29).

Curried Yogurt Marinade

MAKES: ABOUT ⅓ CUP MARINADE (ENOUGH FOR 1 TO 1½ POUNDS OF MEAT OR POULTRY)

- ¼ cup plain yogurt
- 1 tablespoon curry powder
- 1 tablespoon honey
- 1 tablespoon olive oil or vegetable oil
- ½ teaspoon salt

1 In a small bowl stir together yogurt, curry powder, honey, oil, and salt.

2 To use, pour marinade over beef, pork, lamb, or poultry in a resealable plastic bag set in a shallow dish; seal bag. Turn to coat meat or poultry. Marinate in the refrigerator for 4 to 6 hours, turning bag occasionally. Drain meat or poultry, discarding marinade. Grill as directed (see pages 25 to 28).

Wine-Shallot Marinade

MAKES: ABOUT 2½ CUPS (ENOUGH FOR 2 POUNDS OF CHICKEN)

- 2 cups dry white wine
- ½ cup chopped onion (1 medium)
- ½ cup chopped shallots or green onions (4)
- 1 teaspoon olive oil or vegetable oil
- ½ teaspoon cracked black pepper
- ½ teaspoon dried basil, crushed
- ¼ teaspoon dried rosemary, crushed
- 1 bay leaf

1 In a medium bowl stir together wine, onion, shallots, oil, pepper, basil, rosemary, and bay leaf.

2 To use, pour marinade over chicken in a resealable plastic bag set in a shallow dish; seal bag. Turn to coat chicken. Marinate in the refrigerator for 8 to 24 hours, turning bag occasionally. Drain chicken, discarding marinade. Grill as directed (see pages 25 to 26).

Apple-Mustard Marinade

MAKES: ABOUT 1 CUP (ENOUGH FOR 1½ POUNDS OF PORK, POULTRY, OR FISH)

- ½ cup apple juice or apple cider
- ¼ cup cider vinegar
- ¼ cup coarse-grain brown mustard
- 2 tablespoons olive oil
- 1 tablespoon packed brown sugar
- 4 cloves garlic, minced
- 1½ teaspoons soy sauce
- Dash black pepper

1 In a small bowl stir together apple juice, vinegar, mustard, oil, brown sugar, garlic, soy sauce, and pepper.

2 To use, pour marinade over pork, poultry, or fish in a resealable plastic bag set in a shallow dish; seal bag. Turn to coat pork, poultry, or fish. Marinate in the refrigerator for 30 minutes, turning bag occasionally. Drain pork, poultry, or fish, reserving marinade. Grill as directed (see pages 25 to 29).

3 Meanwhile, in a small saucepan bring reserved marinade to boiling; reduce heat. Simmer, uncovered, about 8 minutes or until reduced to ⅔ cup. Serve with grilled pork, poultry, or fish.

Orange-Fennel Marinade

MAKES: ABOUT 1¼ CUPS (ENOUGH FOR ¾ POUND OF PORK, HAM, POULTRY, OR FISH)

- ⅔ cup orange juice
- ⅓ cup water
- 2 tablespoons thinly sliced green onion (1)
- 1 tablespoon snipped fresh sage or ½ teaspoon ground sage
- 1 tablespoon Dijon-style mustard
- 1 teaspoon fennel seeds, crushed

1 In a small bowl stir together orange juice, the water, onion, sage, mustard, and fennel seeds.

2 To use, pour marinade over pork, ham, poultry or fish in a resealable plastic bag set in a shallow dish; seal bag. Turn to coat pork, ham, poultry, or fish. Marinate in the refrigerator for 30 minutes to 4 hours, turning bag occasionally. Drain pork, ham, poultry, or fish, discarding marinade. Grill as directed (see pages 25 to 29).

ALTHOUGH PRIME CUTS OF BEEF AND PORK ARE ALREADY TENDER, THESE EXPENSIVE GRILLING CHOICES STILL BENEFIT FROM FLAVOR-INFUSING POWERS OF SIMPLE, SAVORY MARINADES.

Rubs

WET OR DRY, SAVORY BLENDS OF HERBS, SPICES, AND SEASONINGS ADD POTENT FLAVORS TO MEATS, POULTRY, AND FISH.

Mustard-Peppercorn Rub

MAKES: ABOUT 3 TABLESPOONS (ENOUGH FOR 3 POUNDS OF MEAT)

1 tablespoon coarse-grain brown mustard
2 teaspoons cracked black pepper
2 teaspoons snipped fresh tarragon
2 teaspoons olive oil
1 teaspoon coarse salt

1 In a small bowl stir together mustard, pepper, tarragon, oil, and salt. To use, spoon rub over beef, pork, or lamb; rub in with your fingers. Cover and chill for at least 15 minutes or up to 4 hours. Grill as directed (see pages 26 to 28).

BBQ Rub

MAKES: ABOUT 3 TABLESPOONS (ENOUGH FOR 3 POUNDS OF MEAT)

2 tablespoons barbecue seasoning
1 tablespoon garlic powder
1 teaspoon onion salt
½ teaspoon celery seeds, ground
¼ teaspoon cayenne pepper

1 In a small bowl stir together barbecue seasoning, garlic powder, onion salt, celery seeds, and cayenne pepper. To use, sprinkle rub evenly over beef, pork, or lamb; rub in with your fingers. Grill as directed (see pages 26 to 28).

Double-Pepper Barbecue Rub

MAKES: ABOUT ⅔ CUP RUB (ENOUGH FOR 4 TO 6 POUNDS OF MEAT OR POULTRY)

¼ cup paprika
1 tablespoon salt
1 tablespoon ground cumin
1 tablespoon packed brown sugar
1 tablespoon chili powder
1 tablespoon black pepper
1½ teaspoons cayenne pepper
¼ teaspoon ground cloves

1 In a small bowl stir together paprika, salt, cumin, brown sugar, chili powder, black pepper, cayenne pepper, and cloves. To use, sprinkle rub evenly over beef, pork, lamb, or poultry about 10 minutes before grilling; rub in with your fingers. Grill as directed (see pages 25 to 28).

Paprika Rub

MAKES: ABOUT 2½ TABLESPOONS (ENOUGH FOR 2½ POUNDS MEAT OR POULTRY)

4 teaspoons paprika
1½ teaspoons sugar
1 teaspoon garlic powder
½ teaspoon black pepper
¼ teaspoon salt

1 In a small bowl stir together paprika, sugar, garlic powder, pepper, and salt. To use, sprinkle rub evenly over beef, pork, lamb, or poultry; rub in with your fingers. Grill as directed (see pages 25 to 28).

Summer Breeze Rub

MAKES: ABOUT ⅔ CUP (ENOUGH FOR 4 POUNDS OF MEAT, POULTRY, OR FISH)

¼ cup packed brown sugar
2 teaspoons seasoned salt
2 teaspoons chili powder
¼ cup yellow mustard

1 In a small bowl stir together brown sugar, seasoned salt, and chili powder. To use, brush pork, poultry, or fish evenly with mustard. Sprinkle rub evenly over meat or fish. Cover and refrigerate for at least 6 hours or up to 24 hours. Grill as directed (see pages 25 to 29).

Mint Rub

MAKES: ABOUT 3 TABLESPOONS (ENOUGH FOR 3 POUNDS OF LAMB)

2 tablespoons dried mint
1 tablespoon coarsely ground black pepper
½ teaspoon salt
3 tablespoons honey

1 In a small bowl stir together mint, pepper, and salt. To use, drizzle lamb with honey. Sprinkle rub evenly over lamb; rub in with your fingers. Grill as directed (see pages 27 to 28).

Four-Herb Rub

MAKES: ABOUT ¼ CUP (ENOUGH FOR 1½ POUNDS OF MEAT OR POULTRY)

- 2 cloves garlic
- ¼ cup fresh basil leaves
- 2 tablespoons fresh thyme leaves
- 1 tablespoon fresh rosemary leaves
- 1 tablespoon fresh mint leaves
- 2 tablespoons olive oil
- ½ teaspoon salt
- ½ teaspoon black pepper

1 Place garlic in a food processor or blender. Process until garlic is finely chopped. Add basil, thyme, rosemary, and mint. Cover and process or blend until herbs are chopped. With food processor running, add oil in a thin, steady stream through feed tube. (When necessary, stop and scrape the inside of container with a rubber scraper.) Stir in salt and pepper. To use, spread rub evenly over beef, pork, lamb, or poultry. Grill as directed (see pages 25 to 28).

Cajun Rub

MAKES: 2½ TABLESPOONS (ENOUGH FOR 2½ POUNDS OF PORK, POULTRY, OR FISH)

- 1½ teaspoons ground white pepper
- 1½ teaspoons black pepper
- 1 teaspoon cayenne pepper
- 1 teaspoon dried thyme, crushed
- 1 teaspoon onion powder
- 1 teaspoon garlic powder
- ½ teaspoon salt

1 In a small bowl stir together white pepper, black pepper, cayenne pepper, thyme, onion powder, garlic powder, and salt. To use, sprinkle rub evenly over pork, poultry, or fish; rub in with your fingers. Grill as directed (see pages 25 to 29).

Indian Curry Rub

MAKES: ABOUT 2 TABLESPOONS (ENOUGH FOR 4 TO 5 POUNDS OF MEAT OR POULTRY)

- 2 teaspoons ground cinnamon
- ½ teaspoon sugar
- ½ teaspoon ground cumin
- ½ teaspoon ground turmeric
- ½ teaspoon ground coriander
- ¼ teaspoon salt
- ¼ teaspoon ground cardamom
- ¼ teaspoon ground cloves
- ¼ teaspoon ground nutmeg
- ¼ teaspoon cayenne pepper
- Vegetable oil

1 In a small bowl stir together cinnamon, sugar, cumin, turmeric, coriander, salt, cardamom, cloves, nutmeg, and cayenne pepper. To use, brush a little oil evenly over beef, pork, or poultry. Sprinkle rub evenly over meat or poultry; rub in with your fingers. Grill as directed (see pages 25 to 28).

Rosemary-Thyme Rub

MAKES: ABOUT ⅓ CUP (ENOUGH FOR 1 TO 2 POUNDS OF MEAT)

- ¼ cup finely snipped fresh parsley
- 2 tablespoons Dijon-style mustard
- 1 tablespoon snipped fresh rosemary
- 2 teaspoons snipped fresh thyme
- 2 cloves garlic, minced
- 1 teaspoon olive oil or vegetable oil
- ½ teaspoon coarsely ground black pepper

1 In small bowl stir together parsley, mustard, rosemary, thyme, garlic, oil, and pepper. To use, spread rub evenly over beef or pork. Grill as directed (see pages 26 to 28).

Spanish Olive Rub

MAKES: ABOUT ⅓ CUP (ENOUGH FOR 1 POUND OF MEAT)

- ½ cup pimiento-stuffed green olives
- 1 tablespoon capers, drained
- 3 cloves garlic, minced
- 1½ teaspoons finely shredded orange peel
- ½ teaspoon black pepper

1 In a blender or food processor combine olives, capers, garlic, orange peel, and pepper. Cover and blend until chunky. To use, spread rub evenly over beef, pork, or lamb. Grill as directed (see pages 26 to 28).

PREPARING BASIC RUB, STEP-BY-STEP

1. Crush dried herbs between your fingers to release the flavorful oils. In a small bowl combine all of the ingredients for the rub.

2. Stir the rub until all of the ingredients are completely incorporated and are evenly distributed.

3. Using your fingers, spread the rub over the surface of the meat, pressing slightly to help it adhere. Cook meat immediately or cover and chill according to the recipe.

Mediterranean Rub

MAKES: ABOUT ½ CUP (MAKES ENOUGH FOR 2½ TO 3 POUNDS OF MEAT)

- 3 tablespoons Dijon-style mustard
- 2 tablespoons olive oil or cooking oil
- 1 tablespoon dried oregano, crushed
- 1 tablespoon dried basil, crushed
- 1½ teaspoons garlic powder
- ¾ teaspoon salt
- ¾ teaspoon cracked black pepper

1 In a storage container combine mustard, oil, oregano, basil, garlic powder, salt, and pepper. Cover and store in the refrigerator up to 3 days.

2 To use, toss a couple tablespoons with fresh vegetables before grilling. Rub on fish, chicken, pork, and beef before grilling. (If using a cut of meat that is long-cooking, brush on the rub only about the last 20 minutes.) Grill as directed (see pages 24 to 29).

Lip-Smackin' Rub

MAKES: ABOUT 2 CUPS (ENOUGH FOR 12 POUNDS OF MEAT)

- ½ cup paprika
- ⅓ cup black pepper
- ¼ cup salt
- ¼ cup chili powder
- ¼ cup ground cumin
- ¼ cup packed brown sugar
- 3 tablespoons granulated sugar
- 2 tablespoons cayenne pepper

1 In a small bowl stir together paprika, black pepper, salt, chili powder, cumin, brown sugar, granulated sugar, and cayenne pepper.

2 To use, rub mixture evenly onto beef, pork, or chicken. Grill as directed (see pages 25 to 28).

Sweet and Spicy Rub

MAKES: ABOUT 3 TABLESPOONS (ENOUGH FOR 3 POUNDS OF MEAT)

- 2 tablespoons butter
- 1 teaspoon ground cinnamon
- ½ teaspoon salt
- ½ teaspoon ground cumin
- ½ teaspoon ground turmeric
- ½ teaspoon cayenne pepper
- ½ teaspoon black pepper
- ¼ teaspoon ground cardamom
- ⅛ teaspoon ground cloves
- ⅛ teaspoon ground nutmeg
- 1 tablespoon sugar

1 In a small saucepan melt butter. Stir in cinnamon, salt, cumin, turmeric, cayenne pepper, black pepper, cardamom, cloves, and nutmeg. Remove saucepan from heat. Stir in sugar; cool.

2 To use, rub mixture evenly onto meat. Grill as directed (see pages 26 to 28).

Lemon-Coriander Rub

MAKES: ABOUT ⅓ CUP (ENOUGH FOR 2 POUNDS OF MEAT)

- 2 tablespoons coriander seeds, crushed
- 2 tablespoons finely shredded lemon peel
- 1 tablespoon olive oil
- 1 teaspoon cumin seeds, crushed
- ½ teaspoon salt
- ½ teaspoon whole black peppercorns, crushed

1 In a small bowl stir together crushed coriander seeds, lemon peel, oil, cumin seeds, salt, and crushed peppercorns. Rub evenly onto beef, pork, lamb, or chicken. Cover and refrigerate up to 24 hours, if desired. Grill as directed (see pages 24 to 29).

Garlic-Fennel Rub

MAKES: ABOUT 1 TABLESPOON (ENOUGH FOR 1½ POUNDS OF MEAT OR CHICKEN

- 1 teaspoon black pepper
- 2 cloves garlic, minced
- ½ teaspoon celery seeds
- ½ teaspoon fennel seeds, crushed
- ½ teaspoon cayenne pepper
- ¼ teaspoon dried thyme, crushed
- ¼ teaspoon ground cumin

1 In a small bowl stir together black pepper, garlic, celery seeds, fennel seeds, cayenne pepper, thyme, and cumin.

2 To use, rub mixture evenly onto beef, lamb, pork, or chicken before grilling. Grill as directed (see pages 25 to 28).

Chili Rub

MAKES: ABOUT 3 TABLESPOONS (ENOUGH FOR 3 POUNDS OF MEAT OR CHICKEN)

- 1 tablespoon paprika
- 1 teaspoon ground cumin
- 1 teaspoon chili powder
- ½ teaspoon salt
- ½ teaspoon ground coriander
- ¼ to ½ teaspoon ground black pepper
- ¼ to ½ teaspoon cayenne pepper

1 In a small bowl stir together paprika, cumin, chili powder, salt, coriander, black pepper, and cayenne pepper.

2 To use, rub mixture evenly onto beef, pork, or chicken before grilling. Grill as directed (see pages 25 to 28).

Jamaican Jerk Rub

MAKES: ABOUT ⅓ cup (ENOUGH FOR 2 POUNDS OF PORK OR CHICKEN)

- 1 tablespoon onion powder
- 1 tablespoon packed brown sugar
- 1 tablespoon dried thyme, crushed
- 1½ teaspoons salt
- 1½ teaspoons ground allspice
- 1 teaspoon cracked black pepper
- ½ teaspoon ground nutmeg
- ½ teaspoon ground cinnamon
- ½ teaspoon ground cloves
- ¼ teaspoon cayenne pepper

1 In a small bowl stir together onion powder, brown sugar, thyme, salt, allspice, black pepper, nutmeg, cinnamon, cloves, and cayenne pepper.

2 To use, rub mixture evenly onto pork or chicken before grilling. Grill as directed (see pages 25 to 28).

WHAT A PAYOFF! FOR A LITTLE BIT OF EFFORT, HANDMADE RUBS MOVE MEATS FROM MUNDANE TO MASTERPIECE.

Salsas

DANCE THROUGH THESE ZESTY EMBELLISHMENTS TO DISCOVER DELIGHTFULLY FLAVORFUL DRESS-UPS.

Sweet or Savory Salsa

MAKES: ABOUT 3 CUPS (ABOUT TWELVE ¼-CUP SERVINGS)

- 2 cups coarsely chopped strawberries
- 1 cup coarsely chopped fresh pineapple or avocado
- ½ cup coarsely chopped mango, peach, or seeded cucumber
- 1 teaspoon finely shredded lime peel
- 2 tablespoons lime juice
- 2 tablespoons honey
- ½ teaspoon grated fresh ginger or 1 to 2 tablespoons seeded and finely chopped jalapeño pepper (see Hot Tip, page 45)
- ¼ teaspoon cracked black pepper

1 For sweet salsa, in a medium bowl stir together strawberries, pineapple, mango, lime peel, lime juice, honey, ginger, and cracked black pepper.

2 For savory salsa, in a medium bowl stir together strawberries, avocado, cucumber, lime peel, lime juice, honey, jalapeño pepper, and cracked black pepper.

3 Cover and refrigerate for 2 to 24 hours before serving. Serve with grilled beef, pork, or chicken.

Tomatillo-Apple Salsa

MAKES: 5 CUPS (TWENTY ¼-CUP SERVINGS)

- 24 fresh tomatillos, husked and chopped* (4⅔ cups)
- 3 medium tart apples, peeled, cored, and finely chopped (2 cups)
- ½ cup chopped red sweet pepper (1 small)
- ½ cup cider vinegar
- 4 to 6 fresh or canned jalapeño peppers, seeded and finely chopped (see Hot Tip, page 45) (¼ to ⅓ cup)
- ¼ cup snipped fresh cilantro
- ¼ cup sugar
- 1 teaspoon salt

1 In a 4- to 6-quart Dutch oven combine tomatillos, apples, sweet pepper, vinegar, jalapeño peppers, cilantro, sugar, and salt. Bring to boiling; reduce heat. Simmer, uncovered, for 15 minutes. Serve with grilled beef, pork, or poultry.

***NOTE:** If you can't find fresh tomatillos, use four 18-ounce cans tomatillos, drained and chopped.

Apricot-Rosemary Salsa

MAKES: 1 CUP (FOUR ¼-CUP SERVINGS)

- ½ cup chopped fresh apricots or peaches
- ¼ cup chopped avocado
- ¼ cup chopped tomato
- 2 tablespoons lime juice or lemon juice
- 1 tablespoon chopped green onion
- 1 teaspoon honey
- ½ to 1 teaspoon snipped fresh rosemary

1 In a small bowl stir together apricots, avocado, tomato, lime juice, green onion, honey, and rosemary. Cover and chill for up to 4 hours. Serve with grilled chicken or fish.

Blueberry Salsa

MAKES: 2 CUPS (EIGHT ¼-CUP SERVINGS)

- 1½ cups fresh blueberries
- 2 oranges
- ¼ cup finely chopped red onion
- 2 tablespoons balsamic vinegar
- 1 tablespoon snipped fresh mint
- ⅛ teaspoon salt

1 Coarsely chop ½ cup of the blueberries. Place all of the blueberries in a medium bowl; set aside. Peel and section the oranges; coarsely chop orange sections. Add chopped oranges and any juice to the blueberries. Stir in red onion, vinegar, mint, and salt. Serve with grilled pork, chicken, or fish.

Double Peach Salsa

MAKES: 3 CUPS (TWELVE ¼-CUP SERVINGS)

- 2 cups chopped peaches
- 1 cup chopped white peaches or peaches
- ¼ cup chopped sweet onion
- 3 tablespoons lime juice
- 2 to 3 tablespoons finely chopped, seeded fresh jalapeño chile peppers (see Hot Tip)
- 1 tablespoon snipped fresh cilantro
- 1 clove garlic, minced

1 In a medium bowl stir together peaches, onion, lime juice, jalapeño peppers, cilantro, and garlic. Cover and chill for 1 to 2 hours. Serve with grilled pork, chicken, or fish.

Fresh Tomato Salsa

MAKES: 3 CUPS (TWELVE ¼-CUP SERVINGS)

- 1½ cups finely chopped tomatoes (3 medium)
- 1 fresh Anaheim pepper, chopped, or 1 4-ounce can diced green chile peppers, drained
- ¼ cup chopped green sweet pepper
- ¼ cup sliced green onions (2)
- 3 to 4 tablespoons snipped fresh cilantro or parsley
- 2 tablespoons lime juice or lemon juice
- 1 to 2 fresh jalapeño, serrano, Fresno, or banana peppers, seeded and finely chopped (see Hot Tip)
- 1 clove garlic, minced
- ⅛ teaspoon salt
- ⅛ teaspoon cracked black pepper

1 In a medium bowl stir together tomatoes, Anaheim pepper, sweet pepper, green onions, cilantro, lime juice, jalapeño pepper, garlic, salt, and cracked black pepper.

2 If desired, for a smooth salsa, place 1 cup salsa in a food processor or blender container. Cover and process just until smooth; stir into remaining salsa. Cover and refrigerate until ready to serve. Serve with grilled beef, pork, or chicken.

Hot Tip!

BECAUSE CHILE PEPPERS CONTAIN VOLATILE OILS THAT CAN BURN SKIN AND EYES, AVOID DIRECT CONTACT WITH THEM AS MUCH AS POSSIBLE. WHEN WORKING WITH CHILE PEPPERS, WEAR PLASTIC OR RUBBER GLOVES. IF YOUR BARE HANDS TOUCH THE PEPPERS, WASH YOUR HANDS AND NAILS WELL WITH SOAP AND WARM WATER.

Tangy Avocado Salsa

MAKES: 2 CUPS (EIGHT ¼-CUP SERVINGS)

- 6 fresh tomatillos, husked and halved
- 1 cup water
- 1 ripe avocado, halved, seeded, and peeled
- ½ cup coarsely chopped green onions (4)
- ½ cup loosely packed fresh cilantro leaves
- ⅓ cup dairy sour cream
- 1 fresh jalapeño pepper, seeded and coarsely chopped (see Hot Tip)
- ½ teaspoon salt

1 In a medium saucepan combine tomatillos and the water. Bring to boiling; reduce heat. Simmer, uncovered, for 5 to 7 minutes or until tender, stirring occasionally. Using a slotted spoon, transfer tomatillos to a food processor or blender; cool slightly. Add 2 tablespoons of the cooking liquid.

2 Add avocado, green onions, cilantro, sour cream, jalapeño pepper, and salt to the food processor or blender. Cover and process until slightly chunky. Transfer to a covered container; chill for 1 to 24 hours. Serve with grilled meat or poultry.

PREPARING BASIC SALSA, STEP-BY-STEP

1. Begin with garden-fresh, fully ripe fruits or vegetables. Chop evenly—and scrape any flavor-rich juices from the cutting board into the mixing bowl.

2. Acidity, usually in the form of lime or lemon juice, makes salsa flavor shine brightly. For best results, avoid bottled citrus juices and go for the glory of fresh-squeezed juice instead.

3. Allow salsa flavors to meld in the refrigerator for 20 to 30 minutes, then spoon the colorful concoction on meat, poultry, or seafood.

Watermelon, Mango, and Jicama Salsa

MAKES: 6 CUPS (TWENTY-FOUR ¼-CUP SERVINGS)

- 3 cups chopped, seeded watermelon
- 1½ cups chopped, peeled jicama
- 1 cup chopped, peeled mango
- 2 tablespoons chopped green onion (1)
- 1 medium fresh jalapeño chile pepper, seeded and finely chopped (see Hot Tip, page 45)
- 1 tablespoon snipped fresh cilantro
- 1 tablespoon lime juice
- ⅛ teaspoon cayenne pepper

1 In a medium bowl stir together watermelon, jicama, mango, green onion, jalapeño pepper, cilantro, lime juice, and cayenne pepper. Cover and chill up to 24 hours. Serve with grilled pork, chicken, or fish.

Fresh Strawberry Salsa

MAKES: 2 CUPS (EIGHT ¼-CUP SERVINGS)

- 3 tablespoons bottled plum sauce
- 3 tablespoons lime juice
- ½ teaspoon grated fresh ginger
- ¼ teaspoon salt (optional)
- ⅛ teaspoon black pepper
- 1 cup coarsely chopped strawberries
- ½ cup chopped seeded cucumber
- 2 tablespoons thinly sliced green onion (1)
- 2 tablespoons snipped fresh cilantro
- ½ of a small fresh jalapeño chile pepper, seeded and finely chopped (see Hot Tip, page 45)

1 In a small bowl combine plum sauce, lime juice, ginger, salt (if desired), and black pepper. Stir in strawberies, cucumber, green onion, cilantro, and jalapeño pepper. Cover and chill for up to 8 hours. Serve with grilled pork, chicken, or fish.

Mango-Mint Salsa

MAKES: ABOUT 2 CUPS (ABOUT EIGHT ¼-CUP SERVINGS)

- 1 cup chopped, peeled mango
- ½ cup chopped, peeled jicama
- ¼ cup finely chopped red onion
- ¼ cup snipped fresh mint
- ½ to 1 teaspoon finely chopped canned chipotle pepper in adobo sauce
- 1 tablespoon honey
- 1 tablespoon olive oil

1 In a medium bowl stir together mango, jicama, red onion, mint, and chipotle pepper. Drizzle with honey and oil; toss gently to coat. Cover and chill for 2 to 24 hours. Let stand at room temperature for 30 minutes before serving. Serve with grilled meat, poultry, fish, or seafood.

Corn Salsa

MAKES: 4 CUPS (SIXTEEN ¼-CUP SERVINGS)

- 4 large ears fresh corn or one 10-ounce package frozen whole kernel corn (2 cups)
- 1 cup coarsely chopped onion (1 large)
- 1 cup coarsely chopped green or red sweet pepper (1 large)
- 1 fresh jalapeño pepper, seeded and finely chopped (see Hot Tip, page 45)
- 1 tablespoon vegetable oil
- 1 cup chopped, peeled tomatoes or one 14.5-ounce can diced tomatoes, drained
- ¼ cup lime juice
- ½ teaspoon salt
- ½ teaspoon ground cumin
- ½ teaspoon black pepper

1 Remove husks from fresh ears of corn; discard. Scrub with a stiff brush to remove silks; rinse. Cook, covered, in enough lightly salted boiling water to cover for 5 to 7 minutes or until tender; drain. Let cool. Cut kernels from cobs. Or cook frozen corn according to package directions; drain.

2 In a large saucepan cook onion, sweet pepper, and jalapeño pepper in hot oil over medium heat until onion is tender. Stir in corn, tomatoes, lime juice, salt, cumin, and black pepper. Cook and stir until heated through. Let cool. Serve with grilled beef, pork, or poultry.

Spicy Melon Salsa

MAKES: 4 CUPS (SIXTEEN ¼-CUP SERVINGS)

- ½ of a medium cantaloupe, seeded, peeled, and chopped (about 2½ cups)
- 1 8-ounce can crushed pineapple (juice pack), drained
- ¾ cup chopped red sweet pepper (1 medium)
- ¼ cup thinly sliced green onions (2)
- 2 tablespoons snipped fresh cilantro
- 2 tablespoons white wine vinegar or rice vinegar
- 2 tablespoons vegetable oil
- 1 fresh jalapeño chile pepper, seeded and finely chopped (see Hot Tip, page 45)
- ⅛ teaspoon salt

1 In a large bowl stir together cantaloupe, pineapple, sweet pepper, green onions, cilantro, vinegar, oil, jalapeño pepper, and salt. Cover and chill for up to 2 days. Serve with grilled meat, poultry, fish, or seafood.

Chipotle Avocado Salsa

MAKES: 2½ CUPS (TEN ¼ CUP SERVINGS)

- 2 cups finely chopped tomatoes
- 1 avocado, halved, seeded, peeled, and diced
- ½ cup finely chopped sweet onion
- ½ cup chopped fresh cilantro
- 1 canned chipotle pepper in adobo sauce, seeded and finely chopped
- 1 tablespoon adobo sauce
- 2 tablespoon packed brown sugar
- 1 tablespoon lemon juice
- ½ teaspoon ground cumin
- ½ teaspoon kosher salt

1. In a medium bowl combine all ingredients. Serve immediately or cover and chill up to 1 hour. Serve with grilled meat, poultry, or fish.

EVEN SOMETHING AS PLAIN AS GRILLED CHICKEN BREAST BECOMES BELLE-OF-THE-BALL-BEAUTIFUL WHEN DRESSED WITH SALSA.

Brines

BRINES POSSESS A NEARLY MAGICAL ABILITY—TO MAKE MEATS SUPER-MOIST, TENDER, AND SUCCULENT.

Italian Brine

MAKES: 6 CUPS

- 6 cups water
- ¼ cup kosher salt*
- ¼ cup red wine vinegar
- 1 cup chopped fresh basil
- ¼ cup chopped fresh oregano
- 1 tablespoon packed brown sugar
- 6 cloves garlic, minced
- ½ teaspoon crushed red pepper
- Desired meat or poultry
- 1 recipe Basil Pesto

1 In a large bowl combine the water, salt, vinegar, basil, oregano, brown sugar, garlic, and crushed red pepper. Stir until salt and brown sugar dissolve.

2 Place meat or poultry in a very large resealable plastic bag set in a deep dish. Pour brine over meat; seal bag. Marinate as directed. Drain meat, discarding brine. Grill as directed (see pages 25 to 28). Serve with Basil Pesto.

BASIL PESTO: In a food processor or blender combine ¼ cup olive oil; 2 cups firmly packed fresh basil leaves; ½ cup pine nuts; ½ cup finely shredded Parmesan or Romano cheese; 4 cloves garlic, peeled and quartered; and ¼ teaspoon salt. Cover and process until nearly smooth, stopping and scraping sides of container as necessary.

***NOTE** If your meat or poultry has been injected with a sodium solution (packaged meat or poultry that isn't labeled "natural"), reduce the kosher salt to 2 tablespoons.

ONE 3- TO 3½-POUND WHOLE BROILER-FRYER CHICKEN: Marinate in the refrigerator for 6 to 8 hours, turning occasionally. Makes 4 servings.

TWO 1¼- TO 1½-POUND CORNISH GAME HENS: Marinate in the refrigerator for 4 hours, turning occasionally. Makes 4 servings.

FOUR PORK RIB OR LOIN CHOPS, CUT 1¼ INCHES THICK: Marinate in the refrigerator for 4 to 6 hours, turning occasionally. Makes 4 servings.

ONE 2½- TO 3-POUND BONELESS PORK TOP LOIN ROAST: Marinate in the refrigerator for 7 to 8 hours, turning occasionally. Makes 8 servings.

TWO 12- TO 16-OUNCE PORK TENDERLOINS: Marinate in the refrigerator for 4 to 6 hours, turning occasionally. Makes 8 servings.

Chimichurri Brine

MAKES: ABOUT 7 CUPS

- 6 cups water
- ⅓ cup finely chopped onion (1 small)
- ¼ cup kosher salt*
- 1 tablespoon finely shredded lime peel
- ¼ cup lime juice
- ¼ cup snipped fresh parsley
- 1 tablespoon snipped fresh oregano
- 1 tablespoon sugar
- 4 cloves garlic, minced
- ½ teaspoon black pepper
- ¼ teaspoon crushed red pepper
- Desired meat or poultry
- 1 recipe Chimichurri Sauce

1 In a large bowl combine the water, onion, salt, lime peel, lime juice, parsley, oregano, sugar, garlic, black pepper, and crushed red pepper. Stir until salt and sugar dissolve.

2 Place meat or poultry in a very large resealable plastic bag set in a deep dish. Pour brine over meat; seal bag. Marinate as directed. Drain meat, discarding brine. Grill as directed (see pages 25 to 28). Serve with Chimichurri Sauce.

CHIMICHURRI SAUCE: In a medium bowl combine 3 cups snipped fresh parsley; 15 cloves garlic, minced; 3 tablespoons snipped fresh oregano; ¾ teaspoon crushed red pepper; and ¾ teaspoon salt. Add ¾ cup vegetable oil and ½ cup white vinegar. Using a fork, toss to combine. Serve immediately or cover and chill up to 3 days.

***NOTE:** If your meat or poultry has been injected with a sodium solution (packaged meat or poultry that isn't labeled "natural"), reduce the kosher salt to 2 tablespoons.

ONE 3- TO 3½-POUND WHOLE BROILER-FRYER CHICKEN: Marinate in the refrigerator for 6 to 8 hours, turning occasionally. Makes 4 servings.

TWO 1¼- TO 1½-POUND CORNISH GAME HENS: Marinate in the refrigerator for 4 hours, turning occasionally. Makes 4 servings.

FOUR PORK RIB OR LOIN CHOPS, CUT 1¼ INCHES THICK: Marinate in the refrigerator for 4 to 6 hours, turning occasionally. Makes 4 servings.

ONE 2½- TO 3-POUND BONELESS PORK TOP LOIN ROAST: Marinate in the refrigerator for 6 to 8 hours, turning occasionally. Makes 8 servings.

TWO 12- TO 16-OUNCE PORK TENDERLOINS: Marinate in the refrigerator for 4 to 6 hours, turning occasionally. Makes 8 servings.

Herbes de Provence Brine

MAKES: 7 CUPS

- 6 cups water
- ¼ cup kosher salt*
- 2 tablespoons finely shredded lemon peel
- ¼ cup lemon juice
- 1 tablespoon honey
- 2 tablespoons chopped fresh basil
- 1 tablespoon dried lavender
- 1 tablespoon snipped fresh marjoram
- 1 tablespoon snipped fresh rosemary
- 1 tablespoon snipped fresh sage
- 1 tablespoon snipped fresh thyme
- 1 teaspoon fennel seeds, crushed
- Desired meat
- 1 recipe Sauce Verte

1 In a large bowl combine the water, salt, lemon peel, lemon juice, honey, basil, lavender, marjoram, rosemary, sage, thyme, and fennel seeds. Stir until salt and honey dissolve.

2 Place meat or poultry in a very large resealable plastic bag set in a deep dish. Pour brine over meat; seal bag. Marinate as directed. Drain meat, discarding brine. Grill as directed (see pages 25 to 28). Serve with Sauce Verte.

SAUCE VERTE: Blanch ½ cup fresh spinach and ¼ cup Italian parsley leaves in boiling water for 1 minute; drain. Immediately place in ice water to stop cooking. Drain again; pat dry with paper towels. In a blender or food processor combine 1 cup mayonnaise, the blanched parsley and spinach, 1 teaspoon snipped fresh tarragon, 1 teaspoon lemon juice, 1 anchovy fillet, and 1 clove smashed garlic. Cover and blend until smooth. Stir in 2 teaspoons capers.

***NOTE:** If your meat or poultry has been injected with a sodium solution (packaged meat or poultry that isn't labeled "natural"), reduce the kosher salt to 2 tablespoons.

ONE 3- TO 3½-POUND WHOLE BROILER-FRYER CHICKEN: Marinate in the refrigerator for 6 to 8 hours, turning occasionally. Makes 4 servings.

TWO 1¼- TO 1½-POUND CORNISH GAME HENS: Marinate in the refrigerator for 4 hours, turning occasionally. Makes 4 servings.

FOUR PORK RIB OR LOIN CHOPS, CUT 1¼ INCHES THICK: Marinate in the refrigerator for 4 to 6 hours, turning occasionally. Makes 4 servings.

ONE 2½- TO 3-POUND BONELESS PORK TOP LOIN ROAST: Marinate in the refrigerator for 6 to 8 hours, turning occasionally. Makes 8 servings.

TWO 12- TO 16-OUNCE PORK TENDERLOINS: Marinate in the refrigerator for 4 to 6 hours, turning occasionally. Makes 8 servings.

Maple Brine for Turkey

MAKES: ABOUT 7 QUARTS

- 1½ gallons water
- 1½ cups pure maple syrup or maple-flavor syrup
- 1 cup coarse salt
- ¾ cup packed brown sugar
- 1 10-pound turkey (not a self-basting type)

1 For brine, in a 10-quart pot combine the water, syrup, salt, and brown sugar. Stir until sugar and salt dissolve. Set aside.

2 Rinse the turkey body cavity. Add turkey to brine in pot; cover. Marinate in the refrigerator for 12 to 24 hours.

3 Remove turkey from brine; discard brine. Drain turkey; pat dry with paper towels. Grill as directed (see pages 25 to 26).

PREPARING BASIC BRINE, STEP-BY-STEP

1. Add salt and sugar to cold clear water, stirring until the crystals are completely dissolved.

2. Add remaining ingredients called for in your brine recipe. Stir well to combine all ingredients.

3. Pour brine over poultry or pork in a large resealable plastic bag. Squeeze bag to release air, then fasten tightly. Roll bag to distribute brine before refrigerating.

Steaks & Chops

SATISFYING, SUBSTANTIAL, AND OH-SO-GOOD, THESE TOP-SHELF MEATS ARE A GUY'S GO-TO CUTS FOR THE GRILL.

Checking for Doneness

WHEN EVERYONE PREFERS STEAK AND CHOPS GRILLED TO DIFFERENT TEMPERATURES, HERE'S HOW TO PLEASE THEM ALL.

THERMOMETER TEST

A thermometer is the most reliable way to determine doneness. Whether it's a fork-style meat themometer or an instant-read probe, insert it into the thickest part of the meat without touching any bone. To test thin meats, such as hamburgers and boneless chicken breasts, insert the thermometer at the outer edge of the meat and press it flat toward the center.

TOUCH TEST

With a little practice, you can evaluate the temperature of grilling meat by pressing on the thickest part of the steak or chop with your finger.

When meat is rare, it will feel soft and yielding, like the flesh between your thumb and index finger when you pinch them together.

Medium rare meat will feel a bit resistant to the touch, like the flesh between your thumb and your middle finger when you touch them loosely together.

Meat grilled to medium will feel increasingly firm and taut, like the flesh between your thumb and ring finger when you touch those digits gently together.

When meat is well done, it will yield only slightly to the touch and will feel like the flesh between your thumb and little finger when they meet together.

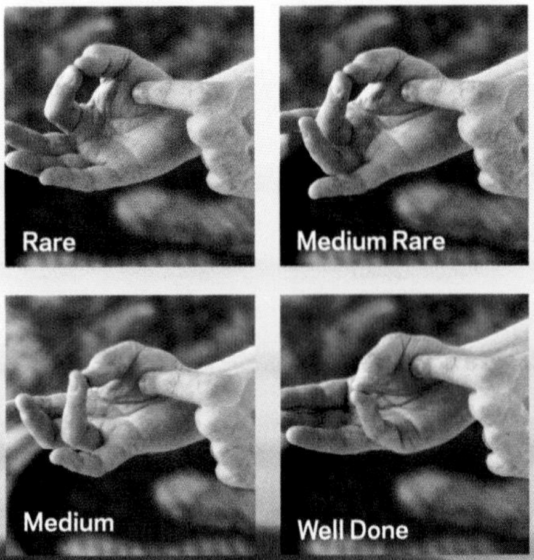

The temperature of rare beef (far left) is about 140°F.

Medium rare beef (left) is about 150°F.

Medium beef, pork, or poultry (lower far left) is approximately 160°F.

Well-done beef, pork, or poultry (left) measures 170°F or more.

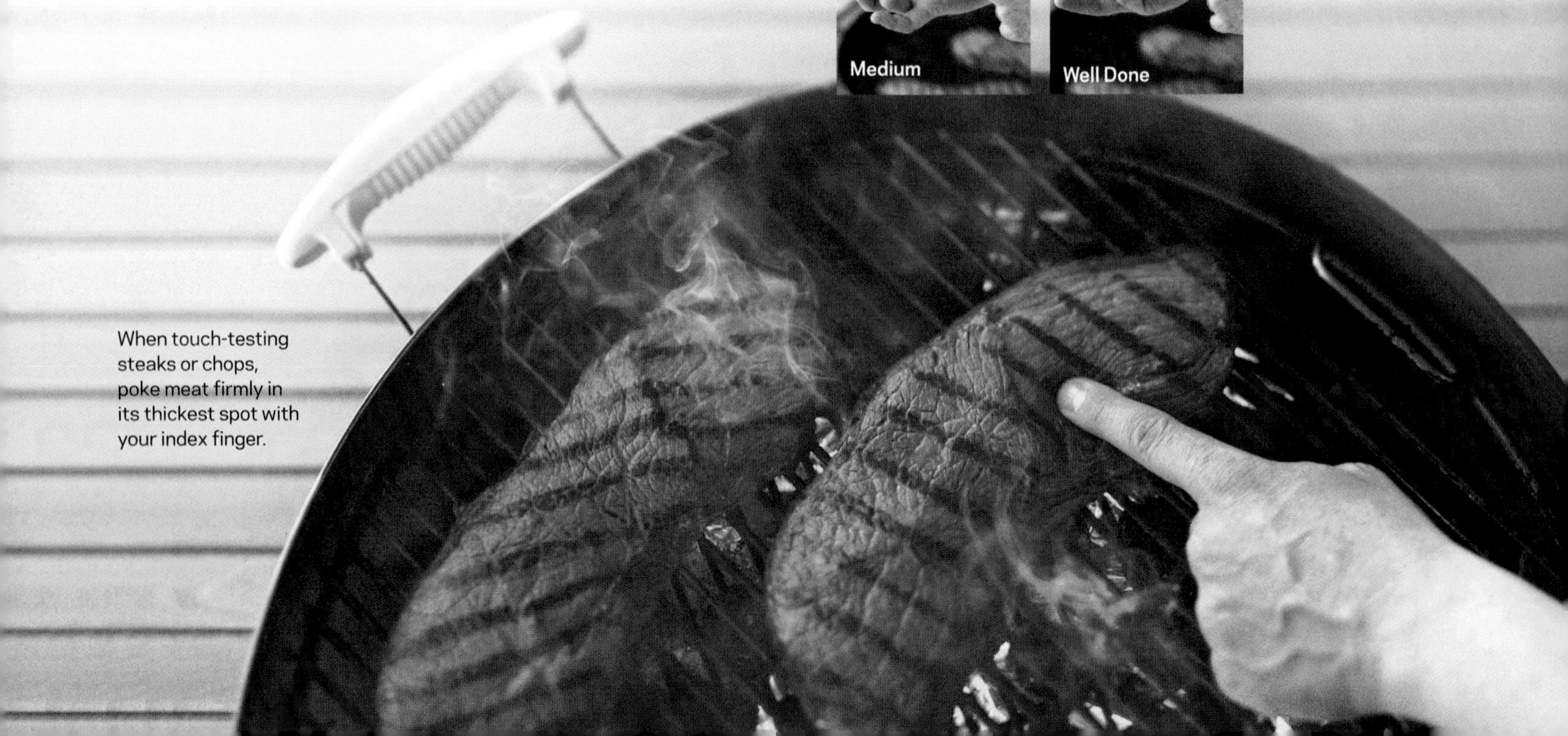

When touch-testing steaks or chops, poke meat firmly in its thickest spot with your index finger.

Meat Cuts

CHOOSE FROM THIS LINEUP OF GRILLERS AND GET YOUR FLAME ON.

When purchasing steaks and chops, make sure the fat is in the right place. Thin streaks of intramuscular fat—marbling—indicate the most flavorful cuts. Excessive pads of fat surrounding the muscle, however, should be trimmed off to prevent fire flare-ups. When in doubt, consult butchers—no one knows or appreciates the potential of a steak or chop like they do.

BEEF

Top sirloin steak

Top loin (strip) steak

Flank steak

Top blade (flat-iron)

Skirt steak

T-bone/porterhouse steak

Tenderloin steaks

Ribeye steak

PORK

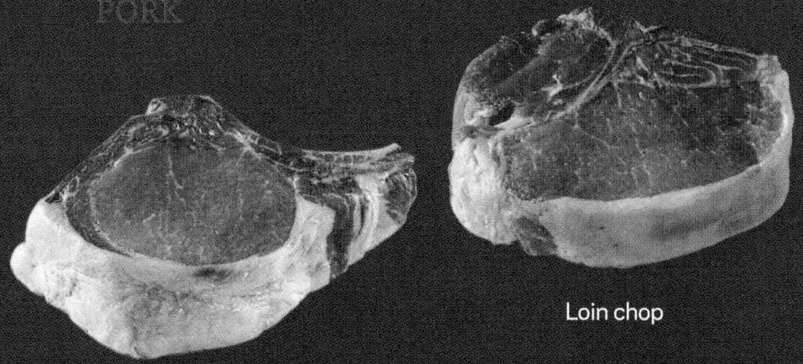

Loin chop

Rib chop

LAMB

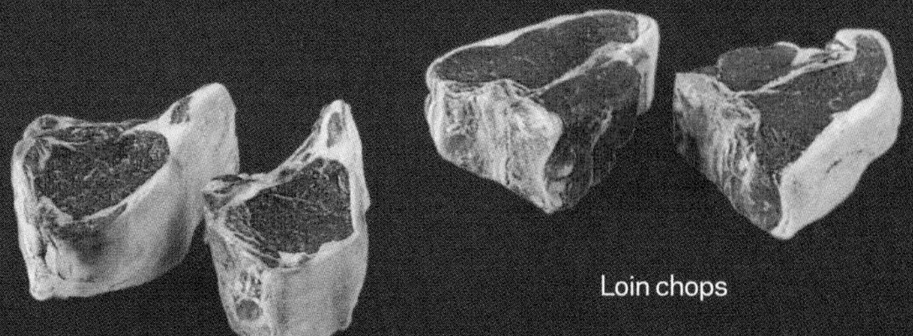

Loin chops

Rib chops

STEP-BY-STEP

1. Halve the peppers and scrape the seeds from halves. Cut the halves into thin strips. Line up the strips and cut crosswise into small pieces.

2. To score the steak, make shallow diagonal cuts on the steak about 1 inch apart and ⅛ inch deep. Make additional cuts in the opposite direction, forming a diamond pattern.

3. Place the steak between two sheets of plastic wrap. Using the flat side of the mallet, pound the meat to ¼-inch thickness, beginning in the center and working to the edges.

Argentinean Rolled Flank Steak (Matambre)

ALTHOUGH IT LOOKS COMPLICATED, MAKING THIS SOUTH AMERICAN MASTERPIECE IS EASIER THAN YOU THINK—AND YOUR GUESTS WILL THINK YOU LABORED ALL DAY.

PREP: 40 MINUTES **CHILL:** 2 HOURS
GRILL: 40 MINUTES **STAND:** 10 MINUTES
MAKES: 6 SERVINGS

- 1 1¼- to 1½-pound beef flank steak
- 2 medium Anaheim peppers, chopped*
- ½ cup chopped sweet onion (1 small)
- 2 cloves garlic, minced
- 1 tablespoon vegetable oil
- 1 tablespoon snipped fresh oregano
- ½ teaspoon salt
- ¼ teaspoon black pepper
- 4 ounces sliced Black Forest ham or cooked ham
- ½ cup shredded fontina cheese (2 ounces)
- 12 corn tortillas or 7- to 8-inch flour tortillas**
- 1 recipe Chimichurri Sauce

1 Trim fat from steak. Score both sides of steak in a diamond pattern by making shallow diagonal cuts at 1-inch intervals. Place steak between 2 pieces of plastic wrap. Using the flat side of a meat mallet, pound steak lightly to about ¼ inch thick, working from the center to the edges (about a 12×8-inch rectangle). Discard plastic wrap.

2 In a large skillet cook Anaheim peppers, onion, and garlic in hot oil over medium heat about 3 minutes or until tender. Stir in oregano, salt, and black pepper.

3 Arrange ham slices evenly over the steak. Spread pepper mixture over the ham. Sprinkle with cheese. Starting from a long side, roll meat into a spiral. Tie in 3 or 4 places with heavy 100%-cotton kitchen string.

4 For a charcoal grill, arrange medium-hot coals around a drip pan. Test for medium heat above the pan. Place rolled flank steak on grill rack over pan. Cover and grill for 40 to 45 minutes or until thermometer registers 150°F, tuning once halfway through grilling. (For a gas grill, preheat grill. Reduce heat to medium. Adjust for indirect cooking. Place rolled steak on grill rack over the burner that is turned off. Grill as directed.)

5 Remove steak roll. Cover with foil; let stand 10 minutes. (Temperature of the meat after standing should be 155°F.) Remove string. Cut steak roll crosswise into 1-inch slices. Serve with tortillas and Chimichurri Sauce.

CHIMICHURRI SAUCE: In a food processor or blender combine 1¼ cups packed fresh Italian parsley, ¼ cup olive oil, 2 tablespoons fresh oregano, 1 peeled shallot, 4 cloves garlic, 2 tablespoons red wine vinegar, 1 tablespoon lemon juice, ½ teaspoon salt, and ½ teaspoon crushed red pepper. Cover and process just until chopped and a few herb leaves are still visible. Cover and chill for 2 hours before serving. (Cover and chill any leftovers for up to 1 week.)

***NOTE** Because hot chile peppers, such as Anaheims, contain volatile oils that can burn skin and eyes, avoid direct contact with chiles as much as possible. When working with chile peppers, wear plastic or rubber gloves. If your bare hands touch the chile peppers, wash your hands well with soap and warm water.

****NOTE** If desired, wrap tortillas in foil and place on side of grill rack for 10 minutes to warm, turning once.

PER ⅙ ROLL: 631 cal., 28 g total fat (7 g sat. fat), 61 mg chol., 1,273 mg sodium, 58 g carbo., 1 g fiber, 36 g pro.

4. Starting from a long side, roll up the steak firmly but not too tightly, enclosing the ham, pepper mixture, and cheese and forming a spiral.

5. To secure the filling and maintain the shape of the roll, tie the steak in several places with clean 100%-cotton string. Allow about 1½ inches between ties.

6. Place steak over drip pan and cover the grill. After 25 minutes, use tongs to turn the meat. Cover and grill for 15 to 20 minutes more or until the center reaches 150°F.

Blue Cheese and Caramelized Onion-Stuffed Flank Steak

BLUE CHEESE LOVERS WILL REJOICE WHEN THEY DISCOVER THEIR FAVORITE CHEESE ALONG WITH SWEET, GOLDEN ONIONS, TUCKED INTO LEAN AND LOVELY FLANK STEAK.

PREP: 30 MINUTES **GRILL:** 17 MINUTES
STAND: 10 MINUTES **MAKES:** 4 SERVINGS

- 1 tablespoon butter
- 1 large sweet onion, halved and thinly sliced
- 1 teaspoon snipped fresh thyme
- ¼ teaspoon salt
- ¼ teaspoon black pepper
- 1 1¼- to 1½-pound beef flank steak
- ½ cup crumbled blue cheese (2 ounces)
- ¼ cup mayonnaise
- ¼ cup dairy sour cream
- 2 tablespoons crumbled blue cheese
- ⅛ teaspoon cayenne pepper
- Thyme sprig (optional)

1 To caramelize onions, in a large skillet melt butter over medium heat. Add onion, thyme, salt, and pepper; cook, covered, for 13 to 15 minutes or until onion is tender, stirring occasionally. Uncover; cook for 4 to 6 minutes more or until onion is golden, stirring occasionally. Cool slightly.

2 Trim fat from steak. Cut a pocket in the steak by using a long sharp knife to cut horizontally through the steak to, but not through, the opposite side. Gently stir ½ cup blue cheese into the caramelized onions. Spoon caramelized onion mixture into the pocket. Secure opening with wooden toothpicks.* Sprinkle outside of steak with additional salt and pepper.

3 For a charcoal grill, grill steak on the rack of an uncovered grill directly over medium coals for 17 to 21 minutes for medium doneness (160°F), turning once halfway through grilling. (For a gas grill, preheat grill. Reduce heat to medium. Place steak on grill rack over heat. Cover and grill as directed.)

4 Remove steak. Cover with foil; let stand 10 minutes. Meanwhile, for blue cheese sauce, in a small bowl stir together mayonnaise, sour cream, the 2 tablespoons blue cheese, and cayenne pepper. Remove toothpicks. Slice steak across the grain. Serve with blue cheese sauce. If desired, garnish with thyme sprig.

***NOTE:** Soak wooden toothpicks in water for 30 minutes to prevent them from burning during grilling.

PER ¼ STEAK: 427 cal., 29 g total fat (12 g sat. fat), 80 mg chol., 653 mg sodium, 5 g carbo., 1 g fiber, 35 g pro.

STEP-BY-STEP

1. Cook the onion, covered, until it is tender. If the onion browns too quickly, reduce the heat. Uncover and cook until golden, stirring occasionally.

2. Using a long sharp knife with a thin blade, cut a pocket in one of the long sides of the steak. Cut to within ½ to 1 inch of the opposite side and the short sides.

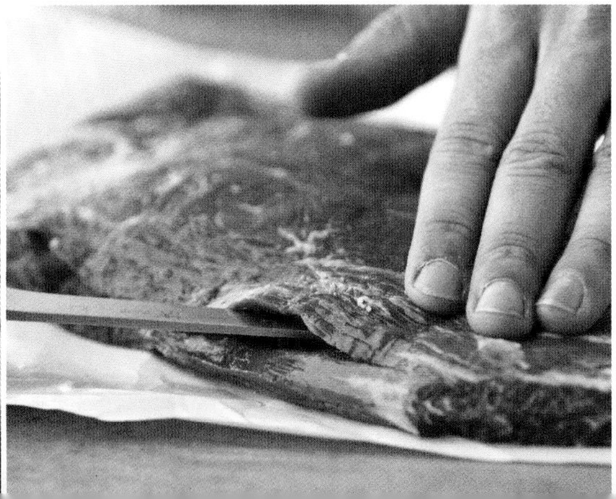

3. Spoon the caramelized onion mixture and the blue cheese into the pocket. Spread the filling in an even layer inside the pocket.

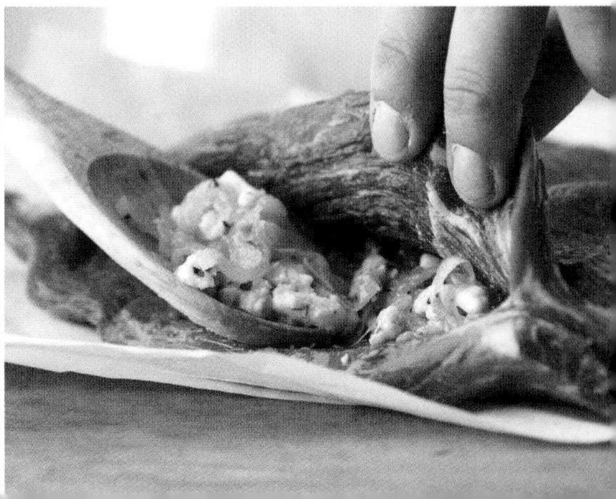

4. To avoid charring, soak wooden toothpicks in water for 30 minutes. Use the toothpicks to fasten the pocket closed and to hold the filling inside the steak.

5. Turn the steak over halfway through grilling. Grill until the inside of the steak registers 150°F. Use tongs to turn the steak to avoid piercing the meat.

6. After allowing the steak to stand for 10 minutes, remove and discard the toothpicks. Use a sharp knife to cut the steak crosswise into slices.

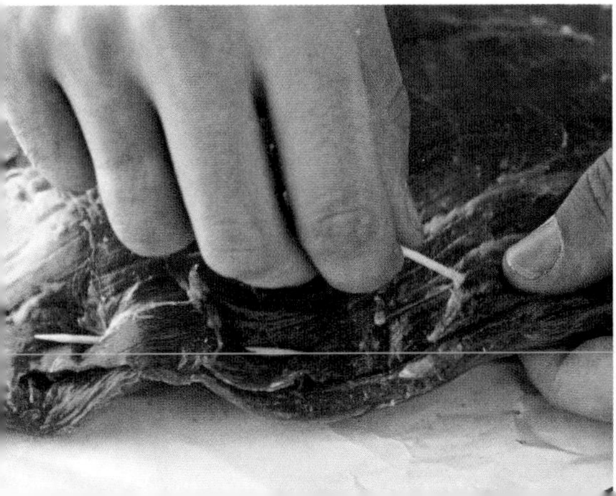

Espresso-Marinated Flank Steak

STRONG COFFEE LENDS A WHOLLY UNEXPECTED, EYE-OPENING FLAVOR TO THIS STEAK MARINADE. WHEN TIME PERMITS, GO FOR THE FULL 12-HOUR MARINATION—YOU'LL BE RICHLY REWARDED WITH TERRIFIC TASTE.

PREP: 20 MINUTES **MARINATE:** 4 HOURS
GRILL: 17 MINUTES **MAKES:** 4 SERVINGS

- 1 1½- to 2-pound beef flank steak
- 1 cup espresso coffee, chilled
- ¼ cup finely chopped red onion
- 2 tablespoons packed brown sugar
- 2 tablespoons Dijon-style mustard
- 2 tablespoons balsamic vinegar
- 1 tablespoon olive oil
- 1 teaspoon cracked black pepper
- 2 cloves garlic, minced
- 1 teaspoon instant espresso coffee powder
- ¼ teaspoon salt
- ¼ teaspoon black pepper

1 Trim fat from steak. Score both sides of steak in a diamond pattern by making shallow diagonal cuts at 1-inch intervals. Place steak in a large resealable plastic bag set in a shallow dish.

2 For marinade, in a small bowl combine coffee, onion, brown sugar, mustard, vinegar, oil, cracked pepper, and garlic. Pour marinade over steak in bag; seal bag. Turn to coat steak. Marinate in the refrigerator for 4 to 12 hours, turning bag occasionally.

3 Drain steak, discarding marinade. Sprinkle espresso coffee powder evenly over both sides of steak; rub in with your fingers.

4 For a charcoal grill, grill steak on the rack of an uncovered grill directly over medium coals for 17 to 21 minutes for medium doneness (160°F), turning once halfway through grilling. (For a gas grill, preheat grill. Reduce heat to medium. Place steak on grill rack over heat. Cover and grill as directed.)

5 Sprinkle steak with salt and black pepper. Thinly slice steak diagonally across the grain.

PER ¼ STEAK: 271 cal., 12 g total fat (5 g sat. fat,) 60 mg chol., 253 mg sodium, 1 g carbo., 0 g fiber, 36 g pro.

STEP-BY-STEP

1. Place the steak in a large resealable plastic bag. Pour the marinade over the steak in the bag. Seal the bag and turn it a few times to evenly coat the steak.

2. Sprinkle the drained steak with half the coffee powder and rub in with your fingers. Turn the steak over and rub the remaining coffee powder over the second side.

3. To serve, using a sharp knife cut the steak diagonally into thin slices. Cutting the steak on the diagonal cuts across the grain, producing more tender slices.

RUB ESPRESSO POWDER—GROUND FROM DARK-ROASTED COFFEE BEANS—ONTO STEAK SURFACES TO PERK UP THE FLAVOR OF FLANK STEAK AND GIVE IT RICH COLOR.

Skirt Steak Tacos with Guacamole and Lime Crema

TO EXPERTLY GRILL INEXPENSIVE SKIRT STEAK, DO IT THE WAY CHEFS IN MEXICO DO—OVER HIGH HEAT FOR JUST A FEW MINUTES ON EACH SIDE.

PREP: 55 MINUTES **MARINATE:** 2 HOURS
GRILL: 4 MINUTES **STAND:** 10 MINUTES
MAKES: 16 TACOS

- ½ cup chopped onion (1 medium)
- ⅓ cup freshly squeezed lime juice
- 2 tablespoons ground cumin
- 6 cloves garlic, minced
- 2 teaspoons ground chipotle chile pepper
- ½ teaspoon salt
- 3½ pounds beef skirt steak
- 1 recipe Guacamole
- 1 recipe Lime Crema
- 16 8-inch flour tortillas, warmed
- 1 head napa cabbage, shredded
- 1½ cups chopped, seeded tomatoes (2 large)
- ½ of a large red onion, quartered, then slivered
- 1 cup cilantro leaves

1 In a food processor or blender combine onion, lime juice, cumin, garlic, ground chipotle pepper, and salt. Cover and process to form a thick paste.

2 Spread paste over both sides of skirt steak; rub in with your fingers. Place skirt steak in a large resealable plastic bag set in a shallow dish; seal bag. Marinate in the refrigerator for 2 to 24 hours.

3 Prepare Guacamole and Lime Crema.

4 For a charcoal grill, grill steak on the rack of an uncovered grill directly over medium coals about 4 minutes or until steak is lightly charred, turning once halfway through grilling. (For a gas grill, preheat grill. Reduce heat to medium. Place steak on grill rack over heat. Cover and grill as directed.)

5 Remove steak. Cover with foil; let stand 10 minutes. Coarsely chop steak. Serve in warm tortillas topped with cabbage, tomatoes, onion, cilantro, Guacamole, and Lime Crema.

GUACAMOLE: In a medium bowl combine 4 ripe avocados, halved, seeded, and mashed; 1 cup chopped roma tomatoes (3 medium); 1 cup coarsely chopped fresh cilantro; ⅓ cup finely chopped red onion (1 small); ¼ cup lime juice; and 1 teaspoon salt. Serve immediately or cover and chill up to 4 hours.

LIME CREMA: In a small bowl stir together one 8-ounce carton dairy sour cream and 3 tablespoons lime juice. Serve immedieately or cover and chill up to 4 hours.

PER 2 TACOS: 752 cal., 40 g total fat (13 g sat. fat), 110 mg chol., 1,027 mg sodium, 51 g carbo., 9 g fiber, 49 g pro.

STEP-BY-STEP

1. Use your fingers to rub the paste over the steak. Apply enough pressure to press the paste into the meat fibers. Turn the steak over and repeat.

2. For Guacamole, place the avocado halves in a bowl. Use the back of a fork to mash the avocado until almost smooth.

3. Stir the remaining Guacamole ingredients into the mashed avocado. Cover the bowl with plastic wrap and chill until serving time. Guacamole may begin to discolor after 4 hours.

4. Grill the steak over medium-hot coals until char marks appear. Cover the steak with foil and let it stand for 5 minutes before chopping the meat for tacos.

5. Use a sharp knife to coarsely chop the meat into ½-inch pieces. Scrape the meat and any paste clinging to the meat into a bowl.

6. To assemble tacos, fill tortillas with chopped steak. Top meat with cabbage, tomatoes, onion, and cilantro. Serve tacos with Guacamole and Lime Crema on the side.

STEP-BY-STEP

1. Score the steak by making shallow diagonal cuts in opposite directions. Cut the steak lengthwise in half.

2. Place each steak piece between two pieces of plastic wrap. Starting in the center and working to the edges, pound each piece into a 10×6×2-inch rectangle with the flat side of the mallet.

3. Cook the bacon just until it browns and is still pliable. Arrange four slices of cooked bacon on each piece of meat, covering as much of the meat as possible.

Stuffed Steak Pinwheels

THE SMOKY FLAVOR OF BACON INVIGORATES THE MEDITERRANEAN FILLING IN THESE, PARTY-PERFECT SPIRALS. IF YOU LIKE, SAVE A STEP BY USING PRECOOKED PACKAGED BACON.

PREP: 30 MINUTES **GRILL:** 12 MINUTES
MAKES: 12 PINWHEELS

8 slices bacon
1 1¼- to 1½-pound beef flank steak or boneless top round steak
¾ teaspoon lemon-pepper seasoning
¼ teaspoon salt
1 10-ounce package frozen chopped spinach, thawed and well drained
⅓ cup crumbled feta cheese
2 tablespoons fine dry bread crumbs
½ teaspoon dried thyme, crushed
Fresh thyme sprigs (optional)
Grilled cherry tomatoes and/or halved small tomatoes (optional)

1 In a large skillet cook bacon over medium heat just until brown but not crisp. Drain bacon on paper towels.

2 Trim fat from steak. Score both sides of steak in a diamond pattern by making shallow diagonal cuts at 1-inch intervals. Cut meat in half lengthwise. Place portions of meat between 2 pieces of plastic wrap. Using the flat side of a meat mallet, pound steak lightly to a 10×6-inch rectangle, working from the center to the edges. Discard plastic wrap. Sprinkle meat with ½ teaspoon of the lemon-pepper seasoning and the salt. Arrange bacon slices lengthwise on meat.

3 For stuffing, in a medium bowl combine spinach, feta, bread crumbs, the dried thyme, and the remaining ¼ teaspoon lemon-pepper seasoning. Spread stuffing over meat. Starting from a short side, roll each portion of meat into a spiral. Secure with wooden toothpicks at 1-inch intervals, starting ½ inch from 1 end. Cutting between the toothpicks, slice each roll into six 1-inch-thick pinwheels. On each of six 6-inch skewers,* thread 2 pinwheels.

4 For a charcoal grill, grill pinwheels on the rack of an uncovered grill directly over medium coals for 12 to 14 minutes for medium doneness (160°F), turning once halfway through grilling. (For a gas grill, preheat grill. Reduce heat to medium. Place pinwheels on grill rack over heat. Cover and grill as directed.)

5 To serve, remove pinwheels from skewers; remove toothpicks. If desired, garnish pinwheels with fresh thyme sprigs and serve with grilled tomatoes.

***NOTE:** If using wooden skewers, soak them in water for at least 30 minutes before grilling.

PER 2 PINWHEELS: 225 cal., 12 g total fat (5 g sat. fat), 50 mg chol., 671 mg sodium, 4 g carbo., 2 g fiber, 24 g pro.

4. Spoon the spinach stuffing over the bacon. Carefully spread the stuffing, completely covering the steak and bacon.

5. Starting from a short side, roll up one of the steak pieces to form a spiral. Starting ½ inch from the end, insert wooden toothpicks at 1-inch intervals. Repeat with remaining piece.

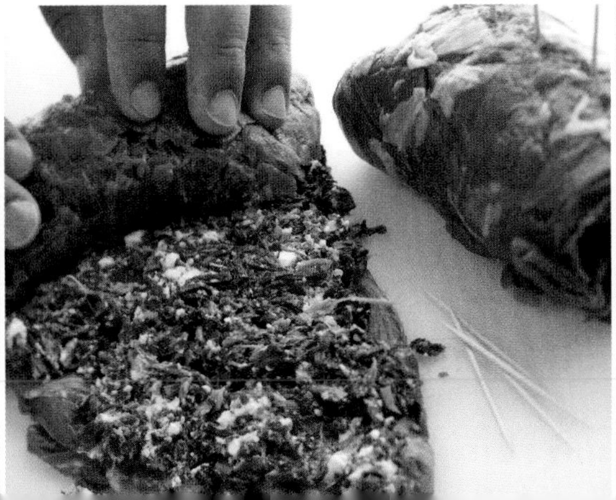

6. Use a sharp knife to cut the steak rolls between the toothpicks ,making a total of twelve 1-inch pinwheels.

Spanish Olive-Stuffed Ribeyes

TINY CAPERS, THE PICKLED FLOWER BUDS OF A MEDITERRANEAN BUSH, ADD EVEN MORE PIQUANCY TO THE OLIVE STUFFING. BE SURE TO RINSE CAPERS BEFORE USING TO REMOVE EXCESS SALT.

PREP: 20 MINUTES **GRILL:** 22 MINUTES
MAKES: 4 SERVINGS

½ cup pimiento-stuffed green olives
1 tablespoon drained capers
3 cloves garlic, minced
1½ teaspoons finely shredded orange peel
½ teaspoon black pepper
2 boneless beef ribeye steaks, cut 1¼ to 1½ inches thick (about 1½ pounds total)

1 In a blender or food processor combine olives, capers, garlic, orange peel, and pepper. Cover and blend until chunky.

2 Trim fat from steaks. Cut each steak in half crosswise. Cut a pocket in each portion by using a sharp knife to cut horizontally through the steaks to, but not through, the opposite side. Spoon about 1 tablespoon olive mixture into each pocket. Spoon any remaining olive mixture over the steaks; rub in with your fingers.

3 For a charcoal grill, arrange medium-hot coals around a drip pan. Test for medium heat above pan. Place steaks on grill rack over pan. Cover and grill to desired doneness, turning once halfway through grilling. Allow 22 to 25 minutes for medium rare (145°F) or 25 to 28 minutes for medium (160°F). (For a gas grill, preheat grill. Reduce heat to medium. Adjust for indirect cooking. Place steaks on grill rack over the burner that is turned off. Grill as directed.)

PER ½ STEAK: 278 cal., 13 g total fat (4 g sat. fat), 81 mg chol., 533 mg sodium, 2 g carbo., 0 g fiber, 38 g pro.

Herb Cheese-Stuffed Steaks

MAKE THIS WINNER WHEN YOUR GARDEN BRIMS WITH FRESH BASIL OR WHEN FARMER'S MARKET VENDORS OFFER BUNCHES OF THE FRAGRANT HERB FOR PENNIES.

PREP: 25 MINUTES **GRILL:** 8 MINUTES
MAKES: 6 SERVINGS

6 beef tenderloin steaks, cut 1 inch thick (2½ to 3 pounds)
1 12-ounce jar roasted red sweet peppers, drained
1 5.2-ounce container semisoft cheese with garlic and herbs
12 fresh basil leaves, torn
¼ cup bottled red wine vinaigrette salad dressing
¼ teaspoon salt
¼ teaspoon black pepper
2 tablespoons sliced green onion (1)
1 tablespoon snipped fresh basil
3 cloves garlic, quartered
1 recipe Roasted Garlic Kabobs (optional)

1 Trim fat from steaks. Cut a pocket in each steak by using a sharp knife to cut horizontally through the steaks to, but not through, the opposite side.

2 Coarsely chop enough of the roasted peppers to equal ⅓ cup. Reserve the remaining peppers for sauce. In a small bowl combine the chopped roasted peppers, the cheese, and the torn basil. Spoon pepper mixture evenly into pockets in steaks. Secure openings with wooden toothpicks. Brush steaks with 2 tablespoons of the vinaigrette; reserve the remaining vinaigrette for sauce. Sprinkle steaks with salt and black pepper.

3 For a charcoal grill, grill steaks on the rack of an uncovered grill directly over medium coals to desired doneness, turning once halfway through grilling. Allow 8 to 12 minutes for medium rare (145°F) or 10 to 15 minutes for medium (160°F). (For a gas grill, preheat grill. Reduce heat to medium. Place steaks on grill rack over heat. Cover and grill as directed.)

4 Meanwhile, in a food processor or blender combine the reserved roasted peppers, the green onion, the snipped basil, and the garlic. Cover and process until chopped. Transfer to a serving bowl. Stir in the reserved vinaigrette.

5 Remove toothpicks. Serve steaks with sauce and, if desired, Roasted Garlic Skewers.

PER 1 STEAK: 602 cal., 46 g total fat (19 g sat. fat), 147 mg chol., 353 mg sodium, 5 g carbo., 1 g fiber, 39 g pro.

ROASTED GARLIC KABOBS: Preheat oven to 425°F. Divide 1 whole garlic bulb into individual unpeeled cloves; cut cloves in half lengthwise. Place garlic cloves in a custard cup. Drizzle with 1 teaspoon olive oil. Cover with foil. Roast about 20 minutes or until garlic feels soft when pressed. When cool enough to handle, thread garlic cloves on skewers.* Add garlic skewers to the grill rack during the last 5 minutes of grilling, turning once halfway through grilling.

***NOTE:** If using wooden skewers, soak them in water for at least 30 minutes before grilling.

PREPARING SPANISH OLIVE-STUFFED RIBEYES, STEP-BY-STEP

1. Process the stuffing just until the mixture forms small chunks. Be careful to not overprocess the mixture.

2. Using a chef's knife, cut each steak in half crosswise, for a total of four steaks.

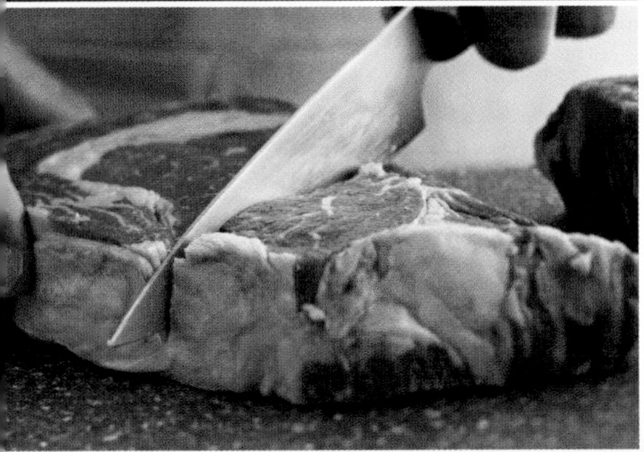

3. Cut a pocket in each piece. Do not cut all the way through the steak; leave some meat uncut on each side.

4. Use a spoon to fill each pocket with the olive stuffing. Push the filling to the back of the pocket and spread evenly.

5. Spread the remaining olive stuffing over the top of each steak. Use your fingers to rub the stuffing over the meat.

Steaks with Roasted Garlic

ROASTING CALMS THE RAMBUNCTIOUS FLAVOR OF GARLIC, MAKING IT SOFT AND SUBTLE—AND PERFECT FOR ENHANCING THE SAVORY, STAND-UP CHARACTER OF BEEF STEAK.

PREP: 20 MINUTES **GRILL:** 30 MINUTES
MAKES: 6 SERVINGS

- 1 or 2 whole bulbs garlic
- 3 to 4 teaspoons snipped fresh basil or 1 teaspoon dried basil, crushed
- 1 tablespoon snipped fresh rosemary or 1 teaspoon dried rosemary, crushed
- 2 tablespoons olive oil or vegetable oil
- 1½ pounds boneless beef ribeye steaks or sirloin steak, cut 1 inch thick
- 1 to 2 teaspoons cracked black pepper
- ½ teaspoon salt

1 Cut off the top ½ inch of garlic bulb to expose the ends of the individual cloves. Leaving garlic bulb whole, remove any loose, papery outer layers. Fold a 20×18-inch piece of heavy foil in half crosswise; trim to make a 10-inch square. Place bulb, cut end up, in the center of foil. Sprinkle with basil and rosemary; drizzle with oil. Bring up 2 opposite edges of foil; seal with a double fold. Fold the remaining ends to completely enclose garlic, leaving space for steam to build.

2 For a charcoal grill, grill packet on the rack of an uncovered grill directly over medium coals about 30 minutes or until garlic feels soft when packet is squeezed, turning occasionally during grilling. (For a gas grill, preheat grill. Reduce heat to medium. Place packet on grill rack over heat. Cover and grill as directed.)

3 Meanwhile, trim fat from steaks. Sprinkle steaks evenly with pepper and salt; rub in with your fingers. While garlic is grilling, add steaks to grill rack. Grill steaks to desired doneness, turning once halfway through grilling. For ribeye steaks, allow 10 to 12 minutes for medium rare (145°F) or 12 to 15 minutes for medium (160°F). For sirloin steak, allow 14 to 18 minutes for medium rare (145°F) or 18 to 22 minutes for medium (160°F).

4 To serve, cut steaks into 6 pieces. Remove garlic from foil, reserving basil mixture. Squeeze garlic pulp onto steaks. Mash pulp slightly, spreading it over steaks. Drizzle steaks with the reserved basil mixture.

PER 3 OUNCE STEAK: 189 cal., 9 g total fat (2 g sat. fat), 52 mg chol., 139 mg sodium, 4 g carbo., 0 g fiber, 22 g pro.

STEP-BY-STEP

1. Slice about ½ inch off the top of a garlic bulb. Cut off enough to remove the tips of the individual cloves. Remove the papery outer layers.

2. Sprinkle the snipped basil and rosemary over the garlic bulb. Using a spoon, drizzle the oil over the garlic and herbs.

3. Place the garlic packet directly over the coals. For even cooking, turn the packet over now and then during grilling.

4. When the garlic is cool enough to handle, squeeze the bulb, releasing the soft garlic over the steaks.

5. Use the tines of a fork to mash the garlic into a paste. Spread the mashed garlic over the steaks.

6. Using a spoon, drizzle the reserved basil and oil mixture over the garlic-topped steaks. Some of the oil will spill off the steaks and pool on the plate.

Ancho-Rubbed Prime Rib Steaks with Grilled Papaya Butter

ALTHOUGH SWEET-TART PAPAYAS ARE AVAILABLE IN SUPERMARKETS YEAR-ROUND, THEY ARE AT THEIR BEST FROM JUNE UNTIL SEPTEMBER, JUST IN TIME FOR GRILLING SEASON.

PREP: 30 MINUTES **GRILL:** 25 MINUTES
MAKES: 10 SERVINGS

- 1 recipe Grilled Papaya Butter
- 2 2-pound boneless beef ribeye steaks, cut 2 to 2½ inches thick
- 2 tablespoons ground ancho chile pepper
- 1 tablespoon unsweetened cocoa powder
- ½ teaspoon kosher salt
- ½ teaspoon black pepper
- 1 tablespoon olive oil

1 Prepare Grilled Papaya Butter.

2 Trim fat from steaks. In a small bowl combine ancho chile pepper, cocoa powder, salt, and black pepper. Brush steaks with oil. Sprinkle chile mixture evenly over steaks; rub in with your fingers.

3 For a charcoal grill, arrange medium-hot coals around a drip pan. Test for medium heat above the pan. Place steaks on grill rack over pan. Cover and grill to desired doneness, turning once halfway through grilling. Allow 25 to 30 minutes for medium-rare (145°F) or 30 to 35 minutes for medium (160°F). (For a gas gill, preheat grill. Reduce heat to medium. Adjust for indirect cooking. Place steaks on grill rack over the burner that is turned off. Grill as directed.)

4 Cut steaks into serving-size pieces. Serve with Grilled Papaya Butter.

GRILLED PAPAYA BUTTER: Peel and seed half a small papaya (reserve remaining papaya for another use); cut into ¼-inch slices. Lightly brush slices with olive oil. For a charcoal grill, grill papaya on the rack of an uncovered grill directly over medium coals for 5 minutes, turning once halfway through grilling. (For a gas grill, preheat grill. Reduce heat to medium. Place papaya on grill rack over heat. Cover and grill as directed.) In a food processor combine grilled papaya and ¾ cup softened butter. Cover and process with several on-off pulses until papaya is finely chopped. Spoon mixture onto a sheet of plastic wrap. Shape into an 8-inch roll. Wrap and chill about 2 hours or until firm.

PER ABOUT 5 OUNCES STEAK: 571 cal., 50 g total fat (23 g sat. fat), 141 mg chol., 282 mg sodium, 2 g carbo., 1 g fiber, 27 g pro.

STEP-BY-STEP

1. Brush the steaks with the olive oil. The oil helps the rub adhere to the steaks. Divide the rub evenly among the steaks.

2. Use your fingers to spread the rub over the steaks. Completely cover the steaks with the rub, pressing the mixture into the meat.

3. For a gas grill, place the steaks on the grill rack over the side of the grill without heat. If using a charcoal grill, place the steaks over the drip pan.

4. After removing the steaks from the grill, let them stand on a plate or cutting board for 5 minutes. Cut into serving-size pieces.

5. To prepare the papaya, use a sharp knife to cut the peel from the fruit. Cut the papaya lengthwise in half.

6. Use a spoon to scrape the seeds and fibers from the cavities of the papaya halves. Wrap one half in plastic wrap and save for another use.

STEP-BY-STEP

1. Use a small sharp knife to halve the habanero. With the tip of the knife, cut away the membranes and scrape away the seeds.

2. Keep your hands protected with plastic gloves. Rub the habanero mixture over both sides of the steaks. For best flavor, cover and chill the steaks up to 24 hours.

3. To finely chop the onion, halve the onion and place, cut side down, on surface. Thinly slice the onion lengthwise, maintaining shape. Then cut crosswise into tiny pieces.

Strip Steaks with Lime and Sweet Onion Salsa

EXTRA-SWEET ONION VARIETIES INCLUDE THE NORTH AMERICAN CULTIVARS WALLA WALLA, RIO SWEET, AND VIDALIA. FROM SOUTH AMERICA COMES THE OSSO SWEET ONION.

PREP: 20 MINUTES **GRILL:** 10 MINUTES
MARINATE: 24 HOURS **MAKES:** 4 SERVINGS

- 4 boneless beef top loin (strip) steaks, cut 1 inch thick
- 1 fresh habanero chile pepper, seeded and finely chopped*
- 2 tablespoons snipped fresh sage
- ½ teaspoon salt
- 1 recipe Lime and Sweet Onion Salsa

1 Trim fat from steaks. In a small bowl combine habanero pepper, sage, and salt. Wearing plastic or rubber gloves, sprinkle mixture evenly over both sides of each steak; rub in with your fingers. If desired, cover and marinate in the refrigerator up to 24 hours.

2 Prepare Lime and Sweet Onion Salsa. Cover and chill until ready to serve.

3 For a charcoal grill, grill steaks on the rack of an uncovered grill directly over medium coals to desired doneness, turning once halfway through grilling. Allow 10 to 12 minutes for medium rare (145°F) or 12 to 15 minutes for medium (160°F). (For a gas grill, preheat grill. Reduce heat to medium. Place steaks on grill rack over heat. Cover; grill as directed.) Serve steaks with salsa.

LIME AND SWEET ONION SALSA: Peel and section 2 large limes; chop lime segments. In a medium bowl stir together chopped lime, ½ cup finely chopped sweet onion (1 medium), 3 tablespoons snipped fresh cilantro, ½ teaspoon sugar, and ¼ teaspoon salt.

***NOTE:** Because hot chile peppers contain volatile oils that can burn your skin and eyes, avoid direct contact with chiles as much as possible. When working with chile peppers, wear plastic or rubber gloves. If your bare hands do touch the chile peppers, wash your hands and fingernails well with soap and warm water.

PER STEAK: 431 cal., 17 g total fat (6 g sat. fat), 166 mg chol., 581 mg sodium, 4 g carbo., 1 g fiber, 62 g pro.

4. To section lime, cut off the top and bottom. Place the lime upright on surface. Cut away the peel, including the bitter-tasting white membrane.

5. Holding the lime in one hand, cut between membranes, releasing the segments. Chop the segments into small pieces.

6. For salsa, place the onion, lime, cilantro, sugar, and salt in a bowl. Stir with a spoon to mix the ingredients. Cover and chill until needed.

Flat-Iron Steaks Cubano

PREVIOUSLY ONLY CONSIDERED SUITABLE FOR GRINDING, THE FLAT-IRON STEAK IS NOW LAUDED FOR BEING ONE OF THE RICHEST, MOST BEEFY-TASTING CUTS. IT TASTES EVEN BETTER WHEN MARINATED.

PREP: 20 MINUTES **MARINATE:** 1 HOUR
GRILL: 7 MINUTES **MAKES:** 4 SERVINGS

- 4 beef shoulder top blade (flat-iron) steaks, cut ¾ to 1 inch thick (1½ pounds)
- ⅔ cup olive oil
- 2 to 3 tablespoons finely shredded orange peel*
- ½ cup orange juice
- ⅓ cup finely chopped red onion (1 small)
- 1 tablespoon finely shredded lime peel*
- ¼ cup lime juice
- 2 teaspoons finely shredded lemon peel*
- 3 tablespoons lemon juice
- 6 cloves garlic, minced
- 2 teaspoons dried oregano, crushed
- 2 teaspoons ground cumin
- 1 teaspoon salt
- ½ teaspoon black pepper

1 Trim fat from steaks. Place steaks in a large resealable plastic bag set in a shallow dish. For marinade, in a medium bowl stir together oil, orange peel, orange juice, onion, lime peel, lime juice, lemon peel, lemon juice, garlic, oregano, cumin, salt, and pepper. Set aside ½ cup of the marinade until ready to serve.

2 Pour the remaining marinade over steaks in bag; seal bag. Turn to coat steaks. Marinate in the refrigerator for 1 to 2 hours, turning bag occasionally. Drain steaks, discarding marinade.

3 For a charcoal grill, grill steaks on the rack of an uncovered grill directly over medium coals to desired doneness, turning once halfway through grilling. Allow 7 to 9 minutes for medium rare (145°F) or 10 to 12 minutes for medium (160°F). (For a gas grill, preheat grill. Reduce heat to medium. Place steaks on grill rack over heat. Cover; grill as directed.)

4 Before serving, drizzle steaks with the reserved ½ cup marinade.

***NOTE:** To get enough citrus peel and juice for the marinade, use 2 oranges, 2 limes, and 1 lemon.

PER STEAK: 374 cal., 25 g total fat (6 g sat. fat), 102 mg chol., 296 mg sodium, 3 g carbo., 1 g fiber, 33 g pro.

STEP-BY-STEP

1. Use a sharp knife to cut away any fat from the edges of the steaks. Place steaks in a resealable plastic bag.

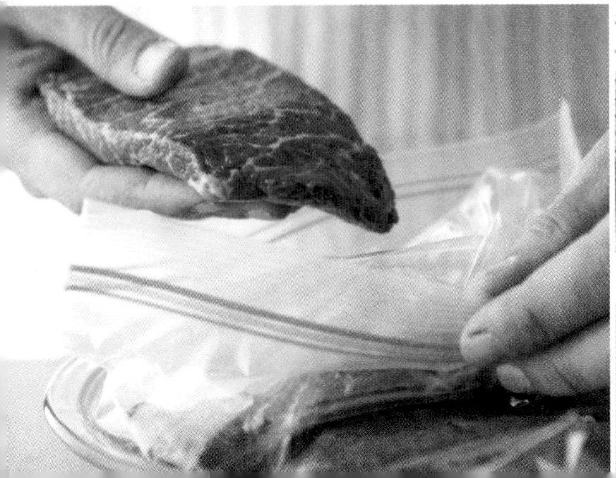

2. Pour the marinade over the steaks in the bag. Close the bag, pressing out excess air. Turn the bag several times to completely coat the steaks with the marinade.

3. Use tongs to remove the steaks from the marinade. Some of the marinade will cling to the steaks, but discard any marinade that remains in the bag.

4. Once the coals are covered with ash, use long-handled tongs to arrange the coals in an even layer on the grill grate. Place the rack and test for medium heat.

5. Place the steaks on the rack over the heat. Turn the steaks once about halfway through cooking or after 4 minutes for medium rare and after 5 minutes for medium.

6. Place steaks on dinner plates. Drizzle each steak with a generous tablespoon of the reserved ½ cup marinade.

CRISP LETTUCES SUCH AS ICEBURG, BOSTON, AND BIBB MAKE THE BEST WRAPS FOR THIS POPULAR ASIAN STREET FOOD. TO MAKE LETTUCE EVEN CRUNCHIER, RINSE LEAVES WITH COOL WATER, WRAP THEM IN DAMP PAPER TOWELS, AND REFRIGERATE UNTIL READY TO USE.

Lettuce-Wrapped Vietnamese Beef

BEFORE CHOPPING LEMONGRASS, BRUISE THE FIBROUS STALKS BY STRIKING THEM FIRMLY IN SEVERAL PLACES WITH THE DULL SIDE OF A CHEF'S KNIFE TO RELEASE LEMONY ESSENCE.

PREP: 30 MINUTES **MARINATE:** 2 HOURS
GRILL: 10 MINUTES **MAKES:** 4 SERVINGS

- 1 pound boneless beef top sirloin steak, cut 1 inch thick
- ¼ cup chopped green onions (2)
- 2 tablespoons sugar
- 2 tablespoons lime juice
- 2 tablespoons fish sauce
- 1 tablespoon chopped fresh lemongrass (2 stalks) or ½ teaspoon finely shredded lemon peel
- 3 cloves garlic, minced
- 8 large lettuce leaves
- Assorted toppings (such as shredded carrots, fresh cilantro leaves, fresh mint leaves, and/or chopped peanuts)
- 1 recipe Rice Vinegar Sauce

1 Trim fat from steak. Place steak in a large resealable plastic bag set in a shallow dish. For marinade, in a small bowl stir together green onions sugar, lime juice, fish sauce, lemongrass, and garlic. Pour marinade over steak in bag; seal bag. Turn to coat steak. Marinate in the refrigerator for 2 to 24 hours, turning bag occasionally. Drain steak, discarding marinade.

2 For a charcoal grill, grill steak on the rack of an uncovered grill directly over medium coals to desired doneness, turning once halfway through grilling. Allow 10 to 12 minutes for medium rare (145°F) or 12 to 15 minutes for medium (160°F). (For a gas grill, preheat grill. Reduce heat to medium. Place steak on grill rack over heat. Cover; grill as directed.)

3 To serve, overlap 2 lettuce leaves on each of 4 dinner plates. Thinly slice steak. Arrange steak slices on lettuce leaves. Add desired toppings; drizzle with Rice Vinegar Sauce. Roll lettuce leaves around filling.

RICE VINEGAR SAUCE: In a small bowl stir together ¼ cup sugar; ¼ cup rice vinegar; 2 tablespoons lime juice; 2 tablespoons fish sauce; 2 cloves garlic, minced; and dash cayenne pepper.

PER 2 LETTUCE WRAPS: 348 cal., 13 g total fat (5 g sat. fat), 76 mg chol., 671 mg sodium, 30 g carbo., 1 g fiber, 29 g pro.

STEP-BY-STEP

1. For each wrap, place two lettuce leaves on a plate so they overlap just a bit. Top lettuce with one-fourth of the meat slices.

2. Sprinkle two or more of the toppings over the beef. Drizzle the Rice Vinegar Sauce over the steak and toppings.

3. Roll up the lettuce leaves, enclosing the beef and toppings. Position the roll so the the seam side rests on the plate. Serve at once.

LUXURIOUS, WELL-MARBLED PORTERHOUSE STEAKS PROVIDE TWO STEAKS IN A SINGLE CUT—ON ONE SIDE OF THE BONE IS A TENDERLOIN OR FILLET AND ON THE OTHER SIDE OF THE BONE LIES A STRIP STEAK.

Rosemary Porterhouse Steaks with Olive Mayo

WHEN TRIMMING EXCESS FAT FROM STEAKS, DON'T TRIM IT ALL AWAY—LEAVE A ½-INCH MARGIN OF FAT. STEAKS COVERED WITH A THIN BORDER OF FAT TASTE BETTER THAN PERFECTLY LEAN CUTS OF MEAT.

PREP: 25 MINUTES **MARINATE:** 30 MINUTES
GRILL: 10 MINUTES **STAND:** 5 MINUTES
MAKES: 4 TO 6 SERVINGS

- 2 porterhouse steaks, cut 1 to 1¼ inches thick (about 1 pound each)
- 1 tablespoon olive oil
- 1 tablespoon finely snipped fresh rosemary
- ¾ teaspoon kosher salt or salt
- ½ teaspoon freshly ground black pepper
- 1 recipe Olive Mayo
- Snipped fresh rosemary (optional)

1 Trim fat from steaks. Brush steaks with oil. In a small bowl combine the 1 tablespoon rosemary, salt, and pepper. Sprinkle over both sides of steaks; rub in with your fingers. Let steaks stand at room temperature for 30 minutes.

2 Meanwhile, prepare Olive Mayo. Cover and chill until serving time.

3 For a charcoal grill, grill steaks on the rack of an uncovered grill directly over medium coals to desired doneness, turning once halfway through grilling. Allow 10 to 13 minutes for medium-rare (145°F) or 12 to 15 minutes for medium (160°F). (For a gas grill, preheat grill. Reduce heat to medium. Place steaks on grill rack over heat. Cover; grill as directed.) Let steaks stand for 5 minutes.

4 If desired, sprinkle steaks with additional fresh rosemary. Cut steaks into serving portions. Serve with Olive Mayo.

OLIVE MAYO: In a small bowl stir together ½ cup mayonnaise, 2 tablespoons chopped pitted kalamata olives, 1 tablespoon snipped fresh dill, and 1 clove garlic, minced.

PER 6 OUNCES STEAK: 682 cal., 59 g total fat (18 g sat. fat), 125 mg chol., 654 mg sodium, 1 g carbo., 0 g fiber, 34 g pro.

STEP-BY-STEP

1. Brush the steaks with olive oil. Snip the rosemary and mix with salt and pepper. Rub the rosemary mixture over both sides of steaks.

2. For Olive Mayo, stir together mayonnaise, chopped olives, snipped dill, and garlic. If not serving right away, cover and chill.

3. To serve, cut the meat away from the bones and cut into serving-size pieces. Arrange steak on a platter and sprinkle with additional snipped rosemary.

Pepper-Punched T-Bones

GREEN PEPPERCORNS ARE SOFT, UNRIPE PEPPERCORNS PRESERVED IN BRINE. THEIR FLAVOR IS LESS POTENT THAN THAT OF BLACK OR WHITE PEPPERCORNS, BUT THEY PROVIDE AN UNUSUAL, FRESH-TASTING PIQUANCY TO THE FOODS THEY MEET.

PREP: 15 MINUTES **GRILL:** 7 MINUTES
MAKES: 4 SERVINGS

- ½ cup steak sauce
- 2 tablespoons snipped fresh thyme
- 2 tablespoons whole green peppercorns in brine, drained and chopped
- 2 teaspoons cracked black pepper
- ½ teaspoon cayenne pepper
- 4 beef T-bone steaks, cut ¾ inch thick

1 In a small bowl stir together steak sauce, thyme, green peppercorns, black pepper, and cayenne pepper. Trim fat from steaks. Spread half the pepper mixture on 1 side of each steak.

2 For a charcoal grill, place steaks, pepper sides down, on the rack of an uncovered grill directly over medium coals. Spread the remaining pepper mixture on tops of steaks. Grill for 7 to 10 minutes for medium rare (145°F) or 10 to 13 minutes for medium (160°F), turning once halfway through grilling. (For a gas grill, preheat grill. Reduce heat to medium. Place steaks on grill rack over heat. Cover; grill as directed.)

PER 1 STEAK: 583 cal., 38 g total fat (15 g sat. fat), 146 mg chol., 567 mg sodium, 5 g carbo., 1 g fiber, 52 g pro.

STEP-BY-STEP

1. To chop the peppercorns, spread them on a cutting board. Move a chef's knife in an up-and-down motion over the peppercorns until chopped.

2. Place the steaks in a pan or on a platter. Spoon half the peppercorn mixture over steaks. Use the back of the spoon to spread the mixture over the steaks.

3. After grilling the peppered sides and flipping the steaks, spread the remaining peppercorn mixture over the steaks. Grill steaks to desired doneness.

STEP-BY-STEP

1. Use a chef's knife in an up and down motion to quickly chop the nuts. After a few chops, reposition the knife and chop in the opposite direction.

2. For the Gorgonzola Butter, stir together the Gorgonzola cheese, cream cheese, soft butter, and nuts. Mix well.

3. Place a piece of plastic wrap on the work surface. Shape the cheese mixture into an 1-inch-diameter log. Roll the plastic wrap around the log and chill until firm.

New York Strips with Gorgonzola Butter

GORGONZOLA, A BLUE-VEINED CHEESE PRODUCED IN ITALY, MAY BE A BIT SWEETER THAN FRENCH BLEU CHEESE OR AMERICAN BLUES, BUT ANY VARIETY OF BLUE CHEESE WILL BE OUTSTANDING IN THIS SENSATIONAL STEAK RECIPE.

PREP: 15 MINUTES **CHILL:** 1 HOUR
GRILL: 10 MINUTES **MAKES:** 4 SERVINGS

- 2 tablespoons crumbled Gorgonzola cheese or other blue cheese
- 2 tablespoons cream cheese spread with chives and onion
- 1 to 2 tablespoons butter, softened
- 1 tablespoon chopped pine nuts or walnuts, toasted*
- 4 boneless beef top loin (strip) steaks, cut 1 inch thick (about 3 pounds)
- Salt

1 For Gorgonzola butter, in a small bowl stir together Gorgonzola cheese, cream cheese, butter, and nuts. Shape mixture into a 1-inch-diameter log. Wrap in plastic wrap and chill about 1 hour or until firm.

2 Trim fat from steaks. Sprinkle steaks lightly with salt. For a charcoal grill, grill steaks on the rack of an uncovered grill directly over medium coals to desired doneness, turning once halfway through grilling. Allow 10 to 12 minutes for medium rare (145°F) or 12 to 15 minutes for medium (160°F). (For a gas grill, preheat grill. Reduce heat to medium. Place steaks on grill rack over heat. Cover; grill as directed.)

3 To serve, cut butter into 8 slices. Place 2 slices on each steak.

***NOTE:** To toast the nuts, spread them in a single layer in a shallow pan. Bake in a 350°F oven for 5 to 10 minutes or until golden brown, shaking pan once or twice. Watch pine nuts closely; they burn easily.

PER STEAK: 700 cal., 42 g total fat (18 g sat. fat,), 216 mg chol., 429 mg sodium, 1 g carbo., 0 g fiber, 75 g pro.

4. Unwrap the Gorgonzola butter and place on a cutting board. Cut the roll into eight even-size pieces.

5. Once the coals are covered in ash, use long-handled tongs to arrange the coals in a single layer on the grill grate. Position the grill rack and test for medium heat.

6. To serve, place steaks on dinner plates. Top each steak with two pieces of Gorgonzola butter. The heat from the steak will partially melt the butter.

Hanger Steak with Asian Dipping Sauce

HANGER STEAK ALSO GOES BY THE NAME "BUTCHER STEAK," BECAUSE BUTCHERS OFTEN SAVE THIS UNKNOWN, YET FLAVORFUL CUT FOR THEMSELVES.

PREP: 15 MINUTES **GRILL:** 10 MINUTES
MAKES: 4 SERVINGS

- ½ cup beef broth
- ¼ cup water
- ¼ cup reduced-sodium soy sauce
- 1 tablespoon oyster sauce
- 1 tablespoon rice vinegar
- 2 teaspoons cornstarch
- 1 teaspoon sugar
- 1 1½-pound beef hanger steak*
- ¼ teaspoon salt
- 2 tablespoons cream sherry
- ⅓ cup chopped green onions (3)
- 1 tablespoon minced fresh ginger
- 2 cloves garlic, minced
- 3 cups hot cooked ramen noodles or rice
- Radish strips (optional)
- Sliced green onions (optional)

1 In a small bowl stir together broth, the water, soy sauce, oyster sauce, vinegar, cornstarch, and sugar; set aside. Trim fat from steak. Sprinkle steak with salt.

2 For a charcoal grill, grill steak on the rack of an uncovered grill directly over medium coals for 10 to 12 minutes for medium (160°F), turning once halfway through grilling. (For a gas grill, preheat grill. Reduce heat to medium. Place steak on grill rack over heat. Cover; grill as directed.)

3 Meanwhile, for sauce, in a small saucepan bring sherry to simmering over medium heat; simmer for 1 minute. Stir in the ⅓ cup green onions, ginger, and garlic; simmer for 1 minute. Stir in the broth mixture; simmer about 2 minutes more or until slightly thickened. Cool slightly.

4 Thinly slice steak diagonally across the grain. Arrange meat slices on top of hot cooked noodles; drizzle with a few tablespoons of the sauce. If desired, garnish with radish strips and additional green onions. Serve with the remaining sauce.

***NOTE:** Hanger steak, part of the diaphragm that hangs between the last rib and the loin, is better known in France (as *onglet*) than in the United States, so you might have to ask your butcher to cut it for you. You can substitute flank or skirt steak.

PER 5 OUNCES STEAK + ¾ CUP NOODLES: 438 cal., 10 g total fat (4 g sat. fat), 56 mg chol., 1,442 mg sodium, 40 g carbo., 1 g fiber, 42 g pro.

STEP-BY-STEP

1. For best flavor, sprinkle the steak with the salt before grilling. Distribute the salt evenly over each steak and rub it in with your fingers.

2. Cook and stir the sauce about 2 minutes or until it bubbles and is slightly thickened. As the sauce cools, it will continue to thicken to a consistency that nicely coats the meat.

3. To serve, cut the steak into thin slices. Arrange the slices on plates with the noodles. Spoon the sauce over the meat.

Stuffed Pork Rib Chops

IN THE FOOD COMMUNITY THERE ARE FEW FLAVOR MARRIAGES AS HAPPY AS THAT OF PORK AND DRIED FRUITS. COUPLE TENDER CHOPS WITH ANY COMBINATION OF YOUR FAVORITE FRUIT BITS.

PREP: 20 MINUTES **GRILL:** 35 MINUTES
MAKES: 4 SERVINGS

- 4 ounces semisoft goat cheese (chèvre) or feta cheese, crumbled (1 cup)
- ½ cup dried cherries, blueberries, or cranberries; golden raisins; and/or mixed dried fruit bits
- 1 tablespoon snipped fresh oregano or 1 teaspoon dried oregano, crushed
- 1 tablespoon snipped fresh rosemary or 1 teaspoon dried rosemary, crushed
- 2 cloves garlic, minced
- ¼ to ½ teaspoon crushed red pepper
- ¼ teaspoon salt
- ⅛ teaspoon black pepper
- 4 bone-in pork rib chops or boneless pork top loin chops, cut 1½ inches thick
- ¼ teaspoon salt
- ⅛ teaspoon black pepper
- ½ cup bottled raspberry-chipotle barbecue sauce or other barbecue sauce

1 For stuffing, in a medium bowl stir together goat cheese, cherries, oregano, rosemary, garlic, crushed red pepper, ¼ teaspoon salt, and ⅛ teaspoon black pepper.

2 Trim fat from chops. Make a pocket in each chop by cutting horizontally from the fat side almost to the bone (or the opposite side). Spoon one-fourth of the stuffing into each pocket. Secure the openings with wooden toothpicks. Sprinkle chops with ¼ teaspoon salt and ⅛ teaspoon black pepper.

3 For a charcoal grill, arrange medium-hot coals around a drip pan. Test for medium heat above the pan. Place chops on the grill rack over pan. Cover and grill for 35 to 40 minutes (30 to 35 minutes for boneless chops) or until chops are slightly pink in center (160°F), turning once and brushing frequently with barbecue sauce during the last 10 minutes of grilling. (For a gas grill, preheat grill. Reduce heat to medium. Adjust for indirect cooking. Place chops on grill rack over the burner that is turned off. Grill as directed.) Remove toothpicks.

PER STUFFED CHOP: 359 cal., 14 g total fat (8 g sat. fat), 70 mg chol., 556 mg sodium, 32 g carbo., 2 g fiber, 26 g pro.

Mix It Up!

PICK ONE FROM EACH COLUMN TO CUSTOMIZE THE RIB CHOPS TO YOUR TASTE.

SEASON IT

Instead of salt and pepper, season chops with one of the following:

- ½ teaspoon fajita seasoning
- ½ teaspoon chili powder plus ¼ teaspoon salt
- ½ teaspoon ground chipotle chile powder plus ¼ teaspoon salt
- 1 teaspoon steak seasoning
- 1 teaspoon barbecue spice
- 1 teaspoon purchased pork rub

MIX IT IN

Replace ¼ cup of the dried fruit with one of the following:

- ¼ cup chopped pitted olives
- ¼ cup toasted pine nuts
- 2 tablespoons snipped fresh mint
- ¼ cup chopped red or green sweet pepper
- ¼ cup toasted chopped walnuts
- ¼ cup toasted chopped almonds
- 2 tablespoons drained capers

TOP IT

Instead of the barbecue sauce, brush and/or top chops with one of the following:

- Purchased salsa
- Purchased basil pesto
- Orange marmalade
- Seedless raspberry jam
- Bottled Italian or Caesar dressing
- Purchased dried tomato pesto
- Purchased onion jam

STEP-BY-STEP

1. For the stuffing, stir together the goat cheese, dried fruit, herbs, and seasonings until well mixed.

2. Evenly spoon the stuffing among the pockets of the pork chops.

3. Insert wooden toothpicks through the openings in the chops, securing the filling inside the pockets.

4. Halfway through grilling, turn the chops over. Brush the chops several times with barbecue sauce during the last 10 minutes of grilling.

5. Remove the toothpicks before serving the chops. Place the chops on plates and serve at once.

Beer-Brined Pork Loin Chops

THE BRINING PROCESS DRAWS THE FULL-FLAVOR PERSONALITY OF STOUT INTO THE CHOPS, INFUSING THEM WITH ENTICING NOTES OF ROASTED COFFEE AND RIPE FRUIT.

PREP: 15 MINUTES **MARINATE:** 8 HOURS
GRILL: 30 MINUTES **MAKES:** 4 SERVINGS

- 4 boneless pork top loin chops, cut 1½ inches thick
- 1¾ cups water
- 1¾ cups stout (dark beer)
- 3 tablespoons coarse salt
- 2 tablespoons mild-flavor molasses
- 2 teaspoons coarsely cracked black pepper
- 4 cloves garlic, minced

1 Trim fat from chops. Place chops in a large resealable plastic bag set in a shallow dish. For brine, in a large bowl combine the water, stout, salt, and molasses; stir until salt dissolves. Pour brine over chops in bag; seal bag. Marinate in the refrigerator for 8 to 24 hours, turning bag occasionally.

2 Drain chops, discarding brine. Pat chops dry with paper towels. In a small bowl combine pepper and garlic. Sprinkle pepper mixture over both sides of each chop; rub in with your fingers.

3 For a charcoal grill, arrange medium-hot coals around a drip pan. Test for medium heat above pan. Place chops on the grill rack over pan. Cover and grill for 30 to 35 minutes or until chops are slightly pink in center (160°F), turning once halfway through grilling. (For a gas grill, preheat grill. Reduce heat to medium. Adjust for indirect cooking. Place chops on grill rack over the burner that is turned off. Grill as directed.)

PER CHOP: 345 cal., 12 g total fat (4 g sat. fat), 123 mg chol., 702 mg sodium, 3 g carbo., 0 g fiber, 50 g pro.

STEP-BY-STEP

1. For the brine, slowly pour the stout into a 4-cup glass measure.

2. Sprinkle the salt into the stout in the measuring cup. The salt will cause foam.

3. Add the molasses. Stir well to dissolve the salt and distribute the molasses throughout the mixture.

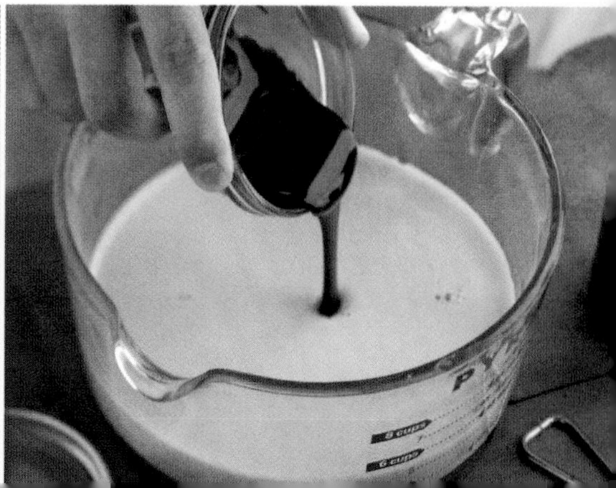

4. Pat the chops dry with paper towels and sprinkle with the pepper and garlic mixture. Rub the pepper and garlic evenly over both sides of the chops.

5. Carefully pour water into the drip pan. Adjust the grill rack and place the chops on the rack over the drip pan.

6. The pork chops are done when the internal temperature reaches 160°F. Begin testing a minute or two before the minimum timing.

GREEK COOKING IS CHARACTERIZED BY SIMPLE, FRESH, AND BRIGHT FLAVORS. LOCALLY GROWN LEMONS, HONEY, AND MINT—CALLED UPON IN THIS MEDITERRANEAN-STYLE CHOP RECIPE—ARE CULINARY MAINSTAYS.

Greek Honey-Lemon Pork Chops

WHEN PURITY IS PARAMOUNT—AS IT IS IN THIS DISH—PURCHASE EUROPEAN OR AMERICAN HONEY. INEXPENSIVE ASIAN HONEY PRODUCTS ARE OFTEN DILUTED WITH CORN SYRUP.

PREP: 15 MINUTES **MARINATE:** 4 HOURS
GRILL: 11 MINUTES **MAKES:** 4 SERVINGS

- 4 bone-in pork rib chops, cut ¾ inch thick (about 1¾ pounds)
- ½ cup honey
- 3 tablespoons finely shredded lemon peel
- ¼ cup lemon juice
- ¼ cup snipped fresh mint or 2 teaspoons dried mint, crushed
- ¼ cup olive oil
- 2 teaspoons salt
- 1 teaspoon cayenne pepper

1 Trim fat from chops. Place chops in a large resealable plastic bag set in a shallow dish. For marinade, in a small bowl stir together honey, lemon peel, lemon juice, mint, oil, salt, and cayenne pepper. Pour over chops in bag; seal bag. Turn to coat chops. Marinate in the refrigerator for 4 to 24 hours, turning bag occasionally. Drain chops, discarding marinade.

2 For a charcoal grill, grill chops on the rack of an uncovered grill directly over medium coals for 11 to 14 minutes or until chops are slightly pink in center (160°F), turning once halfway through grilling. (For a gas grill, preheat grill. Reduce heat to medium. Place chops on grill rack over heat. Cover; grill as directed.)

PER 1 CHOP: 272 cal., 15 g total fat (5 g sat. fat), 75 mg chol., 219 mg sodium, 5 g carbo., 0 g fiber, 27 g pro.

STEP-BY-STEP

1. Cut away the fat around the bone and along the edges of the meat. This reduce flare-ups and gives the chops a pleasing shape.

2. Pour the marinade over the chops in the bag. Turn the bag a few times to ensure that all of the chops are coated with marinade. Return the bag to the dish and place it in the refrigerator.

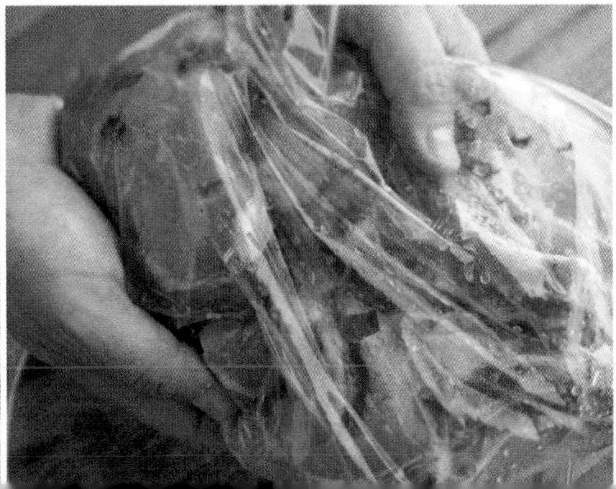

3. Grill the chops for 5 to 6 minutes. Use long-handled tongs to turn the chops and continue grilling until the chops reach 160°F and are slightly pink in centers.

APPLE CIDER AND WARM SPICES LEND CRISP AUTUMNAL ATTRIBUTES TO THESE THICK AND HEARTY FIRE-GRILLED PORK CHOPS.

Apple Cider-Brined Pork Chops

ADDING ICE CUBES TO THE CIDER BRINE COOLS THE BRINE QUICKLY—SAVING YOU TIME—AND MELTING ICE DILUTES BRINE TO THE PERFECT CONSISTENCY TO PRODUCE EXTRA-MOIST AND TENDER CHOPS.

PREP: 30 MINUTES **MARINATE:** 6 HOURS
GRILL: 7 MINUTES **MAKES:** 4 SERVINGS

- 2 cups cold water
- 1 cup kosher salt
- 1 cup packed light brown sugar
- 2 teaspoons dried thyme, crushed, or 2 sprigs fresh thyme
- 1 teaspoon whole black peppercorns
- 1 teaspoon whole cloves
- 4 cups unfiltered apple cider
- 2 cups ice cubes
- 4 boneless pork chops, cut ¾ inch thick
- Olive oil
- Miniature sweet peppers (optional)
- Sliced French bread (optional)

1 For brine, in a large saucepan bring water, salt, brown sugar, thyme, peppercorns, and cloves to boiling over medium heat. Cook for 2 to 3 minutes or until sugar and salt dissolve, stirring occasionally. Remove from heat; stir in apple cider and ice cubes. Stir until ice cubes melt and brine is cool.

2 Place pork chops in a large resealable plastic bag set in a shallow dish. Pour cooled brine over chops in bag; seal bag. Refrigerate for 6 to 12 hours, turning bag occasionally. Drain chops, discarding brine. Pat chops dry with paper towels. Lightly brush chops with olive oil.

3 For a charcoal grill, grill chops on the rack of an uncovered grill directly over medium coals for 7 to 9 minutes or until chops are slightly pink in center (160°F), turning once halfway through grilling. (For a gas grill, preheat grill. Reduce heat to medium. Place chops on grill rack over heat. Cover; grill as directed.)

4 If desired, brush peppers and bread slices with olive oil. Add peppers to grill rack with chops. Grill about 8 minutes or until tender, turning occasionally. Add bread to grill rack during the last 2 to 4 minutes of grilling, turning once. Serve chops with peppers and bread.

PER 1 CHOP: 214 cal., 6 g total fat (2 g sat. fat), 105 mg chol., 1,481 mg sodium, 5 g carbo., 0 g fiber, 33 g pro.

STEP-BY-STEP

1. To minimize splashing, pour the apple cider in a thin stream into the hot mixture. Stir in ice cubes until melted and let the brine cool completely.

2. Place the chops in a resealable plastic bag placed in a bowl. Pour the cooled brine over the chops. Seal the bag and turn it over a few times to be sure all of the chops are coated with brine.

3. Brush the whole peppers with oil. Place the peppers on the grill perpendicular to the grates on the grill rack so they don't fall into the coals.

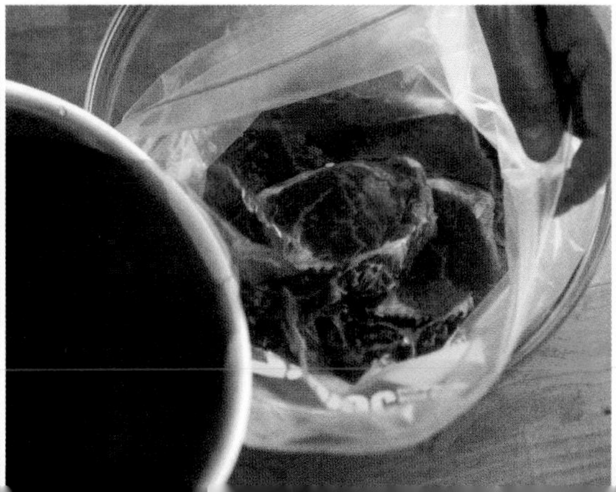

Pork Chops Stuffed with Blue Cheese

CREAMY-RICH BLUE CHEESE, CRUNCHY PECANS, AND BUTTERY, FORK-TENDER PORK GIVE THIS CROWD-THRILLING DISH A TRUE TEXTURAL REVELATION.

PREP: 20 MINUTES **GRILL:** 35 MINUTES
MAKES: 4 SERVINGS

- ⅓ cup shredded carrot (1 large)
- ⅓ cup crumbled blue cheese
- ¼ cup chopped pecans
- 2 tablespoons thinly sliced green onion (1)
- 1 teaspoon Worcestershire sauce
- 4 bone-in pork loin chops or pork rib chops, cut 1¼ inches thick (about 2¼ pounds)
- Barbecue sauce
- Crumbled blue cheese (optional)

1 For stuffing, in a small bowl combine carrot, the ⅓ cup cheese, pecans, green onion, and Worcestershire sauce. Set aside.

2 Trim fat from chops. Make a pocket in each chop by cutting horizontally from the fat side almost to the bone. Spoon one-fourth of the stuffing into each pocket. Secure the openings with wooden toothpicks.

3 For a charcoal grill, arrange medium-hot coals around a drip pan. Test for medium heat above the pan. Place chops on the grill rack over pan. Cover and grill for 35 to 40 minutes or until chops are slightly pink in center (160°F), turning once and brushing frequently with barbecue sauce during the last 10 minutes of grilling. (For a gas grill, preheat grill. Reduce heat to medium. Adjust for indirect cooking. Place chops on grill rack over the burner that is turned off. Grill as directed.) Remove toothpicks.

4 If desired, sprinkle chops with additional cheese.

PER CHOP: 406 cal., 27 g total fat (9 g sat. fat), 106 mg chol., 272 mg sodium, 3 g carbo., 1 g fiber, 37 g pro.

STEP-BY-STEP

1. For the stuffing, shred the carrot and crumble the blue cheese into a bowl. Add green onions and Worcestershire and mix well.

2. Starting from the fat side and cutting almost to the bone, cut a pocket in each chop. Divide the stuffings in fourths and spoon one-fourth into each chop.

3. Test for medium heat over the drip pan where the chops will cook. To avoid piercing the meat, use tongs to carefully place the stuffed chops on the grill rack. Cover and grill.

GRILLING PORK—AS WELL AS OTHER MEAT—ON THE BONE RESULTS IN FULL, INTENSE FLAVOR THAT'S OFTEN MISSING FROM MILD, BONELESS CUTS.

Honey-Citrus Pork Quesadillas

WHEN YOU GO TO THE TROUBLE OF MAKING A DIVINE DISH LIKE THIS, BE SURE TO USE FRESHLY SQUEEZED LIME JUICE FOR THE BRIGHTEST CITRUS FLAVOR.

PREP: 30 MINUTES **MARINATE:** 20 MINUTES
GRILL: 9 MINUTES **MAKES:** 6 QUESADILLAS

- 1 pound boneless pork loin chops, cut ¾ inch thick
- ½ cup lime juice
- 2 tablespoons snipped fresh cilantro
- 1 tablespoon honey
- 2 cloves garlic, thinly sliced
- 1 medium red onion, sliced ½ inch thick
- 1 medium green sweet pepper, seeded and cut lengthwise into quarters
- 3 tablespoons lime juice
- 2 tablespoons snipped fresh cilantro
- ¼ cup thinly sliced green onions (2)
- ¼ teaspoon salt
- ¼ teaspoon black pepper
- 2 cups shredded Monterey Jack cheese with jalapeño peppers (8 ounces)
- 12 6-inch flour tortillas
- Dairy sour cream and/or bottled salsa (optional)

1 For marinade, combine ½ cup lime juice, 2 tablespoons cilantro, honey, and garlic in a large resealable plastic bag set in a shallow dish. Place chops in bag; seal bag. Turn to coat chops. Marinate in the refrigerator for 20 minutes. Drain chops, discarding marinade.

2 For a charcoal grill, grill chops, onion slices, and pepper quarters on the rack of an uncovered grill directly over medium coals. Grill vegetables for 5 to 7 minutes or until browned and crisp-tender, turning once halfway through grilling. Grill chops for 7 to 9 minutes or until slightly pink in center (160°F), turning once halfway through grilling. (For a gas grill, preheat grill. Reduce heat to medium. Place chops, onion, and sweet pepper on grill rack over heat. Cover; grill as directed.)

3 Meanwhile, in a large bowl combine 3 tablespoons lime juice, 2 tablespoons cilantro, the green onions, salt, and black pepper. Chop cooked pork chops, red onion, and sweet pepper; add to green onion mixture.

4 For quesadillas, spoon cheese evenly over half of each tortilla. Top cheese with pork mixture. Fold tortilla over filling. For a charcoal grill, place folded tortillas on the rack of an uncovered grill directly over medium coals. Grill for 2 to 3 minutes or until tortillas are light brown, turning once halfway through grilling. (For a gas grill, place folded tortillas on grill rack over medium heat. Cover; grill as directed.)

5 Cut each quesadilla into 3 wedges. If desired, serve with sour cream and/or salsa.

PER QUESADILLA: 161 cal., 8 g total fat (3 g sat. fat), 40 mg chol., 197 mg sodium, 11 g carbo., 3 g fiber, 13 g pro.

Mix It Up!

PICK ONE FROM EACH COLUMN TO CUSTOMIZE THE QUESADILLA TO YOUR TASTE.

SEASON IT

Add one of the following to the chopped pork and vegetable mixture:

- 1 teaspoon ground cumin
- 1 teaspoon chili powder
- 1 teaspoon barbecue seasoning
- 1 teaspoon blackened seasoning
- 1 teaspoon Cajun seasoning
- 1 teaspoon fajita seasoning
- 1 teaspoon mesquite grilling seasoning blend

MIX IT IN

Instead of the green sweet peppers, use one of the following:

- 1 medium red or yellow sweet pepper, seeded and cut lengthwise into quarters
- 1 small zucchini or yellow summer squash, sliced lengthwise
- 2 medium roma tomatoes, halved lengthwise
- 1 portobello mushroom, stemmed and gills removed

TOP IT

Instead of Monterey Jack cheese with jalapeño peppers, use one of the following:

- Smoked cheddar cheese
- Queso Chihuahua
- Queso fresco
- Shredded Mexican-style four-cheese blend
- Colby and Monterey Jack cheese
- Manchego cheese
- Muenster cheese

STEP-BY-STEP

1. Peel the garlic cloves. Use a sharp paring knife to cut the cloves lengthwise into thin slices.

2. Pour the marinade into a resealable plastic bag. Add the chops to the bag. Seal the bag and turn to coat chops.

3. Place the onion slices and pepper quarters on the grill rack. After 3 or 4 minutes of grilling, turn them over.

4. Sprinkle cheese on half of each tortilla. Spoon the pork mixture on the cheese. Fold the the tortilla over the filling.

5. Use tongs to place the quesadillas on the grill. Grill until the cheese melts and grill marks appear on tortillas, turning to grill second sides.

Lamb Chops with Garlic and Lavender

LAVENDER, A RELATIVE OF MINT, IS OFTEN USED FOR COOKING IN THE SOUTH FRANCE. IF CULINARY LAVENDER IS UNAVAILABLE IN YOUR SUPERMARKET, PURCHASE IT AT NATURAL FOOD STORES OR FROM ONLINE HERB AND SPICE COMPANIES.

PREP: 45 MINUTES **CHILL:** 4 HOURS
GRILL: 10 MINUTES **MAKES:** 8 SERVINGS

- 16 to 20 lamb rib or loin chops, cut ¾ inch thick (4 to 5 pounds)
- 1 tablespoon dried lavender or finely shredded lemon peel
- 1 tablespoon dried Italian seasoning, crushed
- 1½ teaspoons freshly ground black pepper
- 1 teaspoon sea salt or salt
- 4 whole bulbs garlic, separated into cloves and peeled
- 2 tablespoons olive oil
- 2 lemons, halved (optional)
- Fresh lavender (optional)

1 Trim fat from chops. In a small bowl combine dried lavender, Italian seasoning, pepper, and sea salt. Sprinkle evenly over both sides of chops; rub in with your fingers. Cover; chill chops up to 4 hours.

2 In a medium skillet cook garlic cloves in hot oil over medium heat for 15 to 20 minutes or until golden and soft, stirring occasionally and reducing heat if cloves begin to brown. Remove from heat; cover and keep warm.

3 Meanwhile, for a charcoal grill, grill chops on the rack of an uncovered grill directly over medium coals until desired doneness, turning once halfway through grilling. Allow 10 to 14 minutes for medium rare (145°F) and 15 to 17 minutes for medium (160°F). (For a gas grill, preheat grill. Reduce heat to medium. Place chops on grill rack over heat. Cover; grill as directed.)

4 To serve, transfer chops to serving plates. Spoon garlic cloves on grilled chops. If desired, squeeze fresh lemon juice on chops and top with fresh lavender.

MAKE-AHEAD DIRECTIONS: Peel garlic; cover and chill for up to 24 hours. Prepare chops as directed through Step 1. Cover and chill lamb for up to 4 hours. Serve as directed. Grill lamb and cook garlic as directed.

PER 2 CHOPS: 215 cal., 12 g total fat (3 g sat. fat), 64 mg chol., 263 mg sodium, 6 g carbo., 2 g fiber, 21 g pro.

STEP-BY-STEP

1. Cook the garlic cloves in olive oil over medium heat. Stir often to evenly brown the cloves. If the cloves begin to brown too quickly, reduce heat to low.

2. Use your fingers to spread the lavender rub over both sides of the chops, gently pressing the rub into the meat fibers.

3. For each serving, arrange two chops on a plate. Top with several garlic cloves. If you like, squeeze a little lemon juice over the chops or serve with lemon wedges.

WHILE LAMB IS UNCOMMON IN MOST PARTS OF THE UNITED STATES, ITS UTTERLY TENDER TEXTURE MAKES IT A PRIZED CHOICE THROUGHOUT MOST OF THE WORLD. TRY IT ON YOUR GRILL AND YOU'LL SEE WHY.

STEP-BY-STEP

1. Peel the pear and cut it into four wedges. Cut the core portions from each quarter.

2. Cut each wedge into two or three pieces. Cut the pieces into approximately ½-inch chunks.

3. Heat the oil over medium heat. Add the pear and onions to the oil and sprinkle with cloves. Cook, stirring occasionally, until the pear pieces are tender.

Lamb Chops with Blackberry-Pear Chutney

LUSCIOUS LAMB CHOPS PAIR WONDERFULLY WITH PEARS AND BRAMBLEBERRIES, RIPENED TO JUICY PERFECTION IN ORCHARDS AND FIELDS FROM MAY THROUGH SEPTEMBER.

PREP: 20 MINUTES **GRILL:** 12 MINUTES
MAKES: 4 SERVINGS

- 1 large pear, peeled, cored, and coarsely chopped (about 1⅓ cups)
- ¼ cup sliced green onions (2)
- ⅛ teaspoon ground cloves
- 2 teaspoons vegetable oil
- 1 cup fresh blackberries or frozen blackberries, thawed
- 1 tablespoon red wine vinegar
- ½ teaspoon ground allspice
- ¼ teaspoon salt
- ¼ teaspoon coarsely ground black pepper
- 8 lamb loin chops, cut 1 inch thick

1 For chutney, in a medium skillet cook pear, green onions, and cloves in hot oil over medium heat about 3 minutes or just until pear is tender, stirring occasionally. Add blackberries; reduce heat to medium-low. Cook and stir for 3 minutes; remove from heat. Stir in vinegar. Set aside to cool.

2 In a small bowl, stir together allspice, salt, and pepper. Sprinkle evenly over both sides of chops; rub in with your fingers.

3 For a charcoal grill, grill chops on the rack of an uncovered grill directly over medium coals until desired doneness, turning once halfway through grilling. Allow 12 to 14 minutes for medium rare (145°F) or 15 to 17 minutes for medium (160°F). (For a gas grill, preheat grill. Reduce heat to medium. Place chops on grill rack over heat. Cover; grill as directed.)

4 Serve lamb with chutney.

PER 2 LOIN CHOPS: 161 cal., 8 g total fat (3 g sat. fat) 40 mg chol., 197 mg sodium, 11 g carbo., 3 g fiber, 13 g pro.

4. Stir blackberries into the pear mixture. Cook for 3 minutes, then remove the skillet from the heat. Add the vinegar, tossing gently to coat.

5. Sprinkle lamb chops with the spice mixture. Rub the mixture into the chops, evenly coating both sides.

6. When the coals are ready, use long-handled tongs to spread them in an even layer.

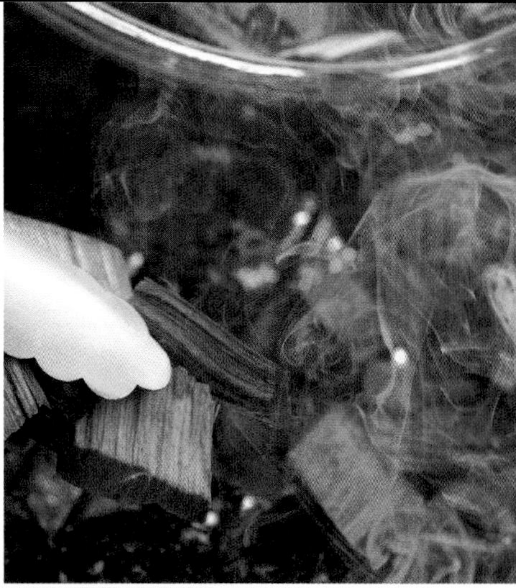

Ribs

MANY PEOPLE AGREE THAT RIBS ARE THE QUINTESSENTIAL AMERICAN MEAL, BUT THEY SURE CAN'T AGREE ON HOW TO COOK THEM. TAKE THE SUMMER TO TRY THEM ALL. EXPERIMENT FOR A FINGER-LICKING GOOD TIME.

How do you like your ribs?

EVERY PART OF THE U.S.A. IS PROUD OF ITS UNIQUE STYLE OF RIBS AND BELIEVES THAT ITS VERSION BEATS ALL OTHERS.

Few grillers know this little secret: To achieve the most tender, fall-off-the-bone ribs, remove the slippery membrane that covers the bones. Grab it with a paper towel to slip it off easily.

RIBS

Ribs are relatively inexpensive, have succulent formidable flavor, and best of all, the handheld pieces provide a fabulously efficient way to taste all sorts of wonderful sauces.

Whichever cut you choose—from super-tender baby back pork ribs to meaty, caveman-style beef ribs—shop for grill-bound ribs that have ample meat and little excess surface fat. Avoid ribs that look dry or discolored. For best quality, skip over "enhanced" ribs, which have been plumped up with saline solutions to be extra-moist; they may also taste overly salty and hamlike.

Be prepared—ribs packed in Cryovac, or vacuum packaging, may release a slightly unpleasant odor when the package is opened. This is perfectly normal. A quick rinse under cool water will remove the odor. If it does not, and if ribs smell putrid, return them to the market where you purchased them.

As a general rule, a slab of spareribs will feed two to four people. A rack of loin back or baby back ribs serves one to two people. When serving country-style pork ribs, plan ½ pound per diner, and when serving beef ribs, grill up a full pound per guest.

HOW DO YOU LIKE YOUR RIBS?

There is great debate over the perfect rib. No matter where you stand this chart should help you satisfy your craving.

Style	Cut	Description	Method
Kansas City	baby back ribs	Dry rub and a thick, sweet, tomato-based sauce	Appy rub, bake, grill, and baste with thick sauce.
Memphis	spareribs	Mild dry rub, with a mustard- or vinegar-based mop	Apply rub, bake, grill, and mop with thin sauce.
North Carolina	pork loin back	Tangy, hot vinegar-based sauce	Bake with sauce, grill, and baste with more mop.
Texas	beef ribs	Dry rub and stout sauce with coffee and chipotles	Apply rub, bake, and grill. Serve sauce on the side.

Rib Cuts

BEEF OR PORK, MEATY OR LEAN, THESE BONES ARE BEAUTIFUL.

Until you have more rib-choosing practice under your belt, depend on the expertise of a butcher or the meat department staff. These people know their stuff. If your market displays unwrapped rib cuts, all the better—allow the butcher to move through the stacks and help you choose the best slab or rack in the display.

TRY THIS UNIQUE, OLD-SCHOOL METHOD FOR GRILLING RIBS. THERE ARE TWO BENEFITS TO THIS APPROACH—IT PREVENTS THE SPICE RUB FROM SCORCHING OVER OPEN FLAME AND IT BRINGS THE RIBS TO PERFECTION OVER LOW, SLOW HEAT.

Memphis Dry Ribs

MOP SAUCES ARE THIN, VINEGARY MIXTURES FOR BASTING RIBS. MOPS MAKE RIBS EXTRA MOIST AND SUCCULENT.

PREP: 25 MINUTES **BAKE:** 2 HOURS
GRILL: 10 MINUTES **OVEN:** 350°F
MAKES: 6 SERVINGS

- 4 pounds pork loin back ribs or meaty pork spareribs
- 1 tablespoon smoked paprika or sweet paprika
- 1½ teaspoons packed brown sugar
- 1 teaspoon ground pasilla or ancho chile pepper
- ½ teaspoon ground coriander
- ½ teaspoon dry mustard
- ½ teaspoon garlic powder
- ½ teaspoon salt
- ¼ teaspoon celery salt
- ¼ teaspoon coarsely ground black pepper
- ⅛ teaspoon cayenne pepper
- ½ cup cider vinegar
- 2 tablespoons yellow mustard
- 2 cups hickory or oak wood chips*

1 Preheat oven to 350°F. Trim fat from ribs. Place ribs in a shallow roasting pan. For rub, in a small bowl stir together paprika, brown sugar, pasilla pepper, coriander, dry mustard, garlic powder, salt, celery salt, black pepper, and cayenne pepper. Reserve 1 teaspoon of the rub mixture. Sprinkle remaining rub evenly over both sides of ribs; rub in with your fingers. Cover pan with foil.

2 Bake ribs for 2 to 2½ hours or until very tender. Carefully drain off fat in roasting pan.

3 For mop sauce, in a medium bowl whisk together vinegar and mustard. Stir in the 1 teaspoon reserved rub mixture.

4 For a charcoal grill, sprinkle the wood chips over coals. Grill ribs on the rack of a covered grill directly over the coals for 10 to 15 minutes or until ribs are brown, turning once halfway through grilling and brushing occasionally with mop sauce. (For a gas grill, preheat grill. Reduce heat to medium. Add wood chips according to manufacturer's directions. Place ribs on grill rack over heat. Cover; grill as directed.)

***NOTE:** For the most smoke production, soak wood chips in enough water to cover for at least 1 hour before grilling. Drain wood chips before using.

PER ⅙ RIBS: 526 cal., 39 g total fat (16 g sat fat), 148 mg chol., 446 mg sodium, 3 g carbo., 1 g fiber, 31 g pro.

STEP-BY-STEP

1. Test the coals for medium heat. Using tongs, scatter soaked or dry wood chips over the coals. Soaked chips produce more smoke than dry.

2. Spread the rub over both sides of the ribs. Cover the pan with foil and bake for 2 to 2½ hours. Covering the ribs will keep them moist and help tenderize them.

3. To make the mop sauce, use a wire whisk to beat together the vinegar, mustard, and the 1 teaspoon of rub set aside in Step 1.

Kansas City Ribs

THE FACT THAT THERE ARE MORE THAN 100 BARBEQUE JOINTS IN KANSAS CITY SHOWS HOW SERIOUSLY THE AREA TAKES RIBS. KANSAS CITY-STYLE, BORN IN THE INNER CITY, NOW REACHES TO DISTANT SUBURBS.

PREP: 25 MINUTES **BAKE:** 2 HOURS
COOK: 20 MINUTES **GRILL:** 10 MINUTES
OVEN: 350°F **MAKES:** 6 SERVINGS

4 to 5 pounds pork loin back ribs
1 tablespoon packed brown sugar
1 tablespoon paprika
1 teaspoon garlic powder
1 teaspoon celery salt
½ teaspoon dry mustard
½ teaspoon black pepper
¼ teaspoon cayenne pepper
½ cup finely chopped onion (1 medium)
2 cloves garlic, minced
1 tablespoon butter
1 cup ketchup
¼ cup molasses
¼ cup cider vinegar
¼ cup water
2 tablespoons brown sugar
1 tablespoon chili powder
1 tablespoon yellow mustard
1 tablespoon Worcestershire sauce
2 cups hickory chips*

1 Preheat oven to 350°F. Trim fat from ribs. Place ribs in a shallow roasting pan. For rub, in a small bowl stir together brown sugar, paprika, garlic powder, celery salt, dry mustard, black pepper, and cayenne pepper. Sprinkle rub evenly over both sides of ribs; rub in with your fingers. Cover pan with foil.

2 Bake ribs for 2 to 2½ hours or until very tender. Carefully drain off fat in roasting pan.

3 Meanwhile, for sauce, in a medium saucepan cook onion and garlic in hot butter over medium heat about 5 minutes or until tender. Stir in ketchup, molasses, vinegar, the water, brown sugar, chili powder, yellow mustard, Worcestershire sauce, and ½ teaspoon *salt*. Bring to boiling; reduce heat. Simmer for 20 to 25 minutes or until desired consistency.

4 For a charcoal grill, sprinkle the wood chips over the coals. Grill ribs on the rack of a covered grill directly over the coals for 10 to 15 minutes or until ribs are brown, turning once halfway through grilling and brushing occasionally with sauce. (For a gas grill, preheat grill. Reduce heat to medium. Add wood chips according to manufacturer's directions. Place ribs on grill rack over heat. Cover; grill as directed.) Serve ribs with remaining sauce.

***NOTE:** For the most smoke production, soak wood chips in enough water to cover for at least 1 hour before grilling. Drain wood chips before using.

PER ⅙ RIBS: 653 cal., 42 g total fat (17 g sat. fat), 153 mg chol., 1,122 mg sodium, 32 g carbo., 2 g fiber, 32 g pro.

STEP-BY-STEP

1. Place ribs on a shallow roasting pan and sprinkle with the rub. Spread over the meat with your fingers. Turn ribs over and repeat with second sides.

2. Cook the sauce, uncovered, until it is thick enough to coat the ribs. Stir the sauce occasionally to avoid scorching.

3. Use a basting brush to spread the sauce on the ribs before turning them. Turn the ribs and brush again with sauce. Continue brushing occasionally with sauce until ribs are done.

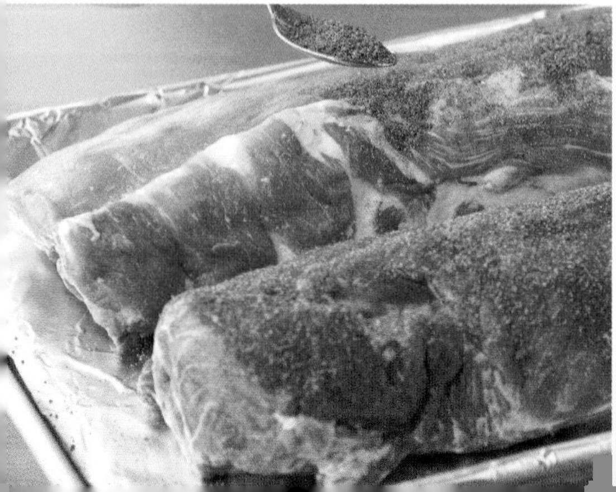

KANSAS CITY-STYLE RIBS ARE CHARACTERIZED BY LIBERAL APPLICATION OF SLIGHTLY SWEET, STICKY SAUCES MADE WITH TOMATO AND MOLASSES.

North Carolina-Style Ribs

THE NORTH CAROLINA BBQ STYLE IS THE NATION'S OLDEST, DATING TO COLONIAL TIMES. BECAUSE PEOPLE AT THAT TIME THOUGHT THAT TOMATOES WERE POISONOUS, THEY SEASONED RIBS WITH VINEGAR.

PREP: 15 MINUTES **BAKE:** 2 HOURS
GRILL: 10 MINUTES **OVEN:** 350°F
MAKES: 6 SERVINGS

- 4 pounds pork loin back ribs or meaty pork spareribs
- 2 cups cider vinegar
- 1 medium onion, thinly sliced
- 2 tablespoons packed brown sugar
- 2 serrano chile peppers, thinly sliced*
- 2 teaspoons salt
- 1 teaspoon crushed red pepper
- 1 teaspoon black pepper
- 2 cups hickory or oak chips**

1 Preheat oven to 350°F. Trim fat from ribs. Place ribs in a shallow roasting pan. For sauce, in a medium bowl combine vinegar, onion, brown sugar, serrano peppers, salt, crushed red pepper, and black pepper. Reserve ½ cup for mop sauce. Pour remaining sauce over ribs. Turn ribs to coat. Place ribs, meaty sides down, in the pan; cover with foil.

2 Bake ribs for 2 to 2½ hours or until very tender, turning ribs once after 1½ hours of baking. Carefully drain off liquid in pan. Pat ribs dry with paper towels.

3 For a charcoal grill, sprinkle the wood chips over the coals. Grill ribs on the rack of a covered grill directly over the coals for 10 to 15 minutes or until ribs are brown, turning once halfway through grilling and brushing occasionally with mop sauce. (For a gas grill, preheat grill. Reduce heat to medium. Add wood chips according to manufacturer's directions. Place ribs on grill rack over heat. Cover; grill as directed.) Brush ribs with any remaining mop sauce before serving.

***NOTE:** Because chile peppers, such as serranos, contain volatile oils that can burn your skin and eyes, avoid direct contact with them as much as possible. When working with fresh chile peppers, wear plastic or rubber gloves. If your bare hands do touch the chiles, wash your hands and nails well with soap and hot water.

****NOTE:** For the most smoke production, soak wood chips in enough water to cover for at least 1 hour before grilling. Drain wood chips before using.

PER ⅙ RIBS: 553 cal., 39 g total fat (16 g sat. fat), 148 mg chol., 908 mg sodium, 8 g carbo., 1 g fiber, 31 g pro.

STEP-BY-STEP

1. Wear plastic gloves when preparing the chile peppers. Cut off and discard the stem ends and tips. Slice the remaining pepper.

2. Spoon the sauce over the ribs, arranging the onion and chile pepper slices on top of the ribs.

3. After baking the ribs, carefully pour off the liquid in the roasting pan. Use paper towels to blot excess moisture from the ribs.

4. Arrange either dry or soaked and drained wood chips on medium coals. Soaked wood chips produce more smoke than dry chips.

5. A rib rack is handy if grill space is limited. To use one, spray the rack with nonstick cooking spray and place ribs in the rack. Place the rack and ribs on the grill and grill as directed.

6. Remove the ribs from the grill and place on cutting board. Stand the ribs on a long side and cut between the ribs into serving-size pieces.

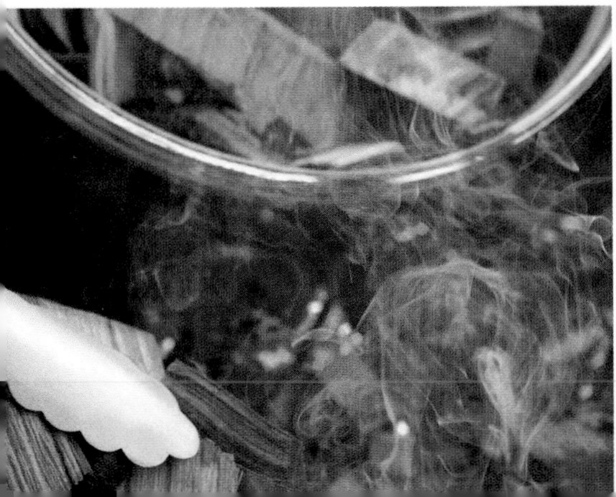

CALL THEM REGGAE RIBS IF YOU LIKE—THESE JUICY LOIN BACK RIBS PRACTICALLY DANCE WITH JAMAICA'S FAVORITE FLAVORS.

Caribbean Baby Back Ribs

GUAVA PASTE IS A THICK GEL THAT USUALLY COMES IN SMALL TINS AND IS AVAILABLE IN MOST LATINO MARKETS. TRY THIN LEFTOVER SLICES OF GUAVA PASTE WITH YOUR FAVORITE CHEESE—THE COMBINATION IS SUBLIME.

PREP: 30 MINUTES **MARINATE:** 8 HOURS
GRILL: 90 MINUTES **MAKES:** 6 SERVINGS

- 4 pounds pork loin back ribs, cut into 6- to 8-rib portions
- ¼ cup packed brown sugar
- 2 tablespoons grated fresh ginger
- 2 teaspoons salt
- 2 teaspoons finely shredded lime peel
- 1 teaspoon ground cumin
- ½ teaspoon ground cinnamon
- ½ cup chicken broth
- ¼ cup dark rum
- 3 tablespoons lime juice
- 1 tablespoon vegetable oil or olive oil
- 1 small habañero chile pepper, finely chopped*
- 1 recipe Mango-Guava BBQ Sauce

1 Trim fat from ribs. For rub, in a small bowl stir together brown sugar, ginger, salt, lime peel, cumin, and cinnamon. Sprinkle rub evenly over both sides of ribs; rub in with your fingers. Place ribs in a large resealable plastic bag set in a shallow dish; seal bag. Marinate in the refrigerator for 8 to 24 hours.

2 For mop sauce, in a medium bowl stir together broth, rum, lime juice, oil, and habañero pepper. Cover and chill for 8 to 24 hours.

3 For a charcoal grill, arrange medium-hot coals around a drip pan. Test for medium heat above pan. Place ribs, bone sides down, on the grill rack over drip pan. Cover and grill for 90 to 105 minutes or until ribs are tender, brushing with mop sauce every 15 to 20 minutes. (For a gas grill, preheat grill. Reduce heat to medium. Adjust for indirect cooking. Place ribs in roasting pan; place pan on grill rack over burner that is off. Grill as directed.)

4 Meanwhile, prepare Mango-Guava BBQ Sauce. About 15 minutes before ribs are done, brush some of the mango sauce over ribs. Serve ribs with the remaining sauce.

MANGO-GUAVA BBQ SAUCE: In a small saucepan combine 1⅓ cups chopped mangoes; ⅔ cup packed brown sugar; ⅔ cup chopped onion; ⅓ cup lime juice; ¼ cup olive oil; ¼ cup guava paste; 3 tablespoons honey; 2 tablespoons tomato paste; 2 cloves garlic, minced; and ¾ teaspoon ground cumin. Bring to boiling; reduce heat. Cover and simmer for 15 minutes. Cool slightly. Transfer to a food processor or blender. Cover and process until slightly chunky.

***NOTE:** Because chile peppers, such as habañeros, contain volatile oils that can burn your skin and eyes, avoid direct contact with them as much as possible. When working with fresh chile peppers, wear plastic or rubber gloves. If your bare hands do touch the chiles, wash your hands and nails well with soap and hot water.

PER ⅙ RIBS: 877 cal., 51 g total fat (17 g sat. fat), 148 mg chol., 1,039 mg sodium, 64 g carbo., 2 g fiber, 31 g pro.

STEP-BY-STEP

1. After cooking the Mango-Guava BBQ Sauce, the mangoes will be tender and the liquid syrupy. Remove the saucepan from heat and cool for a few minutes.

2. Spoon the Mango-Guava BBQ Sauce into a food processor or blender. Process or blend the mixture until it is almost smooth but still has a few small chunks.

3. Using a basting brush, generously brush the Mango-Guava BBQ Sauce on the ribs 15 minutes before they are done. Serve the remaining sauce with ribs.

PREPARING ALABAMA RIBS, STEP-BY-STEP

1. Trim the excess fat from the ribs with a small sharp knife.

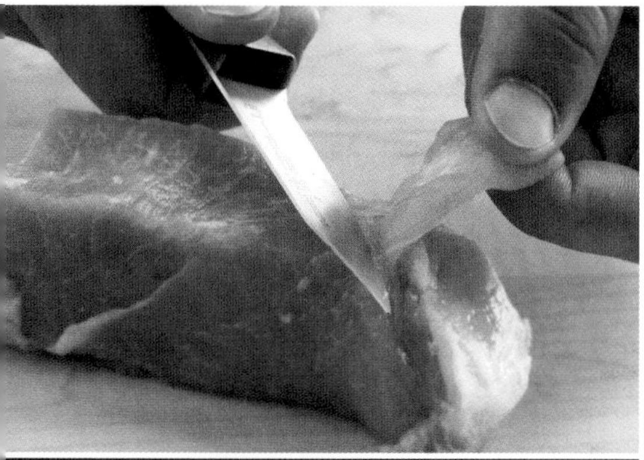

2. Bake the ribs until they are very tender. Transfer the ribs from roasting pan to a tray lined with paper towels.

3. Whisk together the sauce ingredients. Cover the bowl and chill the sauce while you grill the ribs.

4. Sprinkle either soaked and drained or dry wood chips over medium coals. The soaked wood chips produce more smoke.

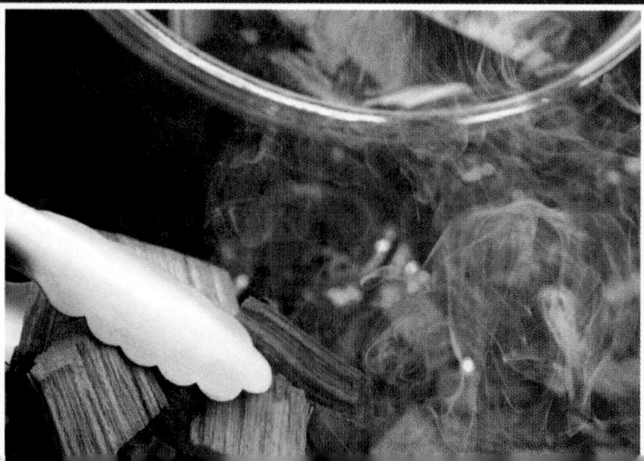

5. Grill the ribs until browned on both sides. The ribs are precooked in the oven but finished on the grill to give them smoky flavor.

Alabama Ribs

ALABAMIANS DOUSE THEIR COUNTRY-STYLE RIBS WITH A DOLLOP OF MAYO SAUCE—A DELICIOUS, EMBELLISHMENT THAT YOU MUST TRY.

PREP: 15 MINUTES **BAKE:** 1¾ HOURS
GRILL: 15 MINUTES **OVEN:** 350°F
MAKES: 6 SERVINGS

- 3 pounds bone-in pork country-style ribs
- Salt and ground black pepper
- ½ cup mayonnaise
- 2 tablespoons cider vinegar
- 2 teaspoons sugar
- 2 teaspoons cracked black pepper
- 2 teaspoons prepared horseradish
- ½ teaspoon finely shredded lemon peel
- 1 teaspoon lemon juice
- 1 clove garlic, minced
- ¼ teaspoon cayenne pepper
- 2 cups hickory chips*

1 Preheat oven to 350°F. Trim fat from ribs. Place ribs in a shallow roasting pan. Generously sprinkle ribs with salt and ground black pepper. Cover pan with foil.

2 Bake ribs for 1¾ to 2 hours or until very tender. Carefully drain off fat in roasting pan.

3 For sauce, in a small bowl stir together mayonnaise, vinegar, sugar, cracked black pepper, horseradish, lemon peel, lemon juice, garlic, ¼ teaspoon *salt*, and cayenne pepper. Cover and refrigerate until serving time.

4 For a charcoal grill, sprinkle the wood chips over the coals. Grill ribs on the rack of a covered grill directly over the coals about 15 minutes or until ribs are brown, turning once halfway through grilling. (For a gas grill, preheat grill. Reduce heat to medium. Add wood chips according to manufacturer's directions. Place ribs on grill rack over heat. Cover; grill as directed.) Serve ribs with sauce.

***NOTE:** For the most smoke production, soak wood chips in enough water to cover for at least 1 hour before grilling. Drain wood chips before using.

PER ⅙ RIBS: 626 cal., 47 g total fat (12 g sat. fat), 173 mg chol., 741 mg sodium, 5 g carbo., 1 g fiber, 43 g pro.

Floribbean Ribs

THESE RIBS GRAB THE BEST OF CARIBBEAN STYLE AND FLORIDIAN FLAIR, THEN THEY WRAP IT ALL UP IN ONE EXTRA-TASTY PACKAGE.

PREP: 20 MINUTES **BAKE:** 2 HOURS
GRILL: 10 MINUTES **OVEN:** 350°F
MAKES: 6 SERVINGS

- 1 tablespoon whole allspice
- 1 tablespoon cumin seeds
- 2 teaspoons fennel seeds
- 1 teaspoon mustard seeds
- 4 to 5 pounds meaty pork spareribs or pork loin back ribs
- 2 medium mangoes, halved, seeded, peeled, and chopped
- 2 tablespoons honey
- 2 tablespoons grated fresh ginger
- 2 tablespoons key lime juice or lime juice
- 2 tablespoons bourbon (optional)
- 1 jalapeño pepper, seeded and finely chopped*
- ¼ cup chopped green onions (2)
- 2 cups hickory or oak chips**

1 Preheat oven to 350°F. For rub, heat a medium skillet over medium heat. Add allspice, cumin seeds, fennel seeds, and mustard seeds to skillet. Toast about 3 minutes or until seeds are fragrant, stirring occasionally. Crush seeds with a mortar and pestle or in a clean coffee grinder. Stir in 1 teaspoon *salt*.

2 Trim fat from ribs. Place ribs in a shallow roasting pan. Sprinkle rub evenly over both sides of ribs; rub in with your fingers. Cover pan with foil.

3 Bake ribs for 2 to 2½ hours or until very tender. Carefully drain off fat in roasting pan.

4 Meanwhile, for mango mojo sauce, in a food processor or blender combine mangoes, honey, ginger, key lime juice, and, if desired, bourbon. Cover and process until smooth. Stir in jalapeño pepper and green onions.

5 For a charcoal grill, sprinkle the wood chips over the coals. Grill ribs on the rack of a covered grill directly over the coals for 10 to 15 minutes or until ribs are brown, turning once halfway through grilling and brushing occasionally with mango mojo sauce. (For a gas grill, preheat grill. Reduce heat to medium. Add wood chips according to manufacturer's directions. Place ribs on grill rack over heat. Cover; grill as directed.) Serve ribs with any remaining sauce.

***NOTE:** Because chile peppers, such as jalapeños, contain volatile oils that can burn your skin and eyes, avoid direct contact with them as much as possible. When working with fresh chile peppers, wear plastic or rubber gloves. If your bare hands do touch the chiles, wash your hands and nails well with soap and hot water.

****NOTE:** For the most smoke production, soak wood chips in enough water to cover for at least 1 hour before grilling. Drain wood chips before using.

PER ⅙ RIBS: 664cal., 44g total fat (15 g sat. fat), 165 mg chol., 548 mg sodium, 20 g carbo., 2 g fiber, 34 g pro.

South Carolina-Style Ribs

SOUTH CAROLINA SWEARS THAT ITS SIMPLE MUSTARDY RIBS—TOUCHED WITH A BIT OF HEAT—ARE THE COUNTRY'S BEST.

PREP: 42 MINUTES **BAKE:** 1¾ HOURS
GRILL: 15 MINUTES **OVEN:** 350°F
MAKES: 4 SERVINGS

- 3 pounds bone-in pork country-style ribs
- Salt and black pepper
- ½ cup yellow mustard
- ¼ cup honey
- ¼ cup cider vinegar
- ¼ cup apple juice
- 1 tablespoon Worcestershire sauce
- ½ teaspoon salt
- ½ teaspoon bottled hot pepper sauce
- 2 cups hickory or oak chips*

1 Preheat oven to 350°F. Trim fat from ribs. Place ribs in a foil-lined shallow roasting pan. Sprinkle ribs with salt and black pepper. Cover pan with foil.

2 Bake ribs for 1¾ to 2 hours or until very tender. Carefully drain off fat in roasting pan.

3 Meanwhile, for sauce, in a small saucepan stir together mustard, honey, vinegar, apple juice, Worcestershire sauce, the ½ teaspoon salt, and hot pepper sauce. Bring to boiling; reduce heat. Simmer, uncovered, for 12 to 15 minutes or until desired consistency, stirring occasionally.

4 For a charcoal grill, sprinkle the wood chips over the coals. Grill ribs on the rack of a covered grill directly over the coals about 15 minutes or until ribs are brown, turning once halfway through grilling and brushing occasionally with the sauce. (For a gas grill, preheat grill. Reduce heat to medium. Add wood chips according to manufacturer's directions. Place ribs on grill rack over heat. Cover; grill as directed.) Serve ribs with any remaining sauce.

***NOTE:** For the most smoke production, soak wood chips in enough water to cover for at least 1 hour before grilling. Drain wood chips before using.

PER ¼ RIBS: 510 cal., 26 g total fat (9 g sat. fat), 162 mg chol., 1,109 mg sodium, 22 g carbo., 1 g fiber, 44 g pro.

Mix It Up!

PICK ONE FROM EACH COLUMN TO CUSTOMIZE THE RIBS TO YOUR TASTE.

SEASON IT

To salt and pepper add one of the following:

- 1 tablespoon chili powder
- 1 tablespoon Cajun seasoning
- 1 tablespoon Jamaican Jerk seasoning
- 1 tablespoon Italian seasoning
- 1 tablespoon Chinese five-spice powder
- 1 tablespoon smoked paprika
- 1 tablespoon ground cumin

MIX IT IN

Instead of yellow mustard, use one of the following:

- ½ cup Dijon-style mustard
- ½ cup spicy brown mustard
- ½ cup Creole mustard
- ¼ cup Chinese-style hot mustard
- ½ cup cranberry mustard
- ½ cup horseradish mustard
- ¼ cup wasabi mustard
- ½ cup sweet-hot mustard

TOP IT

Serve ribs with one of the following:

- Sweet tea
- Hush puppies
- French fries
- Potato salad
- Baked beans
- Coleslaw
- Biscuits
- Cornmeal muffins

STEP-BY-STEP

1. Place the ribs in a foil-lined roasting pan and season with salt and pepper. Cover and bake the ribs until they are very tender.

2. Stir together the sauce ingredients in a small saucepan. Cook the sauce until it reaches a consistency that is thick enough to adhere to the ribs, yet spreads smoothly.

3. Turn the ribs when the first sides brown and grill until second sides are brown. Every few minutes, generously brush the ribs with the sauce.

Santa Maria-Style Ribs

COUNT ON CALIFORNIA TO MARCH TO THE BEAT OF A DIFFERENT DRUMMER. THIS STATE'S MOST POPULAR RIB IS BEEF, NOT PORK, AND THE DENSE, MEATY RIBS ARE HEAVY ON THE GARLIC.

PREP: 15 MINUTES **BAKE:** 1¼ HOURS
GRILL: 15 MINUTES **OVEN:** 350°F
MAKES: 6 SERVINGS

- 4 pounds bone-in beef short ribs
- 1 tablespoon salt
- 1 tablespoon paprika
- 1 tablespoon coarsely ground black pepper
- ¼ cup snipped fresh parsley
- 6 cloves garlic, minced
- 2 tablespoons olive oil
- 2 tablespoons red wine vinegar
- 2 cups red oak or oak chips or chunks*

1 Preheat oven to 350°F. Trim fat from ribs. Place ribs in a shallow roasting pan. In a small bowl stir together salt, paprika, and pepper. Sprinkle rub evenly over all sides of ribs; rub in with your fingers. Cover pan with foil.

2 Bake ribs for 1¼ to 1½ hours or until very tender. Carefully drain off fat in roasting pan.

3 In a small bowl stir together parsley, garlic, olive oil, and red wine vinegar.

4 For a charcoal grill, sprinkle the wood chips over the coals. Spoon half of the parsley mixture on ribs. Grill ribs on the rack of a covered grill directly over the coals about 15 minutes or until ribs are brown, turning once halfway through grilling and spooning the remaining parsley mixture on ribs after turning. (For a gas grill, preheat grill. Reduce heat to medium. Add wood chips according to manufacturer's directions. Place ribs on grill rack over heat. Cover; grill as directed.)

***NOTE:** For the most smoke production, soak wood chips in enough water to cover for at least 1 hour before grilling. Drain wood chips before using.

PER ⅙ RIBS: 778 cal., 70 g total fat (28 g sat. fat), 152 mg chol., 1,274 mg sodium, 2 g carbo., 1 g fiber, 32 g pro.

STEP-BY-STEP

1. When buying beef short ribs, look for ones with lots of meat. Because this cut requires long, slow cooking to become tender, they are baked first.

2. Toss together olive oil, vinegar, snipped parsley, and minced garlic.

3. Place the baked ribs on the grill rack. Spoon the parsley mixture over the ribs. Cover the grill and grill until the ribs are brown on both sides.

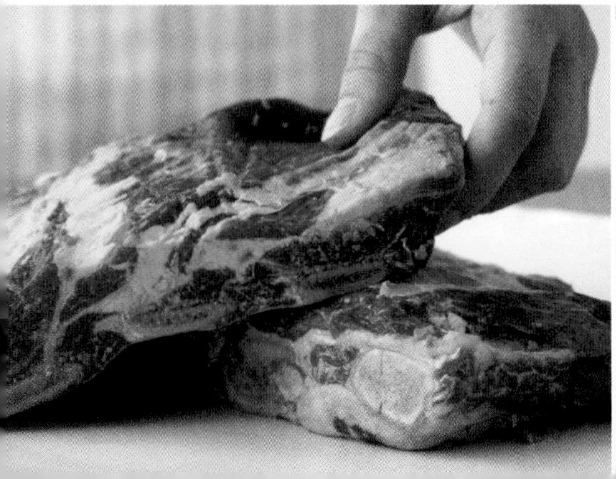

FOR A TRUE TASTE OF BARBEQUE HEAVEN, BITE INTO ONE OF THESE CALIFORNIA DREAMERS.

Texas Cowboy-Style Ribs

TEXAS BARBEQUE DEPENDS ON THE SWEET SMOKE OF THE STATE'S LOW-SLUNG LOCAL HARDWOOD. IT'S JUST NOT TEXAN WITHOUT MESQUITE. AND FORTUNATELY THE WOOD IS EASY TO FIND ELSEWHERE.

PREP: 30 MINUTES **BAKE:** 1½ HOURS
COOK: 35 MINUTES **GRILL:** 15 MINUTES
OVEN: 350°F **MAKES:** 6 SERVINGS

- 4 pounds bone-in beef short ribs
- 1 tablespoon chili powder
- 1 tablespoon packed brown sugar
- 1 teaspoon garlic powder
- 1 teaspoon onion powder
- 1 teaspoon ground cumin
- 1 teaspoon cracked black pepper
- ¼ teaspoon cayenne pepper
- ½ cup finely chopped onion (1 medium)
- 2 cloves garlic, minced
- 1 tablespoon vegetable oil
- 1½ cups ketchup
- ¼ cup Worcestershire sauce
- ¼ cup strong brewed coffee
- ¼ cup red wine vinegar
- 2 tablespoons packed brown sugar
- 1 canned chipotle pepper in adobo sauce, chopped*
- 2 teaspoons dry mustard
- 2 cups mesquite chips**

1 Preheat oven to 350°F. Trim fat from ribs. Place ribs in a shallow roasting pan. For rub, in a small bowl stir together chili powder, the 1 tablespoon brown sugar, 1 teaspoon *salt*, garlic powder, onion powder, cumin, black pepper, and cayenne pepper. Sprinkle rub evenly over all sides of ribs; rub in with your fingers. Cover pan with foil.

2 Bake ribs for 1½ to 2 hours or until very tender. Carefully drain off fat in roasting pan.

3 For sauce, in a medium saucepan cook onion and garlic in hot oil over medium heat about 5 minutes or until tender. Stir in ketchup, Worcestershire sauce, coffee, vinegar, the 2 tablespoons brown sugar, chipotle pepper, dry mustard, and ½ teaspoon *salt*. Bring to boiling; reduce heat. Simmer, uncovered, about 30 minutes or until desired consistency, stirring occasionally.

4 For a charcoal grill, sprinkle the wood chips over the coals. Grill ribs on the rack of a covered grill directly over the coals about 15 minutes or until ribs are brown, turning once halfway through grilling. (For a gas grill, preheat grill. Reduce heat to medium. Add wood chips according to manufacturer's directions. Place ribs on grill rack over heat. Cover; grill as directed.) Serve ribs with sauce.

***NOTE:** Because chile peppers, such as jalapeños, contain volatile oils that can burn your skin and eyes, avoid direct contact with them as much as possible. When working with fresh chile peppers, wear plastic or rubber gloves. If your bare hands do touch the chiles, wash your hands and nails well with soap and hot water.

****NOTE:** For the most smoke production, soak wood chips in enough water to cover for at least 1 hour before grilling. Drain wood chips before using.

STEP-BY-STEP

1. To keep track of the rub ingredients, place them one at a time in a bowl, keeping them in separate sections, and then stir them all together.

2. After cooking the onion and garlic in the oil, stir in the ketchup, Worcestershire sauce, coffee, vinegar, brown sugar, chipotle pepper, dry mustard, and salt.

3. Simmer the mixture, uncovered, for 30 minutes until it is thick and saucy. Reduce heat if the sauce starts to boil and stir occasionally to prevent scorching.

135.0°F

Big Meats

WHY HEAT UP THE KITCHEN WHEN IT'S SO EASY TO ROAST LARGE CROWD-FEEDING ENTRÉES—SUCH AS WHOLE CHICKEN, TURKEY, BEEF, AND PORK ROASTS—IN THE BACKYARD?

Preparing the Meat

LEARN A FEW SIMPLE TECHNIQUES TO PREPARE LARGE CUTS OF MEAT FOR GRILLING.

BUTTERFLY

To evenly cook and expedite the grilling time of large cuts of meat, such as shoulder, butt, or leg butterfly them. Simply snip away the cotton netting and pull the roast apart on a clean work surface.

Using a sharp chef's knife, slice deeply into thick muscle areas. Being careful not to remove meat completely, cut into the deepest, thickest part of the muscle until a flap of meat folds out like a book.

Butterflying creates an even thickness. With practice, you will butterfly meats quickly and easily.

TYING LARGE CUTS

Sometimes a recipe instructs you to tie two parts of a large roast together. Tying is common for a loin—like the pork loin above—that will be stuffed or filled.

To accomplish this task efficiently, place long lengths of clean cotton cooking twine across a cutting board. Be sure the lengths are long enough to wrap around the roast with string to spare.

Place roast on top of strings, then firmly pull each string around the roast. Tie ends of string together securely.

Using scissors, trim excess string. Good job—your nicely tied roast is ready to season and place on the grill.

Big Meat Cuts

SURVEY THESE JUMBO-SIZE SELECTIONS, THEN CHOOSE ONE FOR THE DINNER TABLE TONIGHT.

Don't wait for a holiday or special occasion to treat family and friends to the slow-roasted aromas and enticing flavor of whole birds, beef rib roasts, and pork loins. Each of these big meat cuts will feed a houseful of guests or make a family-size meal with leftovers. So give them a go on the grill.

Grilled Chili-Garlic Tri-Tip

TRI-TIP STEAK BECAME POPULAR IN CALIFORNIA. THEN—AS WITH MANY CALIFORNIAN EXPORTS—THE SENSATIONAL STEAK GATHERED A NATIONAL AND ABSOLUTELY LOYAL FAN BASE.

PREP: 25 MINUTES **MARINATE:** 2 HOURS
GRILL: 35 MINUTES **STAND:** 15 MINUTES
MAKES: 6 SERVINGS

- 2 teaspoons caraway seeds
- 2 teaspoons cumin seeds
- ½ teaspoon coriander seeds
- 2 tablespoons tomato sauce
- 1 tablespoon red chili paste
- 1 tablespoon olive oil
- 1¼ teaspoons chili powder
- 3 cloves garlic, minced
- 1 2-pound boneless beef tri-tip roast (bottom sirloin)
- ½ teaspoon salt
- ¼ teaspoon black pepper

1 In a medium skillet combine caraway seeds, cumin seeds, and coriander seeds. Cook over medium-high heat for 2 to 3 minutes or until seeds are lightly toasted and fragrant, shaking the skillet constantly. Cool. Transfer seeds to a clean coffee grinder; pulse to form a fine powder.

2 For spice paste, in a small bowl combine the tomato sauce, chili paste, oil, chili powder, and garlic. Stir in spice seed powder.

3 Trim fat from roast. Place meat in a shallow dish; sprinkle with salt and pepper. Spread spice paste over both sides of meat. Cover and marinate in the refrigerator for 2 hours.

4 For a charcoal grill, arrange medium-hot coals around a drip pan. Test for medium heat above pan. Place roast on grill rack over pan. Cover and grill to desired doneness, turning once halfway through grilling. Allow 35 to 40 minutes for medium rare (135°F) and 40 to 45 minutes for medium (150°F). (For a gas grill, preheat grill. Reduce heat to medium. Adjust for indirect cooking. Place roast in roasting pan; place pan on grill rack over the burner that is turned off. Grill as directed.)

5 Remove meat from grill. Cover meat with foil; let stand for 15 minutes. Temperature of meat will rise 10°F during standing.

PER 4 OUNCES: 290 cal., 16 g total fat (5 g sat. fat), 98 mg chol., 426 mg sodium, 4 g carbo., 1 g fiber, 32 g pro.

Spice-Rubbed Beef Tenderloin

BEEF TENDERLOIN OFFERS DINING LUXURY AT ITS FINEST. BE SURE TO SPECIFY CENTER-CUT TENDERLOIN AT THE MEAT MARKET—ONLY THE CENTER CUT PROVIDES A PERFECT SHAPE FOR THE PIECE OF MEAT AND KNIFE-FREE PREPARATION.

PREP: 15 MINUTES **GRILL:** 60 MINUTES
STAND: 15 MINUTES **MAKES:** 12 SERVINGS

- 1 tablespoon chili powder
- 1 tablespoon ground coriander
- 1 tablespoon packed brown sugar
- 1 teaspoon paprika
- 1 teaspoon dry mustard
- 1 teaspoon salt
- ½ teaspoon garlic powder
- ¼ teaspoon cayenne pepper
- 1 3- to 4-pound center-cut beef tenderloin roast

1 For rub, in a small bowl combine chili powder, coriander, brown sugar, paprika, dry mustard, salt, garlic powder, and cayenne pepper. Sprinkle rub over roast and rub in with your fingers.

2 For a charcoal grill, arrange hot coals around a drip pan. Test for medium-high heat above the pan. Place roast on grill rack over pan. Cover and grill for 60 to 75 minutes for medium rare (135°F). (For a gas grill, preheat grill. Reduce heat to medium-high. Adjust for indirect cooking. Place roast on a rack in a shallow roasting pan; place pan on grill rack over the burner that is turned off. Grill as directed.)

3 Remove meat from grill. Cover meat with foil; let stand for 15 minutes. Temperature of meat after standing should be 145°F.

PER 4 OUNCES: 193 cal., 10 g total fat (4 g sat. fat), 70 mg chol., 253 mg sodium, 2 g carbo., 0 g fiber, 24 g pro.

PREPARING GRILLED CHILI-GARLIC TRI-TIP, STEP-BY-STEP

1. Toast the seeds to enhance the flavor. To avoid burning, shake the skillet; reduce heat if necessary.

2. Spoon the toasted seeds into a coffee grinder. Pulse until the seeds are ground to a fine powder.

3. For spice paste, mix the tomato sauce, chili paste, oil, chili powder, and garlic. Stir in the ground spice mixture.

4. Place the meat in a rectangular dish. Spread all sides of the roast with the spice paste. Cover with plastic wrap and chill for 2 hours.

5. To check for doneness, insert an instant-read meat thermometer into the thickest part of the meat after the minimum grilling time.

STEP-BY-STEP

1. Use a sharp knife to cut 20 small slits into the top of the roast. Make each hole about 1 inch deep and space them evenly over the roast.

2. Cut each garlic clove lengthwise into fourths, for a total of 20 pieces. Press a piece of garlic into each slit in the roast.

3. To crack the peppercorns, place them in a resealable plastic bag. Close the bag and place it on a work surface. Pound the peppercorns with the flat side of a meat mallet to crack them.

Pepper-and-Garlic-Studded Beef Rib Roast

PEPPERCORN MÉLANGE—A COLORFUL MIX OF DRIED GREEN, PINK, AND BLACK TELLICHERRY PEPPERS—COATS THIS ROAST WITH SPRITELY FLAVOR AND A PICTURE-PERFECT, NUBBY CRUST.

PREP: 30 MINUTES **GRILL:** 2 HOURS
STAND: 15 MINUTES **MAKES:** 14 SERVINGS

- 1 6- to 6½-pound beef rib roast
- 5 cloves garlic, quartered lengthwise
- 1 tablespoon olive oil
- 3 tablespoons peppercorn melange, cracked
- 1 tablespoon kosher salt or coarse sea salt
- 2 cups hickory or mesquite wood chips*

1 Trim fat from meat. With a small sharp knife, make 20 evenly spaced small holes, about 1 inch deep, in the roast. Insert a piece of garlic in each hole. Brush roast with olive oil. Rub peppercorn melange and salt over the roast; pat gently to hold in place. Insert an oven-going meat thermometer into center of roast. The thermometer should not touch bone.

2 For a charcoal grill, arrange medium-hot coals around a drip pan. Test for medium-low heat above pan. Sprinkle wood chips over the coals. Place roast, fat side up, on grill rack over pan. Cover and grill until desired doneness. Allow 2 to 2¾ hours for medium rare (135°F) and 2½ to 3¼ hours for medium (150°F). (For a gas grill, preheat grill. Reduce heat to medium-low. Adjust for indirect cooking. Add wood chips according to manufacturer's directions. Place roast on a rack in a shallow roasting pan; place pan on grill rack over the burner that is turned off. Grill as directed.)

3 Remove meat from grill. Cover meat with foil; let stand for 15 minutes. Temperature of the meat will rise 10°F during standing.

***NOTE:** For the most smoke production, soak wood chips in enough water to cover for at least 1 hour before grilling. Drain wood chips before using.

PER 4 OUNCES: 281 cal., 16 g total fat (6 g sat. fat), 92 mg chol., 221 mg sodium, 1 g carbo., 0 g fiber, 31 g pro.

4. Rub the cracked peppercorns evenly over the top and sides of the meat, pressing pepper into the meat. Insert a meat thermometer into the roast.

5. If using a charcoal grill, arrange medium-hot coals on one side of the grill and place a drip pan on the other side. Sprinkle wood chips over the coals and add water to the drip pan.

6. To carve the meat, hold the roast so the bones are to one side. Cut the meat from the bones in one piece.

Indian-Spiced Leg of Lamb

WARM INDIAN SPICES WRAP THIS RICH LEG OF LAMB IN A DUVET OF DELICIOUSNESS. TANGY YOGURT, COOL CUCUMBER, AND FRESH MINT—INGREDIENTS OF TRADITIONAL TZATZIKI SAUCE—COMPLEMENT THE RICH, WARM MEAT.

PREP: 20 MINUTES **GRILL:** 50 MINUTES
STAND: 15 MINUTES **MAKES:** 8 SERVINGS

- 1 tablespoon ground cumin
- 1 tablespoon ground coriander
- 1 teaspoon black pepper
- 1 teaspoon salt
- ½ teaspoon garlic powder
- ½ teaspoon ground cardamom
- ½ teaspoon ground ginger
- ⅛ teaspoon ground cinnamon
- ⅛ teaspoon ground cloves
- ⅛ teaspoon ground nutmeg
- 1 3½- to 4-pound boneless leg of lamb, rolled and tied
- 1 recipe Tzatziki Sauce

1 In a small bowl combine cumin, coriander, pepper, salt, garlic powder, cardamom, ginger, cinnamon, cloves, and nutmeg; set aside.

2 Untie and unroll lamb. Trim fat from meat. Using the flat side of a meat mallet, pound lamb to an even thickness (1½ to 2 inches thick). Sprinkle spice mixture evenly over both sides of meat; rub in with your fingers. To keep meat from curling, insert 2 long metal skewers through meat, forming an X.

3 For a charcoal grill, arrange medium-hot coals around a drip pan. Test for medium-low heat above pan. Place meat on grill rack over pan. Cover and grill for 50 to 60 minutes or until medium rare (135°F), turning once halfway through grilling. (For a gas grill, preheat grill. Reduce heat to medium-low. Adjust for indirect cooking. Place meat on grill rack over the burner that is turned off. Grill as directed.)

4 Remove meat from grill. Cover meat with foil; let stand for 15 minutes. Temperature of meat will rise 10°F during standing. Remove metal skewers. Thinly slice lamb and serve with Tzatziki Sauce.

TZATZIKI SAUCE: In a small bowl stir together one 6-ounce carton plain Greek-style yogurt, ⅓ cup finely chopped cucumber, 1 teaspoon snipped fresh mint, ¼ teaspoon black pepper, and 1 small clove garlic, minced.

PER SERVING: 260 cal., 8 g total fat (3 g sat. fat) 127 mg chol., 399 mg sodium, 3 g carbo., 1 g fiber, 42 g pro.

STEP-BY-STEP

1. Unroll the lamb onto a cutting board. Use a sharp knife to cut large sections of separable fat away from the meat.

2. Using the flat side of a meat mallet, pound the meat, from the center toward the edges, until it is an even 1½ to 2 inches thick.

3. Insert a long metal skewer from one corner of the meat diagonally to the opposite corner. Insert another skewer so the two skewers cross in the center.

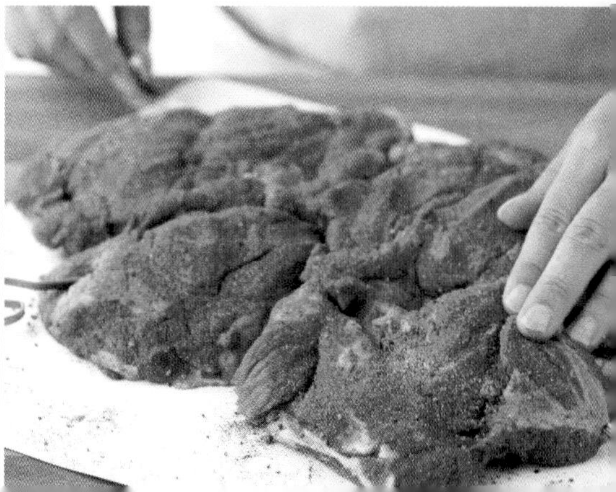

4. For a charcoal grill, move the medium-hot coals to opposite sides of the grill, leaving space for the drip pan. Add the drip pan and test for heat over pan.

5. After the minimum grilling time, insert an instant-read meat thermometer into the meat, being sure to avoid fat. Lamb is best cooked to medium rare.

6. Remove the meat from the grill. Cover it loosely with foil and let stand for 15 minutes. Remove the skewers. Cut the meat crosswise into thin slices.

STEP-BY-STEP

1. For marinade, combine the citrus juices and onion in a glass bowl. Stir in the olive oil until the liquids are well blended and no longer separate.

2. Stir in the ground cumin and crushed dried oregano. (Crushing the oregano releases flavorful oils.) Add the garlic and stir well until all the ingredients are mixed.

3. Place the meat over the drip pan and the peppers and onions directly over the coals. Turn the vegetables occasionally during grilling to roast them evenly.

Mojo Pork Fajitas with Orange-Avocado Salsa

MOJO—A SPICY, EASY-TO-MAKE SAUCE THAT HAILS FROM THE CARIBBEAN ISLANDS—PUNCTUATES PORK WITH RAMBUNCTIOUS FLAVOR THAT'S WORTH RAVING ABOUT.

PREP: 45 MINUTES **MARINATE:** 8 HOURS
GRILL: 30 MINUTES **STAND:** 10 MINUTES
MAKES: 4 SERVINGS

- ⅓ cup olive oil
- ¼ cup chopped onion
- ⅓ cup lime juice
- ⅓ cup orange juice
- 1 teaspoon ground cumin
- 1 teaspoon dried oregano, crushed
- 6 cloves garlic, minced
- 1 1-pound pork tenderloin
- 2 large red sweet peppers, halved lengthwise and seeded
- 2 medium onions, cut into thick slices
- 8 8-inch flour tortillas, warmed*
- 1 recipe Orange-Avocado Salsa
- ¼ cup dairy sour cream
- Fresh cilantro leaves (optional)
- Lime wedges (optional)

1 For marinade, in a small bowl combine olive oil, the ¼ cup onion, lime juice, orange juice. Add cumin, oregano, and garlic; stir well. Trim fat from meat. Place meat in a large resealable plastic bag set in a shallow dish. Pour marinade over meat; seal bag. Marinate in the refrigerator for 8 to 24 hours, turning bag occasionally.

2 Drain meat, reserving marinade. Brush sweet pepper quarters and onion slices with some of the marinade; discard the remaining marinade.

3 For a charcoal grill, arrange hot coals around a drip pan. Test for medium-hot heat above the pan. Place meat on the grill rack over pan. Place pepper quarters and onion slices on the grill directly over coals. Cover and grill for 8 to 10 minutes for peppers and 10 to 12 minutes for onions or until vegetables are crisp-tender, turning occasionally. Remove vegetables from grill; keep warm. Cover grill and grill meat for 20 to 25 minutes more or until thermometer registers 155°F. (For a gas grill, preheat grill. Reduce heat to medium-high. Adjust for indirect cooking. Grill vegetables and meat as directed.)

4 Remove meat from grill. Cover with foil and let stand for 10 minutes. (Meat temperature after standing should be 165°F.) Meanwhile, if desired or if skin of peppers is too charred, peel skin from peppers. Cut peppers into thin strips and chop onions. Slice meat. Serve meat and vegetables on warm tortillas with Orange-Avocado Salsa and sour cream. If desired, sprinkle with cilantro and serve with lime wedges.

***NOTE:** Wrap tortillas tightly in foil. Place on edge of grill rack for 10 minutes, turning once.

ORANGE-AVOCADO SALSA: In a medium bowl combine 2 medium oranges, peeled, sectioned, and chopped; 1 ripe large avocado, halved, seeded, peeled, and chopped; ¼ cup chopped red onion; ¼ cup snipped fresh cilantro; 2 tablespoons lime juice; ½ to 1 teaspoon bottled hot pepper sauce; and ¼ teaspoon salt. If desired, cover and chill up to 4 hours.

PER 2 FAJITAS: 739 cal., 32 g total fat (7 g sat. fat), 80 mg chol., 723 mg sodium, 80 g carbo., 8 g fiber, 36 g pro.

4. To section an orange, cut a thin slice off each end of the fruit. Place the orange on a cutting board and cut off the peel from top to bottom.

5. To remove the sections, use a small sharp knife to cut from the outside to the center of each section on each side of the membrane. The sections will easily pop out of the fruit.

6. When the vegetables are cool enough to handle, cut the grilled onions and peppers into thin strips.

Pork Loin Stuffed with Dried Fruit and Gorgonzola

MELLOW GARLIC, FRESH ROSEMARY, AND TANGY BLUE CHEESE MAKE THIS ITALIAN-STYLE DISH A PERFECT PICK FOR COMPANY-SPECIAL GRILLED LOIN.

PREP: 25 MINUTES **GRILL:** 1½ HOURS
STAND: 15 MINUTES **MAKES:** 8 SERVINGS

- ⅓ cup chopped onion (1 small)
- 2 tablespoons butter
- 1½ cups snipped dried pears or dried apples
- ½ cup chopped walnuts, toasted
- ¼ cup crumbled Gorgonzola or other blue cheese (1 ounce)
- 1 tablespoon balsamic vinegar
- 1 3- to 4-pound boneless pork top loin roast (double loin, tied)
- 1 tablespoon snipped fresh rosemary
- 2 large cloves garlic, minced
- ½ teaspoon coarsely ground black pepper
- Grilled lengthwise carrot slices (optional)
- Grilled nectarine slices (optional)
- Fresh rosemary sprigs (optional)

1 For stuffing, in a medium saucepan cook onion in hot butter over medium heat until tender. Remove from heat. Stir in dried pears, walnuts, Gorgonzola cheese, and balsamic vinegar. Set aside.

2 Untie meat; separate halves and trim fat from meat. Spoon stuffing onto the flat side of 1 portion of meat. Top with second portion of meat; retie meat with heavy 100%-cotton kitchen string.

3 For rub, in a small bowl stir together the snipped rosemary, garlic, and pepper. Sprinkle rub evenly over meat; rub in with your fingers.

4 For a charcoal grill, arrange medium coals around a drip pan. Test for medium-low heat above pan. Place roast on grill rack over pan. Cover and grill for 1½ to 2 hours or until thermometer inserted into center of meat registers 150°F, turning once halfway through grilling. (For a gas grill, preheat grill. Reduce heat to medium-low. Adjust for indirect cooking. Place roast in roasting pan; place pan on grill rack over the burner that is turned off. Grill as directed.)

5 Remove meat from grill. Cover meat with foil; let stand for 15 minutes. Temperature of the meat will rise 10°F during standing. If desired, serve meat with grilled nectarine slices and grilled carrot slices and garnish with rosemary sprigs.

PER 5 OUNCES MEAT: 420 cal., 18 g total fat (6 g sat. fat), 104 mg chol., 148 mg sodium, 26 g carbo., 3 g fiber, 40 g pro.

STEP-BY-STEP

1. Use kitchen scissors to snip the dried pears. Spraying the scissors with nonstick cooking spray will prevent the fruit from sticking to the blades.

2. After cooking the onion, remove the saucepan from the burner. Stir in the snipped pears, walnuts, Gorgonzola, and vinegar. Let the stuffing stand while preparing the roast.

3. Untie the roast and discard the string. Separate the roast into two pieces. Use a sharp knife to trim as much fat as you can from each piece of meat.

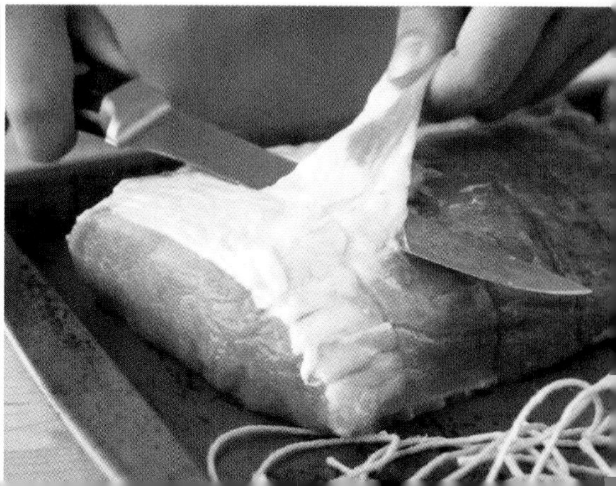

4. Place one piece of meat on the work surface, flat side up. Spread the stuffing on top of the meat. Pat the stuffing in an even layer.

5. Place the second piece of meat on the stuffing, rounded side up. Use clean string to tie the roast in 1-inch intervals to secure the two pieces of meat and stuffing.

6. Combine the garlic, rosemary, and pepper and rub over the stuffed roast. If any stuffing spills out, use your fingers to slip it back between the two pieces of meat.

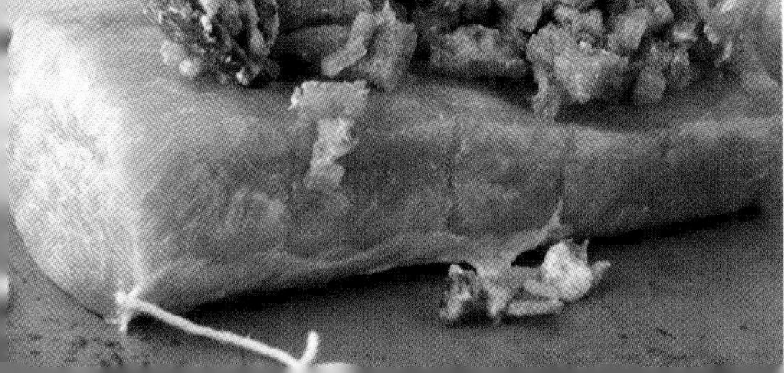

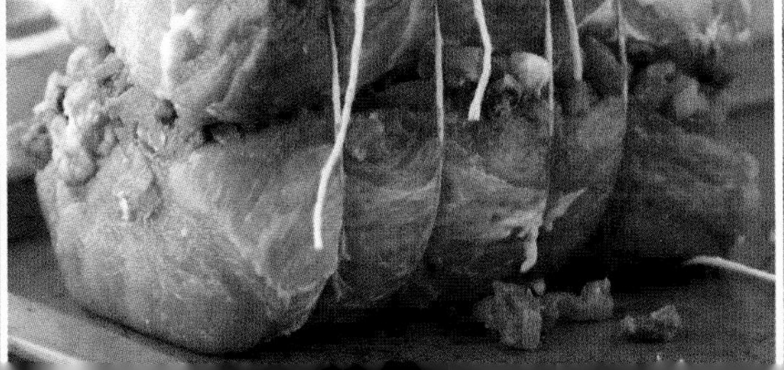

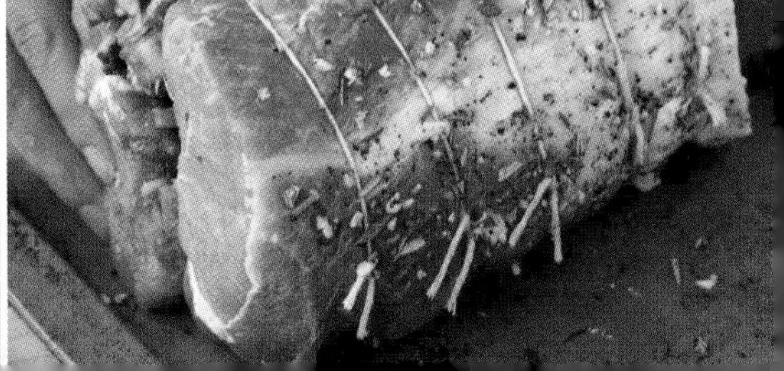

STEP-BY-STEP

1. Use a sharp knife to cut the excess fat from the meat. Hold the knife parallel to the meat and cut away the fat a little at a time.

2. Brush the honey and lime mixture on the top, sides, and bottom of the roast. After contact with raw meat, wash the pastry brush in hot soapy water or in the dishwasher.

3. Sprinkle the chili powder mixture on the meat. Rub it in with your fingers. The honey and lime mixture will help the spices adhere to the roast.

Southwestern Rotisserie Pork Roast

THE AGES-OLD TECHNIQUE OF SPIT-ROASTING MEATS IS MAKING A COMEBACK—FOR GOOD REASON. CONTINUOUS BASTING AS THE MEAT TURNS ON THE SPIT CREATES EXTRA-MOIST MEAT WITH A BEAUTIFUL CARAMELIZED EXTERIOR.

PREP: 20 MINUTES **GRILL:** 1½ HOURS
STAND: 15 MINUTES **MAKES:** 6 SERVINGS

- 3 tablespoons honey
- 1 teaspoon finely shredded lime peel
- 1 tablespoon lime juice
- 2 tablespoons chili powder
- 1 tablespoon salt
- 1 tablespoon onion powder
- 1 tablespoon garlic powder
- 2 teaspoons ground cumin
- 2 teaspoons black pepper
- 1 teaspoon paprika
- ¼ teaspoon cayenne pepper
- 1 2½- to 3-pound boneless pork top loin roast (single loin)

1 In a small bowl stir together honey, lime peel, and lime juice; set aside. In another small bowl stir together chili powder, salt, onion powder, garlic powder, cumin, black pepper, paprika, and cayenne pepper; set aside.

2 Trim fat from meat. Brush meat evenly with the honey mixture. Sprinkle chili powder mixture evenly over roast; pat in with your fingers.

3 To secure the roast on a rotisserie rod, place one holding fork on the rod with tines toward the point. Insert rod through the narrow end of the roast, pressing the tines of the holding fork firmly into meat. Place second holding fork on rod with tines toward roast; press tines of holding fork firmly into meat. Adjust forks and tighten screws. Test balance, making adjustments as necessary.

4 For a charcoal grill, arrange medium coals around a drip pan. Test for medium-low heat above the pan. Secure rotisserie rod; turn on rotisserie motor. Cover and grill about 1½ hours or until thermometer inserted into center of roast registers 150°F. Add fresh coals as needed to maintain temperature. (For a gas grill, preheat grill. Reduce heat to medium. Adjust for indirect cooking. Secure rotisserie rod so roast is over burner that is turned off. Grill as directed.)

5 Remove roast from rotisserie rod. Cover roast with foil; let stand for 15 minutes. Temperature will rise 10°F during standing.

PER 5 OUNCES MEAT: 338 cal., 15 g total fat (5 g sat. fat), 109 mg chol., 1,242 mg sodium, 13 g carbo., 2 g fiber, 37 g pro.

4. Insert the rotisserie rod into the roast and press the tines of the fork into the meat. Place the second holding fork on the rod and press into meat.

5. Adjust the forks so the roast is evenly balanced on the rod. Insert the rod into the motor. Reposition as necessary so the meat will be over the burner that is turned off.

6. Remove one holding fork from the meat. With a meat fork, push the roast from the rotisserie rod. Cover with foil and let stand for 15 minutes before slicing.

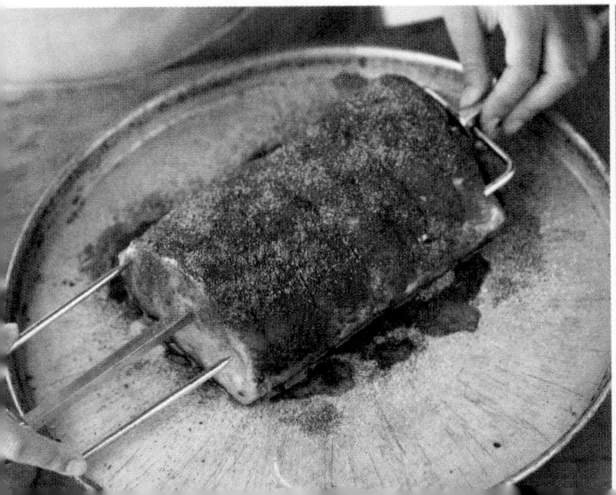

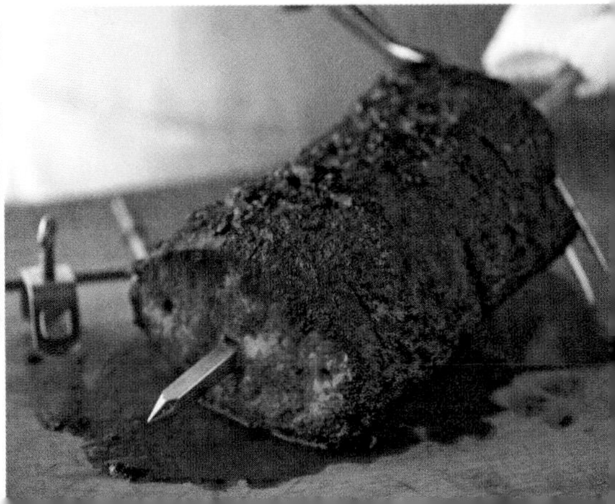

Bayou Rotisserie Chicken

BRINE THE BIRD IN BOURBON AND HONEY. RUB IT WITH SPIRITED CAJUN SPICE. AND SERVE IT WITH SPICY SLAW. BY THE TIME YOU SIT DOWN TO THIS PLATE OF PLENTY, YOU'LL FEEL AS IF YOU WERE BORN ON THE BAYOU.

PREP: 30 MINUTES **MARINATE:** 6 HOURS
GRILL: 1 HOUR **STAND:** 10 MINUTES
MAKES: 8 SERVINGS

- 2 3- to 3½-pound whole broiler-fryer chickens
- 8 cups water
- ½ cup kosher salt
- ½ cup bourbon
- ½ cup honey
- 2 tablespoons finely shredded lemon peel
- ¼ cup lemon juice
- ¼ cup bottled hot pepper sauce
- 6 cloves garlic, minced
- 1 recipe Cajun Spice Rub
- 1 recipe Cajun Broccoli Slaw

1 Remove neck and giblets from chickens; reserve for another use or discard. Rinse the chicken body cavity; pat dry with paper towels. Place chickens in a 2-gallon resealable plastic bag set in a large bowl. For brine, in a large bowl combine the water, salt, bourbon, honey, lemon peel, lemon juice, hot pepper sauce, and garlic. Stir until salt and honey are dissolved. Pour brine over chickens; seal bag. Marinate in the refrigerator for 6 to 8 hours, turning bag occasionally.

2 Remove chickens from brine; discard brine. Pat chickens dry with paper towels. Sprinkle Cajun Spice Rub evenly over chickens; rub in with your fingers.

3 To secure chickens on a rotisserie rod, place 1 holding fork on the rod with tines toward the point. Insert rod through 1 of the chickens, neck end first, pressing the tines of the holding fork firmly into breast meat. To tie wings, slip a 24-inch length of 100%-cotton kitchen string under back of chicken; bring ends of string to front, securing each wing tip. Tie in center of breast, leaving equal string ends. To tie legs, slip a 24-inch piece of string under tail. Loop string around tail, then loop around crossed legs. Tie very tightly to hold bird securely on rod, leaving string ends. Pull together strings attached to wings and legs; tie tightly. Trim off excess string. Place second holding fork on rod with tines toward the chicken; press tines of holding fork firmly into thigh meat. Adjust forks and tighten screws. Repeat with remaining chicken. Test balance, making adjustments as necessary.

4 For a charcoal grill, arrange medium-hot coals around a drip pan. Test for medium heat above the pan. Secure rotisserie rod; turn on rotisserie motor. Cover and grill for 1 to 1¼ hours or until chicken is no longer pink (180°F in thigh muscle). (For a gas grill, preheat grill. Reduce heat to medium. Adjust for indirect cooking. Secure rotisserie rod so chickens are over burner that is turned off. Grill as directed.)

5 Remove chickens from rotisserie rod. Cover chickens with foil; let stand for 10 minutes. Serve with Cajun Broccoli Slaw.

CAJUN SPICE RUB: In a small bowl stir together 2 tablespoons packed brown sugar; 2 teaspoons paprika; 1 teaspoon garlic powder; 1 teaspoon onion powder; 1 teaspoon dried thyme, crushed; ½ teaspoon ground allspice; ¼ teaspoon cayenne pepper; and ¼ teaspoon black pepper.

CAJUN BROCCOLI SLAW: For dressing, in a small bowl stir together ½ cup mayonnaise, 2 tablespoons snipped fresh parsley, 1 tablespoon white wine vinegar, 2 teaspoons packed brown sugar, 1 teaspoon snipped fresh thyme, ½ teaspoon salt, ¼ teaspoon black pepper, and ¼ teaspoon cayenne pepper; set aside. In a bowl combine one 16-ounce package shredded broccoli (broccoli slaw mix); 6 tablespoons sliced green onions (3); and ¾ cup finely chopped red sweet pepper. Add dressing; toss to coat. Chill until ready to serve. Before serving, top with ¼ cup chopped toasted pecans.

PER ¼ CHICKEN: 672 cal., 47 g total fat (11 g sat. fat), 182 mg chol., 1,113 mg sodium, 14 g carbo., 3 g fiber, 45 g pro.

Mix It Up!

PICK ONE FROM EACH COLUMN TO CUSTOMIZE THE CHICKEN TO YOUR TASTE.

SEASON IT

Instead of the Cajun Spice Rub, season chicken with one of the following:

- 1 tablespoon purchased Cajun seasoning
- 1 to 2 tablespoons freshly ground multicolored peppercorns
- 1 to 2 tablespoons Jamaican jerk seasoning
- 2 tablespoons taco seasoning mix

MIX IT IN

Instead of sweet red pepper, mix one of the following into the broccoli mixture:

- ½ cup raisins plus ¼ cup chopped mixed olives
- ¾ cup chopped pickled vegetables
- ½ cup snipped dried cherries
- ¾ cup chopped jicama
- ¾ cup quartered cherry tomatoes

TOP IT

Instead of pecans, top salad and chicken with one of the following:

- Crumbled queso fresco
- Crumbled blue cheese
- Toasted pine nuts
- Chopped assorted pitted olives
- Shredded cheddar cheese
- French-fried onion rings
- Crushed herb-seasoned croutons

STEP-BY-STEP

1. Starting at the neck end, insert the rod through one of the chickens. Press the fork into the breast meat.

2. Place the string under the chicken. Bring the string up around the breast, securing wing tips to the breast.

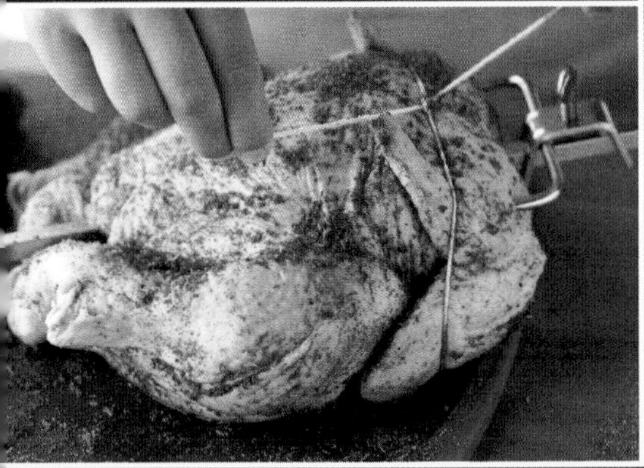

3. Wrap another piece of string around the tail; twist it, then wrap around drumstick tips. Tie tightly.

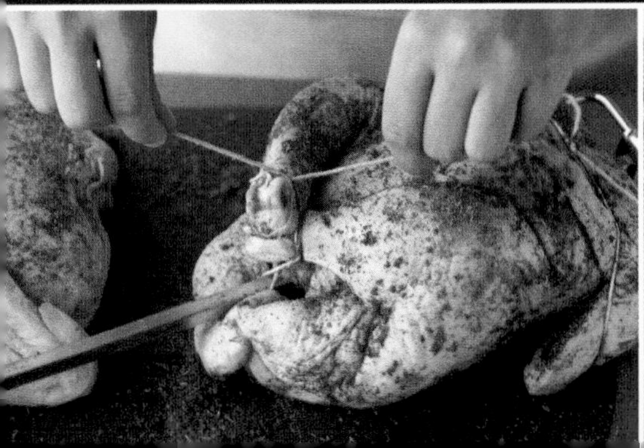

4. Bring together ends of string, securing the wings and the tail together. Tie tightly.

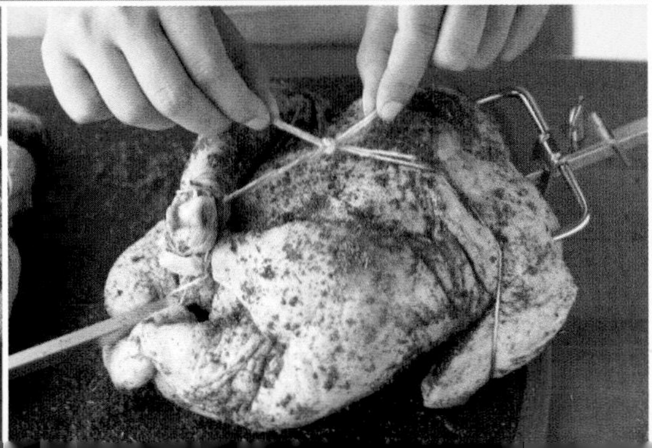

5. Place second chicken on rod and tie as directed for first chicken. Insert the holding fork tightly into thigh meat of second chicken.

STEP-BY-STEP

1. Pour out half the beer and discard. Spoon 1 teaspoon of the spice rub into the beer remaining in the can. The spices will cause the beer to foam.

2. Mix together the softened butter and the remaining rub. With your fingers, spread the butter-rub mixture evenly over the chicken.

3. Carefully lower the chicken onto the beer can so the can fills the cavity. Pull the legs forward. The upright chicken will be supported by the beer can and the legs.

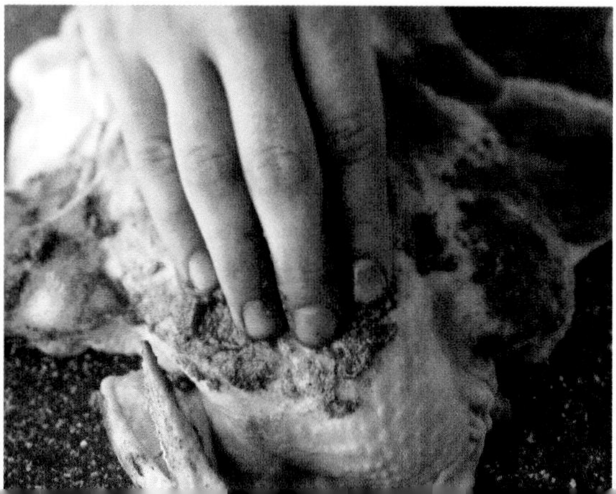

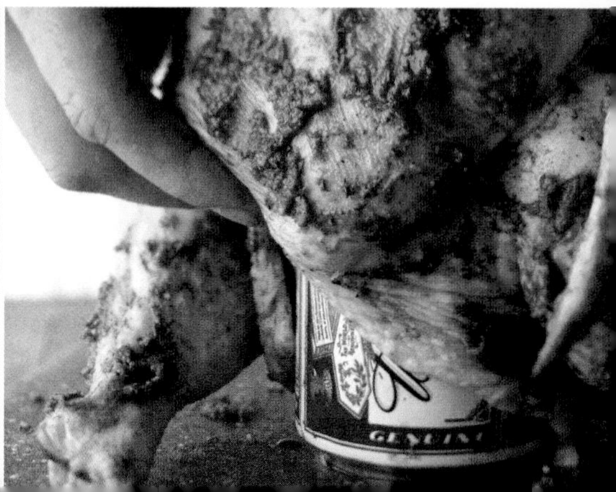

Beer-Can Chicken

THIS UNUSUAL METHOD—IN WHICH CHICKEN GRILLS WHILE ON A CAN OF BEER—IS MORE THAN JUST A GIMMICK. THE TECHNIQUE PRODUCES THE MOST TENDER, MOIST, AND SUCCULENT CHICKEN YOU MAY EVER TASTE.

PREP: 25 MINUTES **GRILL:** 75 MINUTES
STAND: 10 MINUTES **MAKES:** 4 SERVINGS

- 2 teaspoons salt
- 2 teaspoons packed brown sugar
- 2 teaspoons paprika
- 1 teaspoon dry mustard
- ½ teaspoon dried thyme, crushed
- ½ teaspoon black pepper
- ¼ teaspoon garlic powder
- 1 12-ounce can beer
- 1 3½- to 4-pound whole broiler-fryer chicken
- 2 tablespoons butter or margarine, softened
- 1 lemon wedge

1 For rub, in a small bowl combine salt, brown sugar, paprika, dry mustard, thyme, pepper, and garlic powder. Discard about half of the beer from the can. Add 1 teaspoon of the rub mixture to the half-empty can (beer will foam up).

2 Remove neck and giblets from chicken; reserve for another use or discard. Rinse the chicken body cavity; pat dry with paper towels. Sprinkle 1 teaspoon of the rub inside the body cavity. Add the softened butter to the remaining rub mixture in bowl; mix well. Rub butter mixture over the outside of the chicken.

3 Hold the chicken upright with the opening of the body cavity at the bottom and lower it onto the beer can so the can fits into the cavity. Pull the chicken legs forward so the bird rests on its legs and the can. Twist wing tips behind back. Stuff the lemon wedge in the neck cavity to seal in steam.*

4 For a charcoal grill, arrange medium-hot coals around a drip pan. Test for medium heat above pan. Stand chicken upright on grill rack over drip pan. Cover and grill for 75 to 105 minutes or until chicken is no longer pink (180°F in thigh muscle). If necessary, tent chicken with foil to prevent overbrowning. (For a gas grill, preheat grill. Reduce heat to medium. Adjust for indirect cooking. Place chicken on grill rack as directed above a burner that is turned off. If necessary, remove upper grill racks so chicken will stand upright. Grill as directed.) With hot pads or oven mitts, carefully remove chicken from grill, holding by the can. Cover with foil; let stand for 10 minutes. To pull the can from the chicken, use a hot pad to grasp the can and heavy tongs to carefully remove the chicken.

***NOTE:** To grill the chicken without the beer can, prepare chicken as directed. Place the chicken, breast side up, on grill rack directly over drip pan. Cover and grill as directed.

PER ¼ CHICKEN: 670 cal., 47 g total fat (15 g sat. fat), 218 mg chol., 1,399 mg sodium, 6 g carbo., 2 g fiber, 51 g pro.

4. For a charcoal grill, move the coals to the edge of the grill, leaving enough room for a drip pan. Place the pan in the center of the coals; replace the grill rack.

5. Carefully place the chicken with the beer can upright on the grill over the drip pan. If needed, reposition the legs to steady the chicken so the chicken rests on the grill rack.

6. Use hot pads and tongs to carefully lift chicken and can from the grill. Then use the hot pad or a thick towel to pull the can from the chicken cavity.

Grilled Turkey with Southwestern Spices

PLACING CHILE- AND SPICE-INFUSED BUTTER BENEATH TURKEY'S SKIN MAKES FOR SUPER-MOIST AND FLAVORFUL MEAT. LEFTOVER TURKEY MAKES THE WORLD'S BEST SANDWICHES, TACOS, AND QUESADILLAS. PLAN FOR EXTRA.

PREP: 25 MINUTES **GRILL:** 2½ HOURS
STAND: 15 MINUTES **MAKES:** 8 SERVINGS

- 1 8- to 10-pound whole turkey
- ½ cup butter, softened
- 1 teaspoon ground sage
- 1 teaspoon ground pasilla or ancho chile pepper
- ½ teaspoon ground cumin
- ¼ teaspoon garlic powder
- ⅛ teaspoon ground cinnamon
- ⅛ teaspoon cayenne pepper
- Salt and black pepper
- 1 recipe Grilled Butternut Squash (optional)

1 Remove neck and giblets from turkey; reserve for another use or discard. Rinse turkey body cavity; pat dry with paper towels.

2 In a small bowl combine butter, sage, pasilla pepper, cumin, garlic powder, cinnamon, and cayenne pepper; set aside. Starting at the neck on 1 side of the breast, slip your fingers between skin and meat, loosening skin as you work toward the tail end. Once your entire hand is under the skin, free the skin around the thigh and leg area up to, but not around, the tip of the drumstick. Repeat on the other side of the breast. Rub butter mixture under the skin, directly on the meat. Skewer neck skin to the back. Twist wing tips behind back. Sprinkle surface and cavity of turkey with salt and black pepper. Tuck drumsticks under band of skin or tie to tail. Insert a meat thermometer into center of an inside thigh muscle.

3 For a charcoal grill, arrange medium-hot coals around a drip pan. Test for medium heat above the pan. Place turkey in a foil pan on grill rack over drip pan. Cover; grill for 2½ to 3 hours or until thermometer registers 180°F and turkey is no longer pink, adding fresh coals every 45 to 60 minutes and cutting band of skin or string the last hour of grilling. (For a gas grill, preheat grill. Reduce heat to medium. Adjust for indirect cooking. Place turkey in a foil pan; place pan on grill rack over burner that is turned off. Grill as directed.)

4 Remove turkey from grill. Cover with foil; let stand for 15 minutes before carving. If desired, serve with Grilled Butternut Squash.

PER 4 OUNCES TURKEY: 539 cal., 33 g total fat (13 g sat. fat), 215 mg chol., 335 mg sodium, 0 g carbo., 0 g fiber, 56 g pro.

GRILLED BUTTERNUT SQUASH: Cut a medium butternut squash crosswise into ½-inch-thick slices. Remove and discard seeds. Brush slices with 1 tablespoon olive oil and sprinkle with salt. For a charcoal grill, grill slices on the rack of an uncovered grill directly over medium coals about 8 minutes or until tender, turning once halfway through grilling. (For a gas grill, preheat grill. Reduce heat to medium. Place squash slices on grill rack over heat. Cover and grill as directed.)

STEP-BY-STEP

1. Starting at the neck cavity, slip your hand between the skin and the meat and gently separate the skin from the meat.

2. Tie drumsticks together with 100%-cotton string. If the tail is present, tie the drumsticks to the tail. Securing the drumsticks will give the finished turkey a pleasing appearance.

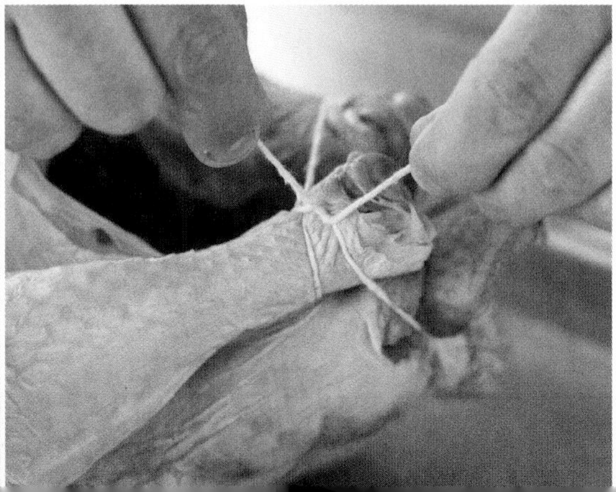

3. Pull the neck skin to the back of the turkey. Use a wooden skewer to fasten the neck skin to the back skin.

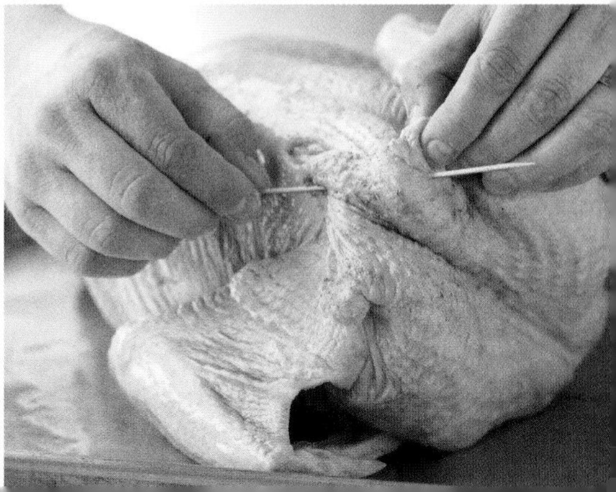

4. To keep the wings in place, twist them behind the back so they will rest beneath the turkey when you place it on the grill.

5. Check for medium heat over the drip pan. Place the turkey, breast side up, on the grill rack over the drip pan. Cover and grill until a thermometer registers 180°F.

6. To maintain grill temperature at medium above the drip pan, lift the turkey and rack and add fresh coals every 45 to 60 minutes during grilling.

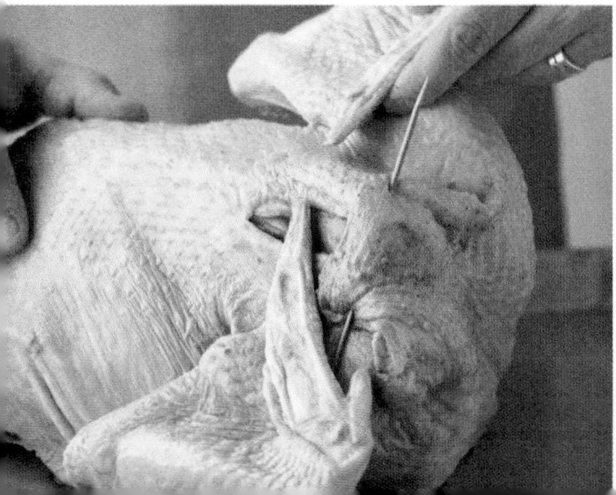

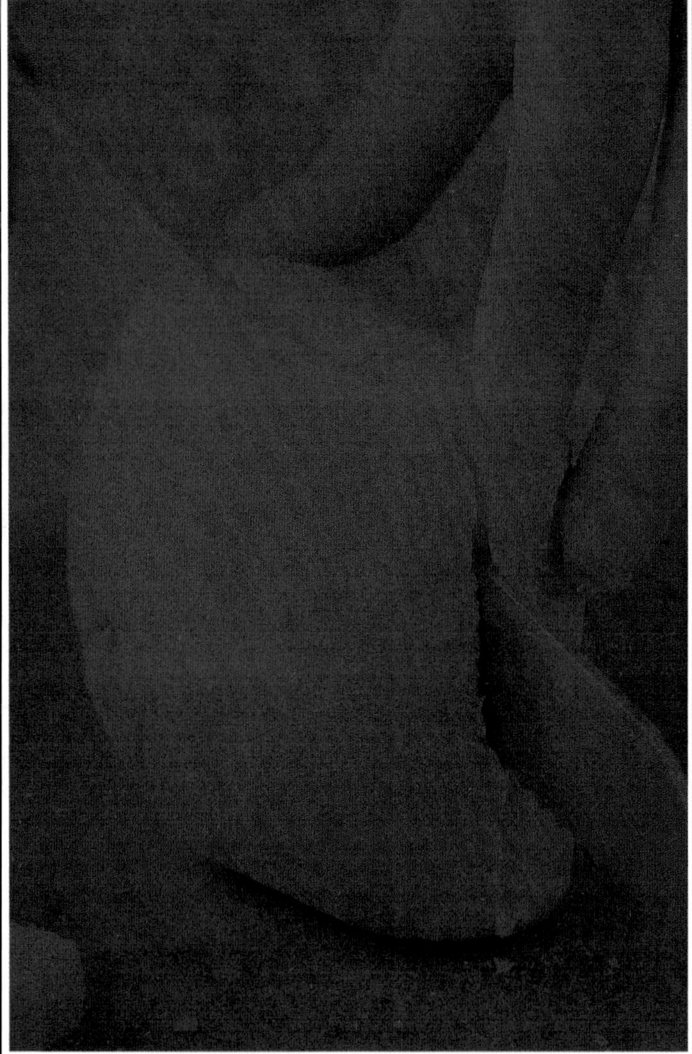

Burgers & Brats

ANYONE CAN GRILL A PATTY OR A SAUSAGE, BUT NO ONE ELSE CAN TAKE THIS ECONOMICAL DUO FROM HO-HUM TO HOLY COW LIKE YOU WILL—WITH THE HELP OF THESE REMARKABLE RECIPES.

Perfect Patties

SKIP MEAT DEPARTMENT FROZEN DISKS AND READY-MADE PATTIES. THE BEST BURGERS LIE IN YOUR OWN TWO HANDS.

Here's how to choose the best gound beef for burgers.

First, go for the most flavorful ground cuts. Three cuts guarantee the beefiest flavor—ground sirloin, ground chuck, and ground round. Ground sirloin is the most expensive; ground chuck and ground round are economical.

Second, don't choose the leanest ground beef. For juicy burger goodness, purchase ground beef that contains 15 to 20 percent fat.

STEP-BY-STEP

1. Use your hands to mix the meat. Don't overwork it or the cooked burgers will be tough.

2. Place the meat mixture on a clean work surface or cutting board. Pat into a square or rectangle of even thickness.

3. Evenly cut the meat mixture into the number of patties specified in the recipe.

4. To shape a patty, pick up one portion and shape it into a ball.

5. Flatten the ball into an evenly thick patty. Most recipes specify thickness or diameter of the patty.

6. To ensure an evenly cooked burger, make an indentation in the center of the patty with your thumb.

Better Buns

OH SURE, YOU CAN BUY THE STANDARD 8-PACK OF SESAME SEED BUNS, BUT A VARIETY OF OTHER BUNS AND BREADS WILL BREAK THE BASIC BUN ROUTINE.

Scan bakery shelves for breads and buns that appeal to you. Chances are if you like a certain bread or bun, you'll like it even better with a savory burger or sizzling sausage. Ciabatta, focaccia, sourdough baguettes, rye loaves, whole wheat breads, and bagels are all fair game. To really rock the burger boat, consider pita bread, naan, and other ethnic specialties.

TOASTED BUNS

A hot, toasty bun is like icing on a cake—it's an extra touch. To toast buns, spread butter or brush on olive oil, then place over indirect heat on the grill for about 2 minutes or until nicely browned.

Best-Ever Grilled Burgers

MARK THIS PAGE! THIS BEEF-PLUS-PORK MIXTURE—ALL JAZZED UP WITH ITALY'S BEST SEASONINGS—IS ONE YOU WILL RETURN TO AGAIN AND AGAIN. BY SUMMER'S END, YOU MAY EVEN HAVE IT MEMORIZED.

PREP: 30 MINUTES **GRILL:** 14 MINUTES
MAKES: 8 BURGERS

- 1 egg, lightly beaten
- ½ cup water
- ¼ cup finely chopped onion, leek, shallot, or green onion
- ¼ cup grated Parmesan, Romano, or Asiago cheese
- 2 tablespoons snipped fresh basil or parsley or 1 teaspoon dried basil or parsley, crushed
- 2 tablespoons Worcestershire sauce
- 1½ teaspoons instant beef bouillon granules
- 1 teaspoon garlic powder
- ½ teaspoon black pepper
- 1 pound ground beef*
- 1 pound ground pork*
- 8 onion buns, hamburger buns, or kaiser rolls, split and toasted
- 1 recipe Mustard Sauce
- Lettuce leaves (optional)
- Thin tomato slices (optional)
- Thin red onion slices (optional)
- Dill pickle spears (optional)

1 In a large bowl combine egg, the water, onion, Parmesan cheese, basil, Worcestershire sauce, bouillon granules, garlic powder, and pepper. Add beef and pork; mix well. Shape meat mixture into eight ¾-inch-thick patties.

2 For a charcoal grill, grill patties on the rack of an uncovered grill directly over medium coals for 14 to 18 minutes or until done (160°F), turning once halfway through grilling. (For a gas grill, preheat grill. Reduce heat to medium. Place patties on grill rack over heat. Cover; grill as directed.)

3 Serve burgers on buns with Mustard Sauce. If desired, top with lettuce, tomato slices, and onion slices. If desired, serve with pickle spears.

MUSTARD SAUCE: In a small bowl combine ⅓ cup stone-ground mustard, 2 tablespoons beer or apple juice, 1 tablespoon honey, and ½ teaspoon Worcestershire sauce or steak sauce.

***NOTE:** To grind your own meat, cut 1 pound boneless beef chuck roast and 1 pound boneless pork sirloin into 1 to 1½ inch pieces. Using the meat grinder attachment of your mixer, grind the meat according to manufacturer's directions.

PER BURGER + 1 TABLESPOON SAUCE: 343 cal., 15 g total fat (6 g sat. fat), 91 mg chol., 661 mg sodium, 26 g carbo., 1 g fiber, 24 g pro.

STEP-BY-STEP

1. To wash leeks, cut them lengthwise in half. Rinse in cold water, lifting and separating the leaves to flush out any dirt.

2. To grind meat, start with a beef chuck roast and a pork loin roast. Trim off as much fat as you can. Cut the meat into pieces between 1 and 1½ inches.

3. Place a bowl under a meat grinder or an electric mixer with a meat grinder attachment. Feed the beef and pork cubes through the grinder.

WHEN THIS SIMPLE-TO-MAKE—AND SO-GOOD—MUSTARD SAUCE OF ONLY FOUR PANTRY STAPLES CASCADES OVER YOUR HANDMADE AND HOME-GRILLED BURGERS IT WILL BRING PEOPLE TO THEIR FEET.

PREPARING CUBAN BURGERS, STEP-BY-STEP

1. Make indentations in centers of patties. The thinner centers will be done at the same time as the edges.

2. Top each burger with a slice of ham and a slice of cheese. Grill for another minute or until cheese melts.

3. Place the split buns, cut sides down, on the grill rack directly over heat. Grill until golden and grill marks appear.

4. For the sauce, cook and stir the minced garlic in olive oil just until it starts to brown. Don't let the garlic get too brown or it will taste bitter.

5. To assemble burgers, stack tomato, onion, burger, and pickle slices on each bun bottom. Drizzle with sauce and serve with bun top.

Cuban Burgers

INSPIRED BY EL CUBANO—CUBA'S BELOVED HAM AND PORK SANDWICH—THIS BURGER BRINGS CARIBBEAN FLAVOR TO A MOST-AMERICAN MEAL.

PREP: 25 MINUTES **GRILL:** 14 MINUTES
COOK: 5 MINUTES **MAKES:** 4 BURGERS

- 1 pound ground beef
- 1 teaspoon garlic powder
- ½ teaspoon ground cumin
- ½ teaspoon salt
- ½ teaspoon black pepper
- 4 thin slices cooked ham (about 3 ounces)
- 4 slices fontina or provolone cheese (about 3 ounces)
- 4 rolls or buns, split and toasted
- 2 whole dill pickles, sliced horizontally into 8 slices
- 4 slices red onion
- 4 slices tomato
- 1 recipe Mojo Sauce

1 In a large bowl combine beef, garlic powder, cumin, salt, and pepper; mix well. Shape into four ¾-inch-thick patties.

2 For a charcoal grill, grill patties on the rack of an uncovered grill directly over medium coals for 14 to 18 minutes or until done (160°F), turning once halfway through grilling. Add a slice of ham and cheese to each burger the last 1 minute of grilling. (For a gas grill, preheat grill. Reduce heat to medium. Place patties on grill rack over heat. Cover; grill as directed.)

3 Serve burgers on rolls with pickles, onion, and tomato. Drizzle with some of the Mojo Sauce; pass remaining sauce.

MOJO SAUCE: In a medium skillet cook 6 cloves garlic, minced, in 2 tablespoons olive oil over medium heat just until they start to brown. Remove from heat. Carefully add ⅓ cup orange juice, ⅓ cup lemon juice, 1 teaspoon ground cumin, and ½ teaspoon each salt and black pepper. Bring to boiling; reduce heat. Simmer, uncovered, about 5 minutes or until slightly reduced. Remove from heat; cool. Whisk before serving.

PER BURGER + 2 TABLESPOONS SAUCE: 558 cal., 31 g total fat (12 g sat. fat), 108 mg chol., 1,716 mg sodium, 32 g carbo., 3 g fiber, 36 g pro.

Mediterranean Burgers

ANOTHER TIME, CONSIDER TUCKING THE JUICY PATTY AND ALL THE TOPPINGS INTO A SOFT, WARM PITA BREAD HALF.

PREP: 15 MINUTES **GRILL:** 14 MINUTES
MAKES: 4 BURGERS

- 1 pound lean ground lamb or beef
- 2 teaspoons black pepper
- 4 kaiser rolls, split and toasted
- 4 lettuce leaves
- ½ cup crumbled feta cheese (2 ounces)
- 4 tomato slices
- 1 tablespoon snipped fresh mint
- ½ cup thinly sliced cucumber

1 Shape ground lamb into four ¾-inch-thick patties. Sprinkle pepper on patties; press pepper into patties.

2 For a charcoal grill, grill patties on the rack of an uncovered grill directly over medium coals for 14 to 18 minutes or until done (160°F), turning once halfway through grilling. (For a gas grill, preheat grill. Reduce heat to medium. Place patties on grill rack over heat. Cover; grill as directed.)

3 Serve burgers on rolls with lettuce, feta cheese, tomato slices, mint, and cucumber.

PER BURGER: 435 cal., 21 g total fat (9 g sat. fat), 88 mg chol., 535 mg sodium, 33 g carbo., 1 g fiber, 28 g pro.

STEP-BY-STEP

1. Slice the chile peppers lengthwise in half. Use a small knife to scrape the membranes and seeds from the pepper halves.

2. Roast the peppers in a preheated 425°F oven until the skin is dark and charred. At this point, the peppers will be very tender.

3. Lift the foil with peppers from the baking sheet. Bring the long edges up over the peppers and fold foil a couple times. Fold up foil ends, enclosing peppers in a tight package.

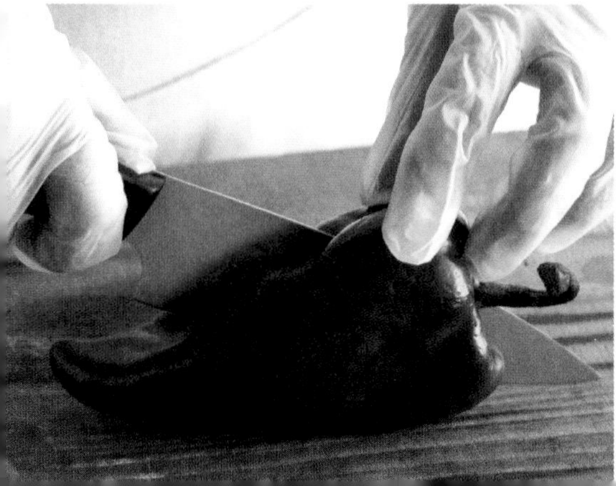

Grilled Poblano Chile Burgers

RICH YET SUBTLE, POBLANO CHILES INFUSE THESE BEEF BURGERS WITH SASSY MEXICAN SPIRIT—BUT WITH A BIT OF HEAT. CHOOSE DARK GREEN, ALMOST BLACK, POBLANOS FOR SWEETEST FLAVOR.

PREP: 25 MINUTES **ROAST:** 20 MINUTES
STAND: 15 MINUTES **GRILL:** 14 MINUTES
OVEN: 425F° **MAKES:** 4 BURGERS

- 2 fresh medium poblano or Anaheim chile peppers
- 1 egg, lightly beaten
- ¾ cup soft bread crumbs (1 slice)
- ½ cup shredded carrot (1 medium)
- 2 tablespoons water
- 1 teaspoon dried oregano, crushed
- 2 cloves garlic, minced
- ½ teaspoon salt
- ¼ teaspoon black pepper
- 1 pound lean ground beef
- 4 kaiser rolls, split and toasted
- 4 slices red and/or yellow tomato
- Frozen avocado dip (guacamole), thawed (optional)

1 Preheat oven to 425°F. To roast chile peppers, cut peppers in half lengthwise; remove stems, seeds, and membranes.* Place pepper halves, cut sides down, on a foil-lined baking sheet. Roast for 20 to 25 minutes or until peppers are charred and very tender. Bring the foil up around the peppers and fold edges together to enclose. Let stand about 15 minutes or until cool enough to handle. Use a sharp knife to loosen edges of the skins; gently pull off the skins in strips and discard. Chop roasted peppers.

2 In a large bowl combine egg, bread crumbs, carrot, the water, oregano, garlic, salt, black pepper, and roasted peppers. Add beef; mix well. Shape meat mixture into four ¾-inch-thick patties.

3 For a charcoal grill, grill patties on the rack of an uncovered grill directly over medium coals for 14 to 18 minutes or until done (160°F), turning once halfway through grilling. (For a gas grill, preheat grill. Reduce heat to medium. Place patties on grill rack over heat. Cover; grill as directed.)

4 Serve burgers on rolls with tomato and, if desired, avocado dip.

***NOTE:** Because chile peppers contain volatile oils that can burn your skin and eyes, avoid direct contact with them as much as possible. When working with fresh chile peppers, wear plastic or rubber gloves. If your bare hands do touch the chiles, wash your hands and nails well with soap and hot water.

PER BURGER: 478 cal., 21 g total fat (7 g sat. fat), 130 mg chol., 751 mg sodium, 41 g carbo., 2 g fiber, 31 g pro.

4. After about 15 minutes, open the packet. If necessary, let peppers cool a little more. Use a sharp knife to remove the charred skins from the peppers.

5. Break egg into a bowl. Beat with a fork until the white and yolk are well combined. Add the crumbs, carrot, water, oregano, garlic, salt, black pepper, and chopped roasted peppers.

6. Add the ground beef. Mix lightly with your hands until all ingredients are evenly dispersed through the meat. Do not overmix or the finished burgers will be tough.

FOR AN EXPERIENCE IN CONTRASTS, BITE INTO THIS DYNAMIC DUO—A SPICY-HOT BURGER TAMED BY A COOLING TROPICAL FRUIT SALSA.

Jerk Burgers with Mango Salsa

LOOK FOR MANGOES WITH UNBLEMISHED YELLOW SKIN AND BRILLIANT RED BLUSHING. MANGOES HAVE ONE LARGE FLAT SEED. CHOOSE THE LARGEST FRUITS TO BE SURE YOU HAVE ENOUGH JUICY, SWEET-TART FLESH FOR THE SALSA.

PREP: 20 MINUTES **GRILL:** 10 MINUTES
MAKES: 4 BURGERS

- 1 cup finely chopped green sweet pepper (1 large)
- ¼ cup finely chopped red sweet pepper
- ¼ cup finely chopped onion
- 1 teaspoon grated fresh ginger
- 1 tablespoon vegetable oil
- 1 mango, pitted, peeled, and chopped (1 cup)
- ¼ cup apple jelly
- 1 tablespoon lime juice
- Dash salt
- 1 egg, lightly beaten
- ⅓ cup bottled jerk sauce
- ¼ cup fine dry bread crumbs
- 1 pound lean ground beef
- 1 cup shredded Monterey Jack cheese (4 ounces)
- 4 ciabatta rolls or hamburger buns, split and toasted

1 For salsa, in a medium saucepan cook sweet peppers, onion, and ginger in hot oil over medium heat for 3 minutes. Add mango, jelly, lime juice, and salt; cook and stir until jelly melts. Set aside.

2 In a large bowl combine egg, ¼ cup of the jerk sauce, and the bread crumbs. Add beef; mix well. Shape meat mixture into four ½-inch-thick patties.

3 For a charcoal grill, grill patties on the rack of an uncovered grill directly over medium coals for 10 to 13 minutes or until done (160°F), turning and brushing once with the remaining jerk sauce halfway through grilling. (For a gas grill, preheat grill. Reduce heat to medium. Place patties on grill rack over heat. Cover; grill as directed.)

4 Divide cheese among bottoms of rolls. Serve burgers on rolls with some of the salsa. Pass the remaining salsa.

PER BURGER: 808 cal., 50 g total fat (20 g sat. fat), 167 mg chol., 740 mg sodium, 60 g carbo., 3 g fiber, 31 g pro.

STEP-BY-STEP

1. To make salsa, stir mango, jelly, lime juice, and salt into the cooked pepper mixture. Stir gently until the jelly melts. Let cool while making the burgers.

2. Split the ciabatta rolls. Place them,cut sides down, on the grill rack next to the burgers. Grill about 1 minute or until toasted.

3. To assemble burgers, sprinkle ¼ cup shredded cheese on each roll bottom. Top with a burger and a little salsa. Add the roll tops.

Feta-Stuffed Pita Burgers

TUCK TANGY FETA CHEESE BETWEEN TWO SUCCULENT LAMB AND BEEF PATTIES, POP THE CAREFULLY CRAFTED CONCOCTION INTO PITA BREAD. WHAT DO YOU HAVE? A BIG FAT GREEK BURGER!

PREP: 20 MINUTES **GRILL:** 12 MINUTES
MAKES: 4 BURGERS

- 2 tablespoons cornmeal
- 2 tablespoons milk
- 1 tablespoon finely chopped onion
- 1 clove garlic, minced
- ¼ teaspoon salt
- ¼ teaspoon dried oregano, crushed
- ⅛ teaspoon lemon-pepper seasoning
- 8 ounces lean ground lamb
- 8 ounces lean ground beef
- ⅓ cup finely crumbled feta cheese
- 1 tablespoon milk
- ¼ teaspoon ground cumin
- ¼ teaspoon cayenne pepper
- 2 large pita bread rounds, halved crosswise
- 2 cups arugula or watercress

1 In a large bowl combine cornmeal, 2 tablespoons milk, onion, garlic, salt, oregano, and lemon-pepper seasoning. Add lamb and beef; mix well. Shape meat mixture into eight ¼-inch-thick patties.

2 In a small bowl combine feta cheese and the 1 tablespoon milk. Spoon cheese mixture evenly onto centers of 4 patties. Top with the remaining patties; press edges to seal. Sprinkle cumin and cayenne evenly on patties.

3 For a charcoal grill, grill patties on the rack of an uncovered grill directly over medium coals for 12 to 16 minutes or until done (160°F), turning once halfway through grilling. (For a gas grill, preheat grill. Reduce heat to medium. Place patties on grill rack over heat. Cover; grill as directed.)

4 Serve burgers in pita halves with arugula.

PER BURGER: 422 cal., 25 g total fat (11 g sat. fat), 92 mg chol., 568 mg sodium, 22 g carbo., 1 g fiber, 25 g pro.

Mix It Up!

PICK ONE FROM EACH COLUMN TO CUSTOMIZE THE STUFFED BURGERS TO YOUR TASTE.

SEASON IT

Instead of the dried oregano and lemon-pepper seasoning, use one of the following:

- ¼ teaspoon dried Italian seasoning and ⅛ teaspoon crushed red pepper
- ¼ teaspoon dried thyme and ¼ teaspoon Cajun seasoning
- ¼ teaspoon ground ginger and ¼ teaspoon ground cinnamon
- ½ teaspoon smoked paprika or paprika

MIX IT IN

Instead of the feta cheese, use ⅓ cup of the following:

- Crumbled blue cheese
- Semisoft cheese with garlic and herbs
- Crumbled goat cheese (chèvre)
- Shredded Monterey Jack cheese with jalapeño peppers (omit milk)
- Shredded smoked cheddar cheese (omit milk)
- Creamy-style Brie (omit milk)

TOP IT

Instead of the arugula or watercress, top with one of the following:

- 1 large tomato, sliced
- ½ cup thinly sliced red onion
- 2 cups finely shredded green cabbage
- 2 cups mesclun greens
- 1 cup thinly sliced roasted red sweet pepper
- 1 medium avocado, sliced

STEP-BY-STEP

1. Divide the feta filling among four of the patties. Spread the filling evenly, leaving a border around the edge.

2. Carefully place a remaining patty on a cheese-topped patty, aligning the edges.

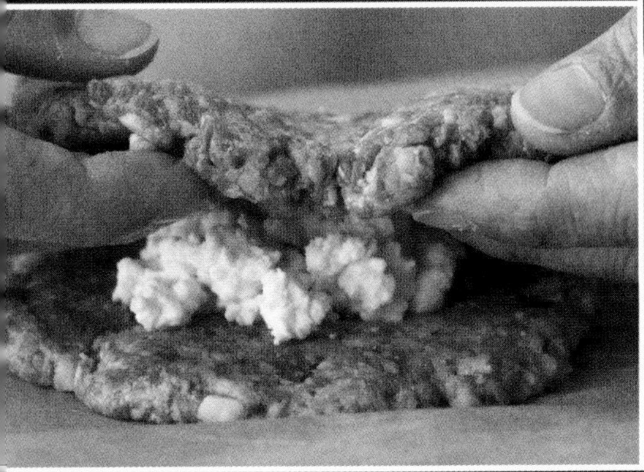

3. Press the edges of the top patty to the edges of the bottom patty, sealing the filling inside the burger.

4. Stack the pita bread rounds. Use a sharp knife to cut through both rounds, making four pita halves.

5. Divide the arugula among the pita halves. Use tongs to slip a stuffed burger into each pita pocket. Serve at once.

HOT, SOUR, SALTY, AND SWEET. GET A BIT OF EACH TASTE IN THESE YUMMY, ASIAN-INSPIRED BURGERS.

Pork and Peanut Burgers

TO PEEL THE THIN TAN SKIN FROM FRESH GINGER, GENTLY SCRAPE IT AWAY WITH THE BACK OF A SMALL SPOON. MOST OF THE GINGERY ESSENCE LIES JUST BENEATH THE PAPERY SKIN, AND A VEGETABLE PEELER TAKES AWAY TOO MUCH.

PREP: 35 MINUTES **GRILL:** 10 MINUTES
MAKES: 4 BURGERS

- 1 recipe Fried Wonton Wrappers or French-style rolls or hamburger buns, split and toasted
- ½ cup finely chopped onion (1 medium)
- ¼ cup finely chopped dry-roasted peanuts
- 1 tablespoon snipped fresh cilantro
- 1 tablespoon grated fresh ginger
- 3 cloves garlic, minced
- 1 teaspoon salt
- ¼ to ½ teaspoon crushed red pepper
- 1 pound lean ground pork
- 1 tablespoon sesame oil (not toasted)
- ⅓ cup Asian sweet chili sauce or chili sauce
- 1 tablespoon creamy peanut butter
- 1 clove garlic, minced
- 1 cup baby bok choy leaves
- Chopped dry-roasted peanuts

1 Prepare Fried Wonton Wrappers. In a large bowl combine onion, ¼ cup peanuts, cilantro, ginger, 3 cloves garlic, salt, and crushed red pepper. Add pork; mix well. Shape mixture into four ½-inch-thick patties that fit on the Fried Wonton Wrappers. Brush patties evenly with oil; set aside.

2 For sauce, in a small bowl whisk together chili sauce, peanut butter, and 1 clove garlic; set aside.

3 For a charcoal grill, grill patties on the rack of an uncovered grill directly over medium coals for 10 to 13 minutes or until done (160°F), turning once halfway through grilling. (For a gas grill, preheat grill. Reduce heat to medium. Place patties on grill rack over heat. Cover; grill as directed.)

4 To serve, place some of the bok choy on the Fried Wonton Wrappers. Top with burgers, sauce, and additional peanuts.

FRIED WONTON WRAPPERS: In a large skillet heat ¼ cup vegetable oil over medium heat. Cook four wonton wrappers, one at a time, in hot oil about 3 minutes or until brown and crisp, turning once. Drain on paper towels.

PER BURGER: 548 cal., 40 g total fat (11 g sat. fat), 82 mg chol., 990 mg sodium, 23 g carbo., 3 g fiber, 25 g pro.

STEP-BY-STEP

1. Prepare the wonton wrappers before making the burgers. Fry wrappers, one at a time, turning when golden brown on the under side.

2. As each wonton is fried, lift it from the oil and place on a plate lined with paper towels to absorb excess oil. Set wrappers aside while preparing burgers.

3. To prepare baby bok choy, cut off the bottom, freeing the leaves. Rinse the leaves in cold water and pat dry with paper towels.

PIZZA IN A BUN? YOU BET! EVEN THE MOST RELUCTANT PINT-SIZE EATERS IN YOUR FAMILY WILL GO FOR THE SPICY, CHEESY GOODNESS OF THIS FAMILY-FRIENDLY BURGER.

Pizza Burgers

GROUND PORK IS OFTEN LESS EXPENSIVE THAN GROUND BEEF. ALTHOUGH GROUND PORK OFTEN CONTAINS MORE FAT THAN GROUND BEEF, EACH PROVIDES EQUAL AMOUNTS OF PROTEIN.

PREP: 20 MINUTES **GRILL:** 14 MINUTES
MAKES: 4 BURGERS

- 1 egg, lightly beaten
- ⅓ cup canned mushroom stems and pieces, drained and chopped
- ¼ cup seasoned fine dry bread crumbs
- 2 tablespoons milk
- 1 teaspoon dried Italian seasoning, crushed
- ¼ teaspoon salt
- 1 pound lean ground pork
- 8 slices French bread (½-inch-thick slices)
- 1 8-ounce can pizza sauce
- ¼ cup sliced pitted ripe olives
- ¼ cup shredded mozzarella cheese (1 ounce)

1 In a large bowl combine egg, mushrooms, bread crumbs, milk, Italian seasoning, and salt. Add pork; mix well. Shape meat mixture into eight ¾-inch-thick patties.

2 For a charcoal grill, grill patties on the rack of an uncovered grill directly over medium coals for 14 to 18 minutes or until done (160°F), turning once halfway through grilling. Toast bread slices on the grill. (For a gas grill, preheat grill. Reduce heat to medium. Place patties, then bread slices, on grill rack over heat. Cover; grill as directed.)

3 Meanwhile, in a small saucepan combine pizza sauce and olives; heat through over low heat.

4 Serve burgers between toasted bread slices with sauce and cheese.

PER BURGER: 546 cal., 23 g total fat (9 g sat. fat), 133 mg chol., 1,133 mg sodium, 48 g carbo., 4 g fiber, 37 g pro.

STEP-BY-STEP

1. Crack the egg into a mixing bowl. Use a fork to lightly beat the egg until the yolk and white are combined.

2. Add mushrooms, bread crumbs, milk, Italian seasoning, and salt to the egg. Break the pork into small pieces and add to the bowl. Use your hands to lightly mix all ingredients together.

3. For sauce, spoon pizza sauce into a small saucepan. Stir in the olives. Heat over low heat, stirring occasionally, until heated through.

Chicken Caesar Burgers

EVERYONE WILL ADORE THIS INGENIOUS TWIST ON A CLASSIC SALAD; ALL THE FLAVORS OF A TOP-SELLING RESTAURANT CHICKEN CAESAR SALAD, WITH NO NEED FOR A FORK.

PREP: 15 MINUTES **GRILL:** 12 MINUTES
MAKES: 4 BURGERS

1 egg, lightly beaten
1 cup soft bread crumbs (2 slices)
¼ cup grated Parmesan cheese
2 teaspoons anchovy paste
1 teaspoon lemon juice
1 teaspoon Worcestershire sauce
1 clove garlic, minced
¼ teaspoon black pepper
1 pound uncooked ground chicken
½ cup sour cream
½ cup bottled Caesar salad dressing
4 small pita bread rounds, split open one-third of the way around
Shredded romaine lettuce
Tomato slices (optional)

1 In a large bowl combine egg, bread crumbs, Parmesan cheese, anchovy paste, lemon juice, Worcestershire sauce, garlic, and pepper. Add chicken; mix well. Shape chicken mixture into four ½-inch-thick patties.

2 For a charcoal grill, grill patties on the lightly greased rack of an uncovered grill directly over medium coals for 12 to 14 minutes or until no longer pink (165°F), turning once halfway through grilling. (For a gas grill, preheat grill. Reduce heat to medium. Place patties on lightly greased grill rack over heat. Cover; grill as directed.)

3 Meanwhile, in small bowl stir together sour cream and dressing. Serve burgers on pitas with some of the sour cream mixture, lettuce, and, if desired, tomato slices.

PER BURGER: 538 cal., 28 g total fat (7 g sat. fat), 167 mg chol., 1,328 mg sodium, 36 g carbo., 2 g fiber, 34 g pro.

STEP-BY-STEP

1. To shape the burgers, divide the mixture into four portions. Cover with waxed paper and press into ½-inch-thick round patties.

2. Chicken burgers are done when the temperature in the centers reaches 165°F. To test for doneness, insert an instant-read thermometer horizontally into the patty.

3. To serve, place tomato and lettuce on a split pita round. Top with a burger and drizzle with the sour cream mixture. Fold the pita over the burger.

LOOK FOR GROUND CHICKEN—RATHER THAN GROUND BREAST ONLY—TO MAKE THESE TENDER PATTIES. BREAST MEAT MAY DRY OUT QUICKLY ON THE GRILL.

STEP-BY-STEP

1. Put the panko crumbs in a bowl. These Japanese-style bread crumbs are light and crisp and coarser than fine dry bread crumbs.

2. To chop the green onion, trim off the root end and about 2 inches from the green top. Cut the onion into slices. Chop the slices into tiny pieces.

3. To prepare the ginger, cut off a piece from the root. Use a spoon to scrape off the thin, light tan skin. To grate, rub the ginger across a fine grater.

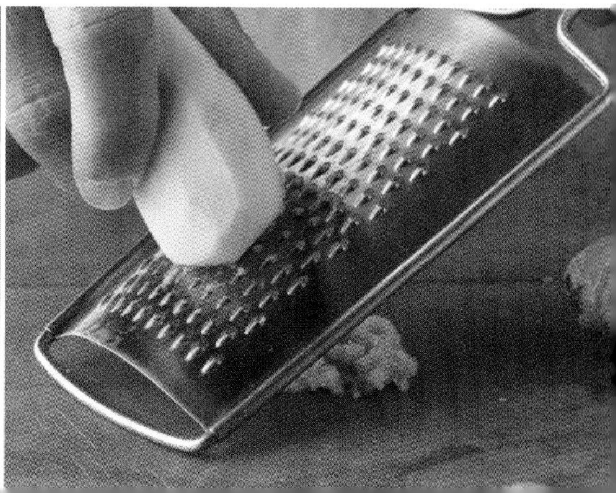

Thai Chicken Burgers

RED CURRY PASTE—A POTENT BLEND OF CHILES, GARLIC, LEMONGRASS, GINGER, LIME, AND SPICES—IS AS COMMON IN THAILAND AS KETCHUP IS IN THE UNITED STATES.

PREP: 30 MINUTES **GRILL:** 14 MINUTES
MAKES: 4 BURGERS

- ¾ cup panko (Japanese-style bread crumbs)
- 2 tablespoons peanut butter
- 2 tablespoons lime juice
- 2 tablespoons toasted sesame oil
- 1 tablespoon finely chopped green onion
- 1 tablespoon soy sauce
- 1 tablespoon red curry paste
- 2 teaspoons grated fresh ginger
- 3 cloves garlic, minced
- 1 pound uncooked ground chicken
- 1 small cucumber, halved lengthwise, seeded, and thinly sliced
- ½ cup mayonnaise
- ¼ cup coconut, toasted
- ¼ cup loosely packed fresh mint leaves, snipped
- 4 seeded hamburger buns, split and toasted

1 In a large bowl combine panko, peanut butter, lime juice, 1 tablespoon of the sesame oil, the green onion, soy sauce, curry paste, ginger, and garlic. Add chicken; mix well. Shape chicken mixture into four ¾-inch-thick patties. Brush patties evenly with the remaining 1 tablespoon sesame oil.

2 In a small bowl stir together cucumber, mayonnaise, coconut, and mint. Set aside.

3 For a charcoal grill, grill patties on the rack of an uncovered grill directly over medium coals for 14 to 18 minutes or until no longer pink (165°F), turning once halfway through grilling. (For a gas grill, preheat grill. Reduce heat to medium. Place patties on grill rack over heat. Cover; grill as directed.)

4 Serve burgers on buns with cucumber mixture.

PER BURGER: 643 cal., 40 g total fat (8 g sat. fat), 90 mg chol., 938 mg sodium, 37 g carbo., 3 g fiber, 34 g pro.

4. Place all the ingredients for the burgers in a bowl. Using your hands, mix until all of the ingredients are combined but avoid overworking the mixture.

5. Divide the chicken mixture into four portions. Gently but firmly pat each portion into a ¾-inch-thick patty. To ensure even cooking, press an indentation in the center of the patty.

6. Place the patties directly over the coals or the heat. Brush with sesame oil. Halfway through cooking, flip the burgers and brush with any remaining oil.

Apricot Chutney Chicken-Bacon Burgers

TREAT FRIENDS AND FAMILY TO THE SENSATION THAT THESE SAVORY-SWEET BURGERS BRING TO THE TABLE.

PREP: 45 MINUTES **GRILL:** 12 MINUTES
MAKES: 6 BURGERS

- 9 thick slices applewood smoked bacon, halved crosswise
- 2 tablespoons pure maple syrup
- 2 teaspoons olive oil
- ⅔ cup finely chopped red onion
- 2 apricots, peeled and finely chopped
- 1 teaspoon grated fresh ginger
- 2 cloves garlic, minced
- 2 tablespoons packed dark brown sugar
- 2 tablespoons cider vinegar
- 1 teaspoon bottled hot pepper sauce
- ½ cup golden raisins
- ½ teaspoon ground allspice
- 1 egg, lightly beaten
- ⅓ cup pecans, toasted and finely chopped
- ¾ teaspoon curry powder
- 1 teaspoon sea salt
- ½ teaspoon black pepper
- 2 pounds uncooked ground chicken
- 6 kaiser rolls, split and toasted

1 In a large skillet cook bacon over medium-low heat until crisp; drain on paper towels. Place bacon on parchment paper; brush evenly with maple syrup.

2 Wipe out skillet. Heat oil in skillet over medium heat. Add ⅓ cup of the onion; cook for 3 minutes or until tender. Stir in apricots, ginger, and garlic. Cook for 2 to 3 minutes more or until apricots soften, stirring occasionally. Stir in brown sugar, vinegar, hot pepper sauce, raisins, and allspice. Cook and stir for 1 minute; remove from heat. Cover and keep warm.

3 In a large bowl combine egg, pecans, curry powder, sea salt, and pepper. Add chicken; mix well. Shape chicken mixture into six ½- to ¾-inch-thick patties.

4 For a charcoal grill, grill patties on the lightly greased rack of an uncovered grill directly over medium coals for 12 to 14 minutes or until no longer pink (165°F), turning once halfway through grilling. (For a gas grill, preheat grill. Reduce heat to medium. Place patties on lightly greased grill rack over heat. Cover; grill as directed.)

5 Serve burgers on buns with apricot mixture and bacon slices.

PER BURGER: 632 cal., 29 g total fat (7 g sat. fat), 180 mg chol., 1,064 mg sodium, 54 g carbo., 3 g fiber, 41 g pro.

STEP-BY-STEP

1. To peel an apricot, make a lengthwise cut around the pit. Twist the halves to separate. Remove the pit. Chop the fruit.

2. Drain the cooked bacon on paper towels to remove excess fat. When cool, place the bacon on a sheet of parchment paper. Brush both sides with maple syrup.

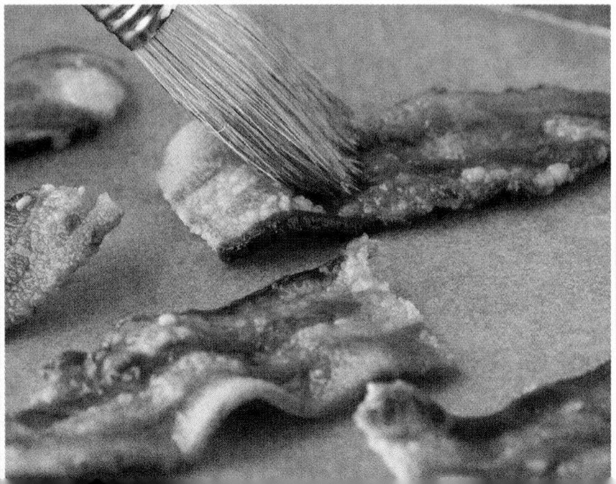

3. To avoid scorching, stir the chutney during cooking. The chutney should be thick and chunky. Remove the pan from the heat and cover to keep warm while you grill the burgers.

BBQ Onion-Cheddar Pork Burgers

THESE AMBROSIAL BURGERS ARE PACKED WITH THE ROWDY, MOUTHWATERING TASTE OF BARBECUED RIBS. BUT THEY'RE BONELESS—AND THEY TAKE MUCH LESS TIME TO PREPARE THAN RIBS.

PREP: 30 MINUTES **CHILL:** 1 HOUR
GRILL: 14 MINUTES **MAKES:** 6 BURGERS

- 2 tablespoons Worcestershire sauce
- ¼ teaspoon salt
- ¼ teaspoon black pepper
- 2 pounds ground pork
- 2 cups shredded cheddar cheese (8 ounces)
- 1 large onion, cut into 1-inch pieces
- 1 clove garlic, minced
- 1 tablespoon olive oil
- 1½ teaspoons chili powder
- ¼ cup ketchup
- 1 tablespoon packed brown sugar
- 1 tablespoon cider vinegar
- 1 tablespoon reduced-sodium soy sauce
- 1 tablespoon coarse-grain mustard
- 6 hamburger buns, split and toasted

1 In a large bowl combine Worcestershire sauce, salt, and pepper. Add pork; mix well. Shape meat mixture into twelve 4-inch-diameter patties. Sprinkle ⅓ cup of the cheese on each of 6 patties. Top with the remaining patties; press edges to seal. Cover and chill for at least 1 hour.

2 For onion sauce, in a large skillet cook onion and garlic in hot oil over medium heat about 10 minutes or until golden. Add chili powder; cook and stir for 1 minute. Stir in ketchup, brown sugar, vinegar, soy sauce, and mustard. Bring to boiling; reduce heat. Simmer, uncovered, for 2 minutes. Cool to room temperature.

3 For a charcoal grill, grill patties on the rack of an uncovered grill directly over medium coals for 14 to 18 minutes or until done (160°F), turning once halfway through grilling. (For a gas grill, preheat grill. Reduce heat to medium. Place patties on grill rack over heat. Cover; grill as directed.)

4 Serve burgers topped with onion sauce in buns.

MAKE-AHEAD DIRECTIONS: Prepare the onion sauce as directed. Cool sauce and transfer to an airtight container. Cover and chill for up to 2 weeks. Bring to room temperature before serving.

PER BURGER: 731 cal., 49 g total fat (21 g sat. fat), 149 mg chol., 946 mg sodium, 31 g carbo., 2 g fiber, 40 g pro.

STEP-BY-STEP

1. Cook the onion and garlic in oil until the onion becomes translucent and golden. To avoid scorching, stir often and reduce heat if needed.

2. Sprinkle the onion mixture with the chili powder. Stir and toss until the onion is evenly coated. Cook and stir for another minute to enhance the flavor of the chili powder.

3. Stir ketchup into onion mixture. Add the brown sugar, vinegar, soy sauce, and mustard. Cook for 2 minutes to blend flavors and dissolve sugar. Let cool while grilling burgers.

EVERYONE LIKES A SURPRISE. ESPECIALLY WHEN IT COMES IN THE FORM OF GOOEY, GOLDEN CHEESE OOZING FROM THE CENTER OF RICH, BARBEQUE-STYLE PORK BURGERS.

STEP-BY-STEP

1. To snip fresh oregano or basil, put several leaves in a custard cup or measuring cup. Snip with kitchen scissors using short, quick strokes.

2. Combine the egg, onion, cheese, herbs, ketchup, garlic, salt, and pepper. Mix these ingredients together before adding the meat to avoid overworking the meat mixture.

3. Turn the meat mixture out onto a cutting board and pat into an evenly thick rectangle. Cut it into eight equal portions. Shape each portion into a ball and then flatten into a patty.

Grilled Herb Burgers

HERB GARDENERS AND FARMER'S MARKET FANS WILL SAVOR THE FRESHLY HARVESTED HERBS INFUSED IN THESE BURGERS.

PREP: 20 MINUTES **GRILL:** 14 MINUTES
MAKES: 8 BURGERS

- 1 egg, lightly beaten
- ⅔ cup chopped onion (1 large)
- ½ cup grated Parmesan cheese (2 ounces)
- ¼ cup snipped fresh oregano and/or basil or 2 teaspoons dried oregano and/or basil, crushed
- ¼ cup ketchup
- 2 cloves garlic, minced
- ¼ teaspoon salt
- ¼ teaspoon black pepper
- 1 pound lean ground beef
- 1 pound uncooked ground turkey
- 8 ciabatta rolls, split and toasted
- 16 slices tomato
- Fresh oregano and/or basil sprigs (optional)

1 In a large bowl combine egg, onion, Parmesan cheese, the ¼ cup oregano, ketchup, garlic, salt, and pepper. Add beef and turkey; mix well. Shape meat mixture into eight ¾-inch-thick patties.

2 For a charcoal grill, place patties on the rack of an uncovered grill directly over medium coals. Grill for 14 to 18 minutes or until no longer pink (165°F), turning once halfway through grilling. (For a gas grill, preheat grill. Reduce to medium. Place patties on grill rack over heat. Cover; grill as directed.)

3 Serve burgers on rolls with tomato slices and, if desired, additional fresh oregano and/or basil sprigs.

PER BURGER: 381 cal., 16 g total fat (6 g sat. fat), 114 mg chol., 611 mg sodium, 29 g carbo., 2 g fiber, 31 g pro.

4. For even cooking, use your thumb to make an indentation in the center of each patty. The thinner middle will cook at the same rate as the outer edges.

5. To split a ciabatta roll, place the roll on its side on a cutting board. Steady the roll with one hand and use a large serrated knife to slice all the the way through the roll.

6. After 7 or 8 minutes of grilling, slide a large metal spatula under each burger and flip to the other side. Continue grilling 7 to 11 minutes more or until burgers test done.

Greek-Style Turkey Burgers

THIS BRIGHT AND COLORFUL, FULL-FLAVOR BURGER HAS A MERE 275 CALORIES. INDULGE—AND FEEL GOOD ABOUT YOURSELF.

PREP: 20 MINUTES **GRILL:** 14 MINUTES
MAKES: 4 BURGERS

- ⅓ cup fine dry whole wheat bread crumbs*
- 1 egg white, lightly beaten
- 1 tablespoon plain low-fat yogurt
- 1 teaspoon snipped fresh rosemary or ½ teaspoon dried rosemary, crushed
- 1 teaspoon snipped fresh oregano or ½ teaspoon dried oregano, crushed
- 1 tablespoon crumbled feta cheese
- ⅛ teaspoon black pepper
- 1 pound uncooked ground turkey breast or chicken breast
- Mixed torn greens (optional)
- 1 recipe Olive-Tomato Salsa
- ¼ cup crumbled feta cheese (1 ounce)
- Plain low-fat yogurt (optional)
- 2 whole wheat pita bread rounds, halved and lightly toasted

1 In a medium bowl combine bread crumbs, egg white, the 1 tablespoon yogurt, rosemary, oregano, the 1 tablespoon feta cheese, and pepper. Add turkey; mix well. Shape turkey mixture into four ¾-inch-thick patties.

2 For a charcoal grill, grill patties on the rack of an uncovered grill directly over medium coals for 14 to 18 minutes or until no longer pink (165°F), turning once halfway through grilling. (For a gas grill, preheat grill. Reduce heat to medium. Place patties on grill rack over heat. Cover; grill as directed.)

3 If desired, divide greens among 4 serving plates; top with burgers. Top burgers evenly with Olive-Tomato Salsa, the ¼ cup feta cheese, and, if desired, additional yogurt. Serve burgers with pita bread.

OLIVE-TOMATO SALSA: In a small bowl stir together 1 cup chopped, seeded tomato; ¼ cup chopped, seeded cucumber; ¼ cup chopped, pitted kalamata or other ripe olives; ½ teaspoon snipped fresh rosemary or ¼ teaspoon dried rosemary, crushed; and ½ teaspoon snipped fresh oregano or ¼ teaspoon dried oregano, crushed. Makes about 1½ cups.

***NOTE:** For fine dry whole wheat bread crumbs, place 1 slice whole wheat bread, toasted, in a food processor. Cover and process until fine crumbs form. Makes ⅓ cup.

PER BURGER: 275 cal., 6 g total fat (2 g sat. fat), 53 mg chol., 507 mg sodium, 23 g carbo., 4 g fiber, 35 g pro.

STEP-BY-STEP

1. To seed a cucumber, halve it lengthwise. Place halves, cut sides up, on a work surface. Use a spoon to scrape the seeds from the cucumber.

2. To pit an olive, place the olive on a cutting board. Crush the olive with the flat side of a knife to split open. If the knife becomes slippery, rinse and dry it.

3. Open the split olives and remove the pits either with your fingers or the tip of a knife. Discard the pits and chop the olives.

4. For the salsa, place the tomato, cucumber, and olives in a bowl. Sprinkle in the rosemary and oregano. Stir gently to mix.

5. Grill the burgers until no longer pink. To be sure they are perfectly done, insert an instant-read thermometer into the centers. The thermometer should register 165°F.

6. Serve the burgers on plates lined with greens. Spoon the salsa over each burger and sprinkle with feta cheese.

Latino Bison Burgers with Tomatillo Salsa

BISON IS A HEALTHFUL ALTERNATIVE TO BEEF, AND ITS LOW-FAT, LOW-CHOLESTEROL MEAT IS GAINING FANS NATIONWIDE. WHEN SEASONED WITH SOUTH-OF-THE-BORDER SPICES NO ONE WILL BE ABLE TO DETECT THE DIFFERENCE BETWEEN BEEF AND BISON IN THE GRILLED BURGER.

PREP: 35 MINUTES **GRILL:** 14 MINUTES
MAKES: 4 BURGERS

- 1½ pounds ground bison (buffalo)
- 2 teaspoons chili powder
- 1 teaspoon ground cumin
- ½ teaspoon onion powder
- ½ teaspoon garlic powder
- ½ teaspoon salt
- 4 1-ounce slices Monterey Jack cheese
- 4 10-inch flour tortillas
- 1 large tomato, sliced
- 2 cups Tomatillo Salsa
- 1 cup shredded fresh spinach leaves

1 In a large bowl combine ground bison, chili powder, cumin, onion powder, garlic powder, and salt; mix well. Shape meat mixture into four ¾-inch-thick oval-shape patties.

2 For a charcoal grill, grill patties on the rack of an uncovered grill directly over medium coals for 14 to 16 minutes or until done (160°F), turning once halfway through grilling. Add cheese to burgers the last 1 minute of grilling. (For a gas grill, preheat grill. Reduce heat to medium. Place patties on grill rack over heat. Cover; grill as directed.)

3 Meanwhile, stack and wrap tortillas in foil. While patties are grilling, add wrapped tortillas to grill rack. Grill about 5 minutes or until warm, turning once.

4 Serve burgers on tortillas with tomato slices, Tomatillo Salsa, and spinach.

TOMATILLO SALSA: In a medium bowl combine 6 medium tomatillos (12 ounces), husked, rinsed, and chopped; 1¼ cups chopped yellow sweet pepper (1 large); 2 tablespoons snipped fresh cilantro; 2 tablespoons lime juice; 1 medium fresh jalapeño chile pepper, seeded and finely chopped;* 1 tablespoon honey; and 6 cloves garlic, minced. Store leftover salsa, covered, in the refrigerator up to 3 days. Makes about 3 cups.

***NOTE:** Because chile peppers contain volatile oils that can burn your skin and eyes, avoid direct contact with them as much as possible. When working with fresh chile peppers, wear plastic or rubber gloves. If your bare hands do touch the chiles, wash your hands and nails well with soap and hot water.

PER BURGER: 542 cal., 25 g total fat (11 g sat. fat), 118 mg chol., 759 mg sodium, 34 g carbo., 3 g fiber, 46 g pro.

STEP-BY-STEP

1. Form the patties into ovals about ¾ inch thick. The oval-shape burgers will be a perfect fit for the folded tortillas.

2. To warm the tortillas, arrange them in a stack and wrap in foil. Place the foil packet on the grill with the burgers for the last 5 minutes of grilling time.

3. To remove the papery skins from a tomatillo, grab one of the loose ends and firmly pull it away from the tomatillo. The remaining skins should slide off easily.

4. Rinse the tomatillas under cold running water to remove the sticky residue left behind. Pat tomatillos dry with paper towels.

5. Cut the chile peppers in half lengthwise. Use the tip of a small knife to cut away membranes and scrape out seeds. The membranes and seeds are the hottest parts of the pepper.

6. On a cutting surface, cut the chile pepper halves into thin lengthwise strips. Line up the strips; cut across the strips into tiny pieces.

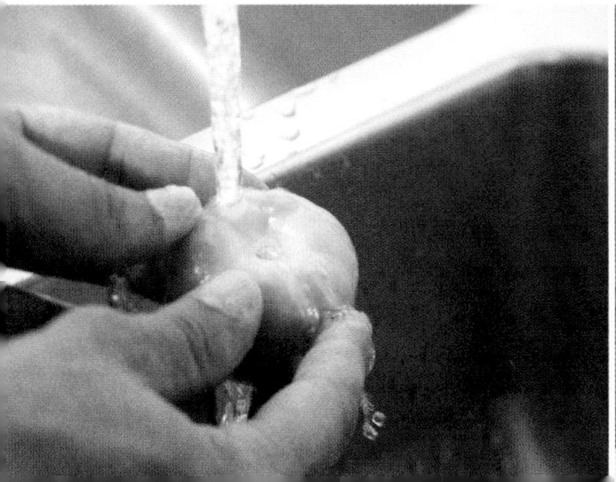

WHEN SWEET, STICKY DATES MEET PUNGENT, SLIPPERY ONIONS ON A CHEDDAR-BLANKETED BUFFALO BURGER, SOME AMAZINGLY GOOD THINGS HAPPEN.

Bison Burgers with Caramelized Dates and Onions

IF YOU'RE PITTING DATES YOURSELF, GO FOR JUMBO-SIZE MEDJOOL DATES. THE SEED-TO-FLESH RATIO WILL REWARD YOU WITH MORE DATE FOR YOUR EFFORT.

PREP: 35 MINUTES **GRILL:** 14 MINUTES
MAKES: 4 BURGERS

- 1 tablespoon Worcestershire sauce
- 2 cloves garlic, minced
- ¼ teaspoon black pepper
- 1 pound ground bison (buffalo)
- 2 medium sweet onions, halved and thinly sliced
- 6 cloves garlic, minced
- 2 tablespoons olive oil
- ½ cup chopped pitted dates
- 2 tablespoons dry red wine
- 4 slices sharp cheddar cheese (4 ounces)
- 4 slices sourdough bread or ciabatta bread (½-inch-thick slices), toasted
- 1 cup arugula leaves

1 In a medium bowl combine Worcestershire sauce, the 2 cloves garlic, and pepper. Add ground bison; mix well. Shape meat mixture into four ¾-inch-thick oval-shape patties. Set aside.

2 In a large skillet cook onions and the 6 cloves garlic in hot oil over medium heat about 10 minutes or until onions are tender and golden, stirring occasionally. Stir in dates and wine. Cook for 1 to 2 minutes more or until wine is evaporated and mixture becomes syrupy. Remove from heat; cover and keep warm.

3 For a charcoal grill, grill patties on the rack of an uncovered grill directly over medium coals for 14 to 16 minutes or until done (160°F), turning once halfway through grilling. Add cheese to burgers the last 2 minutes of grilling. (For a gas grill, preheat grill. Reduce heat to medium. Place patties on grill rack over heat. Cover; grill as directed.)

4 Serve burgers between slices of bread with arugula and onion mixture.

PER BURGER: 617 cal., 25 g total fat (10 g sat. fat), 92 mg chol., 638 mg sodium, 60 g carbo., 4 g fiber, 38 g pro.

STEP-BY-STEP

1. Add the ground bison to the Worcestershire sauce, garlic, and pepper. Use your hands to lightly mix just until the ingredients are combined.

2. Stir the dates and wine into the cooked onion mixture. Cook 1 to 2 minutes. Most of the wine will evaporate, the dates will soften, and the mixture will take on a syrupy consistency.

3. To clean arugula, fill a large bowl with cold water. Add the leaves and swish them around for 30 seconds. Remove the leaves and pat dry with paper towels.

Old-World Veal Burgers

THERE IS NOTHING QUITE LIKE THE VELVETY TEXTURE AND DELICATE, ADAPTABLE FLAVOR OF VEAL. SEE FOR YOURSELF WITH THIS OLD-FASHIONED RECIPE.

PREP: 20 MINUTES **GRILL:** 14 MINUTES
MAKES: 4 BURGERS

- 1 egg, lightly beaten
- ¾ cup soft rye bread crumbs (1 slice)
- 2 tablespoons beer or water
- ½ teaspoon caraway seeds
- ½ teaspoon dried marjoram, crushed
- 1 clove garlic, minced
- ¼ teaspoon salt
- ¼ teaspoon black pepper
- 1 pound ground veal or lean ground beef
- 8 slices rye bread
- 4 1-ounce slices Swiss cheese
- 3 tablespoons German-style mustard, creamy Dijon-style mustard blend, or stone-ground mustard

1 In a large bowl combine egg, bread crumbs, beer, caraway seeds, marjoram, garlic, salt, and pepper. Add veal; mix well. Shape meat mixture into four ¾-inch-thick patties.

2 For a charcoal grill, grill patties on the rack of an uncovered grill directly over medium coals for 14 to 18 minutes or until done (160°F), turning once halfway through grilling. (For a gas grill, preheat grill. Reduce heat to medium. Place patties on grill rack over heat. Cover; grill as directed.)

3 When burgers are nearly done, add rye bread slices to grill. Grill for 1 to 2 minutes or until bottoms are light brown. Turn slices over; top 4 slices with Swiss cheese. Grill for 1 to 2 minutes more or until other sides are light brown.

4 Serve burgers on the cheese-topped bread slices. Spread the plain bread slices with mustard; top burgers.

PER BURGER: 492 cal., 19 g total fat (9 g sat. fat), 172 mg chol., 1,056 mg sodium, 37 g carbo., 4 g fiber, 37 g pro.

STEP-BY-STEP

1. To make bread crumbs, break bread into small pieces and place in a food processor. Process using on/off pulses until finely ground.

2. Crumble the ground veal into small pieces and add to the egg and other ingredients. Small pieces of meat are easier to combine with the other ingredients.

3. When first sides of the bread slices are toasted, turn and top toasted sides with cheese. Return bread to the grill until cheese melts and bottom sides are toasted.

THANK GERMANY FOR THE ROBUST CHARACTER OF THIS SUCCULENT BURGER. GO-FOR-THE-GUSTO INGREDIENTS, SUCH AS CARAWAY MUSTARD AND RYE, FORM THE FLAVORFUL FOUNDATION OF GERMAN CUISINE.

BASIC BRATS BENEFIT FROM CREATIVE TREATMENTS, SUCH AS THE UNEXPECTED PAIRING OF SWEET, CRUNCHY APPLES AND PUNGENT, PICKLY SAUERKRAUT AND HOT-HOT-HOT JALAPEÑOS.

Brats with Jalapeño-Green Apple Kraut

SIMMERING BRATWURST IN APPLE JUICE ADDS A SPUNKY-SWEET NOTE OF APPLE TO THE SAUSAGE, AND THE PROCESS ALSO RELEASES EXCESS FAT,WHICH COULD CAUSE GRILLING FLAR-UPS.

PREP: 10 MINUTES **COOK:** 20 MINUTES
GRILL: 3 MINUTES **MAKES:** 6 SANDWICHES

- 6 uncooked bratwurst (about 1¼ pounds)
- 3 cups apple juice or apple cider
- ⅓ cup apple jelly
- 1 8-ounce can sauerkraut, drained
- 1 tart green apple, cored and cut into thin bite-size pieces
- 2 to 3 fresh jalapeño chile peppers, seeded and cut in thin strips*
- 6 bratwurst or hot dog buns, split and toasted

1 Use the tines of a fork to pierce the skin of each bratwurst several times. In a Dutch oven combine bratwurst and apple juice. Bring to boiling; reduce heat. Simmer, covered, about 20 minutes or until bratwurst are no longer pink and juices run clear (160°F); drain.

2 Meanwhile, in a small saucepan melt apple jelly over low heat. In a medium bowl combine 2 tablespoons of the melted jelly, the sauerkraut, apple, and chile peppers. Set aside remaining melted jelly to brush on bratwurst.

3 Fold a 30×18-inch piece of heavy foil in half to make a 15×18-inch rectangle. Mound sauerkraut mixture in center of foil. Bring up 2 opposite edges of foil; seal with a double fold. Fold in remaining edges to completely enclose sauerkraut mixture, leaving space for steam to build.

4 For a charcoal grill, grill bratwurst and foil packet on the rack of an uncovered grill directly over medium coals for 3 to 7 minutes or until bratwurst are brown, turning bratwurst and foil packet once halfway through grilling and brushing bratwurst with the reserved melted jelly during the last 2 minutes of grilling. (For a gas grill, preheat grill. Reduce heat to medium. Place bratwurst and foil packet on grill rack over heat. Cover; grill as directed.)

5 Serve bratwurst topped with sauerkraut mixture in toasted buns.

***NOTE:** Because chile peppers contain volatile oils that can burn your skin and eyes, avoid direct contact with them as much as possible. When working with fresh chile peppers, wear plastic or rubber gloves. If your bare hands do touch the chiles, wash your hands and nails well with soap and hot water.

PER SANDWICH: 737 cal., 48 g total fat (21 g sat. fat), 101 mg chol., 2,014 mg sodium, 42 g carbo., 3 g fiber, 34 g pro.

STEP-BY-STEP

1. To remove an apple core, cut the apple into four pieces through the stem and blossom ends. Cut away the core, seeds, stem, and blossom end.

2. Place apple quarters on a cutting surface, cut sides down, and cut through the skin into thin slices. Stack a few of the slices and cut into small pieces.

3. Place the sauerkraut mixture in the center of the foil rectangle. Bring up the sides; fold the top over two times, leaving space between the food and foil. Fold up the ends to seal.

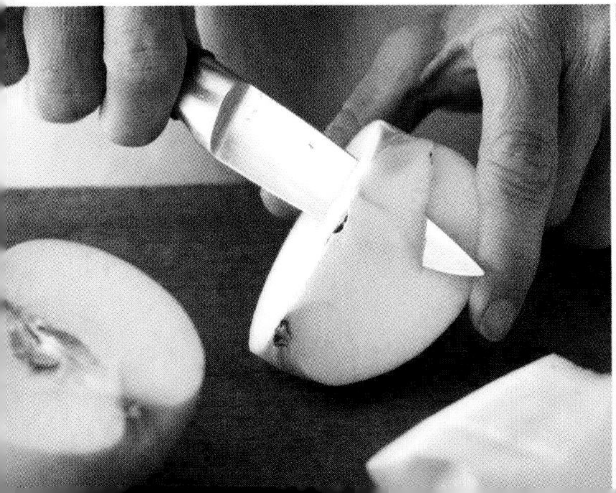

Mustardy Brats with Sauerkraut

HOT DOG AND SAUSAGE AFICIONADOS BELIEVE THAT THE RED STUFF SHOULD NEVER COME NEAR GREAT SAUSAGE. THEY MAY BE RIGHT. WHEN DRESSED WITH VINEGARY PREPARATIONS SUCH AS KRAUT AND MUSTARD, THE TRUE FLAVORS OF SAUSAGE REALLY SHINE THROUGH.

PREP: 25 MINUTES **GRILL:** 20 MINUTES
MAKES: 6 SANDWICHES

- ½ cup chopped green sweet pepper (1 small)
- ⅓ cup chopped onion (1 small)
- 1 tablespoon butter
- 2 tablespoons packed brown sugar
- 1 teaspoon yellow mustard or Dijon-style mustard
- ½ teaspoon caraway seeds
- 1 cup drained sauerkraut
- 6 uncooked bratwurst (about 1¼ pounds)
- 6 hoagie buns, split and toasted
- Yellow mustard or Dijon-style mustard (optional)

1 In a small skillet cook sweet pepper and onion in hot butter over medium heat about 5 minutes or until tender. Stir in brown sugar, the 1 teaspoon mustard, and caraway seeds. Add sauerkraut; toss gently to combine.

2 Fold a 36×18-inch piece of heavy foil in half to make an 18-inch square. Place sauerkraut mixture in the center of foil. Bring up 2 opposite edges of foil; seal with a double fold. Fold the remaining ends to completely enclose sauerkraut mixture, leaving space for steam to build. Use the tines of a fork to pierce the skin of each bratwurst several times.

3 For a charcoal grill, arrange medium-hot coals around a drip pan. Test for medium heat above pan. Place bratwurst and foil packet on the grill rack over drip pan. Cover and grill for 20 to 25 minutes or until bratwurst are no longer pink and juices run clear (160°F), turning bratwurst and foil packet once halfway through grilling. (For a gas grill, preheat grill. Reduce heat to medium. Adjust for indirect cooking. Place bratwurst and foil packet on grill rack over the burner that is turned off. Grill as directed.)

4 Serve bratwurst in toasted buns with sauerkraut mixture and, if desired, additional mustard.

PER SANDWICH: 663 cal., 27 g total fat (11 g sat. fat), 51 mg chol., 1,472 mg sodium, 83 g carbo., 5 g fiber, 22 g pro.

STEP-BY-STEP

1. After cooking the pepper and onion, add the brown sugar, mustard, and caraway seeds; mix well. Add the sauerkraut and gently toss to mix.

2. Spoon the sauerkraut mixture onto the center of the foil, leaving room to fold the foil over the sauerkraut mixture.

3. Lift up the sides of the foil and bring together at the top. Fold the foil over twice. Leave a space at the top. Steam will form during grilling and fill this space.

4. Fold each end over several times, leaving room inside the packet for steam to form. Firmly press the folds to secure the packet.

5. Place the foil packet on the grill alongside the bratwurst. Halfway through grilling, turn over the bratwurst and the packet. Grill until the bratwurst are done.

6. Carefully open the packet to avoid being burned by escaping steam. Keeping fingers away from the openings, unfold the sides and then the top.

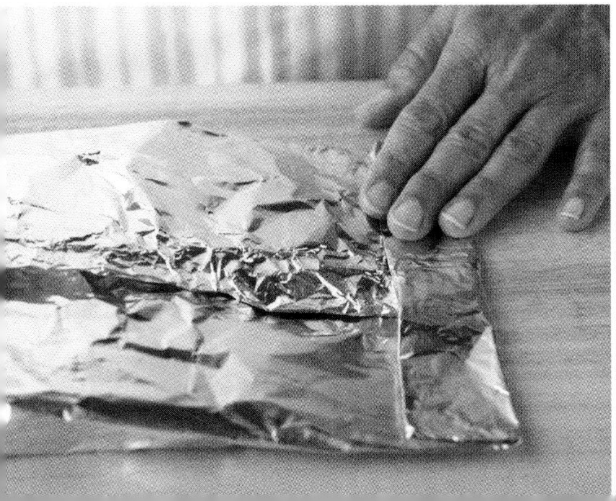

Beer-Braised Brat Sandwiches

IT IS SO NATURAL TO UTTER THE WORDS "BEER" AND "BRAT" IN THE SAME SENTENCE. LIKE APPLE AND PIE, MARTINI AND OLIVE, FRIED AND CHICKEN—THEY'RE JUST MEANT TO GO TOGETHER.

PREP: 30 MINUTES **GRILL:** 20 MINUTES
MAKES: 10 SANDWICHES

- 10 uncooked bratwurst (about 2½ pounds)
- 1 large onion, halved and cut into thin slices
- ¼ cup butter
- 2 12-ounce bottles or cans dark German beer
- 2 tablespoons packed brown sugar
- 2 tablespoons vinegar
- 1 teaspoon caraway seeds
- 1 teaspoon dried thyme, crushed
- 1 teaspoon Worcestershire sauce
- 10 hoagie buns, bratwursts buns, or other crusty rolls, split and toasted
- 1 recipe Easy Cranberry-Pickle Relish

1 Use the tines of a fork to pierce the skin of each bratwurst several times. For a charcoal grill, arrange medium-hot coals around a drip pan. Test for medium heat above pan. Place bratwurst on the grill rack over drip pan. Cover and grill for 20 to 25 minutes or until bratwurst are no longer pink and juices run clear (160°F), turning once halfway through grilling. (For a gas grill, preheat grill. Reduce heat to medium. Adjust for indirect cooking. Place bratwurst on grill rack over the burner that is turned off. Grill as directed.)

2 Meanwhile, in a Dutch oven cook onion in hot butter over medium heat about 5 minutes or until tender. Add beer, brown sugar, vinegar, caraway seeds, thyme, and Worcestershire sauce. Bring to boiling; reduce heat. Place bratwursts in beer mixture; keep warm until serving time.

3 Serve bratwurst in buns. Using a slotted spoon, top with some cooked onion slices and Easy Cranberry-Pickle Relish.

EASY CRANBERRY-PICKLE RELISH: In a small bowl stir together 1 cup canned whole cranberry sauce and ½ cup sweet pickle relish.

PER SANDWICH: 682 cal., 33 g total fat (12 g sat. fat), 76 mg chol., 1,341 mg sodium, 70 g carbo., 3 g fiber, 20 g pro.

STEP-BY-STEP

1. Prick each bratwurst several times with the tines of a fork to release steam that builds while brats cook and keep them from bursting.

2. Use an instant-read thermometer to check for doneness. When the thermometer is inserted in the center of a brat the temperature should register 160°F.

3. When ready to serve, place a brat in a bun. Using a slotted spoon, top it with some of the onion. Add a spoonful of Easy Cranberry-Pickle Relish.

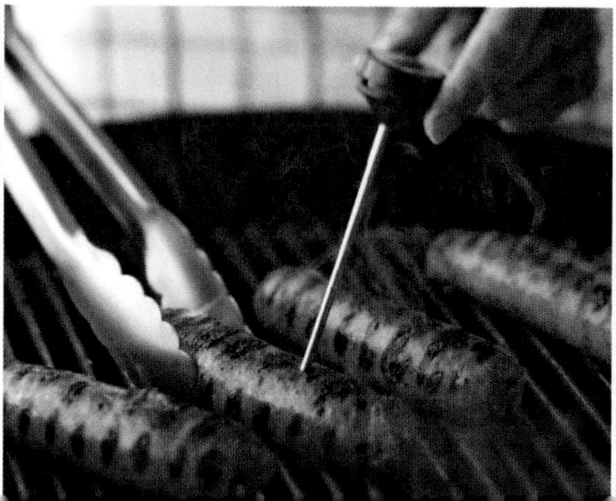

DARK GERMAN BEERS— "DUNKELS" IN GERMANY—INFUSE SAUSAGES, SUCH AS BRATWURST, WITH DISTINCTIVE ROASTED MALT FLAVOR.

PREPARING CHEESE-STUFFED KNOCKWURSTS, STEP-BY-STEP

1. Using a sharp knife and holding one end of the knockwurst, cut a ½-inch-deep slit from end to end.

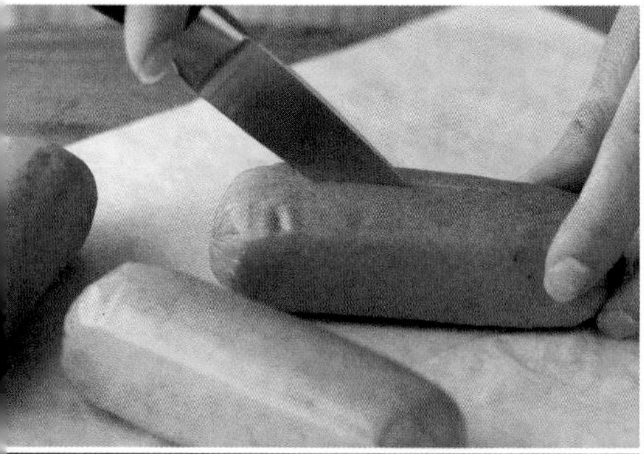

2. Cut the cheese into five strips.

3. Place a green onion in the slit of each knockwurst. Then fit a cheese strip in the slit on top of the onion.

4. Holding the onion and cheese in place, wrap a partially cooked bacon slice in a spiral around the knockwurst.

5. Secure the green onion, cheese, and bacon by inserting wooden toothpicks through the bacon and knockwurst.

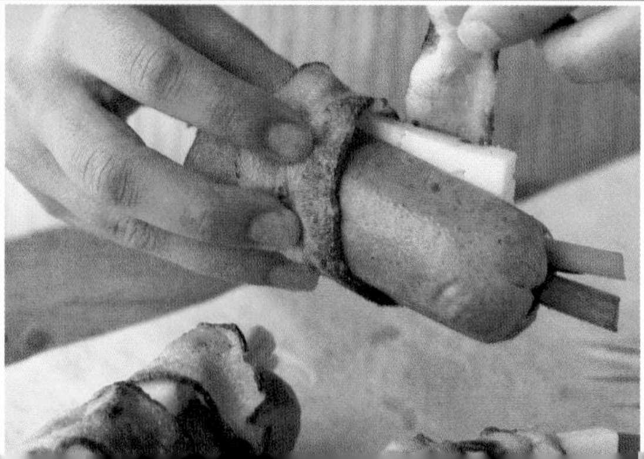

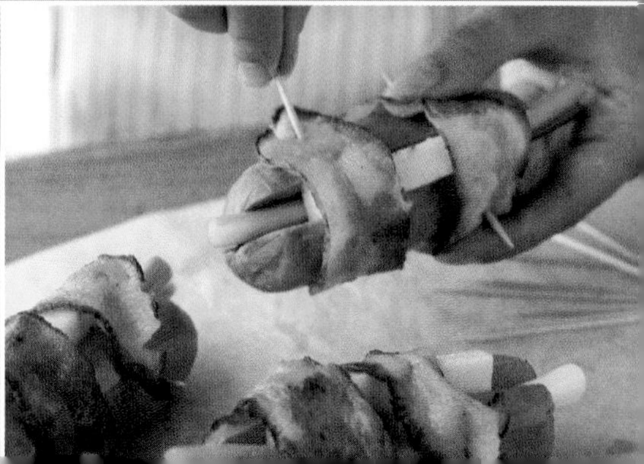

Cheese-Stuffed Knockwursts

KNOCKWURSTS ARE SHORT, FAT SAUSAGES MADE WITH BEEF, PORK, AND A LOT OF GARLIC. THE NAME COMES FROM THE GERMAN WORDS "KNACK" (WHICH MEANS CRACK) AND "WURST" (WHICH MEANS SAUSAGE). CRACK REFERS TO THE SOUND THE NATURAL CASINGS MAKE WHEN PIERCED WITH THE TEETH.

PREP: 15 MINUTES **GRILL:** 8 MINUTES
MAKES: 5 SANDWICHES

- 5 cooked knockwurst or bratwurst (about 1 pound)
- 2 ounces Monterey Jack cheese with caraway seeds
- ¼ cup thinly sliced green onions (2)
- 5 slices bacon
- 5 French-style rolls or frankfurter buns, split
- Ketchup, mustard, pickle relish, and/or crumbled crisp-cooked bacon (optional)

1 Cut a lengthwise slit about ½ inch deep in each knockwurst. Cut cheese into five 2½×½×¼-inch strips. Insert a cheese strip and a scant 1 tablespoon green onions into each slit. Wrap a slice of bacon around each knockwurst; secure with wooden toothpicks.

2 For a charcoal grill, arrange medium-hot coals around a drip pan. Test for medium heat above pan. Place knockwurst, cheese sides up, on grill rack over drip pan. Cover and grill for 8 to 10 minutes or until bacon is crisp and cheese melts. (For a gas grill, preheat grill. Reduce heat to medium. Adjust for indirect cooking. Place knockwurst on grill rack over the burner that is turned off. Grill as directed.)

3 Remove and discard toothpicks from knockwurst. Serve knockwurst in rolls. If desired, top with ketchup, mustard, pickle relish, and/or additional bacon.

PER SANDWICH: 473 cal., 34 g total fat (13 g sat. fat), 77 mg chol., 1,129 mg sodium, 21 g carbo., 1 g fiber, 19 g pro.

Brats with Mango Relish

THE EXOTIC SWEET-TART TASTE OF MANGO IS BEST FRIENDS WITH THE SAVORY SPICE OF SMOKED BRATWURST. AND THERE'S NO PRETTIER COMBO.

START TO FINISH: 20 MINUTES
MAKES: 4 SANDWICHES

- 1 large mango, halved, pitted, and peeled
- 1 small red onion, cut in ½-inch slices
- 3 tablespoons vegetable oil
- 4 cooked smoked bratwurst (12 ounces)
- 2 hearts of romaine lettuce, halved
- 4 hoagie buns, bratwurst buns, or other crusty rolls, split
- ½ teaspoon Jamaican jerk seasoning
- Salt and black pepper

1 Brush mango and onion with 1 tablespoon of the oil.

2 For a charcoal grill, grill mango halves, onion slices, and bratwurst directly over medium coals, about 8 minutes or until mango and brats are brown and heated through and onion is crisp-tender, turning once halfway through cooking. Lightly brush romaine with 1 tablespoon of the oil. Grill romaine for 1 to 2 minutes or until light brown and wilted, turning once. Lightly toast buns for 1 to 2 minutes on grill. (For a gas grill, preheat grill. Reduce heat to medium. Place mango, onion, and bratwurst on grill rack over heat. Cover; grill as directed.)

3 For mango relish, chop grilled mango and onion. In a medium bowl combine mango, onion, the remaining 1 tablespoon oil, and the jerk seasoning. Season with salt and pepper. Serve bratwurst in buns with relish and romaine on the side.

PER SANDWICH: 478 cal., 31 g total fat (6 g sat. fat), 66 mg chol., 1,112 mg sodium, 35 g carbo., 2 g fiber, 15 g pro.

Baconista Brats

BACON IS EVERYWHERE THESE DAYS—IN PAIRINGS AS SEEMINGLY INCOMPATIBLE AS BACON-INFUSED COCKTAILS AND BACON-FLAVOR ICE CREAM. HERE IS ONE PAIRING THAT APPEALS TO EVERYONE—BACON AND BRATS.

PREP: 30 MINUTES **COOK:** 10 MINUTES
GRILL: 5 MINUTES **MARINATE:** 6 HOURS
MAKES: 5 SANDWICHES

- 5 uncooked bratwurst links or turkey bratwursts (about 1 pound)
- 1 12 ounce bottle or can dark German beer, desired beer, or 1½ cups beef broth
- ½ cup coarsely chopped onion (1 medium)
- 3 tablespoons bottled steak sauce
- 2½ teaspoons smoked paprika or sweet paprika
- 4 cloves garlic, coarsely chopped
- 5 slices uncooked bacon
- 5 round hard rolls, bratwurst buns, hoagie buns, or other crusty rolls, split and toasted
- 1 recipe Tangy Midwest Slaw

1 Use the tines of a fork to pierce the skin of each bratwurst several times. Place bratwurst in a large resealable plastic bag set in a shallow dish. For marinade, stir together beer, onion, steak sauce, paprika, and garlic. Pour over bratwurst; seal bag. Marinate in the refrigerator for 6 to 24 hours, turning bag occasionally.

2 Transfer bratwurst and marinade to a large saucepan. Bring to boiling; reduce heat. Cover and simmer for 10 minutes.

3 Meanwhile, in a large skillet cook bacon until brown but not crisp. Drain on paper towels.

4 Using tongs, remove bratwurst from saucepan; discard marinade. Let bratwurst cool slightly. Wrap a slice of bacon around each bratwurst; secure with wooden toothpicks.

5 For a charcoal grill, grill bratwurst on the rack of an uncovered grill directly over medium coals about 5 minutes or until brown and bacon is crisp, turning often. (For a gas grill, preheat grill. Reduce heat to medium. Grill bratwurst on grill rack over heat. Cover; grill as directed.)

6 Remove and discard toothpicks from bratwurst. Serve bratwurst on rolls with Tangy Midwest Slaw.

TANGY MIDWEST SLAW: In medium bowl combine ⅓ cup mayonnaise; 1 tablespoon rice vinegar or white wine vinegar; 1 tablespoon sweet pickle juice; ¼ teaspoon celery seeds; and ⅛ teaspoon bottled hot pepper sauce. Add 2½ cups packaged shredded cabbage with carrot (coleslaw mix) or ½ of a small head green cabbage, shredded. Toss to coat. Makes about 2 cups.

PER SANDWICH: 682 cal., 48 g total fat (10 g sat. fat), 103 mg chol., 1,601 mg sodium, 37 g carbo., 2 g fiber, 23 g pro.

STEP-BY-STEP

1. Place brats in the marinade in the resealable plastic bag. Seal and turn bag so brats are coated.

2. Mix the slaw dressing in a medium bowl. Add the coleslaw mix. Stir, scraping the spoon across the bottom of the bowl, to coat the cabbage with dressing.

3. Wrap partially cooked bacon slices around the partially cooked bratwurst. Insert wooden toothpick through bacon and bratwurst to hold the bacon in place.

4. Once the coals are coated with gray ash, use long-handled tongs to spread the coals over the grate. Position the grill rack and test for medium heat.

5. Grill the bratwurst until the outside is browned and the bacon is crisp. Use tongs to remove brats from the grill. Carefully remove the toothpicks.

6. Place bacon-wrapped brats in toasted rolls. Top each with a spoonful of coleslaw.

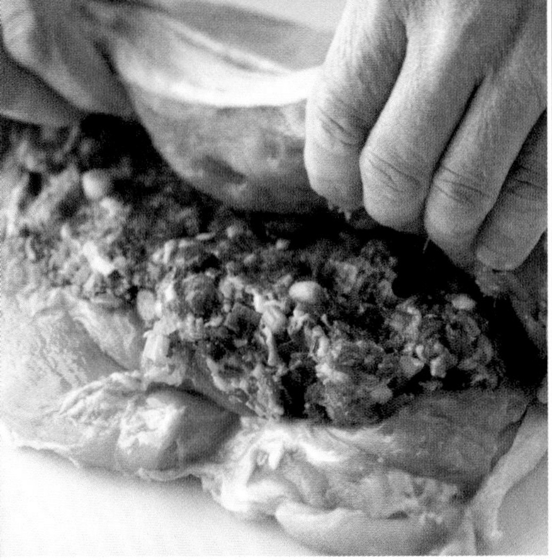

Poultry

POULTRY—IT IS THE LITTLE BLACK DRESS OF THE FOOD WORLD. DRESS IT UP OR DRESS IT DOWN. MAKE IT CASUAL OR TAKE IT UPTOWN. THESE BIRDS ARE GAME FOR ANYTHING THAT TICKLES YOUR GRILLING FANCY.

Cutting Up a Chicken

MASTER THIS TASK TO PROVE YOUR GRILLING AND COOKING PROFICIENCY.

DECONSTRUCTING A CHICKEN STEP-BY-STEP

Pull one leg away from the chicken with your fingers, making the skin taut. With a sharp knife, slice through the skin between the leg and the breast, allowing the leg to hang free.

Slice along the fold that connects the top of the thigh to the body. When the knife hits bone, stop cutting, Set your knife aside. Holding the body with one hand and the leg-thigh section with the other, bend the joint upward until it snaps. With your knife, slice carefully into the hinge between the thigh bone and the body of the chicken. Remove the leg and attached thigh.

To separate the thigh from the leg, wiggle the joint back and forth until you can detect approximately where the leg bone and thigh bone join. Cut through this joint with your knife—it is soft tissue and will cut through easily. Repeat for the other leg and thigh. Remove wings in the same way.

Remove the backbone by slicing down on each side, from the neck to the tail. To halve the breast, place it fleshy side down on the cutting board. Insert your knife at the center of the breast at the neck. Cut forcefully down, on the entire length of the breast, splitting it in half.

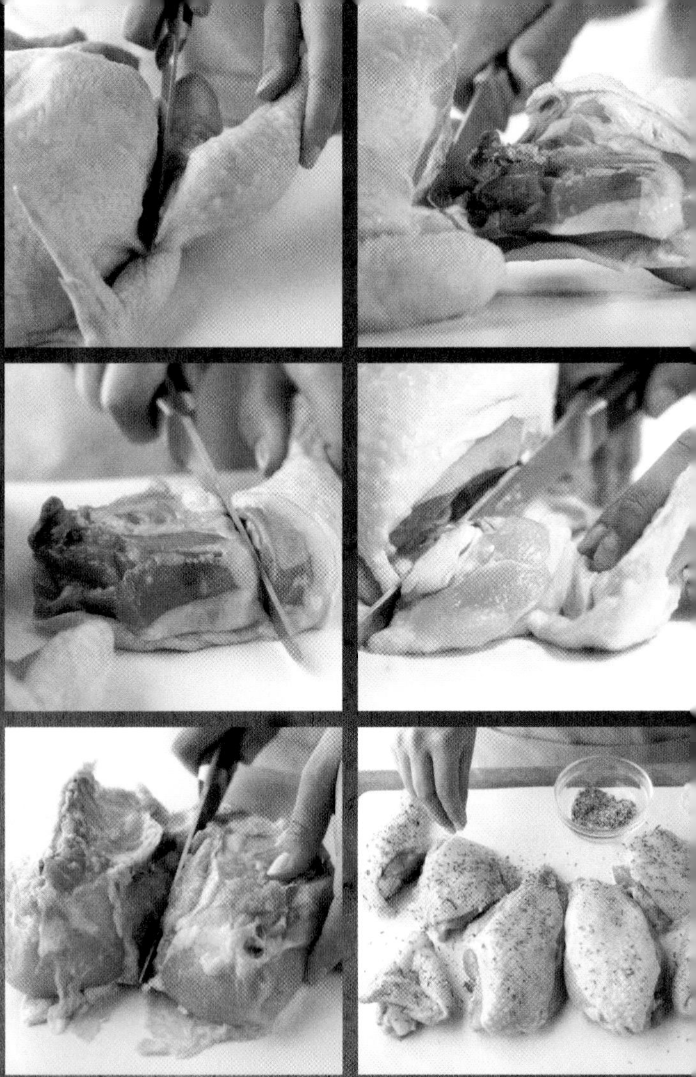

Ta-da! You have eight pieces of chicken ready for the grill. If desired, season chicken pieces with a purchased poultry seasoning blend, ready-to-use lemor pepper, or any poultry-friendly herbs. Seasonings that go well with poultry ar basil, chervil, chives, coriander, marjoram, oregano, rosemary, and thyme.

Poultry Cuts

BIRDS OF A FEATHER FLOCK TO THE GRILL, BRINGING WITH THEM A BEVY OF BEAUTIFUL FLAVORS.

To get the best chicken or turkey, look first at the "sell by" or "use before" date printed on the poultry package. Choose a package with a date several days beyond the date you make your purchase. For best flavor and juiciest flesh, buy poultry that's never been stored below 26°F. Look at the bone ends: If they are nice and pink, the bird is likely fresh. If the cut bone ends are grayish the meat has probably been frozen. Squeeze the package. If you see or feel any icy spots, the bird has been frozen. Store chicken and turkey in the coldest part of the refrigerator and keep it no longer than three days. If plans change and you are unable to cook the bird within three days, wrap and freeze to safely keep for six months.

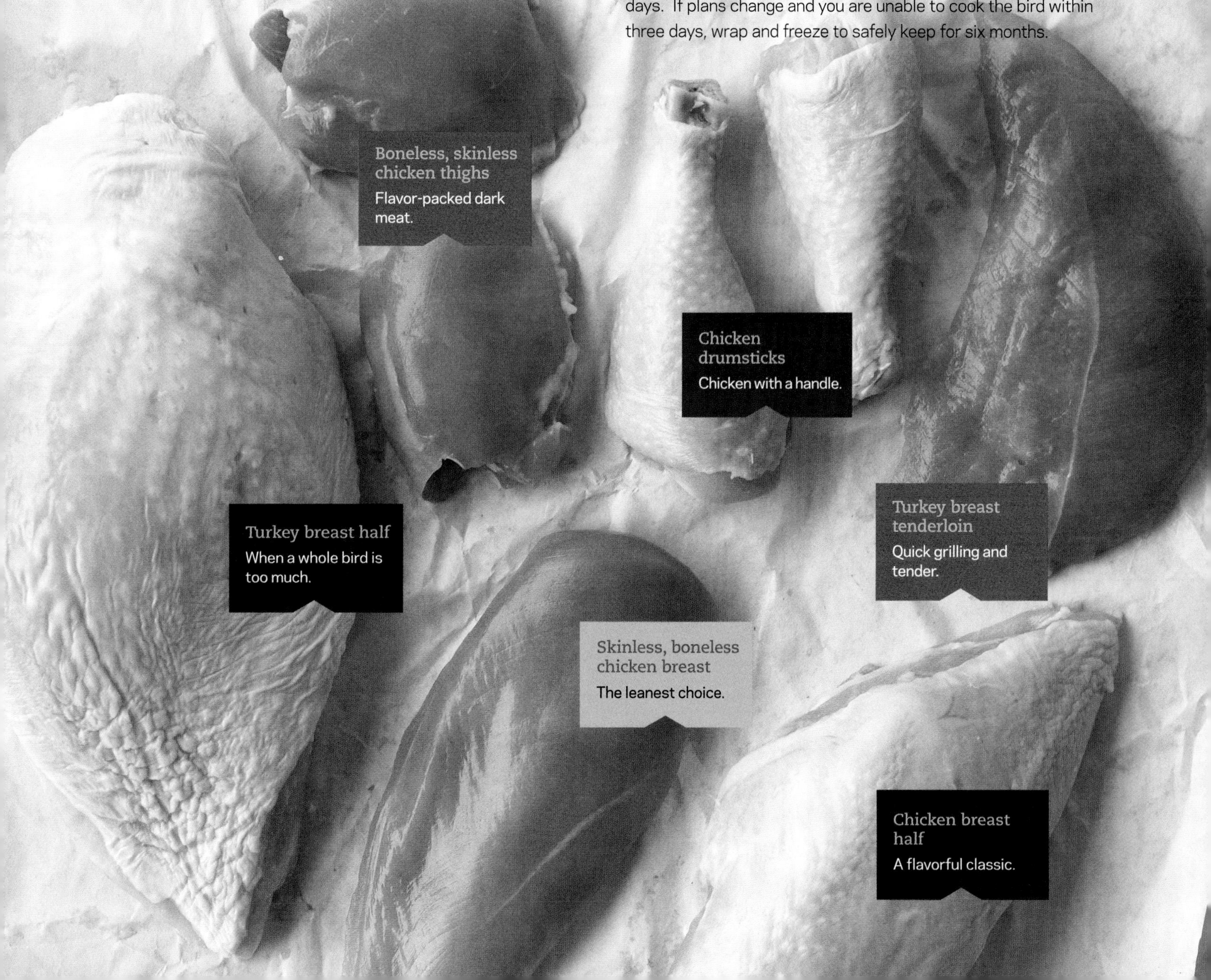

Honey-Mustard Chicken

ALTHOUGH LEGS ARE MUCH MORE FLAVORFUL THAN BREASTS, THEY ARE OFTEN NEGLECTED. GIVE INEXPENSIVE LEGS A CHANCE. MARINATED IN PIQUANT MUSTARD, SWEET HONEY, AND LEMON ZEST, THEN GRILLED, THEY'RE ABSOLUTELY DIVINE.

PREP: 15 MINUTES **MARINATE:** 4 HOURS
GRILL: 50 MINUTES **MAKES:** 6 SERVINGS

- 12 chicken drumsticks
- ½ cup honey
- ¼ cup country Dijon-style mustard
- 2 teaspoons finely shredded lemon peel
- 3 tablespoons lemon juice
- 2 tablespoons olive oil
- 4 cloves garlic, minced
- ½ teaspoon salt
- ½ teaspoon bottled hot pepper sauce
- ¼ teaspoon black pepper

1 Place chicken in a large resealable plastic bag set in a shallow dish. For marinade, in a small bowl stir together honey, mustard, lemon peel, lemon juice, oil, garlic, salt, hot pepper sauce, and black pepper. Pour over chicken; seal bag. Turn to coat chicken. Marinate in the refrigerator for 4 hours, turning bag occasionally.

2 Drain chicken; place any remaining marinade in a saucepan. Bring marinade to a boil; remove from heat. For a charcoal grill, arrange medium-hot coals around a drip pan. Test for medium heat above the pan. Place chicken on grill rack over drip pan. Cover and grill for 50 to 60 minutes or until chicken is no longer pink (180°F), brushing occasionally with sauce during the last 5 minutes of grilling. (For a gas grill, preheat grill. Reduce heat to medium. Adjust for indirect cooking. Place chicken pieces on grill rack over burner that is off. Grill as directed.)

PER 2 DRUMSTICKS: 345 cal., 21 g total fat (6 g sat. fat), 137 mg chol., 240 mg sodium, 6 g carbo., 0 g fiber, 30 g pro.

STEP-BY-STEP

1. To make the marinade, combine all the ingredients except the drumsticks in a bowl. Stir to mix well.

2. Place the drumsticks in a large resealable plastic bag. Stir the marinade again and pour over the drumsticks in the bag. Seal the bag.

3. Remove the chicken from the marinade, shaking each piece gently to remove excess marinade. Reserve the marinade remaining in the bag for the basting sauce.

THESE BEAUTIFULLY GLAZED LEGS PAIR NICELY WITH A SIMPLE SALAD AND CORN BREAD SLATHERED WITH BUTTER—AND MORE HONEY.

Chicken Kabobs and Grilled Pineapple

THAI BASIL HAS A SUBTLE YET INTOXICATING LICORICELIKE FRAGRANCE AND TASTE. TO FIND THE BASIL, IT'S WORTH A STOP AT YOUR LOCAL ASIAN MARKET. IF YOU CANNOT FIND IT, REGULAR BASIL BLENDS NICELY IN THIS RECIPE AS WELL.

PREP: 30 MINUTES **GRILL:** 10 MINUTES
MAKES: 4 KABOBS

- ⅔ cup sweet-and-sour sauce*
- 2 tablespoons snipped fresh Thai basil or basil
- 1 teaspoon Thai seasoning or five-spice powder
- 1 clove garlic, minced
- 1 tablespoon packed brown sugar (optional)*
- 1 tablespoon butter, melted
- 1 small fresh pineapple
- Nonstick cooking spray or vegetable oil
- 1 pound skinless, boneless chicken breast halves, cut into 1½-inch pieces
- 2 cups hot cooked rice (optional)
- Fresh Thai basil or basil sprigs, chopped (optional)
- Fresh red or green chile peppers, sliced (see note, page206) (optional)

1 For Thai sauce, in a small bowl combine sweet-and-sour sauce, snipped basil, Thai seasoning, and garlic. Reserve ¼ cup of the sauce to use for basting. Stir brown sugar (if desired) and melted butter into the remaining sauce; cover and set aside to serve with grilled chicken and pineapple.

2 Cut ends off pineapple, exposing the flesh. Cut pineapple in half lengthwise; cut each half crosswise into 4 slices. Lightly coat pineapple slices with cooking spray or brush with oil. Set aside.

3 For kabobs, thread chicken onto four 10- to 12-inch metal skewers, leaving ¼ inch between pieces.

4 For a charcoal grill, grill kabobs on the rack of an uncovered grill directly over medium coals for 10 to 12 minutes or until chicken is no longer pink, turning occasionally and brushing with the ¼ cup reserved sauce during the first half of grilling. Discard the sauce used for brushing on grilled chicken. Grill pineapple slices for 6 to 8 minutes or until warm and grill marks appear, turning once halfway through grilling. (For a gas grill, preheat grill. Reduce heat to medium. Place skewers, then pineapple, on grill rack over heat. Cover and grill as directed.)

5 Serve chicken and pineapple with Thai sauce and hot cooked rice, if desired. If desired, garnish with chopped basil sprigs and chile peppers.

***NOTE:** Bottled sweet-and-sour sauces vary in sweetness and thickness. If you use a less sweet sauce, add the brown sugar to the Thai sauce. If you use a thick sweet-and-sour sauce, adjust the consistency of the Thai sauce by adding a little water.

PER KABOB: 269 cal., 5 g total fat (2 g sat. fat), 73 mg chol., 333 mg sodium, 29 g carbo., 1 g fiber, 27 g pro.

STEP-BY-STEP

1. After removing ¼ cup of the sauce for basting, stir the melted butter into the sauce remaining in the bowl. For a sweet sauce, stir in the brown sugar.

2. To slice the pineapple, place it on its side on a cutting board. Using a large sharp knife, cut the bottom end off the pineapple. Cut off the top end too.

3. Turn the pineapple upright. Cut the pineapple in half from top to bottom.

4. Place each pineapple half, cut side down, on the cutting board. Cut each half crosswise into four slices.

5. Thread chicken pieces onto the skewers. To ensure even cooking, leave about ¼ inch space between the chicken pieces.

6. Use tongs to turn skewers and pineapple slices halfway through grilling. Grill until the chicken is no longer pink and grill marks appear on pineapple.

Spicy Buffalo Chicken Salad

ROLL A FAVORITE APPETIZER INTO A FRESH, CRISP GRILLED CHICKEN SALAD. THIS IS THE KIND OF LAZY LAWN CHAIR FARE THAT MAKES SUMMER A FAVORITE SEASON.

PREP: 20 MINUTES **MARINATE:** 3 HOURS
GRILL: 12 MINUTES **MAKES:** 4 SERVINGS

- 1 pound skinless, boneless chicken breast halves
- 2 tablespoons olive oil
- 1 tablespoon cider vinegar
- 1 tablespoon bottled hot pepper sauce or Louisiana hot sauce
- 2 cups shredded savoy or green cabbage
- 1 cup bite-size carrot strips (2 medium)
- 1 cup thinly sliced celery (2 stalks)
- ½ cup crumbled blue cheese (2 ounces)
- ⅓ cup bottled blue cheese salad dressing
- ½ teaspoon bottled hot pepper sauce or Louisiana hot sauce

1 Place chicken in a large resealable plastic bag set in a shallow dish. For marinade, in a small bowl stir together oil, vinegar, and the 1 tablespoon hot pepper sauce. Pour over chicken in bag; seal bag. Turn to coat chicken. Marinate in the refrigerator for 3 to 4 hours, turning bag occasionally.

2 Drain chicken, reserving marinade. For a charcoal grill, grill chicken on the rack of an uncovered grill directly over medium coals for 12 to 15 minutes or until chicken is no longer pink (170°F), turning and brushing once with reserved marinade halfway through grilling. (For a gas grill, preheat grill. Reduce heat to medium. Place chicken on grill rack over heat. Cover and grill as directed.) Discard any remaining marinade. Slice chicken diagonally.

3 In a medium bowl combine cabbage, carrots, celery, and three-fourths of the blue cheese. Combine the blue cheese salad dressing and the ½ teaspoon hot pepper sauce. Pour over vegetables. Toss to coat. Arrange sliced chicken on cabbage mixture. Sprinkle with the remaining blue cheese.

PER 3 OUNCES CHICKEN + ¾ CUP SALAD: 367 cal., 23 g total fat (6 g sat. fat), 80 mg chol., 563 mg sodium, 8 g carbo., 3 g fiber, 32 g pro.

STEP-BY-STEP

1. Combine the savoy cabbage, carrots, celery, and blue cheese until mixed. Toss with tongs to mix.

2. Stir the hot sauce into the salad dressing. Pour the dressing mixture over the vegetable mixture and toss again until all the vegetables are coated.

3. Halfway through grilling, brush chicken with reserved marinade and turn to the other sides. Brush second sides with marinade and grill until the chicken is no longer pink.

HOT, COLD, CREAMY, CRISP. OPPOSITES ATTRACT, AND THEY'LL ATTRACT EVERYONE TO THIS SENSATIONAL SUMMERY SALAD.

Mozzarella-and-Tomato-Stuffed Chicken Breasts

WHILE THESE SAVORY STUFFED BREASTS ARE SIMPLE ENOUGH TO SERVE THE FAMILY ANY NIGHT OF THE WEEK, THEY'RE SO GORGEOUS THAT THEY'RE A PERFECTLY DELICIOUS WAY TO IMPRESS GUESTS.

PREP: 20 MINUTES **MARINATE:** 2 HOURS
GRILL: 50 MINUTES **MAKES:** 4 SERVINGS

- 4 6- to 8-ounce chicken breast halves, skinned if desired
- ½ cup bottled Italian salad dressing
- 4 oil-packed dried tomatoes, undrained
- 4 ounces fresh mozzarella cheese, sliced
- 8 large fresh basil leaves
- ¼ teaspoon salt
- ⅛ teaspoon black pepper

1 Using a sharp knife, cut a 2-inch pocket in the thickest part of each chicken breast half by cutting horizontally toward, but not through, the opposite side. Place chicken in a large resealable plastic bag set in a shallow dish. Pour dressing over chicken in bag; seal bag. Turn to coat chicken. Marinate in the refrigerator for 2 to 4 hours, turning bag occasionally.

2 Drain dried tomatoes, reserving 1 tablespoon of the oil. Slice dried tomatoes. Drain chicken, discarding dressing. Divide dried tomatoes, cheese, and basil evenly among pockets in chicken. If necessary, secure openings with wooden toothpicks. Brush chicken with the reserved 1 tablespoon oil; sprinkle evenly with salt and pepper.

3 For a charcoal grill, arrange medium-hot coals around a drip pan. Test for medium heat above pan. Place chicken, bone sides down, on grill rack over pan. Cover and grill for 50 to 60 minutes or until chicken is no longer pink (170°F). (For a gas grill, preheat grill. Reduce heat to medium. Adjust for indirect cooking. Place chicken, bone sides down, on grill rack over the burner that is turned off. Grill as directed.) Remove and discard any toothpicks.

PER BREAST HALF: 437 cal., 31 g total fat (9 g sat. fat), 107 mg chol., 811 mg sodium, 4 g carbo., 0 g fiber, 34 g pro.

STEP-BY-STEP

1. Using a small sharp knife, cut a 2-inch-long pocket in the meaty side of each chicken breast. Cut almost but not all the way to the bone.

2. Slide a cheese slicer across the mozzarella to cut it into thin slices.

3. Using kitchen scissors, cut the dried tomatoes crosswise into thin strips.

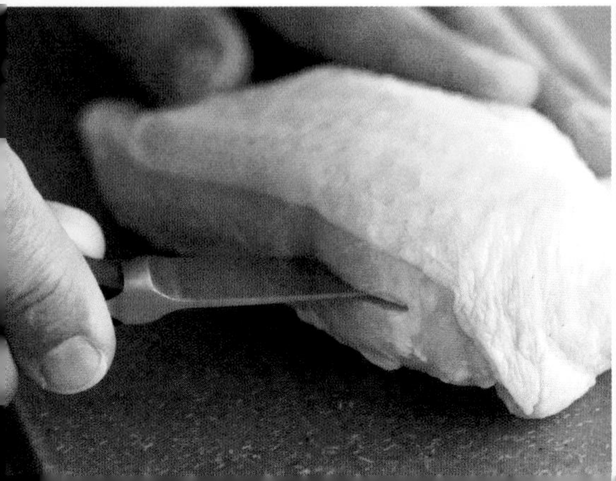

4. Stuff the chicken pockets with the mozzarella slices. Tuck two basil leaves in each pocket on top of the cheese. Add tomato strips to the pocket.

5. Fasten the pockets with wooden toothpicks to secure the cheese, basil, and tomatoes inside the chicken breasts.

6. Place the stuffed chicken breasts on the grill rack with the bone sides down and over the drip pan. Cover and grill. You won't need to turn the chicken during grilling.

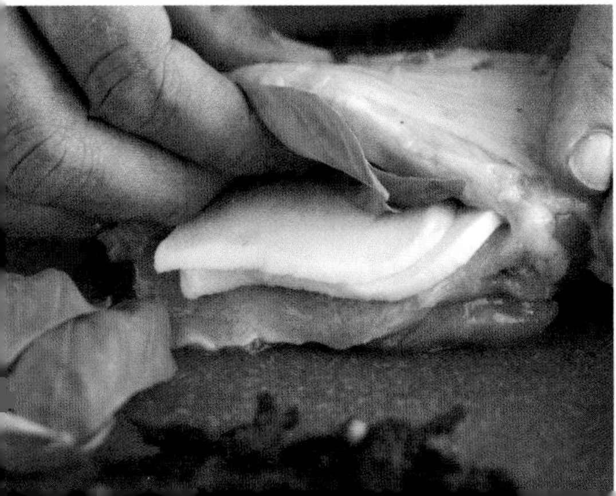

STEP-BY-STEP

1. Trim off root ends of green onions and 2 inches from green tops. Lay onions on a cutting surface and cut across into thin slices.

2. Spoon the green onion and lemongrass paste on chicken breasts. Use your fingers to rub the paste on the surfaces of the chicken breasts.

3. Remove the chicken from the grill and let cool for a few minutes. Cut chicken crosswise into slices.

Ginger-Lemongrass Chicken with Cilantro Rice Noodles

LEMONGRASS IS AN HERB THAT RESEMBLES A WOODY STALK OF PRAIRIE GRASS. ONCE YOU RUB IT BETWEEN YOUR FINGERS, RELEASING ITS MAGICAL LEMONY ESSENCE, YOU'LL UNDERSTAND WHY IT IS SO REVERED IN ASIAN CUSINES.

PREP: 30 MINUTES **GRILL:** 12 MINUTES
MAKES: 4 SERVINGS

- ¼ cup sliced green onions (2)
- ¼ cup sliced fresh lemongrass or 1 teaspoon finely shredded lemon peel
- 2 tablespoons lime juice
- 2 tablespoons vegetable oil
- 1 tablespoon grated fresh ginger
- 6 cloves garlic
- 4 skinless, boneless chicken breast halves
- 1 recipe Cilantro Rice Noodles
- Lime wedges (optional)

1 For rub, in a food processor or blender combine green onions, lemongrass, lime juice, oil, ginger, and garlic. Cover and process until a thin paste forms. Spoon mixture evenly over chicken; rub in with your fingers.

2 For a charcoal grill, grill chicken on the rack of an uncovered grill directly over medium coals for 12 to 15 minutes or until chicken is no longer pink (170°F), turning once halfway through grilling. (For a gas grill, preheat grill. Reduce heat to medium. Place chicken on grill rack over heat. Cover and grill as directed.)

3 Slice chicken; serve over Cilantro Rice Noodles. If desired, serve with lime wedges.

CILANTRO RICE NOODLES: In a large saucepan cook 8 ounces dried rice noodles* (rice sticks) in a large amount of boiling water for 3 to 4 minutes or just until tender; drain. Meanwhile, in a large bowl combine ¼ cup fish sauce, 3 tablespoons lime juice, 2 tablespoons packed brown sugar, and 1 or 2 cloves garlic, minced, stirring until brown sugar is dissolved. Add cooked noodles, 1 cup shredded carrots (2 medium), ¼ cup coarsely snipped fresh cilantro, and ¼ cup peanuts; toss gently to coat.

***NOTE:** If you can't find dried rice noodles, substitute dried vermicelli or capellini.

PER 4 OUNCES CHICKEN + 1 CUP NOODLES: 541 cal., 13 g total fat (2 g sat. fat), 82 mg chol., 1,670 mg sodium, 65 g carbo., 2 g fiber, 39 g pro.

4. To shred carrots, cut the top off a peeled carrot. Rub the cut end against the coarse side of a box grater.

5. Remove cilantro leaves from the stems and place in a measuring cup. To snip the leaves, use kitchen scissors and make short, quick strokes until pieces are desired size.

6. Add the cooked rice noodles, carrots, cilantro, and peanuts to the fish sauce mixture in bowl. Toss until all the ingredients are combined and coated with sauce.

Double-Cherry Chicken Roll-Ups

MASCARPONE—ITALY'S BUTTERY-RICH DOUBLE-CREAM CHEESE—PAIRS PERFECTLY WITH FRUIT AND MILD- FLAVOR MEATS. THAT'S EXACTLY WHAT IT DOES IN THIS RICH RECIPE.

PREP: 30 MINUTES **GRILL:** 20 MINUTES
MAKES: 4 SERVINGS

- ½ of an 8-ounce carton mascarpone cheese or cream cheese spread
- ⅓ cup snipped dried cherries
- 3 tablespoons thinly sliced green onions
- 4 skinless, boneless chicken breast halves
- 1 tablespoon packed brown sugar
- ½ teaspoon salt
- ¼ teaspoon black pepper
- 1 recipe Cherry-Orange Sauce

1 For filling, in a small bowl stir together cheese, dried cherries, and green onions; set aside.

2 Place each chicken breast half between 2 pieces of plastic wrap. Using the flat side of a meat mallet, pound chicken lightly to a rectangle about ¼ inch thick. Discard plastic wrap. Spread filling evenly over each breast half to within ½ inch of the edges. Fold in sides; roll up from bottom edges. Secure with wooden toothpicks.

3 For rub, in a small bowl stir together brown sugar, salt, and pepper. Sprinkle mixture over chicken roll-ups; rub in with your fingers.

4 For a charcoal grill, arrange medium-hot coals around a drip pan. Test for medium heat above pan. Place chicken on grill rack over pan. Cover and grill for 20 to 25 minutes or until chicken is no longer pink (170°F). (For a gas grill, preheat grill. Reduce heat to medium. Adjust for indirect cooking. Place chicken on grill rack over the burner that is turned off. Grill as directed.) Remove and discard toothpicks. Serve chicken with Cherry-Orange Sauce.

CHERRY-ORANGE SAUCE: Finely shred enough peel from 1 orange to equal 1 teaspoon; set aside. Peel and section orange over a bowl to catch the juices. Add enough additional orange juice to equal ¼ cup. In a small saucepan combine the ¼ cup orange juice and ½ cup cherry preserves. Cook and stir over medium heat until preserves melt. Remove from heat. Coarsely chop orange sections. Stir orange sections and the 1 teaspoon orange peel into preserves mixture.

PER ROLL-UP: 459 cal., 15 g total fat (8 g sat. fat), 118 mg chol., 400 mg sodium, 45 g carbo., 2 g fiber, 40 g pro.

Mix It Up!

PICK ONE FROM EACH COLUMN TO CUSTOMIZE THE CHICKEN TO YOUR TASTE.

SEASON IT

Add to the rub mixture one of the following:

- ½ teaspoon dried Italian seasoning
- ½ teaspoon smoked paprika
- ½ teaspoon ground cumin
- ¼ teaspoon crushed red pepper
- ½ teaspoon chili powder
- ½ teaspoon snipped fresh rosemary
- ½ teaspoon Cajun seasoning
- ½ teaspoon ground coriander

MIX IT IN

Instead of the dried cherries in the mascarpone mixture, add one of the following:

- ⅓ cup snipped dried apricots
- ⅓ cup golden raisins
- 3 tablespoons chopped kalamata olives
- ⅓ cup dried cranberries
- ⅓ cup chopped pistachio nuts
- ⅓ cup chopped roasted red sweet pepper

TOP IT

Instead of Cherry-Orange Sauce, use one of the following:

- 1 cup frozen cranberry orange sauce
- 1 cup peach or pineapple salsa
- 1 cup barbecue sauce
- 1 cup marinara sauce
- ¼ cup basil pesto
- 1 cup Alfredo sauce
- ½ cup Asian salad dressing

STEP-BY-STEP

1. Spread the filling over the chicken, leaving a ½-inch border on all sides. Roll up, starting from a short end.

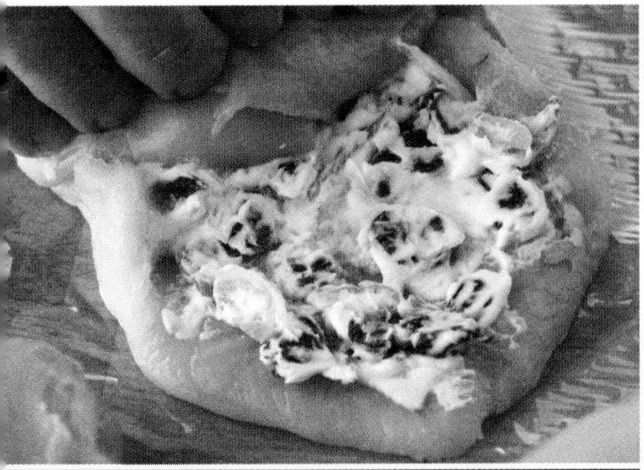

2. Insert a wooden toothpick into each roll to secure. Turn the rolls over so the seam sides are on the bottom.

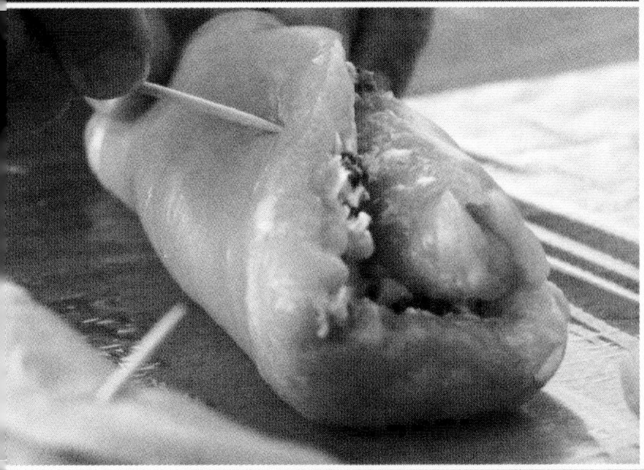

3. Sprinkle the chicken rolls with the brown sugar mixture and use your fingers to spread it over the chicken.

4. Rub a citrus zester over an orange until you have 1 teaspoon finely shredded peel. Turn orange often to scrape only the orange portion.

5. With the saucepan off the heat, add the orange sections and peel to the cherry mixture. Stir gently to avoid breaking up fruit.

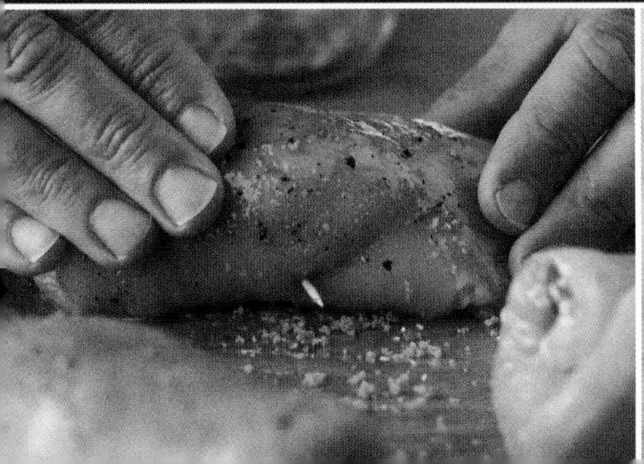

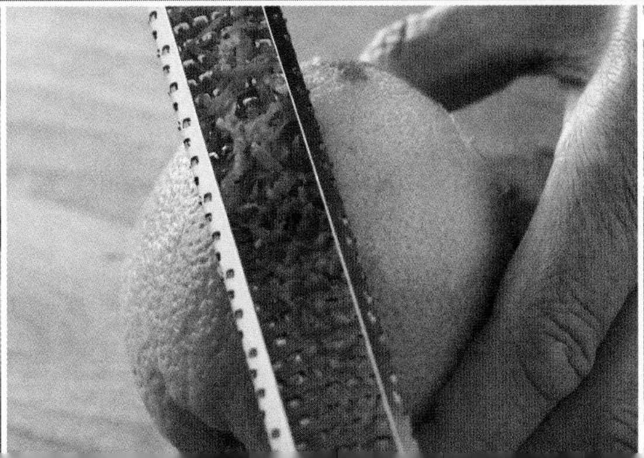

CHIMICHURRI—ARGENTINA'S FAMOUS MELANGE OF OLIVE OIL, VINEGAR, AND CHOPPED PARSLEY—IS AS MUCH FUN TO SAY AS IT IS TO EAT.

Chimichurri Chicken

CONSIDER MAKING A DOUBLE BATCH OF THE VERDANT GREEN SAUCE. IT KEEPS, REFRIGERATED, FOR ABOUT A WEEK, AND IT'S WONDERFUL ON ANY SIMPLE GRILLED MEAT.

PREP: 20 MINUTES **GRILL:** 12 MINUTES
MAKES: 4 SERVINGS

- 4 skinless, boneless chicken breast halves
- 3 tablespoons vegetable oil
- ½ teaspoon salt
- ¼ teaspoon black pepper
- 12 ounces fresh young green beans
- 1 tablespoon water
- ¾ cup packed fresh Italian parsley
- 1 tablespoon cider vinegar
- 2 cloves garlic, halved
- ¼ teaspoon crushed red pepper
- 1 lemon

1 Brush both sides of each chicken breast half with 1 tablespoon of the oil; sprinkle chicken with ¼ teaspoon of the salt and the black pepper.

2 For a charcoal grill, grill chicken on the rack of an uncovered grill directly over medium coals for 12 to 15 minutes or until no longer pink (170°F), turning once halfway through grilling. (For a gas grill, preheat grill. Reduce heat to medium. Place chicken on grill rack over heat. Cover and grill as directed.)

3 Meanwhile, place beans in a grill basket. Grill beans on the rack of an uncovered grill directly over medium coals for 8 minutes or until tender-crisp.

4 For sauce, in a small food processor or blender combine the remaining 2 tablespoons oil, the remaining ¼ teaspoon salt, the parsley, vinegar, garlic, and crushed red pepper. Cover and process until nearly smooth.

5 Finely shred peel from the lemon. Serve chicken and beans topped with sauce and lemon peel. Squeeze lemon juice over all.

PER BREAST HALF + 3 OUNCES BEANS: 281 cal., 12 g total fat (2 g sat. fat), 82 mg chol., 376 mg sodium, 8 g carbo., 3 g fiber, 35 g pro.

STEP-BY-STEP

1. Grill the green beans in a grill basket until they are tender. For even cooking, toss beans with tongs several times during grilling.

2. Combine the sauce ingredients in a food processor. Cover and process until the ingredients are very finely chopped and the sauce is almost smooth.

3. Grill the chicken until it starts to brown and grill marks appear. Sprinkle top sides with additional salt and pepper if you like, and turn to second side.

Cheesy Chicken-Chile Quesadillas

IF YOU'RE LOOKING FOR A SUPER-SIMPLE, FAMILY-FRIENDLY BACKYARD DINNER, HERE'S ONE OF THE BEST. SERVE THE QUESADILLAS WITH FROSTY GRAPES AND SLICED FRESH FRUIT, AND DINNER IS A DONE DEAL.

START TO FINISH: 40 MINUTES
MAKES: 4 QUESADILLAS

- 2 skinless, boneless chicken breast halves
- 2 teaspoons ground cumin
- 1 teaspoon salt
- ½ teaspoon black pepper
- ¼ teaspoon cayenne pepper
- 2 fresh Anaheim or poblano chile peppers*
- ¾ cup shredded cheddar cheese (3 ounces)
- ¾ cup shredded Monterey Jack cheese (3 ounces)
- 4 8-inch flour tortillas

1 Place each chicken breast half between 2 pieces of plastic wrap. Using the flat side of a meat mallet, pound chicken lightly to about ½-inch thickness. Discard plastic wrap. For rub, in a small bowl stir together cumin, salt, black pepper, and cayenne pepper. Sprinkle mixture evenly over chicken; rub in with your fingers.

2 For a charcoal grill, grill chile peppers on the rack of an uncovered grill directly over medium coals about 15 minutes or until peppers are charred on all sides, turning occasionally. Immediately wrap peppers in foil; set aside. Place chicken on grill rack directly over heat. Grill for 8 to 11 minutes or until chicken is no longer pink (170°F), turning once halfway through grilling. (For a gas grill, preheat grill. Reduce heat to medium. Place chile peppers, then chicken on grill rack over heat. Cover and grill as directed.)

3 Cut chile peppers in half lengthwise; remove stems and seeds. Using a sharp knife, gently peel off skins and discard. Cut peppers into 1-inch strips. Cut chicken into 1-inch pieces.

4 In a large bowl combine chile peppers, chicken, cheddar cheese, and Monterey Jack cheese. Spoon chicken mixture over tortillas. Fold tortillas in half, pressing firmly. Grill quesadillas directly over medium heat about 4 minutes or until heated through and light brown, turning once halfway through grilling. To serve, cut quesadillas in half.

***NOTE:** Because chile peppers contain volatile oils that can burn your skin and eyes, avoid direct contact with them as much as possible. When working with fresh chile peppers, wear plastic or rubber gloves. If your bare hands do touch the chiles, wash your hands and nails well with soap and hot water.

PER QUESADILLA: 328 cal., 13 g total fat (6 g sat. fat), 55 mg chol., 834 mg sodium, 29 g carbo., 0 g fiber, 23 g pro.

STEP-BY-STEP

1. Place chicken between sheets of plastic wrap. Starting from the center, lightly pound the chicken until it is about ½ inch thick.

2. Sprinkle the rub over the chicken. Use your fingers to pat the rub into the chicken. Turn the chicken over and repeat with the second sides.

3. Remove the charred chile peppers from the grill and place on foil. Bring up the sides to wrap tightly in foil. The heat will produce steam that will loosen the skins.

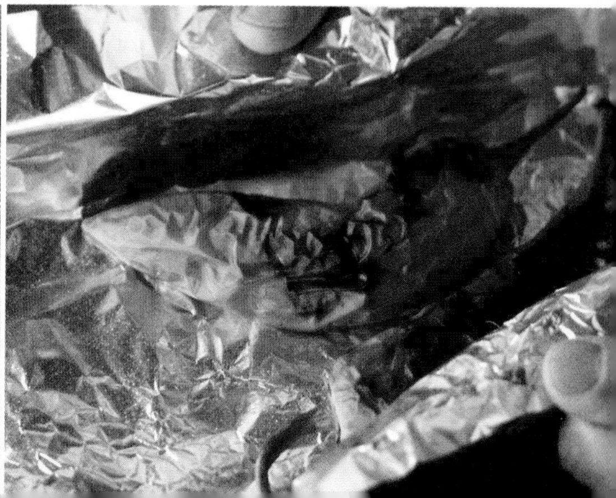

4. Unwrap the peppers. Cut lengthwise in halves and remove stems and seeds. Turn halves over. Use a sharp knife to scrape off skins.

5. Top each tortilla with one-fourth of the filling, spreading filling evenly on half of the tortilla. Fold the remaining half over the filling and press firmly.

6. Place quesadillas on the grill directly over medium heat. Use tongs to turn first sides are light brown. Grill second sides until light brown and filling is hot.

STEP-BY-STEP

1. Toast sesame seeds in a dry skillet over medium heat. Stir often and remove from heat as soon as the seeds start to brown so they don't burn.

2. To grate fresh ginger, rub a piece of ginger across a fine grating surface. You can use a special ginger grater or the fine side of a regular box grater.

3. Combine the sauce ingredients in a small saucepan. Cook on the stove over medium heat until sauce is boiling, stirring often. Reduce heat and simmer 3 minutes to blend flavors.

Sesame-Ginger Barbecued Chicken Breasts

IN ASIA THE GRILL PLAYS A STARRING ROLE IN FOOD PREPARATION, PARTICULARY ON THE STREET, WHERE GRILLS SIZZLE AND SNAP WITH FIRE-COOKED CREATIONS LIKE THIS.

PREP: 15 MINUTES **GRILL:** 12 MINUTES
MAKES: 6 SERVINGS

- ⅓ cup plum sauce or sweet-and-sour sauce
- ¼ cup water
- 3 tablespoons hoisin sauce
- 1½ teaspoons sesame seeds, toasted if desired
- 1 teaspoon grated fresh ginger or ¼ teaspoon ground ginger
- 1 clove garlic, minced
- ¼ to ½ teaspoon Asian chili sauce or several dashes bottled hot pepper sauce
- 6 skinless, boneless chicken breast halves and/or thighs
- Hot cooked rice noodles
- Cooked sugar snap peas (optional)
- Slivered green onions
- Sesame seeds, toasted if desired

1 For sauce, in a small saucepan combine plum sauce, the water, hoisin sauce, 1½ teaspoons sesame seeds, the ginger, garlic, and Asian chili sauce. Bring to boiling over medium heat, stirring frequently; reduce heat. Cover and simmer for 3 minutes. Remove from heat.

2 For a charcoal grill, grill chicken on the rack of an uncovered grill directly over medium coals for 12 to 15 minutes or until chicken is no longer pink (170°F for breast halves, 180°F for thighs), turning once halfway through grilling and brushing once or twice with some of the sauce during the last 5 minutes of grilling. (For a gas grill, preheat grill. Reduce heat to medium. Place chicken on grill rack over heat. Cover and grill as directed.)

3 To serve, slice chicken and serve on rice noodles and, if desired, sugar snap peas. Sprinkle with green onions and additional sesame seeds. Reheat and pass the remaining sauce.

PER BREAST HALF: 166 cal., 4 g total fat (1 g sat. fat), 59 mg chol., 216 mg sodium, 9 g carbo., 0 g fiber, 22 g pro.

4. Once the coals are lightly covered with a gray ash, use tongs to arrange them over the grill grate. Install the grill rack and test for medium heat.

5. About 5 minutes before the chicken is done, brush a little sauce over each breast. Brush with sauce again a minute or two before removing chicken from grill.

6. Cut each chicken breast crosswise into slices. Toss rice noodles with steamed pea pods and arrange on plates. Assemble chicken breasts on top.

Cranberry-Chipotle Drumsticks

THE POTENT CONTENTS OF EVEN A SMALL CAN OF CHIPOTLES LASTS A LONG TIME. TRANSFER LEFTOVER PEPPERS AND ADOBO SAUCE TO A GLASS OR PLASTIC CONTAINER WITH A TIGHT-FITTING LID. THEY WILL KEEP, REFRIGERATED, FOR SEVERAL MONTHS.

PREP: 15 MINUTES **GRILL:** 35 MINUTES
MAKES: 6 SERVINGS

- 1 16-ounce can whole cranberry sauce
- ½ cup barbecue sauce
- 1 canned chipotle pepper in adobo sauce, finely chopped*
- 12 chicken drumsticks or 6 skinless, boneless chicken breast halves

1 In a medium bowl stir together cranberry sauce, barbecue sauce, and chipotle pepper. For dipping sauce, pour 1 cup of the cranberry sauce mixture into a serving bowl; cover and chill. For basting sauce, transfer the remaining cranberry sauce mixture to a blender or food processor. Cover and blend until smooth.

2 For a charcoal grill, grill chicken on the rack of an uncovered grill directly over medium coals until chicken is no longer pink, turning once halfway through grilling and brushing with basting sauce during the last 5 minutes of grilling. Allow 35 to 45 minutes for drumsticks (180°F) or 12 to 15 minutes for breast halves (170°F). (For a gas grill, preheat grill. Reduce heat to medium. Place chicken on grill rack over heat. Cover and grill as directed.) Discard basting sauce. Serve chicken with reserved dipping sauce.

***NOTE:** Because chile peppers contain volatile oils that can burn your skin and eyes, avoid direct contact with them as much as possible. When working with fresh chile peppers, wear plastic or rubber gloves. If your bare hands do touch the chiles, wash your hands and nails well with soap and hot water.

PER 2 DRUMSTICKS: 371 cal., 12 g total fat (3 g sat. fat), 95 mg chol., 415 mg sodium, 36 g carbo., 1 g fiber, 28 g pro.

STEP-BY-STEP

1. Combine the cranberry sauce, barbecue sauce, and chipotle pepper. Stir to break up the cranberry sauce and mix all ingredients together.

2. After removing 1 cup for the dipping sauce, scrape the remaining mixture into a blender. Cover and blend until the sauce is smooth. Some of the seeds will remain.

3. About 5 minutes before it is done, brush the chicken with the pureed sauce. If you brush with sauce too soon, it may burn.

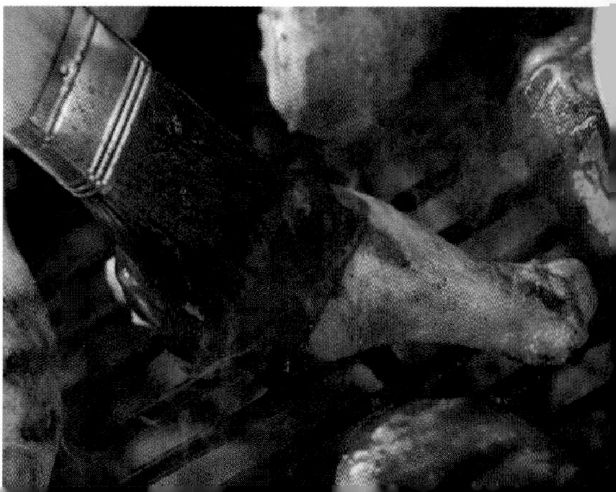

CHIPOTLE PEPPERS COAX CRANBERRIES TO THEIR PERKY BEST AND DOUBLE THE SMOKY FLAVOR OF GRILLED CHICKEN LEGS.

PREPARING GRILLERS STUFFED WITH SPINACH AND SMOKED GOUDA, STEP-BY-STEP

1. Use a small sharp knife to cut a pocket into the thickest side of the breast. Do not cut all the way through.

2. Spoon the filling into the pockets in the chicken breasts. Use the spoon to push the filling into an even layer in the pocket.

3. To prevent the filling from spilling out, fasten the opening with one or two wooden toothpicks. Remember to remove them before serving.

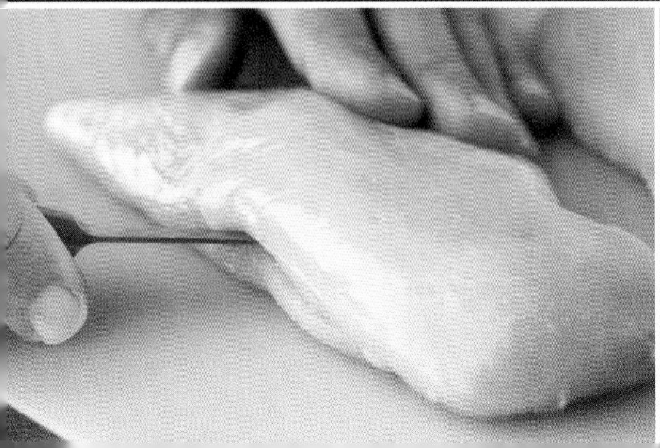

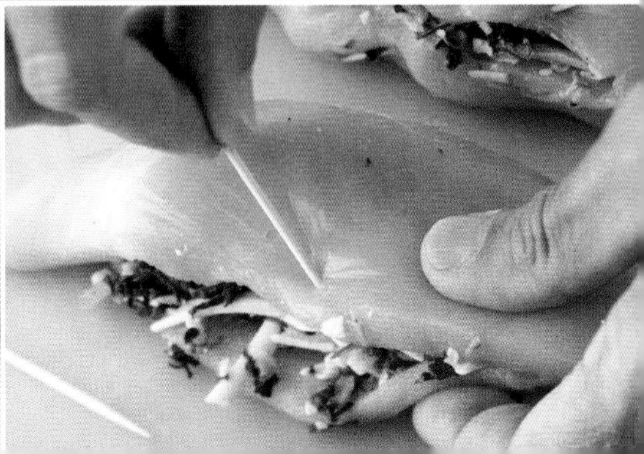

Grillers Stuffed with Spinach and Smoked Gouda

FOR SUCCESS, SQUEEZE EVERY LAST DROP OF WATER FROM THE THAWED SPINACH BY PRESSING THE SPINACH FIRMLY INTO A FINE-MESH SIEVE OR BY SQUEEZING HANDFULS OF THE CHOPPED LEAVES WITH YOUR FISTS.

PREP: 30 MINUTES **GRILL:** 12 MINUTES
MAKES: 4 SERVINGS

- ⅓ cup finely chopped onion (1 small)
- 2 cloves garlic, minced
- 1 tablespoon olive oil
- 1 cup chopped fresh mushrooms
- 1 cup shredded smoked Gouda cheese (4 ounces)
- ½ of a 10-ounce package frozen chopped spinach, thawed and squeezed dry
- ¼ teaspoon ground nutmeg
- 4 skinless, boneless chicken breast halves

1 For filling, in a large skillet cook onion and garlic in hot oil over medium heat about 5 minutes or until onion is tender. Add mushrooms. Cook and stir about 5 minutes more or until mushrooms are tender. Remove from heat. Stir in cheese, spinach, and nutmeg. Set aside.

2 Using a sharp knife, cut a 2-inch pocket in the thickest part of each chicken breast half by cutting horizontally toward, but not through, the opposite side. Divide filling evenly among pockets in chicken. Secure openings with wooden toothpicks.

3 For a charcoal grill, grill chicken on the rack of an uncovered grill directly over medium coals for 12 to 15 minutes or until chicken is no longer pink (170°F), turning once halfway through grilling. (For a gas grill, preheat grill. Reduce heat to medium. Place chicken on grill rack over heat. Cover and grill as directed.) Remove and discard toothpicks.

PER BREAST HALF: 328 cal., 13 g total fat (6 g sat. fat), 121 mg chol., 578 mg sodium, 6 g carbo., 2 g fiber, 47 g pro.

Apricot-Basil Chicken

THE INTRIGUING COMBINATION OF APRICOTS AND BASIL HEIGHTENS THE FLAVOR OF THESE ROLL-UPS.

PREP: 30 MINUTES **GRILL:** 18 MINUTES
MAKES: 4 SERVINGS

- 4 skinless, boneless chicken breast halves
- ½ teaspoon salt
- 1 recipe Apricot-Basil Pesto
- ¼ cup apricot preserves, melted

1 Place each chicken breast half between 2 pieces of plastic wrap. Using the flat side of a meat mallet, pound chicken lightly into a rectangle about ⅛ inch thick. Discard plastic wrap. Spread chicken evenly with salt. Spread pesto evenly over each breast half to within ½ inch of the edges. Fold in sides; roll up from bottom edges. Secure with wooden toothpicks.

2 For a charcoal grill, grill the chicken on the rack of an uncovered grill directly over medium coals for 18 to 20 minutes or until chicken is no longer pink (170°F), turning once halfway through grilling. Brush frequently with preserves during the last 5 minutes of grilling. (For a gas grill, preheat grill. Reduce heat to medium. Place chicken rolls on grill rack over heat. Cover and grill as above.) Remove and discard toothpicks.

APRICOT-BASIL PESTO: In a blender or food processor combine 1 cup loosely packed fresh basil leaves, ⅓ cup dried apricots, ¼ cup chopped pecans, 2 tablespoons grated Parmesan cheese, 2 tablespoons olive oil, and 2 cloves garlic, quartered. Cover and blend with several on-off turns until a paste forms, stopping the machine several times and scraping the sides.

PER ROLL: 324 cal., 16 g total fat (3 g sat. fat), 62 mg chol., 382 mg sodium, 23 g carbo., 1 g fiber, 24 g pro.

Pesto Chicken and Tomatoes

ROMA TOMATOES, ALSO CALLED PLUM OR ITALIAN PLUM TOMATOES, ARE EXTRA-FIRM AND MEATY. THESE QUALITIES MAKE THEM IDEAL CANDIDATES FOR THE GRILL.

PREP: 10 MINUTES **GRILL:** 50 MINUTES
MAKES: 4 SERVINGS

- 1 tablespoon olive oil
- 4 cloves garlic, minced
- 6 roma tomatoes, halved lengthwise
- 1½ to 2 pounds meaty chicken pieces (breast halves, thighs, and drumsticks)
- 3 tablespoons butter or margarine, softened
- 3 tablespoons purchased basil pesto
- 2 tablespoons chopped walnuts, toasted
- 2 tablespoons finely chopped kalamata olives (optional)

1 In a small bowl combine oil and garlic. Lightly brush tomato halves and chicken pieces with oil mixture. Set aside tomatoes. Discard any remaining oil mixture.

2 For a charcoal grill, arrange medium-hot coals around a drip pan. Test for medium heat above the pan. Place chicken, bone sides down, on grill rack over drip pan. Cover and grill for 50 to 60 minutes or until chicken is no longer pink (170°F for breast halves; 180°F for thighs and drumsticks), turning once halfway through grilling. During the last 6 to 8 minutes of grilling, place the tomatoes, cut sides down, on grill rack directly over coals; turn once after 3 minutes of grilling. (For a gas grill, preheat grill. Reduce heat to medium. Adjust for indirect cooking. Place chicken pieces on grill rack over burner that is turned off; place tomatoes on grill rack over heat. Grill as directed.)

3 Meanwhile, in a small bowl stir together butter, pesto, walnuts, and, if desired, olives. To serve, remove chicken from grill. Immediately spread pesto mixture over chicken pieces and cut sides of tomatoes.

PER 5 OUNCES CHICKEN + 3 TOMATO HALVES: 407 cal., 30 g total fat (10 g sat. fat),104 mg chol., 252 mg sodium, 7 g carbo., 1 g fiber, 28 g pro.

STEP-BY-STEP

1. Brush the halved tomatoes with the olive oil and garlic mixture first. Then brush the chicken with the mixture.

2. While the chicken is grilling, combine the softened butter, pesto, walnuts, and olives. Use the back of the fork to mash the butter and mix all the ingredients together.

3. Arrange the chicken on a platter. Spoon a dab of pesto mixture on each piece of chicken and each tomato half; spread with the back of the spoon.

TO ACHIEVE THE MOST ASTONISHING TASTE AND VIVID CRIMSON COLOR, TAKE IT TO THE GRILL IN LATE SUMMER, WHEN LOCAL VINE-RIPENED TOMATOES ARE AT THEIR SEASONAL BEST.

DISCOVER HOW WONDERFULLY TEQUILA ENHANCES THE NATURAL TENDERNESS OF CHICKEN.

Tequila-Marinated Chicken Thighs

WHEN COOKING WITH TEQUILA, CHOOSE ONE THAT CONTAINS 100 PERCENT AGAVE. LESS EXPENSIVE VARIETIES CONTAIN COLORING AND ADDITIVES THAT MASK THE SUBTLE SWEETNESS OF TEQUILA.

PREP: 15 MINUTES **MARINATE:** 4 HOURS
GRILL: 50 MINUTES **MAKES:** 6 SERVINGS

- 12 chicken thighs, skinned if desired
- ½ cup orange juice
- ¼ cup tequila
- 2 tablespoons lime juice
- 1 tablespoon finely chopped canned chipotle pepper in adobo sauce*
- 1 teaspoon snipped fresh oregano
- 2 cloves garlic, minced
- ½ teaspoon salt
- ¼ teaspoon black pepper

1 Place chicken in a large resealable plastic bag set on a baking pan. For marinade, in a small bowl stir together orange juice, tequila, lime juice, chipotle pepper, oregano, garlic, salt, and black pepper. Pour over chicken in bag; seal bag. Turn to coat chicken. Marinate in the refrigerator for 4 to 6 hours, turning bag occasionally.

2 Drain chicken, reserving marinade. For a charcoal grill, arrange medium-hot coals around a drip pan. Test for medium heat above pan. Place chicken, meaty sides down, on grill rack over pan. Cover and grill for 50 to 60 minutes or until chicken is no longer pink (180°F), turning and brushing once with reserved marinade halfway through grilling. (For a gas grill, preheat grill. Reduce heat to medium. Adjust for indirect cooking. Place chicken on grill rack over the burner that is turned off. Grill as directed.) Discard any remaining marinade.

***NOTE:** Because chile peppers contain volatile oils that can burn your skin and eyes, avoid direct contact with them as much as possible. When working with fresh chile peppers, wear plastic or rubber gloves. If your bare hands do touch the chiles, wash your hands and nails well with soap and hot water.

PER 2 THIGHS: 432 cal., 29 g total fat (8 g sat. fat), 158 mg chol., 349 mg sodium, 3 g carbo., 0 g fiber, 33 g pro.

STEP-BY-STEP

1. If you wish to skin the chicken thighs, loosen an edge of skin with your fingers and pull it away from the meat.

2. Place the chicken in a resealable bag set on baking pan. The tray will catch any drips if the bag should leak.

3. Halfway through grilling, turn chicken and brush with the marinade. Throw away any remaining marinade to avoid contamination. Grill chicken to 180°F.

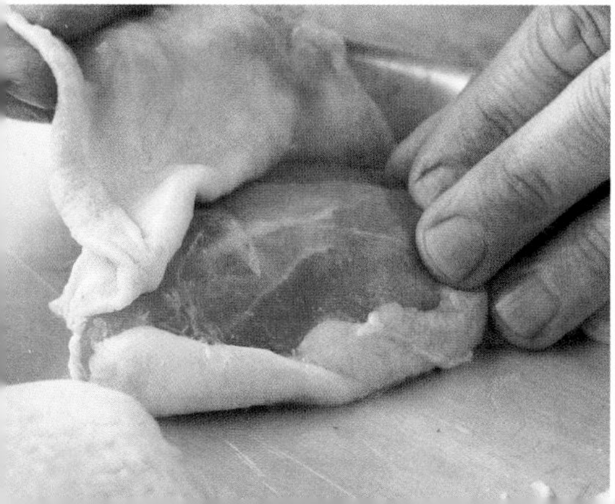

Thai Chicken Thighs

BY REMOVING SKIN FROM THE THIGHS, YOU WILL CUT CALORIES AND THE MARINADE FLAVORS THE MEAT MORE QUICKLY.

PREP: 30 MINUTES **MARINATE:** 4 HOURS
GRILL: 50 MINUTES **MAKES:** 6 SERVINGS

- 12 chicken thighs, skinned if desired
- ⅔ cup snipped fresh basil
- ⅔ cup snipped fresh cilantro
- 2 tablespoons packed brown sugar
- 12 cloves garlic, minced
- 2 tablespoons grated fresh ginger
- 2 tablespoons soy sauce
- 1 tablespoon fish sauce
- 1 tablespoon toasted sesame oil
- 2 teaspoons red curry paste
- ½ cup honey-roasted peanuts, chopped

1 Place chicken in a large resealable plastic bag set in a shallow dish. For marinade, in a small bowl combine ⅓ cup of the basil, ⅓ cup of the cilantro, the brown sugar, garlic, ginger, soy sauce, fish sauce, oil, and curry paste. Pour over chicken in bag; seal bag. Turn to coat chicken. Marinate in the refrigerator for 8 to 24 hours, turning bag occasionally. Drain chicken, scraping off and discarding marinade.

2 For a charcoal grill, arrange medium-hot coals around a drip pan. Test for medium heat above pan. Place chicken, meaty sides down (or skin sides up), on grill rack over drip pan. Cover and grill for 50 to 60 minutes or until chicken is no longer pink (180°F), turning once halfway through grilling. (For a gas grill, preheat grill. Reduce heat to medium. Adjust for indirect cooking. Place chicken on grill rack over the burner that is turned off. Grill as directed.)

3 Meanwhile, in a small bowl combine the remaining ⅓ cup basil, the remaining ⅓ cup cilantro, and peanuts. Sprinkle chicken with basil mixture.

PER 2 THIGHS: 653 cal., 45 g total fat (12 g sat. fat), 224 mg chol., 865 mg sodium, 10 g carbo., 1 g fiber, 49 g pro.

STEP-BY-STEP

1. For marinade, combine basil, cilantro, brown sugar, garlic, ginger, soy sauce, fish sauce, sesame oil, and curry paste. Stir to mix well.

2. Pour over chicken in plastic bag. Close thebag and turn it a few times to coat all the chicken with marinade. Marinate in the refrigerator, turning the bag every hour or two.

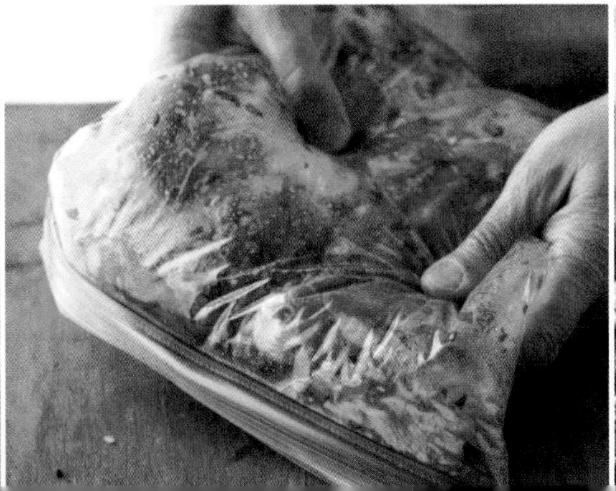

3. Toss together basil, cilantro, and peanuts. Arrange grilled chicken on a platter or serving plates. Sprinkle the basil mixture over chicken.

SPATCHCOCK—IT MUST BE THE SILLIEST-SOUNDING WORD IN THE WORLD OF FOOD. BUT THERE'S NOTHING SILLY ABOUT HOW QUICKLY AND PERFECTLY A SPATCHCOCKED CHICKEN ROASTS TO ABSOLUTE PERFECTION ON THE GRILL.

Spatchcock Barbecue Chicken with Raspberry Glaze

IF YOU LACK CHICKEN-CUTTING CONFIDENCE, DON'T GIVE UP ON THIS RECIPE. JUST ASK A BUTCHER TO DO THE DEED FOR YOU; BUTCHERS ARE PROS WITH THIS OLD EUROPEAN TECHNIQUE.

PREP: 20 MINUTES **GRILL:** 50 MINUTES
MAKES: 4 SERVINGS

- 1 3½- to 4-pound whole broiler-fryer chicken
- ½ cup balsamic vinegar
- 2 tablespoons snipped fresh rosemary
- 1 teaspoon salt
- ¼ teaspoon cayenne pepper
- ½ cup seedless raspberry jam
- ¼ cup dry red wine or cranberry juice

1 To butterfly chicken, using kitchen shears, cut along both sides of backbone to remove. Rinse the chicken body cavity; pat dry with paper towels. Turn chicken skin side up and press down between the breasts to break the breast bone.

2 In a small bowl stir together vinegar, rosemary, salt, and pepper; divide mixture in half. Brush half the vinegar mixture on both sides of chicken.

3 For raspberry glaze, in a small saucepan combine remaining half of the vinegar mixture, the jam, and wine. Bring to boiling over medium heat, stirring frequently; reduce heat. Simmer, uncovered, for 3 to 4 minutes or until slightly thickened. Set aside.

4 Meanwhile, for a charcoal grill, arrange medium-hot coals around a drip pan. Test for medium heat above pan. Place chicken, skin side up, flat on grill rack over pan. Cover and grill for 50 to 60 minutes or until chicken is no longer pink (180°F in thigh muscle), brushing with raspberry glaze during the last 5 minutes of grilling. (For a gas grill, preheat grill. Reduce heat to medium. Adjust for indirect cooking. Place chicken on grill rack over the burner that is turned off. Grill as directed.)

PER ¼ CHICKEN: 730 cal., 39 g total fat (11 g sat. fat), 201 mg chol., 753 mg sodium, 35 g carbo., 1 g fiber, 50 g pro.

STEP-BY-STEP

1. Place the chicken on a work surface with the back on top. Use heavy-duty kitchen scissors to cut along both sides of the backbone.

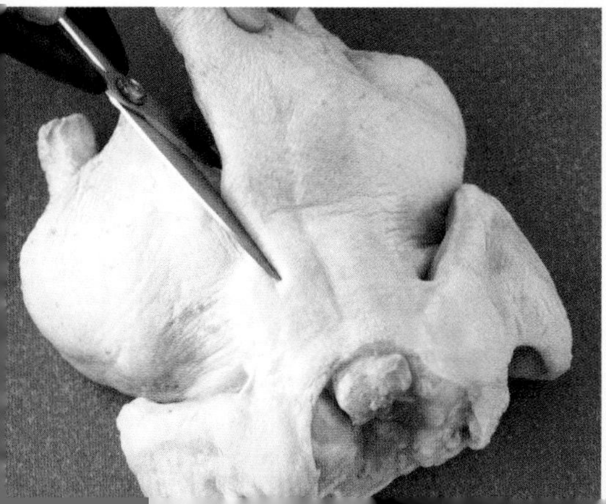

2. Using both hands, firmly press on the breast bone to break bone and flatten the chicken. This step helps the chicken cook evenly.

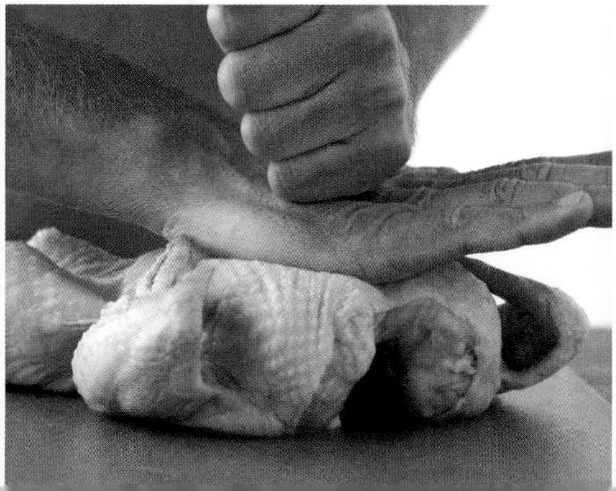

3. Brush the chicken with the raspberry glaze about 5 minutes before it is done.

Turkey Breast Stuffed with Sausage, Fennel, and Figs

WHEN A WHOLE TURKEY IS MORE THAN YOU NEED, BRING ON A BREAST. THIS SAVORY-STUFFED BREAST WILL FEED 8 TO 10 PEOPLE OR PROVIDE DINNER FOR TWO PLUS A WEEK'S WORTH OF TOP-NOTCH BROWN BAGGING.

PREP: 20 MINUTES **GRILL:** 1½ HOURS
STAND: 10 MINUTES
MAKES: 10 TO 12 SERVINGS

- 2 2½- to 3-pound bone-in turkey breast halves or 2 boneless breast halves
- ½ teaspoon salt
- ½ teaspoon black pepper
- 1 pound bulk or link sweet Italian sausage
- 1½ cups thinly sliced green onions (12)
- ⅔ cup snipped dried figs
- 1½ teaspoons fennel seeds
- 2 tablespoons olive oil
- ¼ teaspoon salt
- ¼ teaspoon black pepper

1 Remove bone from turkey.* Place turkey breast, skin side down, between 2 pieces of plastic wrap. Using the flat side of a meat mallet and working from the center to the edges, pound lightly to an even thickness. Discard plastic wrap. Repeat with second breast. Sprinkle turkey evenly with the ½ teaspoon salt and ½ teaspoon pepper.

2 For stuffing, remove casings from sausage if present. In a medium bowl combine sausage, onions, figs, and fennel seeds. On a work surface, lay 1 breast skin side down. Spoon stuffing on top of the breast. Top with second breast skin side up. Tie in several places with heavy 100%-cotton kitchen string. Rub oil over skin; sprinkle with the ¼ teaspoon salt and the ¼ teaspoon pepper.

3 For a charcoal grill, arrange medium-hot coals around a drip pan. Test for medium heat above pan. Place turkey on grill rack over pan. Cover and grill for 1½ to 2 hours or until turkey is no longer pink (170°F) and center of stuffing registers 165°F. (For a gas grill, preheat grill. Reduce heat to medium. Adjust for indirect cooking. Place turkey on grill rack over the burner that is turned off. Grill as directed.)

4 Remove turkey. Cover with foil; let stand for 10 minutes before slicing.

***NOTE:** You may want to ask a butcher to remove the turkey breast bone for you.

PER 6 OUNCES TURKEY: 364 cal., 18 g total fat (6 g sat. fat), 119 mg chol., 577 mg sodium, 8 g carbo., 2 g fiber, 41 g pro.

STEP-BY-STEP

1. Using a sharp, thin boning knife, cut between the meat and the rib cage. Turn the breast over and repeat on the other side.

2. Pull the rib cage away from the meat and cut around the tip. Remove the white cartilage with your fingers.

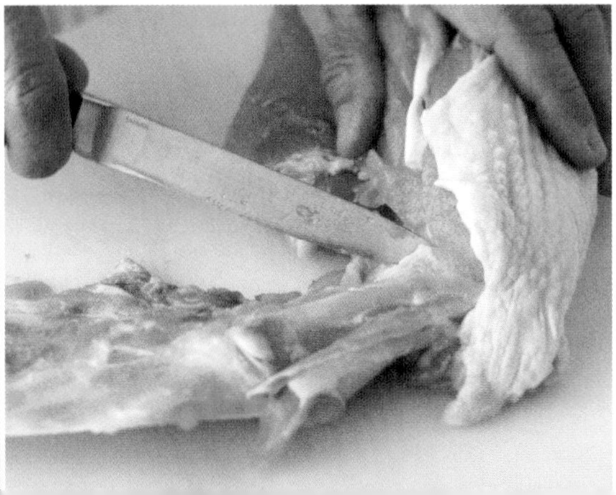

3. Place turkey breast, skin side down, on a sheet of plastic wrap. Cover with another sheet of plastic wrap. Pound with the flat side of a meat mallet until an even thickness.

4. Spread the stuffing on one turkey breast, top with second breast.

5. Tie clean 100%-cotton string around the turkey breast in several places. Tie the string in double knots and cut off long ends.

6. After grilling, let the turkey breast stand, covered with foil, for 10 minutes. Use kitchen scissors to cut the string. Remove the string and slice the turkey.

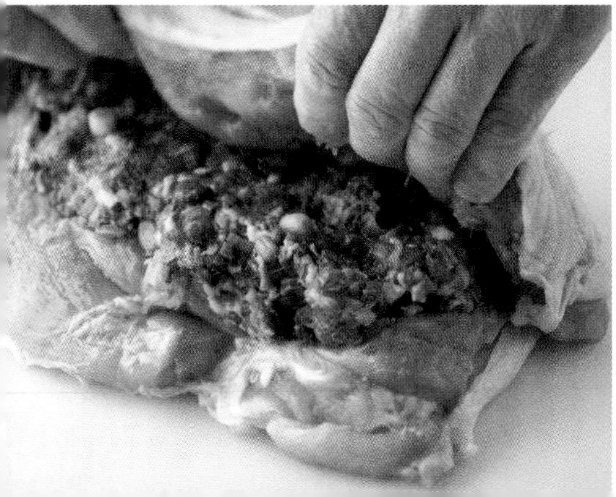

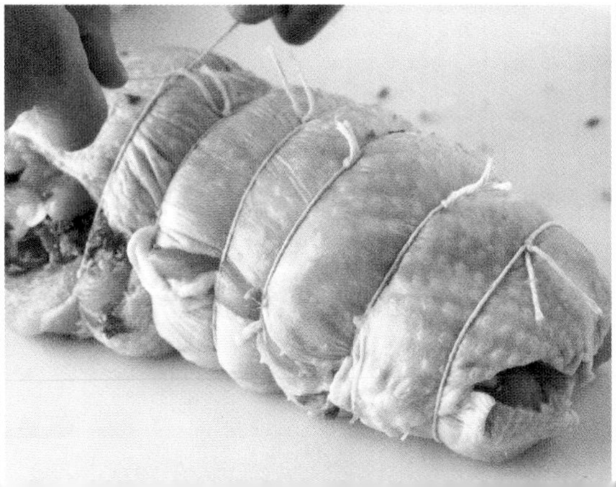

POMEGRANATE GLAZE, SPARKLY WITH TART-SWEET TASTE, BLANKETS TURKEY WITH MEDITERRANEAN FLAIR.

Pomegranate-Glazed Turkey Steaks

IF YOU ARE FORTUNATE ENOUGH TO HAVE A MIDDLE EASTERN MARKET IN YOUR NEIGHBORHOOD, CHANCES ARE THAT YOU WILL BE ABLE TO FIND BOTTLED POMEGRANATE MOLASSES.

PREP: 30 MINUTES **MARINATE:** 4 HOURS
COOK: 45 MINUTES **GRILL:** 12 MINUTES
MAKES: 4 SERVINGS

- 2 turkey breast tenderloins (1 to 1½ pounds)
- 1 cup Pomegranate Molasses
- ⅓ cup olive oil
- 1 tablespoon finely shredded orange peel
- ¼ cup orange juice
- 1 tablespoon fresh thyme leaves
- 1 tablespoon ground coriander
- 2 teaspoons ground cumin
- 2 cloves garlic, minced
- ½ teaspoon salt
- ¼ teaspoon cayenne pepper
- Hot cooked couscous (optional)
- Chopped fresh mint (optional)

1 Cut tenderloins in half horizontally to make 4 steaks. Place turkey steaks in a large resealable plastic bag set in a shallow dish. For marinade, in a small bowl stir together olive oil, orange peel, orange juice, thyme leaves, coriander, cumin, garlic, salt, and cayenne pepper. Stir in pomegranate molasses. Reserve ¾ cup marinade to make sauce; set aside. Pour remaining marinade over turkey in bag; seal bag. Turn to coat turkey. Marinate in the refrigerator for 4 hours to 24 hours.

2 Drain turkey steaks, discarding marinade. For a charcoal grill, grill turkey on the rack of an uncovered grill directly over medium coals for 12 to 15 minutes or until no longer pink (170°F), turning once halfway through grilling time. (For a gas grill, preheat grill. Reduce heat to medium. Place turkey on grill rack over heat. Cover and grill as directed.)

3 Meanwhile, in a small saucepan heat the reserved ¾ cup marinade just until boiling; keep warm.

4 Spoon sauce over turkey steaks. If desired, serve with couscous and fresh mint.

POMEGRANATE MOLASSES: In a medium saucepan bring 3 cups pomegranate juice to boiling; reduce heat. Simmer, uncovered, for 45 minutes or until reduced to 1 cup and slightly thickened.

PER STEAK: 407 cal., 19 g total fat (3 g sat. fat), 70 mg chol., 361 mg sodium, 29 g carbo., 1 g fiber, 28 g pro.

STEP-BY-STEP

1. For the Pomegranate Molasses, cook the juice so bubbles form slowly and burst before reaching the surface. Reduce heat if juice boils.

2. Place the orange peel, thyme, coriander, cumin, garlic, salt, and cayenne pepper in a bowl. Stir in the Pomegranate Molasses, olive oil, and orange juice.

3. Grill the turkey steaks until no longer pink and grill marks appear. Use tongs to flip the steaks to the second sides and grill until cooked through.

Plum-Delicious Bacon-Wrapped Turkey Tenderloins

EVERYTHING'S BETTER WITH BACON. THESE FRUITY GRILLED TENDERLOINS PROVE THE TRUTH OF THE PORK-LOVER'S MAXIM. PACKAGED PRECOOKED BACON SLICES MAKE PREPARATION A SNAP.

PREP: 20 MINUTES **GRILL:** 12 MINUTES
COOK: 10 MINUTES **MAKES:** 6 SERVINGS

- 1 teaspoon black pepper
- 1 teaspoon ground coriander
- 1 teaspoon ground cumin
- ½ teaspoon salt
- 3 turkey breast tenderloins (2 to 2½ pounds)
- 12 slices packaged ready-to-serve cooked bacon
- 3 medium plums, pitted and sliced
- ¼ cup plum jelly
- 1 tablespoon cider vinegar
- Grilled Asparagus (optional)

1 In a small bowl stir together pepper, coriander, cumin, and salt; sprinkle mixture evenly on both sides of turkey tenderloins. Cut each tenderloin crosswise into quarters to make 12 total pieces. Wrap each turkey piece with a slice of bacon and secure with a wooden toothpick.

2 For a charcoal grill, grill turkey on the rack of an uncovered grill directly over medium coals for 12 to 15 minutes or until turkey is no longer pink (170°F), turning once halfway through grilling. (For a gas grill, preheat grill. Reduce heat to medium. Place turkey on grill rack over heat. Cover and grill as directed.)

3 Meanwhile, in a medium saucepan stir together plum slices, jelly, and vinegar. Bring to boiling over medium heat, stirring frequently; reduce heat. Simmer, uncovered, for 4 to 6 minutes or until plums are tender. Serve over turkey pieces. If desired, serve with grilled asparagus.

PER 2 PIECES: 270 cal., 5 g total fat (2 g sat. fat), 104 mg chol., 453 mg sodium, 14 g carbo., 1 g fiber, 40 g pro.

GRILLED ASPARAGUS: For a charcoal grill, place asparagus spears on the rack of an uncovered grill directly over medium coals for 3 to 5 minutes or until asparagus is tender and starting to brown, turning once halfway through grilling. (For a gas grill, preheat grill. Reduce heat to medium. Place asparagus on grill rack over heat. Cover and grill as directed.)

STEP-BY-STEP

1. Sprinkle the whole tenderloins with the spice mixture. With your fingers, rub the mixture over the tenderloins.

2. Cut each tenderloin into four pieces for a total of twelve pieces.

3. Place turkey pieces, cut sides up, on the work surface. Wrap a bacon slice around a turkey piece. Use a wooden toothpick to secure the bacon in place.

4. Grill the turkey directly over medium coals. Use tongs to turn the turkey after the first 6 to 8 minutes of grilling.

5. Cut the plums in half around the pit. Twist the halves to separate. Pry out the pit with the tip of a knife. Cut the halves into slices.

6. Cook the plum slices with the jelly and vinegar until the plums are tender enough to pierce with a fork. Serve the plum sauce over the turkey.

A COVERED GRILL MIMICS THE FLAVOR-BOOSTING COOKERY OF INDIA'S CLAY TANDOOR OVENS QUITE WELL.

Turkey Tenderloin Tandoori

IN KEEPING WITH THE INDIAN THEME, SERVE THESE SPICE-ENHANCED TENDERLOINS WITH A SIMPLE SALAD OF RIPE TOMATOES, SLICED CUCUMBERS, AND RED ONIONS.

PREP: 15 MINUTES **GRILL:** 12 MINUTES
MAKES: 4 SERVINGS

- 2 turkey breast tenderloins (1 to 1½ pounds)
- 1½ teaspoons ground cumin
- 1½ teaspoons coriander seeds, crushed
- 1 teaspoon finely shredded lime peel
- ¾ teaspoon kosher salt
- ¾ teaspoon ground ginger
- ½ teaspoon crushed red pepper
- ½ cup plain low-fat yogurt
- 2 tablespoons lime juice
- Lime wedges (optional)

1 Cut each turkey tenderloin in half horizontally to make 4 steaks; set aside. For rub, in a small bowl stir together cumin, coriander seeds, lime peel, salt, ginger, and crushed red pepper. Set aside ½ teaspoon of the spice mixture for sauce. Sprinkle the remaining spice mixture evenly over turkey steaks; rub in with your fingers.

2 For a charcoal grill, grill turkey on the rack of an uncovered grill directly over medium coals for 12 to 15 minutes or until turkey is no longer pink (170°F), turning once halfway through grilling. (For a gas grill, preheat grill. Reduce heat to medium. Place turkey on grill rack over heat. Cover and grill as directed.)

3 Meanwhile, for sauce, in a small bowl stir together yogurt, lime juice, and the reserved ½ teaspoon spice mixture. Serve turkey with sauce and, if desired, lime wedges.

PER STEAK: 158 cal., 2 g total fat (1 g sat. fat), 70 mg chol., 439 mg sodium, 4 g carbo., 1 g fiber, 29 g pro.

STEP-BY-STEP

1. To crush the coriander seeds, use a mortar and pestle. Place the seeds in the mortar and press and twist the pestle over the seeds.

2. Sprinkle the rub over the turkey steaks. Rub it into the turkey with your fingers.

3. To extract juice from a halved lime, prick the fruit with a fork and squeeze it over a bowl. Pricking the fruit maximizes the juice that comes out of it.

Buffalo-Style Turkey Wraps

THIS RECIPE IS DESTINED FOR TAILGATING. MARINATE TURKEY THE NIGHT BEFORE, THEN PACK IT IN A COOLER ALONG WITH THE REST OF THE INGREDIENTS. LIGHT UP AND GET GRILLING.

PREP: 35 MINUTES **MARINATE:** 2 HOURS
GRILL: 12 MINUTES **MAKES:** 6 WRAPS

- 2 turkey breast tenderloins (1 to 1½ pounds)
- 3 tablespoons bottled hot pepper sauce
- 2 tablespoons vegetable oil
- 2 teaspoons paprika
- ¼ teaspoon salt
- ¼ teaspoon cayenne pepper
- 6 10-inch spinach-flavor flour tortillas
- 1½ cups thin carrot strips (3 medium)
- 1½ cups thinly bias-sliced celery (3 stalks)
- 3 cups shredded lettuce
- 1 recipe Blue Cheese Dressing

1 Cut each tenderloin in half horizontally to make 4 steaks. Place turkey steaks in a resealable plastic bag set in a shallow dish. For marinade, in a small bowl stir together hot pepper sauce, oil, paprika, salt, and cayenne pepper. Pour over turkey in bag; seal bag. Marinate in the refrigerator for 2 to 3 hours, turning bag occasionally.

2 Drain turkey steaks, discarding marinade. For a charcoal grill, place turkey on the rack of an uncovered grill directly over medium coals for 12 to 15 minutes or until turkey is no longer pink (170°F), turning once halfway through grilling time. Wrap tortillas tightly in foil. Place on grill rack with turkey steaks. Heat tortilla packet for 10 minutes, turning once. (For a gas grill, preheat grill. Reduce heat to medium. Place turkey and wrapped tortillas on grill rack over heat. Cover and grill as directed.)

3 Thinly slice turkey. Divide sliced turkey, carrots, celery, and lettuce among the warm tortillas. Spread Blue Cheese Dressing on tortillas. Roll up tortillas tightly; serve immediately.

BLUE CHEESE DRESSING: In a blender or food processor combine ½ cup dairy sour cream; ¼ cup mayonnaise; ¼ cup crumbled blue cheese; 1 tablespoon lemon juice; 1 clove garlic, cut up; and ⅛ teaspoon salt. Cover and blend or process until nearly smooth.

PER WRAP: 416 cal., 22 g total fat (6 g sat. fat), 60 mg chol., 591 mg sodium, 30 g carbo., 4 g fiber, 24 g pro.

STEP-BY-STEP

1. To make turkey steaks, place a tenderloin on a cutting board. Carefully cut the tenderloin horizontally in half.

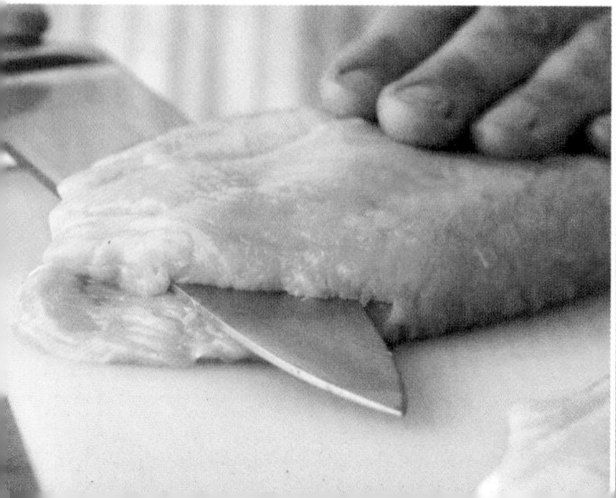

2. Place the turkey steaks in a large resealable plastic bag and add the marinade. Seal the bag. Turn the bag a few times to coat turkey and marinate in the refrigerator for 2 to 3 hours.

3. Place turkey steaks on the grill rack and grill until no longer pink. Turn the steaks only once about halfway through grilling.

4. Place the grilled turkey steaks on a cutting board. Cut crosswise into thin slices.

5. Unwrap the tortillas and place on work surface. Spread Blue Cheese Dressing down the center of a tortilla.

6. Arrange turkey, carrots, celery, and lettuce of the dressing. Fold one side of the tortilla over filling and roll up tightly. Place seam side down on a plate.

Fish & Shellfish

JUMP IN TO DISCOVER HEALTHFUL MEALS AND DEEP-WATER FLAVORS WHEN FISH AND SHELLFISH MEET YOUR GRILL.

Seafood Selection

NET YOURSELF SOME GRILLING PERFECTION WITH ANY ONE OF THESE GREAT CATCHES.

Unless you are fortunate enough to live near rivers, lakes, or the sea, fish and shellfish may represent a significant grilling investment.

To make the most of your seafood dollar, trust a reputable fishmonger and your nose. Fish and shellfish should be displayed on ice, never immersed in pooled water or wrapped in plastic. Ask to sniff selections before purchasing—they should smell briny and sweet as an ocean breeze, never off-putting or stale. Look for fish filets or steaks that appear fresh and moist, and for shrimp, scallops, and bivalves such as clams and mussels that have healthy, shiny flesh or shells.

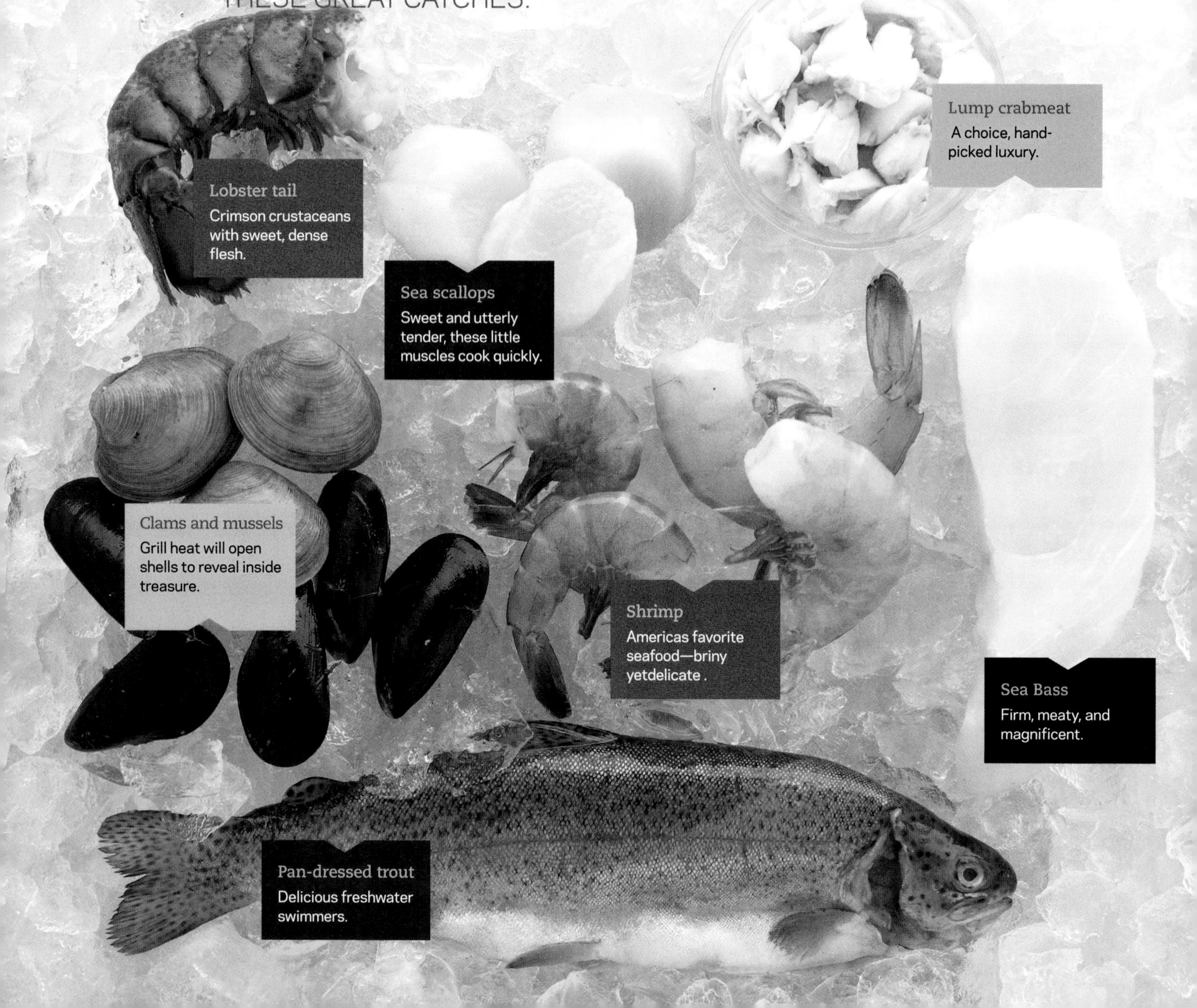

Red snapper
Tasty Gulf-coast favorite.
Halibut
A versatile and plentiful member of the flatfish family.
Catfish
This firm freshwater fish is usually farm-raised.
Cod
Lean and mild, one of the most versatile catches.
Salmon
Packed with flavor and health-enhancing Omega-3's.
Tuna
Distinctively rich-flavored and flaky.
Swordfish
Mild with steaklike texture.

Grilled Salmon Salad Niçoise

VIBRANT COLORS ANNOUNCE WHAT A LEAN AND WHOLLY NUTRITIOUS DINNER CHOICE THIS SALAD IS.

PREP: 20 MINUTES **COOK:** 21 MINUTES
GRILL: 8 MINUTES **MAKES:** 6 SERVINGS

- 6 5- to 6-ounce fresh or frozen salmon fillets
- 1 pound tiny new red or yellow potatoes (1½ to 2 inches)
- 8 ounces fresh haricots verts or green beans, stem ends trimmed
- ½ cup olive oil
- ⅓ cup white wine vinegar
- 3 tablespoons snipped fresh rosemary
- 1 tablespoon olive oil
- 3 cloves garlic, minced
- 1 teaspoon kosher salt
- ½ teaspoon lemon-pepper seasoning
- 6 cups torn mixed salad greens (5 ounces)
- 2 medium ripe tomatoes, cored and cut into thin wedges
- 2 medium red sweet peppers, seeded and cut into thin strips
- 3 hard-cooked eggs, peeled and quartered
- ⅔ cup pitted kalamata olives

1 Thaw fish, if frozen; set aside. In a Dutch oven cook potatoes in enough boiling water to cover for 18 minutes. Add haricots verts; return to boiling. Cook about 3 minutes more or until potatoes are tender and beans are crisp-tender. Drain; immediately plunge potatoes and beans in a large bowl of ice water to cool quickly. Using a slotted spoon, remove slightly cooled potatoes from ice water. Quarter the potatoes; place in a large bowl.

2 In a screw-top jar combine the ½ cup olive oil and vinegar. Cover and shake well. Add half the vinegar mixture to the potatoes; toss gently to coat. Set aside. Drain beans; set aside.

3 Meanwhile, in a small bowl combine rosemary, the 1 tablespoon olive oil, garlic, salt, and lemon-pepper seasoning. Rinse fish; pat dry with paper towels. Spread rosemary mixture on skinless sides of fillets.

4 For a charcoal grill, grill fish, skin sides down, on the greased rack of an uncovered grill directly over medium coals for 8 to 12 minutes or until fish begins to flake when tested with a fork. Do not turn during grilling. (For a gas grill, preheat grill. Reduce heat to medium. Place fish, skin sides down, on greased grill rack over heat. Cover and grill as directed.)

5 Add salad greens to the potato mixture; toss gently to coat. Arrange on a large platter. Top with beans, tomatoes, sweet peppers, eggs, and olives. Using a thin metal spatula, lift the salmon meat off the skin. Place salmon on salad. Drizzle with remaining vinegar mixture.

PER FILLET + 2 CUPS SALAD: 601 cal., 41 g total fat (7 g sat. fat), 190 mg chol., 649 mg sodium, 22 g carbo., 5 g fiber, 35 g pro.

STEP-BY-STEP

1. Test salmon for doneness at minimum grilling time. Insert a fork into the fish and gently twist. The fish is done as soon as it begins to flake.

2. Add the salad greens to the potato mixture. Toss gently to coat the greens with the vinegar mixture. Take care to avoid breaking up the potatoes.

3. Top the greens and potatoes with beans, tomatoes, peppers, eggs, and olives. With a metal spatula, lift the salmon meat from the skin and place on the salad.

Grilled Fish with Moroccan Vinaigrette

FULL FLAVOR FISH—SUCH AS TUNA OR GROUPER—MARRY WELL WITH ASSERTIVE HERBS AND SPICES SUCH AS CUMIN AND CILANTRO.

PREP: 20 MINUTES **GRILL:** 6 MINUTES
MAKES: 4 SERVINGS

- 1¼ to 1½ pounds fresh or frozen tuna fillet or four 5- to 6-ounce skinless red snapper, sea bass, or grouper fillets, ¾ inch thick
- 2 tablespoons olive oil
- ¼ teaspoon kosher salt or sea salt
- ¼ teaspoon black pepper
- ½ cup red wine vinegar
- 2 tablespoons snipped fresh Italian parsley
- 2 tablespoons snipped fresh cilantro
- 2 tablespoons olive oil
- 1 tablespoon fresh lemon juice
- 3 tablespoons finely chopped shallot (1 large)
- 1 clove garlic, minced
- ½ teaspoon kosher salt or sea salt
- ½ teaspoon paprika
- ¼ teaspoon cayenne pepper
- ¼ teaspoon ground cumin
- Hot cooked couscous
- Lemon wedges (optional)
- Mesclun (optional)
- Radish slivers (optional)

1 Thaw fish, if frozen. If using tuna, cut the fillet into ¾-inch steaks. Rinse fish; pat dry with paper towels. If necessary cut fish into 4 serving-size portions. Brush both sides of fish evenly with some of the 2 tablespoons olive oil. Sprinkle both sides of fish with the ¼ teaspoon salt and black pepper.

2 For Moroccan vinaigrette, in a screw-top jar combine vinegar, parsley, cilantro, the 2 tablespoons olive oil, lemon juice, shallot, garlic, the ½ teaspoon salt, paprika, cayenne pepper, and cumin. Cover and shake well. Set aside.

3 For a charcoal grill, grill fish on the greased rack of an uncovered grill directly over medium coals for 6 to 8 minutes or until fish begins to flake when tested with a fork, turning fish once and brushing with the remaining oil halfway through grilling. (For a gas grill, preheat grill. Reduce heat to medium. Place fish on greased grill rack over heat. Cover and grill as directed.)

4 To serve, shake vinaigrette. Using a wide spatula, transfer fish to plates with couscous. Drizzle vinaigrette over fish. If desired, garnish with lemon wedges, mesclun, and radish slivers.

PER SERVING: 261 cal., 15 g total fat (2 g sat. fat), 35 mg chol., 366 mg sodium, 3 g carbo., 0 g fiber, 29 g pro.

Mix It Up!

PICK ONE FROM EACH COLUMN TO CUSTOMIZE THE FISH TO YOUR TASTE.

SEASON IT

To the salt and pepper add one of the following:

- ½ teaspoon ground cumin
- ½ teaspoon Italian seasoning
- ½ teaspoon chili powder
- ½ teaspoon Jamaican jerk seasoning
- ½ teaspoon Chinese five-spice powder
- ½ teaspoon paprika
- ½ teaspoon ground coriander

MIX IT IN

Instead of the Moroccan vinaigrette, use one of the following:

- ¾ cup balsamic vinaigrette with 2 tablespoons chopped fresh basil
- ¾ cup Asian salad dressing with 2 tablespoons chopped fresh cilantro
- ¾ cup Greek vinaigrette with 2 teaspoons chopped fresh oregano

TOP IT

Instead of the couscous and radishes, serve with one of the following combinations:

- Orzo, toasted pine nuts
- Rice, quartered grape or cherry tomatoes
- Mashed potatoes, chopped fresh parsley
- Polenta, toasted chopped hazelnuts
- Angel hair pasta, chopped fresh basil

STEP-BY-STEP

1. To make tuna steaks, cut the tuna fillet into ¾-inch-slices.

2. Brush both sides of each piece of fish with olive oil. Sprinkle with salt and pepper.

3. Place the ingredients for the vinaigrette in a jar. Fasten the lid and shake until well mixed.

4. Let coals burn until they are coated with gray ash. Use long-handled tongs to arrange the coals in a single layer.

5. Turn the fish after 3 to 4 minutes. To turn the fish, gently slide a large wide spatula under the fish and gently turn to the other side.

Fish Tacos with Chipotle Cream

THESE FRESH AND PRETTY CALIFORNIA GIRLS—WEIGHING IN AT A MERE 293 CALORIES FOR TWO—WILL MAKE YOU THINK TWICE ABOUT TURNING IN FOR HEAVY FAST-FOOD TACOS AGAIN.

PREP: 25 MINUTES **GRILL:** 6 MINUTES
MAKES: 6 SERVINGS

- 4 4- to 5-ounce fresh or frozen skinless red snapper, tilapia, or sole fillets, ½ inch thick
- 1 tablespoon cooking oil
- 1 teaspoon ancho chile powder
- ½ teaspoon ground cumin
- ¼ teaspoon salt
- ¼ teaspoon black pepper
- ½ cup dairy sour cream
- 1 teaspoon finely chopped canned chipotle pepper in adobo sauce*
- 12 6-inch corn or flour tortillas
- 2 cups shredded cabbage or romaine lettuce
- 1 ripe avocado, halved, seeded, peeled, and cut into thin slices (optional)
- 1 cup refrigerated fresh salsa
- 1 lime, cut into wedges
- Snipped cilantro (optional)

1 Thaw fish, if frozen. Rinse fish; pat dry with paper towels. Brush oil evenly on both sides of fish. For rub, in a small bowl stir together chili powder, cumin, salt, and pepper. Sprinkle rub over both sides of fish; rub in with your fingers.

2 For chipotle cream, in another small bowl stir together sour cream and chopped chipotle pepper; set aside. Wrap tortillas tightly in foil.

3 For a charcoal grill, grill fish and tortilla packet on the greased rack of an uncovered grill directly over medium coals for 4 to 6 minutes or until fish begins to flake when tested with a fork and tortillas are heated through, turning fish and tortilla packet once halfway through grilling. (For a gas grill, preheat grill. Reduce heat to medium. Place fish and tortilla packet on greased grill rack over heat. Cover and grill as directed.)

4 Fill warm tortillas evenly with cabbage, fish, and avocado slices. Serve with fresh salsa, chipotle cream, lime wedges, and, if desired, cilantro.

***NOTE:** Because chile peppers contain volatile oils that can burn your skin and eyes, avoid direct contact with them as much as possible. When working with fresh chile peppers, wear plastic or rubber gloves. If your bare hands do touch the chiles, wash your hands and nails well with soap and hot water.

PER 2 TACOS: 293 cal., 9 g total fat (3 g sat. fat), 35 mg chol., 493 mg sodium, 34 g carbo., 4 g fiber, 19 g pro.

FISH TOSTADAS: Prepare as above, except substitute 6 tostada shells for the tortillas. Do not grill tostada shells. Break up fish with a fork. Top shells with cabbage, fish, avocado, salsa, chipotle cream, lime wedges, and, if desired, cilantro.

STEP-BY-STEP

1. Holding the avocado in your hands, gently twist the two halves in opposite directions to separate them.

2. To remove the seed, use a quick, firm motion to whack the blade of the knife into the seed; twist and pull the knife to remove the seed.

3. Insert a spoon between the skin and the flesh and slide the spoon beneath the bottom and sides of the avocado. Use the spoon to lift the fruit from the skin.

Grilled Halibut Sarandeado

THIS CHILE-INFUSED FISH FILLET IS PREPARED IN THE STYLE OF THE MEXICAN STATES OF SINALOA AND SONORA. THESE PACIFIC COAST LOCATIONS ARE KNOWN FOR THEIR EXPERTISE IN PREPARING SEAFOOD.

PREP: 15 MINUTES **MARINATE:** 30 MINUTES
GRILL: 8 MINUTES **MAKES:** 4 SERVINGS

- 4 6-ounce fresh or frozen halibut or grouper fillets, about 1 inch thick
- ½ cup freshly squeezed lemon juice
- 1 medium fresh serrano chile, chopped (see below)
- 1 tablespoon Worcestershire sauce
- ½ teaspoon coarse salt
- ½ teaspoon black pepper
- ¼ cup coarsely chopped cilantro
- Salt and black pepper
- 1 lemon, cut into wedges
- Grilled green onions (optional)

1 Thaw fish, if frozen. Rinse fish; pat dry with paper towels. Place fish in a large resealable plastic bag set in a shallow baking dish. In a blender combine lemon juice, chile, Worcestershire sauce, coarse salt, and the ½ teaspoon black pepper. Cover and blend until smooth. Pour over fish in bag; seal bag. Marinate in the refrigerator for 30 minutes, turning bag once. (Do not marinate longer than 30 minutes.)

2 Drain fish, reserving marinade. For a charcoal grill, grill fish on the greased rack of an uncovered grill directly over medium coals for 8 to 12 minutes or until fish begins to flake when tested with a fork, turning once and brushing with reserved marinade halfway through grilling. Discard remaining marinade. (For a gas grill, preheat grill. Reduce heat to medium. Place fish on greased grill rack over heat. Cover and grill as directed.)

3 Sprinkle fish with cilantro. Season to taste with salt and pepper. Serve with lemon wedges and, if desired, grilled green onions.

PER FILLET: 176 cal., 2 g total fat (0 g sat. fat), 63 mg chol., 481 mg sodium, 7 g carbo., 2 g fiber, 34 g pro.

STEP-BY-STEP

1. Always protect your hands with plastic gloves when working with chile peppers. Cut a pepper in half lengthwise.

2. Use the tip of the knife to scrape the seeds from the chile peppers. Cut away the membranes. Most of the heat is contained in the seeds and membranes.

3. Cut the pepper halves into thin lengthwise strips. Line up the strips side by side and cut them across into tiny pieces.

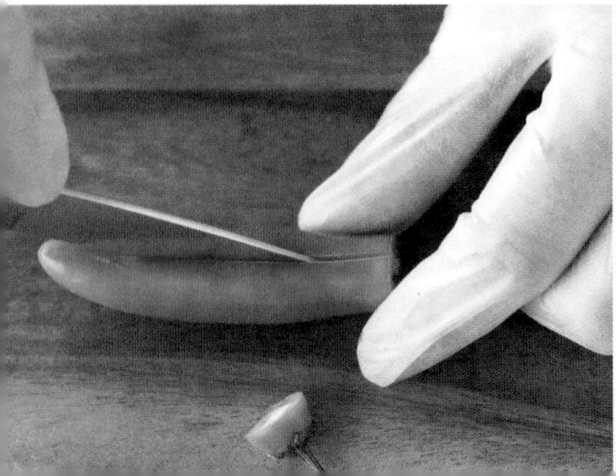

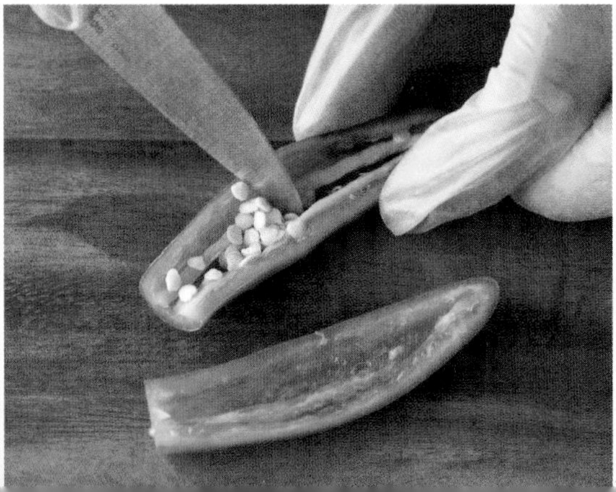

SIMPLE ACCOMPANIMENTS—SUCH AS A GREEN VEGETABLE AND RICE—ALLOW THE ZESTY FISH TO TAKE CENTER STAGE WHERE IT BELONGS.

STEP-BY-STEP

1. Grilling time depends on the thickness of the fish fillets. Measure the fish where it is the thickest.

2. For the stuffing, combine pecans, bread crumbs, softened butter, lemon peel, parsley, salt, black pepper, cayenne pepper, and garlic.

3. Stir the ingredients together. The mixture will be crumbly.

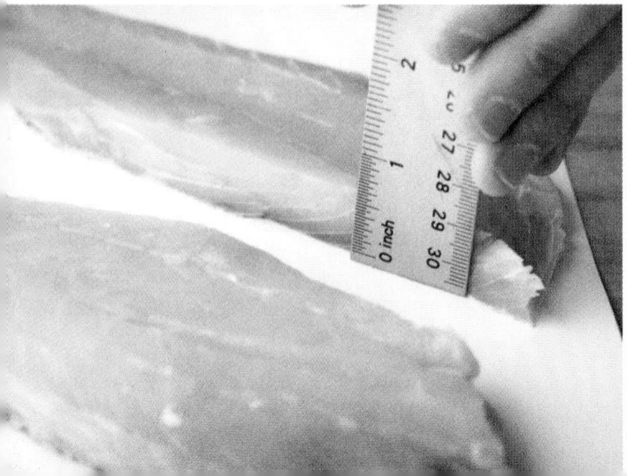

Red Snapper with Herb-Pecan Crust

ANYONE WHOSE ROOTS GROW DEEP IN GULF STATES SOIL—OR EVEN THOSE WHO WOULD LIKE TO PLANT THEMSELVES IN IT—WILL ADORE THE INDIGENOUS FLAVORS OF THIS FIRE-GRILLED FISH.

PREP: 15 MINUTES
GRILL: 4 TO 6 MINUTES PER ½-INCH THICKNESS
MAKES: 4 SERVINGS

- 4 5- to 6-ounce fresh or frozen red snapper fillets, ½ to 1 inch thick
- ⅓ cup finely chopped pecans
- 2 tablespoons fine dry bread crumbs
- 2 tablespoons butter, softened
- 1 teaspoon finely shredded lemon peel
- 1 tablespoon snipped fresh Italian parsley
- ¼ teaspoon salt
- ⅛ teaspoon black pepper
- Dash cayenne pepper
- 2 cloves garlic, minced
- Snipped fresh Italian parsley (optional)
- Lemon wedges (optional)

1 Thaw fish, if frozen. Rinse fish; pat dry with paper towels. Measure thickness of fish; set aside. In a small bowl combine pecans, bread crumbs, butter, lemon peel, the 1 tablespoon parsley, salt, black pepper, cayenne pepper, and garlic. Set aside.

2 For a charcoal grill, grill fish, skin sides down, on the greased rack of an uncovered grill directly over medium coals. Spoon the pecan mixture on fillets; spread slightly. Grill until fish begins to flake when tested with a fork. Allow 4 to 6 minutes per ½-inch thickness of fish. (For a gas grill, preheat grill. Reduce heat to medium. Place fish on greased grill rack over heat. Spoon pecan mixture on fillets. Cover and grill as directed.) If desired, sprinkle fish with additional snipped parsley and serve with lemon wedges.

PER FILLET: 268 cal., 14 g total fat (4 g sat. fat,), 67 mg chol., 287 mg sodium, 7 g carbo., 8 g fiber, 30 g pro.

4. Divide the stuffing among the fishfillets. Spread the stuffing over the fillets.

5. Let the coals burn until lightly covered with gray ash. Use long-handled tongs to arrange them in a single layer in the grill.

6. Check fish after the minimum grilling time. To test for doneness, insert fork into fish and twist. Fish is done as soon as it begins to flake.

Grilled Hazelnut Salmon with Watercress Salad

THE PEPPERY SNAP OF FRESH WATERCRESS IS A PERFECT FOIL FOR SALMON'S BUTTERY-RICH CHARACTER AND THE HAZELNUT'S SWEET CRUNCH.

PREP: 30 MINUTES **GRILL:** 14 MINUTES
MAKES: 4 SERVINGS

- 1 24-ounce fresh salmon fillet, about 1 inch thick, or four 6-ounce fresh or frozen skinless fillets, thawed if frozen
- 1 tablespoon hazelnut oil
- ⅓ cup finely ground hazelnuts
- 2 tablespoons all-purpose flour
- 1 teaspoon kosher salt
- ⅓ cup white balsamic vinegar
- ¼ cup hazelnut oil
- 2½ cups watercress
- 1 cup yellow or red tiny pear-shape or grape tomatoes, halved
- 2 ounces Brie cheese, cubed
- 3 tablespoons finely chopped chives

1 Rinse fish; pat dry with paper towels. To remove the skin, grasp the skin with a paper towl at the tail end of the fillet. Insert the blade of a large sharp knife between the fish and the skin. Keeping the blade between the fish and the skin and holding it at a slight downward angle, cut the fish away from the skin. Discard skin. Cut the fillet crosswise into 4 pieces.

2 Brush one side of fillets evenly with the 1 tablespoon hazelnut oil. In a 9-inch pie plate stir together ground hazelnuts, flour, and ½ teaspoon of the salt. Dip the brushed sides of the salmon in the nut mixture; coat well.

3 For a charcoal grill, arrange medium-hot coals around a drip pan. Test for medium heat above the pan. Place fish, coated sides up, on the greased grill rack over pan. Cover and grill for 14 to 18 minutes or until fish begins to flake when tested with a fork. (For a gas grill, preheat grill. Reduce heat to medium. Adjust for indirect cooking. Place fish, coated side up, on greased grill rack over the burner that is turned off. Grill as directed.)

4 Meanwhile, for dressing, in a small bowl combine vinegar and the remaining ½ teaspoon salt; whisk in the ¼ cup hazelnut oil. Reserve ¼ cup of the dressing; set aside. In a large bowl toss watercress, tomatoes, cheese, and chives with the remaining dressing. Divide evenly among serving plates. Add a salmon fillet to each plate. Drizzle salmon with reserved dressing.

PER FILLET + ¾ CUP SALAD: 663 cal., 51 g total fat (9 g sat. fat), 9 mg chol., 693 mg sodium, 10 g carbo., 2 g fiber, 41 g pro.

STEP-BY-STEP

1. Grasp the skin at the tail end of the fillet and insert the blade of a large sharp knife between the fish and the skin.

2. Keeping the blade between the fish and the skin and holding it at a slightly downward angle, cut the fish away from the skin. Throw the skin away.

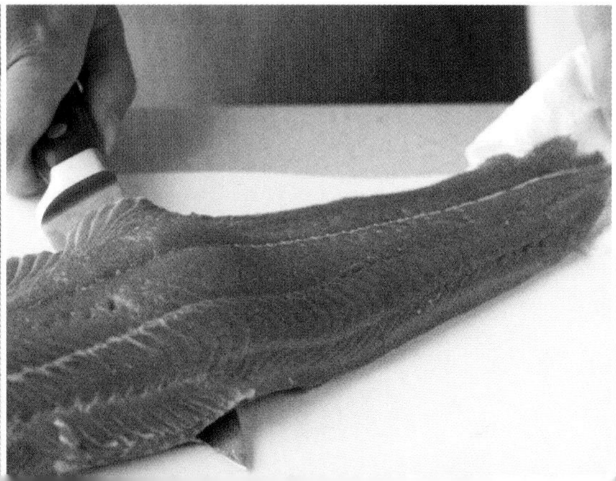

3. Cut the fillet crosswise into four pieces.

4. Brush the tops of the salmon pieces with the hazelnut oil. In addition to providing flavor, the oil helps the coating adhere to the fish.

5. Dip the oil-brushed sides into the nut mixture. Press firmly to hold the coating in place.

6. Check salmon after the minimum grilling time. To test for doneness, insert fork into fish and twist. Fish is done as soon as it begins to flake.

Thai Tuna Kabobs

IF USING FROZEN TUNA STEAKS, BE SURE TO PAT THEM DRY AFTER THAWING AND BEFORE IMMERSING TUNA PIECES IN THE MARINADE.

PREP: 30 MINUTES **MARINATE:** 2 HOURS
GRILL: 10 MINUTES **MAKES:** 4 SERVINGS

- 1 pound fresh or frozen tuna steaks, cut 1 inch thick
- ¼ cup snipped fresh cilantro
- 1 teaspoon finely shredded lemon peel or lime peel
- 3 tablespoons lemon juice or lime juice
- 3 tablespoons rice vinegar
- 1 to 2 fresh Thai, serrano, or jalapeño chile peppers, seeded and finely chopped*
- 1 teaspoon sesame seeds
- 1 teaspoon toasted sesame oil
- 2 medium zucchini, cut into 1-inch slices
- 1 medium red onion, cut into 8 wedges
- Lime wedges (optional)

1 Thaw fish, if frozen. If using wooden skewers, soak skewers in water for at least 30 minutes. Rinse fish; pat dry with paper towels. Cut fish into 1-inch pieces; set aside. For marinade, in a small bowl combine 2 tablespoons of the cilantro, the lemon peel, lemon juice, vinegar, chile pepper, sesame seeds, and oil; set aside.

2 On 8 skewers, alternately thread fish,** zucchini, and red onion, leaving ¼ inch between pieces. Place kabobs on a platter or in a shallow dish. Brush ¼ cup of the marinade over kabobs. Cover and marinate in the refrigerator for 2 to 4 hours. Cover and chill the remaining marinade.

3 For a charcoal grill, grill kabobs on the greased rack of an uncovered grill directly over medium coals for 10 to 12 minutes or until fish begins to flake when tested with a fork but is still slightly pink inside, turning occasionally during grilling. (For a gas grill, preheat grill. Reduce heat to medium. Place kabobs on greased grill rack over heat. Cover and grill as directed.)

4 Transfer kabobs to a serving platter. Sprinkle with the remaining 2 tablespoons cilantro. Serve the remaining chilled marinade as a sauce. If desired, garnish with lime wedges.

***NOTE:** Because chile peppers contain volatile oils that can burn skin and eyes, avoid direct contact with them as much as possible. When working with fresh chile peppers, wear plastic or rubber gloves. If your bare hands touch the chiles, wash your hands and nails well with soap and hot water.

****NOTE:** Thread tuna onto skewers perpendicular to the grain of the fish.

PER 2 KABOBS: 215 cal., 7 g total fat (2 g sat. fat), 43 mg chol., 58 mg sodium, 8 g carbo., 2 g fiber, 28 g pro.

STEP-BY-STEP

1. Thread tuna onto skewers perpendicular to the grain of the fish. Add an onion wedge and zucchini slice, leaving ¼ inch between pieces.

2. Measure ¼ cup of the marinade (chill remaining marinade). Place kabobs on a platter. Brush the tuna and vegetables with the ¼ cup marinade.

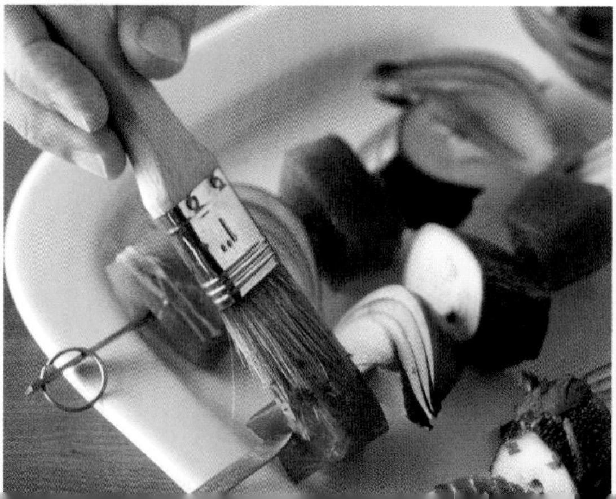

3. For even cooking, use long-handled tongs to turn the kabobs occasionally during grilling. Grill kabobs just until tuna begins to flake and the pieces are still slightly pink on the inside.

STEP-BY-STEP

1. To precook the asparagus, lay the spears in a skillet. If you need two layers, arrange the second layer of spears perpendicular to the first layer.

2. Place hearts of romaine on a cutting board. Cut crosswise into slices.

3. Let the coals burn until lightly covered with gray ash. Use long-handled tongs to arrange them in a single layer in the grill.

Salmon Caesar Salad

TO CREATE WIDE, WINSOME SHARDS OF PARMESAN CHEESE, ALLOW A WEDGE TO WARM SLIGHTLY AT ROOM TEMPERATURE. THEN SHAVE THE WEDGE WITH THE BLADE OF A SHARP VEGETABLE PEELER.

PREP: 25 MINUTES **GRILL:** 8 MINUTES
MAKES: 4 SERVINGS

- 1 pound fresh or frozen skinless salmon fillets, about 1 inch thick
- 1 tablespoon olive oil
- 1 teaspoon finely shredded lemon peel
- 1 tablespoon lemon juice
- ¼ teaspoon black pepper
- 1 pound fresh asparagus spears, trimmed
- 2 cups sliced hearts of romaine lettuce
- 2 cups torn curly endive
- ½ of a medium cucumber, thinly sliced
- ½ cup bottled Caesar salad dressing
- Finely shredded Parmesan cheese (optional)
- Thin slices baguette-style French bread, toasted (optional)

1 Thaw fish, if frozen. Rinse fish; pat dry with paper towels. In a small bowl stir together oil, lemon peel, lemon juice, and pepper. Brush both sides of fish with lemon mixture; set aside.

2 In a large skillet precook asparagus, covered, in a small amount of boiling water for 3 minutes; drain.

3 For a charcoal grill, grill fish on the greased rack of an uncovered grill directly over medium coals for 8 to 12 minutes or until fish begins to flake when tested with a fork, turning once halfway through grilling. Add asparagus to grill during the last 3 to 5 minutes of grilling or until asparagus browns, turning once halfway through grilling. (For a gas grill, preheat grill. Reduce heat to medium. Place fish, then asparagus on greased grill rack over heat. Cover and grill as directed.)

4 In a large bowl combine lettuce and endive. Divide evenly among serving plates. Top with cucumber slices. Using a fork, flake fish into bite-size pieces. Arrange fish and asparagus on lettuce mixture. Drizzle salads with dressing. If desired, sprinkle with cheese and serve with toasted baguette slices.

PER SERVING: 351 cal., 25 g total fat (4 g sat. fat), 59 mg chol., 418 mg sodium, 5 g carbo., 3 g fiber, 26 g pro.

4. Add the asparagus to the grill for the last 3 to 5 minutes of grilling. Place the spears perpendicular to the bars of the rack so they don't fall into the coals.

5. Use a fork to break the grilled salmon into bite-size pieces.

6. Line serving plates with the romaine and endive. Arrange cucumber slices and grilled asparagus on top. Divide salmon pieces among salads.

Mahi Mahi with Tropical Fruit Salsa

THIS WARM-WATER FISH IS BEST PREPARED SIMPLY—AS IT IS HERE—AND ACCOMPANIED BY EXOTIC FLAVORS OF TROPICAL FRUITS. COCONUT AND MACADAMIA NUTS BRING THE IDEA HOME.

PREP: 15 MINUTES **MARINATE:** 30 MINUTES
GRILL: 4 TO 6 MINUTES PER ½-INCH THICKNESS
MAKES: 4 SERVINGS

- 4 5- to 6-ounce fresh or frozen skinless mahi mahi or grouper fillets
- ½ cup reduced-sodium soy sauce
- 2 tablespoons honey
- 2 teaspoons toasted sesame oil or olive oil
- 1 teaspoon grated fresh ginger
- 1 cup peeled and chopped mango
- 1 cup chopped firm, ripe banana or sliced and quartered carambola (star fruit)
- ⅓ cup chopped macadamia nuts
- 2 tablespoons lime juice
- 2 tablespoons toasted coconut
- Lime wedges (optional)

1 Thaw fish, if frozen. Rinse fish; pat dry with paper towels. Measure thickness of fish. Place fish in a shallow dish. For marinade, in a small bowl stir together soy sauce, honey, oil, and ginger. Pour marinade over fish; turn to coat. Cover and marinate in the refrigerator for 30 minutes, turning fish once or twice.

2 Meanwhile, for salsa, in a medium bowl combine mango, banana, macadamia nuts, and lime juice. Cover and chill until ready to serve.

3 Drain fish, discarding marinade. Place fish in a greased grill basket, tucking under any thin edges.

4 For a charcoal grill, grill fish in basket on the rack of an uncovered grill directly over medium coals until fish begins to flake when tested with a fork, turning basket once halfway through grilling. Allow 4 to 6 minutes per ½-inch thickness of fish. (For a gas grill, preheat grill. Reduce heat to medium. Place fish in basket on grill rack over heat. Cover and grill as directed.)

5 Serve fish with salsa. Sprinkle each serving with toasted coconut. If desired, serve with lime wedges.

PER FILLET + ABOUT ½ CUP SALSA: 286 cal., 11 g total fat (3 g sat. fat), 103 mg chol., 368 mg sodium, 20 g carbo., 3 g fiber, 28 g pro.

STEP-BY-STEP

1. Halve the mango, cutting on either side of the pit. Score the flesh in each half in a checkerboard pattern up to, but not through, the skin.

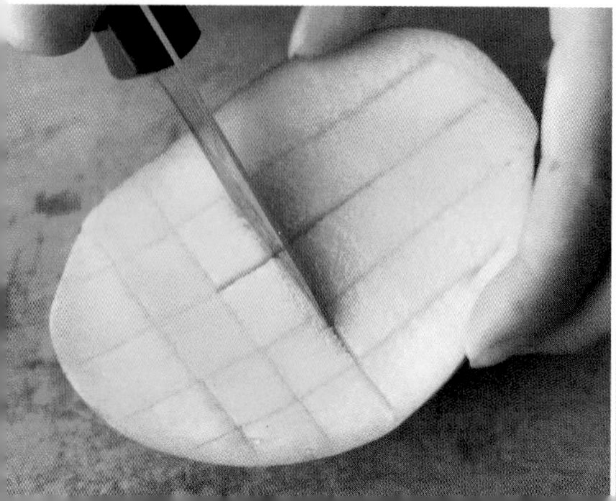

2. Invert the skin to push out the cubes of mango flesh.

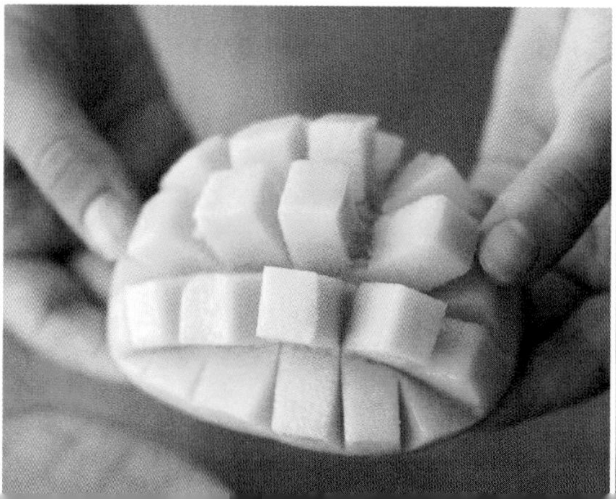

3. Cut the cubes of mango flesh from the skin with the paring knife.

4. To toast coconut, spread shredded coconut in a shallow pan. Bake in 350°F oven for 5 minutes, shaking pan once or twice. Watch closely to avoid burning it.

5. A fish basket keeps fish from sticking to the grill and makes turning the fillets a breeze. Grease the basket, place the fish in the basket, and bring the top down over the fish.

6. Place the fish in the basket on the grill rack. Halfway through grilling, turn the basket over and grill just until fish begins to flake with a fork.

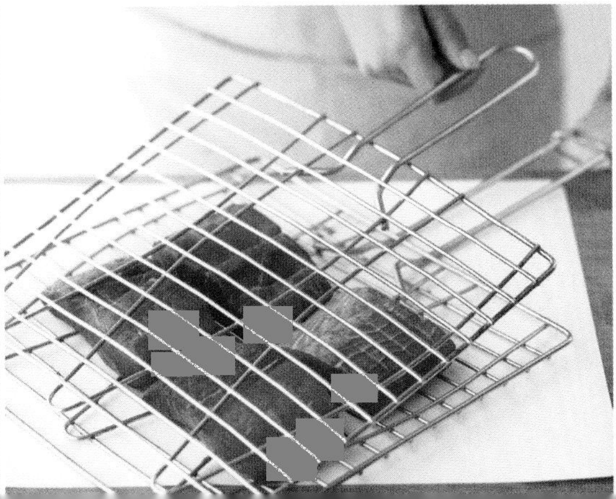

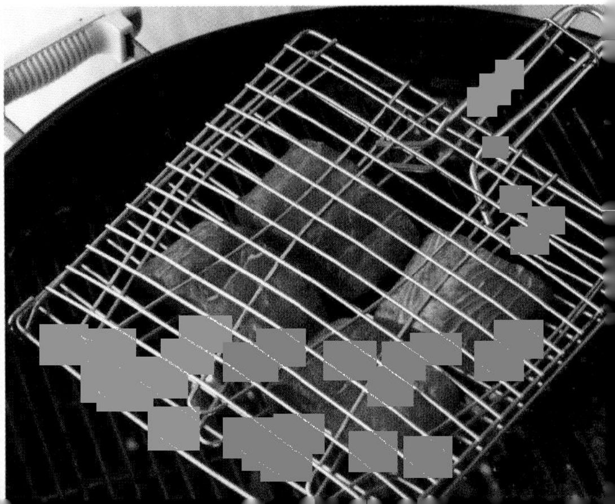

BLACKENED FISH IS A NEW ORLEANS TRADITION. BRING A TASTE OF "THE BIG EASY" TO YOUR GRILL ANY NIGHT OF THE WEEK.

Blackened Swordfish with Hominy Dirty Rice

THIS SPICY SOUTHERN BELLE GOES ALL THE WAY WITH CAJUN FLAVOR AND A BAYOU BENT.

PREP: 30 MINUTES **COOK:** 15 MINUTES
GRILL: 8 MINUTES **MAKES:** 4 SERVINGS

- 4 4- to 5-ounce fresh or frozen swordfish or tuna steaks, cut 1 inch thick
- 1 recipe Hominy Dirty Rice
- 4 cloves garlic, minced
- 1 teaspoon black pepper
- 1 teaspoon paprika
- ½ teaspoon cayenne pepper
- ½ teaspoon ground white pepper
- ½ teaspoon dried thyme, crushed
- ½ teaspoon salt
- 3 tablespoons butter, melted

1 Thaw fish, if frozen. Rinse fish; pat dry with paper towels. Prepare Hominy Dirty Rice. In a small bowl stir together garlic, black pepper, paprika, cayenne pepper, white pepper, thyme, and salt. Stir in melted butter. Brush both sides of fish with melted butter mixture.

2 For a charcoal grill, grill fish on the greased rack of an uncovered grill directly over medium coals for 8 to 12 minutes or until fish begins to flake when tested with a fork, turning once halfway through grilling. (For a gas grill, preheat grill. Reduce heat to medium. Place fish on greased grill rack over heat. Cover and grill as directed.) Serve with Hominy Dirty Rice.

HOMINY DIRTY RICE: In a large skillet cook 8 ounces bulk pork sausage, ¼ cup finely chopped onion, 3 tablespoons finely chopped celery, 3 tablespoons finely chopped green sweet pepper, 3 tablespoons finely chopped red sweet pepper, and 2 tablespoons minced garlic over medium heat for 4 to 5 minutes or until sausage is no longer pink and vegetables are tender. Drain off fat, if necessary. Stir in 1½ cups chilled cooked white rice, ⅔ cup chicken broth, ⅓ cup hominy, ¼ teaspoon black pepper, and ⅛ to ¼ teaspoon cayenne pepper. Bring to boiling; reduce heat. Simmer, uncovered, about 5 minutes or until rice is heated through and most of the liquid has been absorbed, stirring occasionally.

PER STEAK + ¾ CUP RICE: 504 cal., 27 g total fat (12 g sat. fat), 106 mg chol., 1,001 mg sodium, 26 g carbo., 2 g fiber, 34 g pro.

STEP-BY-STEP

1. Place fish steaks on a platter. Brush the melted butter and pepper mixture over both sides of the steaks.

2. Grill the fish just until it begins to flake with a fork. Check the fish at the minimum grilling time because fish can quickly overcook. Use a large metal spatula to remove fish from the grill.

3. Cook the rice mixture until all of the liquid is absorbed by the rice and hominy. Check the bottom of the skillet for any free liquid.

Trout with Mushroom Stuffing

PRISTINE-FRESH, RUSTIC, AND WILD, A DINNER LIKE THIS WILL BRING OUT YOUR INNER FLY FISHERMAN.

PREP: 25 MINUTES **SOAK:** 1 HOUR
COOK: 8 MINUTES **GRILL:** 20 MINUTES
MAKES: 4 SERVINGS

- 4 10- to 12-ounce fresh or frozen pan-dressed trout
- 4 slices bacon, chopped
- 2 cups sliced assorted wild mushrooms (such as cremini, shiitake, chanterelle, oyster, porcini, and/or cepes)
- 3 tablespoons butter, melted
- ½ teaspoon salt
- ½ teaspoon coarsely ground black pepper
- 3 large cloves garlic, thinly sliced
- 8 sprigs fresh thyme
- ¼ cup dry white wine
- 1 cup apple or alder wood chips or chunks*
- 1 recipe Grilled Apple Slices (optional)

1 Thaw trout, if frozen. Rinse trout; pat dry with paper towels. Set aside. For stuffing, in a large skillet cook bacon over medium heat for 3 to 4 minutes or until softened and beginning to brown. Add mushrooms; cook for 5 to 8 minutes or until mushrooms are tender and most of the liquid has evaporated, stirring occasionally. Set aside.

2 Brush the outside and inside of each trout with melted butter. Sprinkle inside of trout with salt, pepper, and garlic slices. Place 2 thyme sprigs in cavity of each trout. Divide stuffing among cavities of each trout. Sprinkle each with 1 tablespoon wine. Secure stuffing in trout with 4 or 5 short metal skewers or toothpicks. Place trout on a sheet of heavy-duty foil.

3 For a charcoal grill, arrange medium-hot coals around a drip pan. Sprinkle the wood chips over the coals. Test for medium heat above the pan. Place foil with fish on grill rack over pan. Cover and grill for 20 to 25 minutes or until trout begins to flake when tested with a fork. (For a gas grill, preheat grill. Reduce heat to medium. Add wood chips according to manufacturer's directions. Adjust for indirect cooking. Place foil with fish on grill rack over the burner that is turned off. Grill as directed.)

4 If desired, serve trout with Grilled Apple Slices.

***NOTE:** For the most smoke production, soak wood chips in enough water to cover for at least 1 hour before grilling. Drain wood chips before using.

PER TROUT: 544 cal., 29 g total fat (12 g sat. fat), 198 mg chol., 614 mg sodium, 3 g carbo., 1 g fiber, 63 g pro.

GRILLED APPLE SLICES: Remove the core from 2 apples. Cut apples crosswise into ½-inch slices; brush with olive oil. Grill apple slices directly over medium heat for 5 to 6 minutes or until apples are tender, turning once. Serve warm with fish.

STEP-BY-STEP

1. Place the wood chips in a large bowl and add enough water to cover. If using wooden skewers, soak them at the same time.

2. Brush outside of trout with melted butter and place on sides on work surface. Lift one side of the trout to expose the cavity. Brush insides of trout with melted butter.

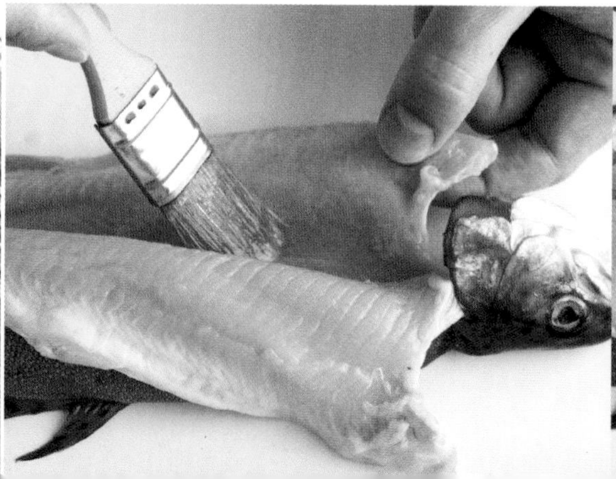

3. Divide the stuffing among the trou,t spreading it to fill the length of the cavities.

4. Place twp sprigs of thyme in each trout.

5. Fold the trout over the stuffing. Insert the toothpicks through both sides of the trout, securing the stuffing inside the fish.

6. If you like, grill the fish on foil pans. To make a foil pan, fold a large piece of heavy foil in half and build up the sides. Place trout on pans and place on grill.

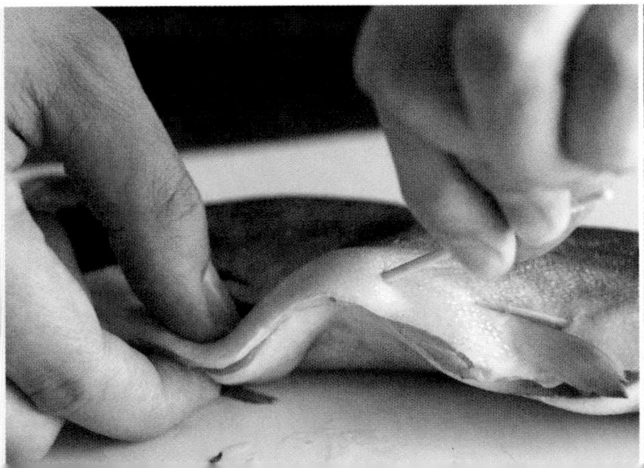

STEP-BY-STEP

1. To chop the pepper, cut it in half from top to bottom. Cut away the membranes and seeds. Cut into strips and then cut the strips into pieces.

2. To peel tomatoes, cut an X in the tomato bottom. Plunge the tomato into boiling water for 30 seconds to loosen the skin. Using a paring knife, peel the skin away from the fruit.

3. When the peppers are tender and tomatoes are soft, spoon the mixture into a blender and blend until smooth. Return the mixture to the skillet and keep warm while grilling fish.

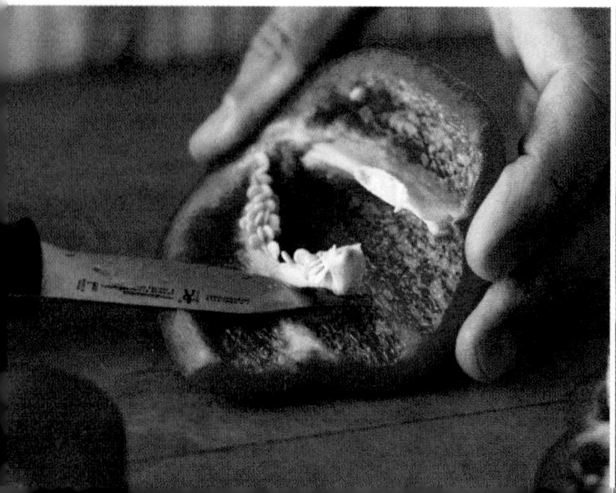

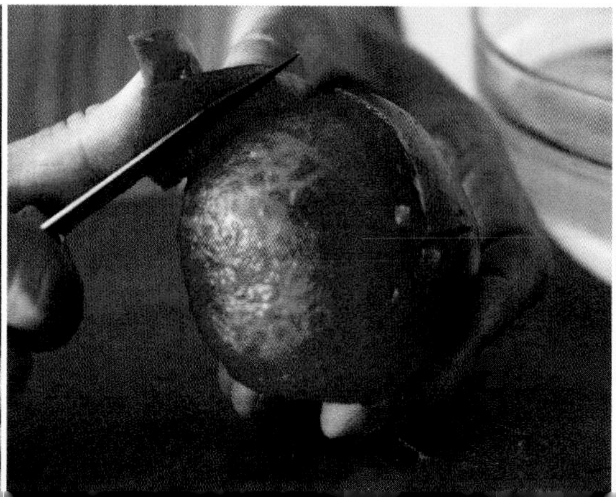

Grilled Cod with Red Pepper Sauce

ALTHOUGH COD IS MOST OFTEN PAN-FRIED, ITS MOIST, DENSE, AND FLAKY WHITE FLESH MAKES IT AN INCREDIBLE CANDIDATE FOR GRILLING GOODNESS.

PREP: 30 MINUTES
GRILL: 4 TO 6 MINUTES PER ½-INCH THICKNESS
MAKES: 4 SERVINGS

- 4 4- to 6-ounce fresh or frozen skinless cod fillets
- 1¼ cups chopped red sweet pepper (1 large)
- 1 tablespoon olive oil
- 1 cup peeled, seeded, and chopped tomatoes (2 medium)
- 2 tablespoons white wine vinegar
- ¼ teaspoon salt
- Dash cayenne pepper
- 1 tablespoon olive oil
- 1 tablespoon snipped fresh basil or oregano or ½ teaspoon dried basil or oregano, crushed
- Red and/or yellow cherry tomatoes (optional)
- Fresh basil or oregano sprigs (optional)

1 Thaw fish, if frozen. Rinse fish; pat dry with paper towels. Measure thickness of fish; set aside.

2 For sauce, in a small skillet cook sweet pepper in 1 tablespoon hot oil over medium heat for 3 to 5 minutes or until tender, stirring occasionally. Stir in chopped tomatoes, 1 tablespoon of the vinegar, the salt, and cayenne pepper. Cook about 5 minutes or until tomatoes are softened, stirring occasionally. Cool slightly. Transfer mixture to a blender or food processor. Cover and blend until smooth. Return sauce to skillet; cover and keep warm.

3 In a small bowl stir together the remaining 1 tablespoon vinegar, 1 tablespoon oil, and snipped fresh or dried basil; brush over both sides of fish. Place fish in a greased grill basket, tucking under any thin edges.

4 For a charcoal grill, grill fish in basket on the rack of an uncovered grill directly over medium coals until fish begins to flake when tested with a fork, turning basket once halfway through grilling. Allow 4 to 6 minutes per ½-inch thickness of fish. (For a gas grill, preheat grill. Reduce heat to medium. Place fish in basket on grill rack over heat. Cover and grill as directed.)

5 Serve fish with sauce. If desired, garnish with cherry tomatoes and fresh basil sprigs.

PER FILLET + ABOUT ⅓ CUP SAUCE: 194 cal., 8 g total fat (1 g sat. fat), 41 mg chol., 223 mg sodium, 4 g carbo., 1 g fiber, 26 g pro.

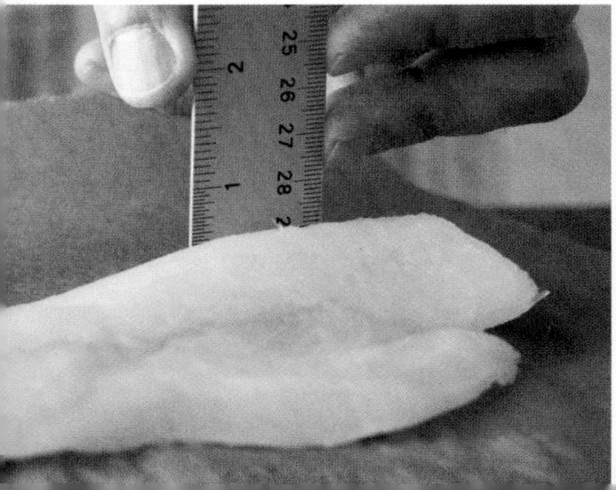

4. Grilling time depends on the thickness of the fish fillets. Measure the fish where it is the thickest.

5. Let the coals burn until lightly covered with gray ash. Use long-handled tongs to arrange them in a single layer in the grill.

6. Place the fish in a greased grill basket and grill until fish begins to flake. The grill basket prevents the fish from sticking to the grill rack and keeps the fish from breaking.

STEP-BY-STEP

1. For finely shredded lime peel, rub a zester over the lime, making sure to remove only the green part. Avoid the bitter white portions.

2. To rinse the beans, empty the can into a colander, letting the liquid drain through. Rinse the beans thoroughy under cold running water. Drain again.

3. Divide the cilantro mixture in half. Pour one half over the beans, avocado, and tomato in a bowl.

Catfish with Black Bean and Avocado Relish

FIRM AND MILD, THE FLAKY FLESH OF CHANNEL CATFISH PAIRS PERFECTLY WITH ZESTY LIME, PUNGENT CILANTRO, AND "NATURE'S BUTTER," THE AVOCADO.

PREP: 20 MINUTES **GRILL:** 4 MINUTES
MAKES: 6 SERVINGS

- 6 4- to 5-ounce fresh or frozen catfish fillets, about ½ inch thick
- 1 teaspoon finely shredded lime peel
- 3 tablespoons lime juice
- 2 tablespoons snipped fresh cilantro
- 2 tablespoons snipped fresh oregano
- 2 tablespoons finely chopped green onion (1)
- 1 tablespoon olive oil
- ¼ teaspoon salt
- ¼ teaspoon cayenne pepper
- 1 15-ounce can black beans, rinsed and drained
- 1 medium avocado, halved, seeded, peeled, and diced
- ½ cup chopped tomato (1 medium)
- Lime wedges

1 Thaw fish, if frozen. Rinse fish; pat dry with paper towels. Set aside.

2 For relish, in a small bowl stir together lime peel, lime juice, cilantro, oregano, green onion, olive oil, salt, and cayenne pepper. In a medium bowl combine beans, avocado, and tomato; stir in half the cilantro mixture. Cover and chill until serving time.

3 For a charcoal grill, grill fish on the greased rack of an uncovered grill directly over medium coals for 4 to 6 minutes or until fish begins to flake when tested with a fork, turning and brushing once with remaining cilantro mixture halfway through grilling. Discard any remaining cilantro mixture. (For a gas grill, preheat grill. Reduce heat to medium. Place fish on the ungreased rack over heat. Grill covered as directed.)

4 Serve catfish with relish and lime wedges.

PER FILLET + ½ CUP RELISH: 273 cal., 15 g total fat (3 g sat. fat), 53 mg chol., 337 mg sodium, 14 g carbo., 6 g fiber, 23 g pro.

4. Gently stir all the ingredients together to mix. Cover the bowl with plastic wrap and chill while grilling the fish.

5. Use a large metal spatula to turn the fish after 2 to 3 minutes of grilling.

6. Brush the fish with the cilantro mixture set aside. Grill for 2 to 3 minutes more or until fish just begins to flake when tested with a fork.

Planked Salmon with Cucumber-Dill Sauce

GRILLING SALMON ON CEDAR IS A TRADITION IN THE PACIFIC NORTHWEST. AS THE FISH COOKS ON THE SMOLDERING WOOD PLANK, IT IS ENHANCED BY SWEET CEDAR SMOKE AND BECOMES INCREDIBLY MOIST.

PREP: 10 MINUTES **MARINATE:** 8 HOURS
GRILL: 18 MINUTES **MAKES:** 4 TO 6 SERVINGS

- 1 1½-pound fresh or frozen salmon fillet, 1 inch thick
- 1 tablespoon brown sugar
- 1 teaspoon salt
- ¼ teaspoon black pepper
- 1 cedar grill plank
- 1 recipe Cucumber-Dill Sauce

1 Thaw fish, if frozen. Rinse fish; pat dry with paper towels. Place fish, skin side down, in a shallow dish. For rub, in a small bowl stir together brown sugar, salt, and pepper. Sprinkle rub evenly over salmon; rub in with your fingers. Cover and marinate in the refrigerator for 8 to 24 hours.

2 Place the cedar grill plank in a container of water; weight down the plank and soak it for at least 1 hour.

3 For a charcoal grill, arrange medium-hot coals around edge of grill. Place fish, skin side down, on cedar grill plank. Place plank in center of grill rack. Cover and grill for 18 to 22 minutes or until fish begins to flake when tested with a fork. (For a gas grill, preheat grill. Reduce heat to medium. Adjust heat for indirect cooking. Place plank on grill rack over the burner that is turned off. Grill as directed.)

4 To serve, cut salmon into 4 or 6 pieces. Slide a spatula between the fish and skin to release pieces from plank. Serve with Cucumber-Dill Sauce.

CUCUMBER-DILL SAUCE: In a small bowl stir together ⅓ cup finely chopped cucumber, 3 tablespoons plain yogurt, 2 tablespoons mayonnaise, 2 teaspoons snipped fresh dill, and 2 teaspoons prepared horseradish. Cover and chill until serving time or up to 4 hours.

PER FILLET + ABOUT 2 TABLESPOONS SAUCE: 314 cal., 17 g total fat (4 g sat. fat), 96 mg chol., 757 mg sodium, 5 g carbo., 0 g fiber, 35 g pro.

Port-Glazed Salmon with Basil-Peach Relish

MARINATING SALMON IN ROSY-HUED PORT IMBUES THE FISH WITH AN EVEN MORE BEAUTIFUL CRIMSON COLOR—AND GRACES IT WITH A MOST WONDERFUL, INTRIGUING TASTE.

PREP: 30 MINUTES **GRILL:** 8 MINUTES
MAKES: 4 SERVINGS

- 4 6-ounce fresh or frozen skinless salmon fillets, about 1 inch thick
- 1 cup port wine or pomegranate juice
- 2 tablespoons honey
- 2 tablespoons lemon juice
- 2 tablespoons olive oil
- 3 cups chopped peeled peaches (3 large)
- ⅓ cup chopped fresh basil
- Small basil leaves (optional)

1 Thaw fish, if frozen. Rinse fish; pat dry with paper towels. Set aside. In a small saucepan bring port to boiling; reduce heat. Simmer, uncovered, for 15 to 20 minutes or until reduced to ¼ cup; set aside.

2 For relish, in a medium bowl stir together honey, lemon juice, and olive oil. Add peaches and chopped basil; toss gently to combine. Set aside.

3 For a charcoal grill, grill salmon on the greased rack of an uncovered grill directly over medium coals for 8 to 12 minutes or until fish begins to flake when tested with a fork, turning once halfway through grilling and brushing fish with port glaze frequently during the last 5 minutes. (For a gas grill, preheat grill. Reduce heat to medium. Place fish on greased grill rack over heat. Cover and grill as directed.)

4 Serve salmon with relish. If desired, garnish with small basil leaves.

PER FILLET + ABOUT ¾ CUP RELISH: 559 cal., 26 g total fat (5 g sat. fat), 100 mg chol., 104 mg sodium, 32 g carbo., 2 g fiber, 36 g pro.

PREPARING PLANKED SALMON WITH CUCUMBER-DILL SAUCE, STEP-BY-STEP

1. Sprinkle the salmon with the rub and, using your fingers, rub it evenly over the salmon. Cover and refrigerate for at least 8 hours.

2. Soak the grill plank in water for at least 1 hour before placing it on the grill. You'll need to weight it down so it doesn't float.

3. Place the fish, skin side down, on the cedar grill plank. Carefully place the plank in the center of the grill.

Zucchini Crab Cakes

THESE INCREDIBLE CAKES MAY BE SHAPED SEVERAL HOURS BEFORE GRILLING. SIMPLY PLACE THE PATTIES ON A BAKING SHEET LINED WITH PARCHMENT OR WAXED PAPER. COVER WITH PLASTIC WRAP AND PLACE ON THE COLDEST SHELF IN YOUR FRIDGE.

PREP: 20 MINUTES **GRILL:** 8 MINUTES
MAKES: 8 CRAB CAKES

- 1 cup coarsely shredded zucchini (1 medium)
- ¼ cup thinly sliced green onions (2)
- 2 teaspoons vegetable oil
- 1 egg, beaten
- ⅓ cup seasoned fine dry bread crumbs
- 1 tablespoon Dijon-style mustard
- 1 teaspoon snipped fresh thyme or ½ teaspoon dried thyme, crushed
- ⅛ to ¼ teaspoon cayenne pepper
- 1 cup fresh lump crabmeat or one 6-ounce can crabmeat, drained, flaked, and cartilage removed
- 2 large red and/or yellow tomatoes, sliced ¼ inch thick
- 1 recipe Tomato Sour Cream Sauce
- Lemon and/or lime wedges (optional)

1 In a medium skillet cook zucchini and green onions in hot oil over medium-high heat for 3 to 5 minutes or until just tender and liquid is evaporated. Cool slightly.

2 In a large bowl combine egg, bread crumbs, mustard, thyme, and cayenne pepper. Add crabmeat and the zucchini mixture; mix well. Using about ¼ cup mixture per crab cake, shape into eight ½-inch-thick patties.

3 For a charcoal grill, grill crab cakes on the greased rack of an uncovered grill directly over medium coals for 8 to 10 minutes or until golden, turning once halfway through grilling. (For a gas grill, preheat grill. Reduce heat to medium. Place crab cakes on greased grill rack over heat. Cover and grill as directed.)

4 To serve, arrange tomato slices and crab cakes on plates. Serve with Tomato-Sour Cream Sauce and, if desired, lemon wedges.

TOMATO-SOUR CREAM SAUCE: In a small bowl stir together ½ cup dairy sour cream, ¼ cup finely chopped, seeded yellow or red tomato, 1 tablespoon lemon or lime juice, and ⅛ teaspoon seasoned salt. Cover and chill until serving time.

PER 2 CRAB CAKES + 3 TABLESPOONS SAUCE: 243 cal., 10 g total fat (4 g sat. fat), 120 mg chol., 835 mg sodium, 20 g carbo., 1 g fiber, 18 g pro.

STEP-BY-STEP

1. Lump crabmeat consists of large pieces of meat and some smaller pieces. Check the crabmeat for any cartilage.

2. Break up the crabmeat with your fingers and add it to the bread crumb mixture. Stir to mix well.

3. For each crab cake, measure about ¼ cup of the mixture and place on work surface. Use your fingers to flattern the crab mixture into a round patty about ½ inch thick.

GROUND ANCHO CHILES AND SMOKED PAPRIKA DUST SCALLOPS WITH A COPPERY PATINA—AND LAYERS OF RICH FLAVOR.

Scallops with Garlicky Tomatillo Salsa

NO NEED TO WRESTLE WITH PAPERY WRAPS AND STICKY SKINS OF FRESH TOMATILLOS. THIS SUPER-SIMPLE, SENSATIONAL SALSA TAKES ADVANTAGE OF THE CONVENIENT CANNED VERSION.

PREP: 35 MINUTES **GRILL:** 2 MINUTES
CHILL: 30 MINUTES **MAKES:** 4 SERVINGS

- 16 fresh or frozen sea scallops (1½ to 2 pounds total)
- 1 tablespoon olive oil
- ½ teaspoon ground ancho chile pepper
- ½ teaspoon smoked paprika
- 1 11- to 12-ounce can tomatillos, rinsed and drained
- ⅓ cup coarsely chopped red onion
- ⅓ cup lightly packed fresh cilantro
- 1 small fresh jalapeño chile pepper, seeded and cut up*
- 1 tablespoon lime juice
- 4 large cloves garlic, halved
- ¾ teaspoon ground cumin
- ¼ teaspoon salt
- 1 cup crumbled queso fresco (4 ounces)

1 If using wooden skewers, soak skewers in water for at least 30 minutes. Thaw scallops, if frozen. Rinse scallops; pat dry with paper towels. Thread 4 scallops onto two 10-inch skewers** that are parallel to each other, leaving ¼ inch between each scallop. Repeat with the remaining scallops and skewers to get 4 sets of kabobs; place on a tray. Brush scallops with olive oil and sprinkle evenly with ancho chile pepper and smoked paprika. Cover and chill for 30 minutes.

2 Meanwhile, for salsa, in a food processor or blender combine tomatillos, onion, cilantro, jalapeño pepper, lime juice, garlic, cumin, and salt. Cover and process until the consistency of a chunky sauce. Set aside.

3 For a charcoal grill, grill scallops on the rack of an uncovered grill directly over medium-hot coals for 2 to 3 minutes or until scallops are opaque, turning once halfway through grilling. (For a gas grill, preheat grill. Reduce heat to medium-high. Place scallops on grill rack over heat. Cover and grill as directed.)

4 To serve, spoon salsa into dipping bowls. Sprinkle kabobs with cheese.

***NOTE:** Because chile peppers contain volatile oils that can burn skin and eyes, avoid direct contact with them as much as possible. When working with fresh chile peppers, wear plastic or rubber gloves. If your bare hands touch the chiles, wash your hands and nails well with soap and hot water.

****NOTE:** Threading the scallops onto 2 skewers helps keep them from rotating and falling off the skewers when grilled.

PER KABOB: 303 cal., 8 g total fat (2 g sat. fat), 100 mg chol., 1,228 mg sodium, 11 g carbo., 2 g fiber, 43 g pro.

STEP-BY-STEP

1. Hold two skewers in one hand and thread four scallops, flat sides up, onto the skewers. Using two skewers stabilizes the scallops for grilling.

2. Brush the scallops on both sides with olive oil. Sprinkle with ancho chile pepper and smoked paprika. The oil will help the spices adhere to the scallops.

3. Scallops cook quickly, so watch them carefully when grilling. Use tongs to turn the skewers after 1 to 2 minutes. Scallops turn opaque when done.

Grilled Paella

IN SPAIN, PAELLA—THE COUNTRY'S CULINARY TREASURE—IS OFTEN COOKED OVER LIVE FIRE. TO SERVE IN TRADITIONAL STYLE, PLACE THE RICE, SAUSAGE, AND SEAFOOD-PACKED PAN IN THE MIDDLE OF THE DINNER TABLE AND LET DINERS DIG IN.

PREP: 45 MINUTES **GRILL:** 40 MINUTES
STAND: 10 MINUTES **MAKES:** 10 SERVINGS

- 1 pound mussels or clams
- 1 cup coarse salt
- 6 bone-in chicken thighs
- Salt and black pepper
- 2 tablespoons vegetable oil
- 4 ounces cooked smoked chorizo sausage, sliced, or kielbasa, sliced
- 2 slices thick-sliced bacon, chopped
- 8 ounces boneless pork loin, cut in 1-inch pieces
- ¾ cup chopped green sweet pepper (1 medium)
- ½ cup chopped onion (1 medium)
- 3 cloves garlic, thinly sliced
- 2 cups uncooked short grain rice
- 5 cups chicken broth
- 1⅓ cups chopped roma tomatoes (4 medium)
- Pinch saffron threads or 1 teaspoon ground turmeric
- 1 teaspoon smoked paprika
- ½ teaspoon salt
- ¼ teaspoon black pepper
- 1 pound large shrimp, peeled and deveined, or 8 ounces calamari, cut into rings
- 1 cup frozen peas or baby lima beans
- 1 tablespoon snipped fresh Italian parsley
- 1 teaspoon finely shredded lemon peel
- 1 teaspoon fresh thyme leaves

1 Scrub live mussels under cold running water. Using your fingers, pull out the beards that are visible between the shells. In a large pot combine 4 quarts cold water and ⅓ cup of the coarse salt. Add mussels; soak for 15 minutes. Drain and rinse, discarding water. Repeat twice more. Set mussels aside.

2 Season chicken thighs with salt and black pepper. For a charcoal grill, place a 16-inch paella pan* on the rack of an uncovered grill directly over medium-hot coals; add oil to pan, swirling to coat evenly. Place chicken, skin sides down, in pan. Cook about 10 minutes or until brown, turning once. (For a gas grill, preheat grill. Reduce heat to medium-high. Place pan on grill rack over heat. Cover and grill as directed.) Remove chicken from pan; set aside.

3 Add chorizo, bacon, and pork to pan; cook and stir about 5 minutes or until brown on all sides. Add sweet pepper, onion, and garlic; cook and stir about 5 minutes or until vegetables begin to soften. Add rice; cook and stir until grains of rice are light brown. Return chicken to pan. Add broth, tomatoes, saffron, paprika, the ½ teaspoon salt, and the ¼ teaspoon black pepper to pan. Bring to boiling; cover grill. Cook, without stirring, for 15 to 20 minutes or until rice is plump but still slightly firm. Stir in mussels, shrimp, peas, parsley, lemon peel, and thyme. Cover and cook for 5 to 7 minutes more or until shrimp are opaque, mussels are open, and chicken is no longer pink (180°F). Discard any unopened mussels. Let stand for 10 minutes before serving.

***NOTE:** If you don't have a paella pan, use a roasting pan that you don't mind getting messy or a double layer of 13×9-inch disposable foil pans. If using foil pans, the time to bring rice mixture to boiling will be increased (to about 20 minutes) and the covered cooking time will increase to about 30 minutes plus 10 minutes after shrimp are added.

PER SERVING: 493 cal., 20 g total fat (5 g sat. fat), 157 mg chol., 1,331 mg sodium, 39 g carbo., 3 g fiber, 37 g pro.

STEP-BY-STEP

1. Use a brush with stiff bristles to thoroughly scrub each mussel.

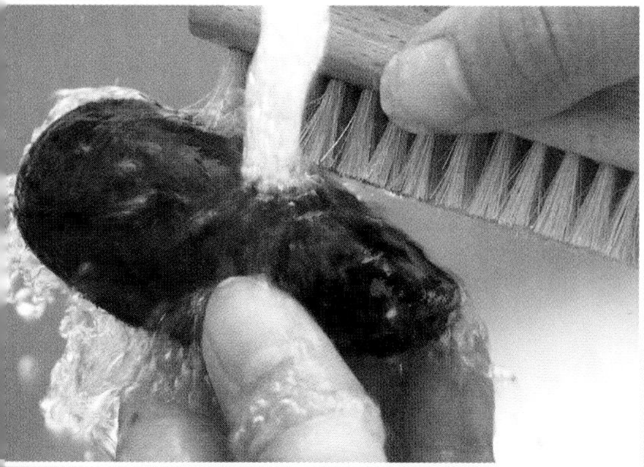

2. With your fingers, pull away the beard on the lower edge of the shell. If needed, cut it away with a knife.

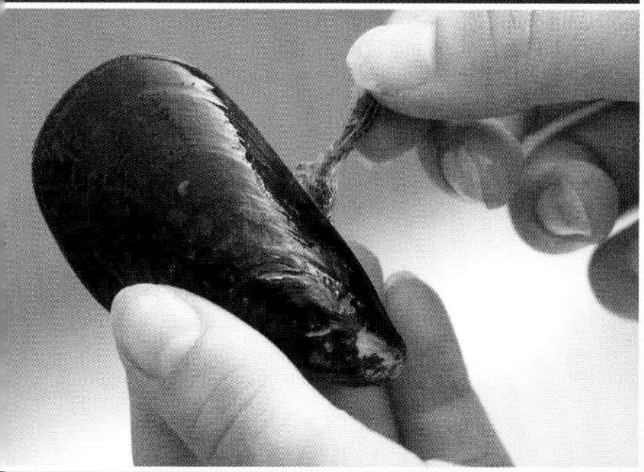

3. To release any sand in the mussels, soak them in salt water for 15 minutes. Drain, rinse, and repeat twice.

4. Place the paella pan with oil on the grill. Add the chicken, skin sides down, and cook until brown, turning to cook evenly. Remove from pan.

5. After the rice cooks, add the mussels, shrimp, and peas. Sprinkle with the parsley, lemon peel, and thyme.

Shrimp Po'Boy with Dried Tomato Aïoli

LOUISIANA'S FAMOUS SUBMARINE SANDWICH IS EVEN BETTER PREPARED ON THE GRILL. BE SURE TO USE TOP-QUALITY "STICKS"—THE COLLOQUIAL NAME FOR LENGTHS OF FRENCH BREAD.

PREP: 30 MINUTES **MARINATE:** 1 HOUR
GRILL: 7 MINUTES + 12 MINUTES
MAKES: 4 SANDWICHES

- 1 pound fresh or frozen jumbo shrimp in shells
- 2 tablespoons lemon juice
- 2 tablespoons olive oil
- 1 teaspoon seafood seasoning (such as Old Bay)
- 1 8-ounce loaf or ½ of a 16-ounce loaf unsliced French bread
- ½ cup mayonnaise
- ¼ cup chopped oil-packed dried tomatoes, drained
- 2 tablespoons dairy sour cream
- 2 cloves garlic, minced
- ½ of a medium red onion, thinly sliced
- Shredded lettuce (optional)

1 Thaw shrimp, if frozen. Peel and devein shrimp, removing tails. Rinse shrimp; pat dry with paper towels. Place shrimp in a large resealable plastic bag set in a shallow dish. For marinade, in a small bowl stir together 1 tablespoon of the lemon juice, 1 tablespoon of the olive oil, and the seafood seasoning. Pour over shrimp in bag; seal bag. Marinate in the refrigerator for 1 hour, turning bag occasionally. Thread shrimp on 4 long metal skewers, leaving ¼ inch between shrimp.

2 Cut bread in half horizontally. Use a spoon to hollow out the top half, leaving a ½-inch shell. Lightly brush cut sides of bread with remaining 1 tablespoon olive oil.

3 For a charcoal grill, grill shrimp on the rack of an uncovered grill directly over medium coals for 7 to 9 minutes or until shrimp are opaque, turning once halfway through grilling. Place bread, cut sides down, on grill rack over heat. Grill about 2 minutes or until lightly toasted. (For a gas grill, preheat grill. Reduce heat to medium. Place shrimp and bread on grill rack over heat. Cover and grill as directed.)

4 Meanwhile, in a small bowl stir together the remaining 1 tablespoon lemon juice, the mayonnaise, dried tomatoes, sour cream, and garlic. Spread on cut sides of toasted bread. Place bottom half of bread in the center of an 18-inch square of heavy-duty foil. Arrange shrimp and red onion slices on top; add the top half of bread. Bring up 2 opposite edges of foil and seal with a double fold. Fold remaining edges together to completely enclose. Place packet on grill over heat; grill for 12 to 15 minutes or until heated through, turning once.

5 To serve, remove foil from sandwich. If desired, remove top and add lettuce; replace top. Cut into 4 equal pieces.

PER SANDWICH: 542 cal., 34 g total fat (5 g sat. fat), 151 mg chol., 829 mg sodium, 34 g carbo., 2 g fiber, 23 g pro.

Mix It Up!

PICK ONE FROM EACH COLUMN TO CUSTOMIZE THE SANDWICH TO YOUR TASTE.

SEASON IT

Instead of the marinade, season or marinate the shrimp with one of the following:

- 1 teaspoon lemon-pepper seasoning
- 1 teaspoon fajita seasoning
- 1 teaspoon chile powder
- 2 tablespoons Caesar salad dressing
- 1 teaspoon Cajun seasoning
- 1 teaspoon fiesta lime seasoning

MIX IT IN

Instead of dried tomatoes, mix one of the following into the mayonnaise:

- ¼ cup raisins
- ¼ cup chopped almonds
- 2 tablespoons snipped dried apricots
- 2 tablespoons capers
- ¼ cup sliced green onions
- ¼ cup chopped assorted olives
- 2 tablespoons pickle relish

TOP IT

Instead of lettuce, top with one of the following:

- Chopped or sliced assorted-color sweet peppers
- Caramelized onions
- Sliced pickled jalapeño peppers
- Pickled mixed vegetables
- Shredded coleslaw mix
- Sauteed sliced zucchini
- Purchased shredded carrots
- Dill pickle slices

STEP-BY-STEP

1. To devein shrimp, make a shallow slit along the back. Place tip of a knife under the vein and lift out. Rinse well.

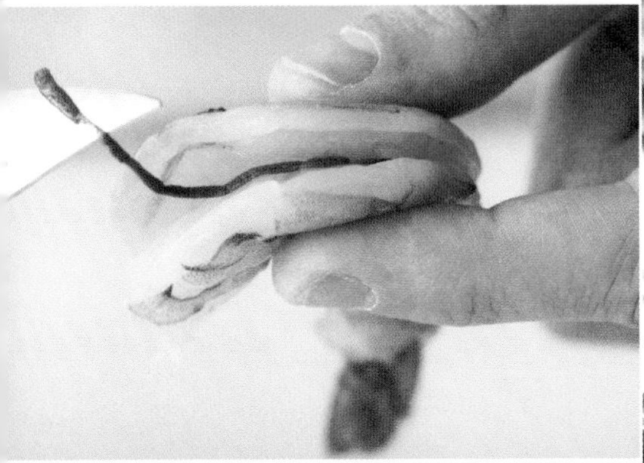

2. To peel shrimp, open the shell on the belly. Starting at the head end, peel away the shell with your fingers.

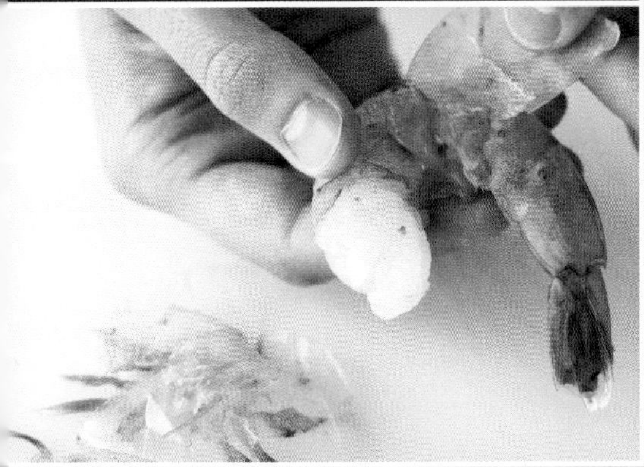

3. Cut off the tails. You can also use your fingers to pull off the tails.

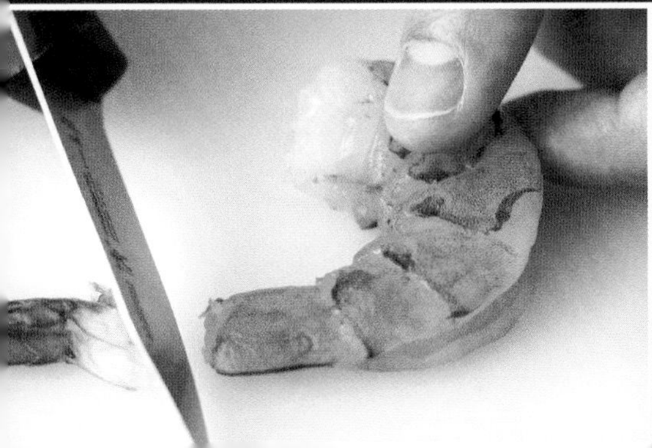

4. Spread bottom half of bread with the mayonnaise mixture and place on the foil. Scatter onion and shrimp on top.

5. Bring up the opposite sides of the foil and fold over twice. Fold up the ends to make a foil packet.

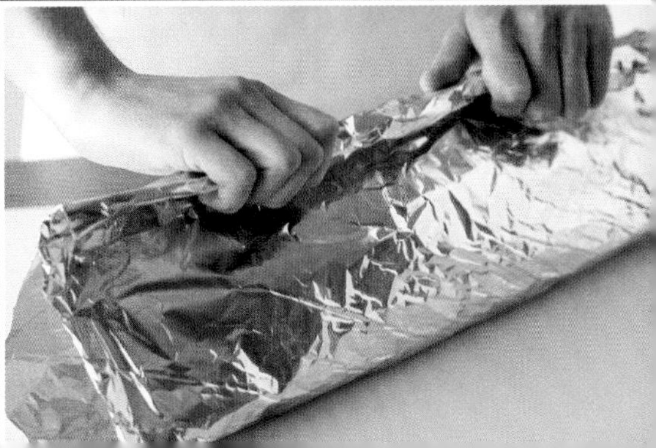

PREPARING CLAM BAKE, STEP-BY-STEP

1. Soak clams and mussels in salt water for 15 minutes to release sand. Drain, rinse, and repeat two times.

2. Place clams and mussels in the foil pan. Add the chorizo.

3. Add the potatoes and corn to the pan. Arrange the lobster tails on top of all.

4. Use tongs to transfer the seafood and vegetables to a serving platter.

5. Pour the liquid remaining in the bottom of the pan into a pitcher. Serve with the clam bake.

Clam Bake

YOU NEED NOT LIVE NEAR A BEACH TO ENJOY THE SIMPLE, NATURAL FLAVORS OF SHELLFISH COOKED AND SERVED ALFRESCO.

PREP: 65 MINUTES **COOK:** 20 MINUTES
MAKES: 4 SERVINGS

- 4 6- to 8-ounce fresh or frozen lobster tails
- 1 pound littleneck clams
- 1 pound mussels
- 1 cup coarse salt
- 1 pound cooked smoked chorizo sausage, sliced ½ inch thick (optional)
- 1 pound small round red potatoes, cut into 1-inch pieces
- 4 ears fresh corn, husks and silks removed
- ½ cup butter, melted

1 Thaw lobster tails, if frozen. Set aside. Scrub live clams and mussels under cold running water. Using your fingers, pull out the beards from the mussels that are visible between the shells. In an extra-large bowl combine 4 quarts cold water and ⅓ cup of the coarse salt. Add clams and mussels; soak for 15 minutes. Drain and rinse, discarding water. Repeat twice.

2 Place clams and mussels in a 13×9×3-inch disposable foil pan. Top with chorizo (if desired), potatoes, and corn. Place lobster tails on top. Cover pan with foil; seal tightly.

3 For a charcoal grill, place foil pan on the rack of an uncovered grill directly over medium coals. Grill for 20 to 30 minutes or until potatoes are tender. (For a gas grill, preheat grill. Reduce heat to medium. Place foil pan on the grill rack over heat. Cover and grill as directed.)

4 Transfer clam mixture to a serving platter, reserving cooking liquid. Discard any unopened clams and mussels. Serve seafood and vegetables with butter and cooking liquid.

PER ¼ CLAM BAKE: 564 cal., 34 g total fat (17 g sat. fat), 166 mg chol., 647 mg sodium, 44 g carbo., 4 g fiber, 25 g pro.

Linguine and Clams in Herbed Wine Sauce

FOR AN ADDITIONAL BURST OF SWEET CLAM FLAVOR, DRIZZLE CLAM LIQUOR—OR PAN JUICES—OVER THE STEAMING LINGUINE.

PREP: 30 MINUTES **GRILL:** 10 MINUTES
STAND: 45 MINUTES **MAKES:** 4 SERVINGS

- 2 dozen clams
- 1 cup coarse salt
- 5 tablespoons olive oil
- 6 cloves garlic, minced
- 2 medium onions, sliced
- 4 anchovy fillets, finely chopped
- ½ cup dry white wine
- ¼ teaspoon sea salt
- ¼ teaspoon coarsely ground black pepper
- ⅛ to ¼ teaspoon crushed red pepper
- 2 cups finely chopped, seeded roma tomatoes (6 medium)
- ¼ cup snipped fresh basil
- 1 tablespoon snipped fresh oregano
- 8 ounces dried linguine or spaghetti
- 8 sprigs fresh thyme
- 2 bay leaves
- 4 slices French bread

1 Scrub live clams under cold running water. In a large pot combine 4 quarts cold water and ⅓ cup of the coarse salt. Add clams and mussels; soak for 15 minutes. Drain and rinse. Repeat twice.

2 For sauce, heat 3 tablespoons of the olive oil in a skillet over medium heat. Cook garlic in oil about 30 seconds. Add onions and anchovies; cook for 4 to 5 minutes or until onions are tender. Add wine, sea salt, black pepper, and crushed red pepper; cook 2 minutes more. Remove from heat. Stir in tomatoes, 2 tablespoons of the basil, and the oregano. Set aside.

3 Prepare linguine according to package directions. Toss with the remaining 2 tablespoons olive oil; cover and keep warm.

4 Place the clams in a 2-quart foil pan. Tie thyme sprigs and bay leaves together in a bundle with 100%-cotton string. Add thyme and bay leaves to pan. Add sauce. Cover pan with foil; seal tightly.

5 For a charcoal grill, place foil pan on the rack of an uncovered grill directly medium-hot coals. Grill for 10 to 12 minutes or until shells open and sauce is hot. (For a gas grill, preheat grill. Reduce heat to medium-high. Place pan on grill rack over heat. Cover and grill as directed.) Discard unopened clams, thyme sprigs, and bay leaves. Sprinkle with remaining basil. Serve over linguine with bread.

PER SERVING: 551 cal., 20 g total fat (3 g sat. fat), 23 mg chol., 448 mg sodium, 69 g carbo., 5 g fiber, 20 g pro.

Rock Lobster Tails

ROCK LOBSTERS—ALSO CALLED "SPINY" LOBSTERS—COME FROM WARM WATERS. THE MEAT, FIRMER THAN THE MEAT OF COLD-WATER LOBSTERS, IS ALL CONTAINED IN THE TAIL. ROCK LOBSTERS HAVE NO CLAWS.

PREP: 15 MINUTES **GRILL:** 10 MINUTES
MAKES: 4 SERVINGS

- 4 6-ounce fresh or frozen rock lobster tails
- 2 tablespoons olive oil
- ½ teaspoon finely shredded lemon or lime peel (set aside)
- 4 teaspoons lemon or lime juice
- 2 cloves garlic, minced
- 1 teaspoon chili powder
- ½ cup mayonnaise
- 1 teaspoon snipped fresh dill or ¼ teaspoon dried dill
- Lemon or lime wedges
- Fresh herb sprigs (optional)

1 Thaw lobster tails, if frozen. Using kitchen shears, cut lobster tails in half lengthwise through centers of hard top shells, meat, and bottoms of shells. Set aside.

2 In a small bowl stir together oil, 2 teaspoons of the lemon juice, the garlic, and chili powder; brush on exposed lobster meat, reserving extra juice mixture.

3 For a charcoal grill, grill lobster tails, cut sides down, on the rack of an uncovered grill directly over medium coals for 10 to 12 minutes or until meat is opaque, turning once and brushing with remaining juice mixture halfway through grilling. Do not overcook. (For a gas grill, preheat grill. Reduce heat to medium. Place lobster tails, cut sides down, on rack over heat. Cover and grill as directed.)

4 Meanwhile, for dipping sauce, stir together mayonnaise, dill, lemon peel, and remaining lemon juice. Serve lobster with dipping sauce and lemon wedges. If desired, garnish with fresh herb sprigs.

PER TAIL: 367 cal., 30 g total fat (4 g sat. fat), 128 mg chol., 462 mg sodium, 2 g carbo., 0 g fiber, 22 g pro.

Lobster Tails with Chive Butter

DON'T BE TEMPTED BY DEHYDRATED CHIVES. THE DRIED VERSION IS ALMOST COMPLETEY DEVOID OF TASTE. IF YOU'RE UNABLE TO FIND FRESH CHIVES, SUBSTITUTE AN EQUAL AMOUNT OF FINELY MINCED GREEN ONION TOPS.

PREP: 10 MINUTES **GRILL:** 10 MINUTES
MAKES: 4 SERVINGS

- 4 6-ounce fresh or frozen rock lobster tails
- ⅓ cup butter
- 2 tablespoons snipped fresh chives
- 1 teaspoon finely shredded lemon peel
- Lemon wedges (optional)

1 Thaw lobster tails, if frozen. Butterfly lobster tails by using kitchen shears to cut lengthwise through centers of hard top shells and meat, cutting to but not through, bottoms of shells. Spread halves of tails apart. Set aside.

2 For sauce, melt butter in a small saucepan. Remove saucepan from heat; stir in chives and lemon peel. Remove 2 tablespoons of the sauce for basting; set remaining sauce aside for dipping.

3 Brush lobster meat with some of the 2 tablespoons sauce. For a charcoal grill, grill lobster tails, cut sides down, on the rack of an uncovered grill directly over medium coals for 10 to 12 minutes or until meat is opaque, turning once and brushing with the remaining basting sauce halfway through grilling. Do not overcook. (For a gas grill, preheat grill. Reduce heat to medium. Place lobster tails, cut sides down, on rack over heat. Cover and grill as directed.)

4 Meanwhile, heat the reserved dipping sauce, stirring occasionally. Transfer sauce to small bowls; serve with lobster. If desired, serve with lemon wedges.

PER TAIL: 214 cal., 17 g total fat (10 g sat. fat), 118 mg chol., 395 mg sodium, 1 g carbo., 0 g fiber, 15 g pro.

PREPARING ROCK LOBSTER TAILS, STEP-BY-STEP

1. Cut through the top and bottom shells with scissors. Use a large knife to cut through meat, halving each tail.

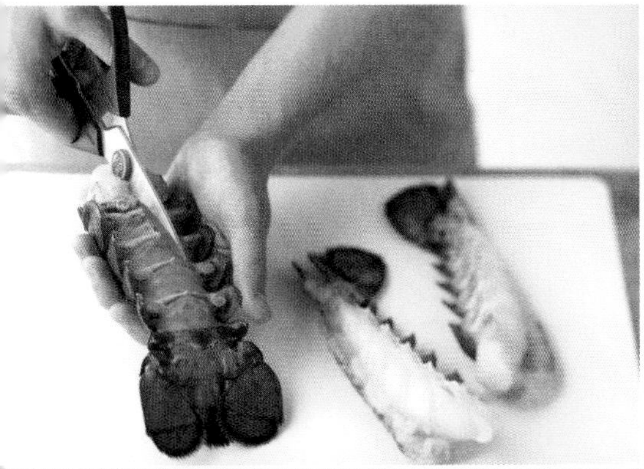

2. Brush the lobster meat with the lemon juice mixture.

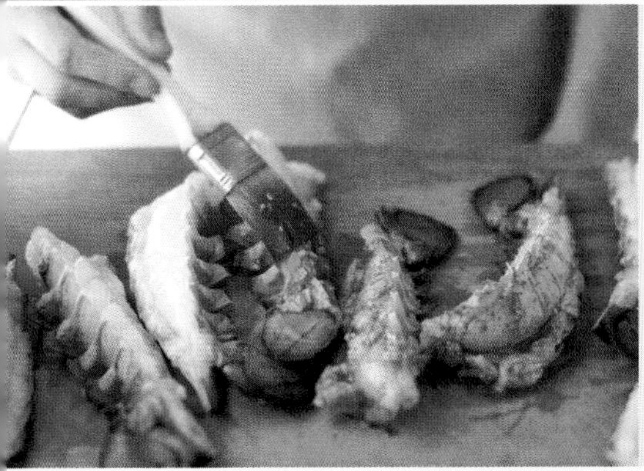

3. Let the coals burn until covered with gray ash. Use long-handled tongs to arrange them in a single layer.

4. Start grilling the lobster tails with meat sides down. Turn meat sides up and brush the meat with the remaining lemon juice mixture.

5. Check lobster at the minimum grilling time. Lobster is done when the meat turns opaque. Lift a piece of meat with a fork to test.

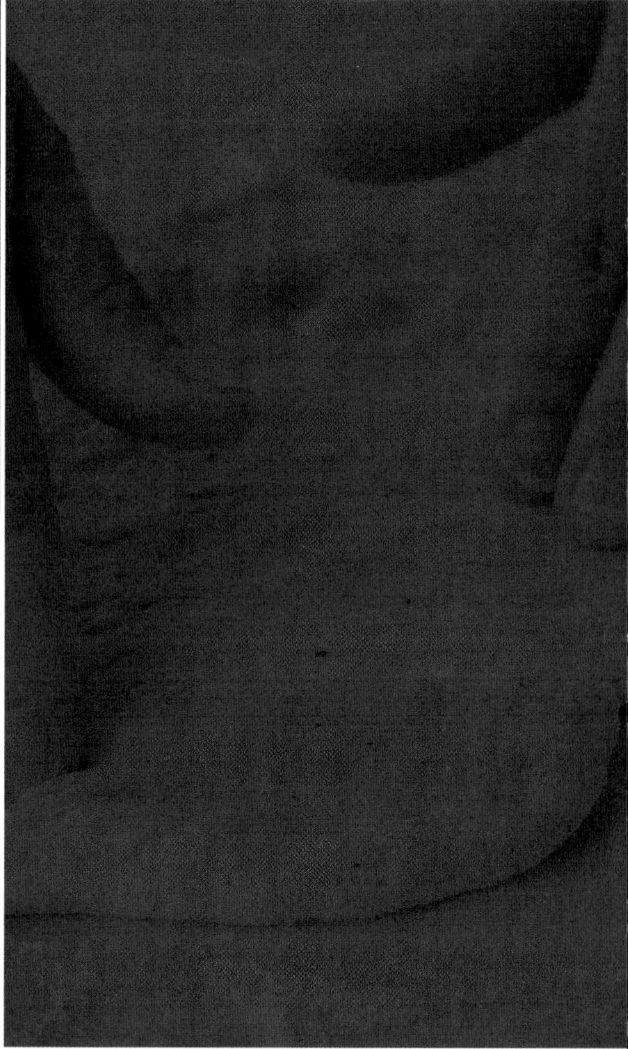

Pizzas & Sandwiches

FORGET FORKS. LIMBER UP YOUR FINGERS. PIZZAS AND SANDWICHES—LIKE THESE BREAD WINNERS HERE—MAKE FOR GREAT GRILLING.

Pizza Dough

CRAFTING HOMEMADE PIZZA DOUGH IS EASIER THAN YOU THINK—AND THE REWARDS ARE DELICIOUS.

Even if you've never made bread before, do not fear. Making pizza dough is beginner-friendly.

All you need are five ingredients, a few simple steps, and a bit of time. The dough will work harder than you do!

Take a tip from efficient pizzanistas: Make double or triple batches of pizza dough at one time. The dough freezes beautifully, and one effort can supply you with a summer's worth of pizza crusts.

MAKING PIZZA DOUGH, STEP-BY-STEP

1. Check the temperature of the water with an instant-read thermometer before adding yeast.

2. Sprinkle the yeast over the warm water. Add the sugar and stir with a fork to mix.

3. Let the yeast mixture stand for 5 minutes or until bubbles appear on the surface.

4. Stir together flour, sugar, salt, and pepper.

5. Add the yeast mixture to the flour mixture in the bowl.

6. Stir with a wooden spoon until the dough looks ropey and pulls away from sides of bowl.

7. Sprinkle the work surface with flour.

8. Scrape the dough from the bowl onto the work surface.

9. To knead, fold the dough and push with your hands. Turn and repeat.

10. Continue to push and fold the dough until it becomes smooth and elastic. Form the dough into a ball.

11. Brush a bowl with oil. Place dough in bowl; turn the dough over to grease the surface.

12. Cover the bowl with a towel and place in warm place until the dough has doubled in size.

13. Make a fist and punch the dough down, pressing out air.

14. Place the dough on the work surface and cut into four portions. Let the dough rest.

15. Pat and stretch a portion of dough into an 8-inch circle.

16. When bottom is light brown and firm, slide a large spatula under the crust and remove from grill.

17. Arrange the pizza toppings on the grilled sides of the crusts. Return pizzas to grill and grill until bottoms of crusts are crisp, cheese is melted, and toppings are heated through.

Four-Way Grilled Pizza

WHAT FUN! YOUR FAMILY WILL LOVE CUSTOMIZING A PIZZA TO THEIR OWN TASTE.

PREP: 30 MINUTES **RISE:** 45 MINUTES
GRILL: 10 MINUTES **STAND:** 15 MINUTES
MAKES: 4 PIZZAS (8 SERVINGS)

- 1 package active dry yeast*
- 1¼ teaspoons sugar*
- 1 cup warm water* (105°F to 115°F)
- ¼ cup olive oil*
- 3 cups all-purpose flour*
- 1 teaspoon salt*
- ½ teaspoon freshly ground black pepper*
- Cornmeal
- Toppings*** (see variations, right)

1 Sprinkle yeast and ¼ teaspoon of the sugar over the warm water in a small bowl. Let stand about 5 minutes or until yeast is bubbly. Stir in 2 tablespoons of the olive oil.

2 In a large bowl combine the flour, remaining 1 teaspoon sugar, the salt, and pepper. Add the yeast mixture to the flour mixture. Stir with a wooden spoon until combined (dough will be sticky). Turn dough out onto a lightly floured surface. Knead until dough is smooth and elastic. Place dough in a lightly greased bowl, turning once to grease surface of dough. Cover; let rise in a warm place until double in size (45 to 60 minutes) or let rise overnight in the refrigerator.

3 Punch dough down. Turn dough out onto a lightly floured surface. Cut dough into 4 equal portions. Cover; let rest for 15 minutes. Pat or roll each piece of dough into an 8-inch circle.** For easy transport to the grill, stack dough circles between sheets of waxed paper or parchment paper sprinkled with cornmeal. Brush tops of dough with some of the remaining 2 tablespoons olive oil.

4 For a charcoal grill, carefully slide 2 of the dough circles, oiled sides down, onto the lightly greased rack of an uncovered grill directly over low coals. Grill about 6 minutes or until light brown and firm enough to transfer. (Top will be dry but soft.) Transfer crusts, cooked sides up, to the back of a baking sheet. (For a gas grill, preheat grill. Reduce heat to low. Place dough circles on lightly greased grill rack over heat. Grill as directed.)

5 Arrange toppings on grilled sides of partially grilled crusts in the order listed. Transfer pizzas from the baking sheet to the grill rack. Cover and grill for 4 to 6 minutes or until crust is crisp and cheese melts, moving pizzas around to brown evenly. Repeat with remaining dough and toppings.

MARGHERITA PIZZA: Top crust with 1 medium tomato, sliced and sprinkled with salt and black pepper, and 2 ounces thinly sliced fresh mozzarella cheese. Grill as directed. Top grilled pizza with ⅓ cup thinly sliced fresh basil leaves.

HAM AND CHEESE PIZZA: Top crust with 2 ounces thinly sliced Camembert or Brie cheese, 1 ounce thinly sliced prosciutto or smoked ham, and 1 teaspoon snipped fresh sage. Grill as directed.

PROVENÇAL PIZZA: Top crust with 2 ounces crumbled goat cheese; 2 tablespoons pitted kalamata olives, chopped; ¼ cup thinly sliced yellow sweet pepper; and ¼ cup thinly sliced roasted red pepper. Grill as directed.

MESCLUN PIZZA: Top crust with 1 teaspoon snipped fresh rosemary and ¼ cup finely shredded Parmesan cheese. Grill as directed. Top grilled pizza with 1¼ cups mesclun. In a screw-top jar combine 2 teaspoons olive oil, 2 teaspoons balsamic vinegar, ¼ teaspoon cracked black pepper, and dash salt. Cover and shake well. Drizzle over pizza.

***NOTE:** If desired, you may substitute 2 packages pizza crust mix, prepared according to package directions, or two 13.8-ounce packages refrigerated pizza dough for the homemade pizza dough.

****NOTE:** If desired, divide the dough into 2 equal portions; roll each portion into a 12-inch circle. Double the amounts of desired toppings for each pizza.

*****NOTE:** The dough cooks quickly, so prepare topping ingredients before you start grilling.

PER ½ PIZZA: 241 cal., 9 g total fat (1 g sat. fa), 0 mg chol., 293 mg sodium, 35 g carbo., 1 g fiber, 5 g pro.

Grilled Vegetable Pizzas

GARDENERS, REJOICE—THIS PIZZA IS A DELIGHTFUL DESTINATION FOR LATE-SUMMER BOUNTY OF JUICY-RIPE TOMATOES, FLAVOR-SPONGING EGGPLANT, AND FRAGRANT LEAVES OF FRESH BASIL.

PREP: 20 MINUTES **FREEZE:** 10 MINUTES
GRILL: 6 MINUTES + 7 MINUTES
MAKES: 2 PIZZAS (6 SERVINGS)

- 1 pound frozen pizza dough, thawed and halved
- ⅓ cup olive oil
- 6 cloves garlic, minced
- 3 medium Japanese eggplants, cut lengthwise into ¼-inch-thick slices
- Salt and black pepper
- ½ pound fresh mozzarella, cut into thin slices
- 3 assorted tomatoes, sliced
- 1 cup fresh basil leaves
- Balsamic vinegar

1 Divide dough into 2 equal portions. On a lightly floured surface roll out each dough portion to a 10×13-inch oval. Stack dough ovals between sheets of waxed paper or parchment paper sprinkled with cornmeal; place on a large baking sheet. Freeze dough about 10 minutes or until firm but not frozen.

2 In a small saucepan heat ¼ cup of the oil over medium heat. Add garlic; cook and stir for 30 seconds. Remove from heat; let garlic oil cool.

3 Brush both sides of eggplant slices with remaining olive oil. For a charcoal grill, grill eggplant on the lightly greased rack of an uncovered grill directly over medium-hot coals for 6 to 8 minutes or until eggplant is golden brown and tender, turning once halfway through grilling. (For a gas grill, preheat grill. Reduce heat to medium-high. Place eggplant on a lightly greased grill rack over heat. Cover and grill as directed.)

4 Remove pizza dough from freezer; discard waxed paper. Brush tops with some of the garlic oil; season to taste with salt and pepper.

5 For a charcoal grill, carefully slide dough, oiled sides down, onto the lightly greased rack of an uncovered grill directly over medium-hot coals. Grill about 4 minutes or until dough is light brown. Working quickly, carefully brush tops with garlic oil. Using tongs, carefully turn the crusts over. Immediately brush tops of crusts with more garlic oil, then top with mozzarella, eggplant, and tomatoes. Cover and grill about 3 minutes more or until cheese melts. Transfer pizzas to a cutting board. Sprinkle with basil and drizzle with balsamic vinegar. (For a gas grill, preheat grill. Reduce heat to medium-high. Place dough on lightly greased grill rack over heat. Grill as directed.)

PER ⅓ PIZZA: 670 cal., 17 g total fat (6 g sat. fat,), 104 mg chol., 144 mg sodium, 93 g carbo., 1 g fiber, 34 g pro.

STEP-BY-STEP

1. Place a portion of dough on a lightly floured work surface. Flour the rolling pin and roll the dough into an oval.

2. Cut the stem ends off the eggplants. Cut lengthwise into thin slices.

3. Let the coals burn until lightly covered with gray ash. Use long-handled tongs to arrange them in a single layer in the bottom of the grill.

4. When crust is light brown on the bottom, brush the top of the crust with oil. Use tongs to flip the crust over.

5. When the pizza is done, use tongs to gently slide the pizza from the grill onto a cutting board.

6. Sprinkle fresh basil leaves over pizza. Use a small spoon to drizzle balsamic vinegar over the tomatoes and cheese.

Chipotle-BBQ Steak Sandwiches

TALK ABOUT MAKING THE MOST OF DELICIOUS INGREDIENTS—THE JAZZED-UP MARINADE FOR FLANK STEAK DOES DOUBLE DUTY, RETURNING AS BARBECUE SAUCE.

PREP: 25 MINUTES **MARINATE:** 4 HOURS
GRILL: 17 MINUTES **STAND:** 5 MINUTES
MAKES: 4 SANDWICHES

- 1 8-ounce can tomato sauce with roasted garlic or one 8-ounce can tomato sauce plus 1 clove garlic, minced
- 3 tablespoons tomato paste
- 2 tablespoons water
- 1 tablespoon Dijon-style mustard
- 1 tablespoon Worcestershire sauce
- 2 teaspoons honey
- 1 teaspoon finely chopped canned chipotle chile peppers in adobo sauce*
- 1 12-ounce beef flank steak
- 1 medium green sweet pepper, seeded and quartered
- 4 slices sweet onion (such as Vidalia) (½ inch thick)
- Nonstick cooking spray
- 4 ciabatta rolls, split and toasted

1 For marinade, in a small bowl stir together tomato sauce, tomato paste, the water, mustard, Worcestershire sauce, honey, and chipotle peppers. Set aside. Trim fat from steak. Score both sides of steak in a diamond pattern by making shallow diagonal cuts at 1-inch intervals. Place steak in a large resealable plastic bag set in a shallow dish. Pour marinade over steak in bag; seal bag. Turn to coat steak. Marinate steak in the refrigerator for 4 to 6 hours, turning bag occasionally.

2 Drain steak, reserving marinade. Lightly coat sweet pepper quarters and onion slices with nonstick cooking spray.

3 For a charcoal grill, grill steak, sweet pepper quarters, and onion slices on the rack of an uncovered grill directly over medium coals until steak is medium doneness (160°F) and vegetables are tender, turning once halfway through grilling. Allow 17 to 21 minutes for the steak and 8 to 12 minutes for the vegetables. (For a gas grill, preheat grill. Reduce heat to medium. Place steak, sweet pepper quarters, and onion slices on grill rack over heat. Cover and grill as directed.)

4 Meanwhile, for sauce, pour reserved marinade into a small saucepan. Bring to boiling; reduce heat. Simmer, uncovered, about 5 minutes or until desired consistency.

5 Let steak stand for 5 minutes. Thinly slice steak across the grain. Thinly slice sweet pepper quarters lengthwise. Place steak slices and sweet pepper strips on the bottom halves of the ciabatta rolls. Top with onion slices. Spoon sauce over onions. Add ciabatta roll tops.

***NOTE:** Because chile peppers contain volatile oils that can burn your skin and eyes, avoid direct contact with them as much as possible. When working with chile peppers, wear plastic or rubber gloves. If your bare hands do touch the peppers, wash your hands and nails well with soap and warm water.

PER SANDWICH: 378 cal., 9 g total fat (3 g sat. fat) 35 mg chol., 1,030 mg sodium, 47 g carbo., 4 g fiber, 25 g pro.

STEP-BY-STEP

1. Lightly spray the pepper quarters and onion slices with cooking spray.

2. Let the coals burn until lightly covered with gray ash. Use long-handled tongs to arrange them in a single layer in the grill.

3. Add the pepper quarters and onion slices to the grill just before you turn the steak. Turn the steak and grill until vegetables are tender and steak reaches medium doneness.

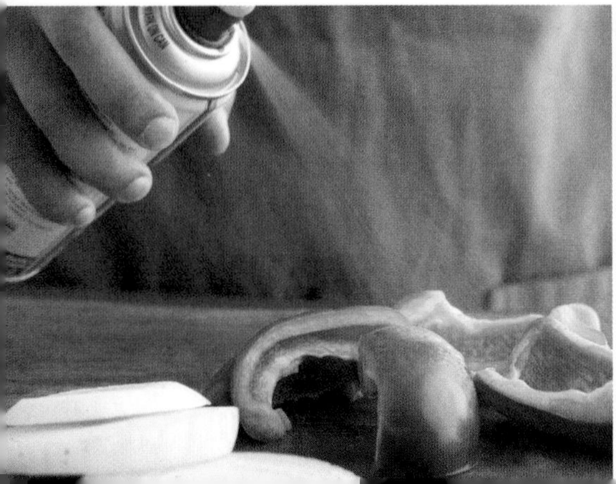

4. Place pepper quarters, skin sides down, on cutting board and cut lengthwise into thin strips.

5. To assemble sandwiches, pile meat onto toasted roll bottoms. Layer pepper strips on meat.

6. Separate the onion slices into rings and layer on pepper strips. Add sauce and roll tops to complete the sandwiches.

STEP-BY-STEP

1. Make a lengthwise cut around a peach, cutting around the pit and through the fruit and skin. Separate the halves and remove the pit.

2. Let the coals burn until lightly covered with gray ash. Use long-handled tongs to arrange them in a single layer.

3. Grill the peach halves until grill marks appear and fruit softens. Remove from grill and cut into thin slices.

Open-Face Beef-Lettuce-Peach Sandwiches

GRILLING PEACHES BRINGS OUT THEIR LUSCIOUS, JUICY SWEETNESS. THEY TASTE AS IF THEY'VE JUST FALLEN OFF THE TREE AND LANDED DIRECTLY ON THE GRILL.

PREP: 25 MINUTES **MARINATE:** 4 HOURS
GRILL: 17 MINUTES **MAKES:** 4 SANDWICHES

- 1 pound beef flank steak
- 6 tablespoons balsamic vinegar
- 2 tablespoons olive oil
- 1 tablespoon snipped fresh rosemary
- 2 cloves garlic, minced
- ¼ teaspoon salt
- ⅛ teaspoon black pepper
- ½ of a 16-ounce round loaf whole grain or multigrain country Italian bread, cut into four ½-inch-thick slices
- 4 leaves romaine lettuce
- 2 medium peaches, halved and pitted

1 Trim fat from steak. Score both sides of steak in a diamond pattern by making shallow diagonal cuts at 1-inch intervals. Place steak in a large resealable plastic bag set in a shallow dish. For marinade, in a small bowl whisk together 4 tablespoons of the balsamic vinegar, 1 tablespoon of the olive oil, the rosemary, and garlic. Pour over steak in bag; seal bag. Marinate in the refrigerator for 4 to 24 hours, turning bag occasionally.

2 Drain steak, discarding marinade. Sprinkle steak with salt and pepper. For a charcoal grill, grill steak on the rack of an uncovered grill directly over medium coals for 17 to 21 minutes for medium doneness (160°F), turning once halfway through grilling. Brush bread slices with the remaining 1 tablespoon oil. Place on grill rack for 1 to 2 minutes or until toasted, turning once. Place peach halves, cut sides down, on grill rack for 1 to 2 minutes or until charred and slightly softened. (For a gas grill, preheat grill. Reduce heat to medium. Place steak, bread, and peach halves on grill rack over heat. Cover and grill as directed.)

3 Thinly slice steak across the grain. Slice peach halves. Top each bread slice with a lettuce leaf. Top lettuce with beef; arrange peach slices on beef. Drizzle sandwiches with the remaining 2 tablespoons balsamic vinegar.

PER SANDWICH: 399 cal., 14 g total fat (3 g sat. fat), 37 mg chol., 385 mg sodium, 35 g carbo., 8 g fiber, 33 g pro.

4. Starting with the stem ends, tear the lettuce leaves to fit the size and shape of bread slices. Place a lettuce leaf on each bread slice.

5. Arrange sliced steak on the lettuce, dividing steak evenly among sandwiches.

6. Layer the peach slices on the steak. Use a small spoon to drizzle sandwiches with balsamic vinegar.

Chicken Sandwiches with Roasted Pepper and Goat Cheese Spread

GOAT CHEESE HAS A DISTINCTIVE TASTE AND TEXTURE. IF THE CHEESE ISN'T A FAVORITE, SUBSTITUTE CRUMBLED FETA CHEESE ON THESE HOT SANDWICHES.

PREP: 30 MINUTES **MARINATE:** 1 HOUR
GRILL: 11 MINUTES **MAKES:** 4 SANDWICHES

- 4 skinless, boneless chicken breast halves
- ¼ cup balsamic vinegar
- 2 tablespoons olive oil
- 1 tablespoon snipped fresh rosemary
- 2 cloves garlic, minced
- Salt and black pepper
- 1 10- to 12-inch rosemary or garlic Italian flatbread (focaccia)
- 1 recipe Roasted Pepper and Goat Cheese Spread
- 1 cup baby spinach leaves or small romaine leaves
- ½ of a medium red onion, thinly sliced

1 Place each chicken breast half between 2 pieces of plastic wrap. Using the flat side of a meat mallet, pound chicken lightly to about ½ inch thick. Discard plastic wrap. Place chicken in a large resealable plastic bag set in a shallow dish. For marinade, stir together vinegar, oil, rosemary, and garlic. Pour over chicken in bag; seal bag. Marinate in the refrigerator for 1 to 2 hours, turning bag occasionally.

2 Drain chicken, discarding marinade. Sprinkle chicken lightly with salt and pepper. For a charcoal grill, grill chicken on the rack of an uncovered grill directly over medium coals for 9 to 11 minutes or until chicken is no longer pink (170°F), turning once halfway through grilling. (For a gas grill, preheat grill. Reduce heat to medium. Place chicken on grill rack over heat. Cover and grill as directed.)

3 Meanwhile, cut flatbread into 4 wedges. Slice each wedge in half horizontally. When chicken is done, grill bread, cut sides down, directly over medium heat about 2 minutes or until toasted. Evenly spread toasted sides of bread with Roasted Pepper and Goat Cheese Spread. Top the 4 bottom wedges with chicken, spinach, and onion slices. Add the top bread wedges.

ROASTED PEPPER AND GOAT CHEESE SPREAD: Drain ¼ cup roasted red sweet peppers, reserving 1 teaspoon liquid. In a food processor combine sweet peppers, reserved liquid, 4 ounces soft goat cheese (chèvre), and 1 teaspoon snipped fresh rosemary. Cover and process until nearly smooth. (Or finely chop the sweet pepper and stir mixture together with a spoon.)

PER SANDWICH: 321 cal., 12 g total fat (5 g sat. fat), 96 mg chol., 392 mg sodium, 11 g carbo., 1 g fiber, 40 g pro.

STEP-BY-STEP

1. Place each chicken piece between sheets of plastic wrap. Starting from the center, lightly pound chicken with flat side of a meat mallet.

2. Use a serrated knife to cut the flatbread into four wedges. Starting from the point of a wedge, split each wedge in half horizontally.

3. For the spread, process the sweet peppers, liquid from the peppers, goat cheese, and rosemary in a food processor until almost smooth, with only tiny pieces of pepper remaining.

4. To toast bread, place the wedges, cut sides down, on the grill for 2 minutes or until crisp and golden.

5. Spoon the goat cheese spread on bottom halves of the wedges, covering all the cut surfaces.

6. To assemble sandwiches, place chicken on bottom wedges. Arrange spinach on chicken. Separate onion slices into rings and place on spinach. Add bread tops.

STEP-BY-STEP

1. To butterfly a chicken breast, slice the breast horizontally, cutting two-thirds of the way through to the opposite side.

2. Open the chicken breast flat. Spread half with the mole sauce. Fold chicken to cover the sauce.

3. When the chicken is no longer pink on the first side, use tongs to turn the chicken over.

Grilled Chicken-Mole Sandwiches

MOLE SAUCE—A BLEND OF ONION, GARLIC, AND CHILES—WITH A SMIDGE OF CHOCOLATE—IS MOST POPULAR IN CENTRAL AND SOUTHERN REGIONS OF MEXICO. IT'S A NATURAL WITH CHICKEN.

PREP: 30 MINUTES **GRILL:** 12 MINUTES
MAKES: 4 SANDWICHES

- 1 small avocado, halved, seeded, peeled, and mashed
- 2 tablespoons mayonnaise
- ¼ teaspoon cayenne pepper
- ¼ teaspoon salt
- 4 skinless, boneless chicken breast halves
- Salt and black pepper
- ⅓ cup bottled molé sauce
- 4 4- to 6-inch ciabata rolls, split and toasted
- Baby romaine or other lettuce leaves
- Tomato slices

1 In a small bowl stir together avocado, mayonnaise, cayenne pepper, and the ¼ teaspoon salt. Cover and chill until serving time.

2 Season chicken breast halves with salt and black pepper. Using a sharp knife, carefully butterfly each chicken breast by cutting a horizontal slit two-thirds of the way through the breast half. Open each breast half and spread with 1 tablespoon of the mole sauce; fold closed.

3 For a charcoal grill, grill chicken on the lightly greased rack of an uncovered grill directly over medium coals for 12 to 15 minutes or until chicken is no longer pink (170°F), turning once halfway through grilling and brushing with the remaining mole sauce during the last 3 minutes of grilling. (For a gas grill, preheat grill. Reduce heat to medium. Place chicken on lightly greased grill rack over heat. Cover and grill as directed.)

4 Cut chicken diagonally into ¼- to ½-inch slices. Spread avocado mixture on rolls; layer with chicken, romaine, and tomato.

PER SANDWICH: 624 cal., 18 g total fat (3 g sat. fat), 85 mg chol., 1,101 mg sodium, 67 g carbo., 7 g fiber, 46 g pro.

4. When the chicken is almost done, brush it with the remaining mole sauce.

5. Thinly slice the chicken, holding the knife at an angle to make bias slices.

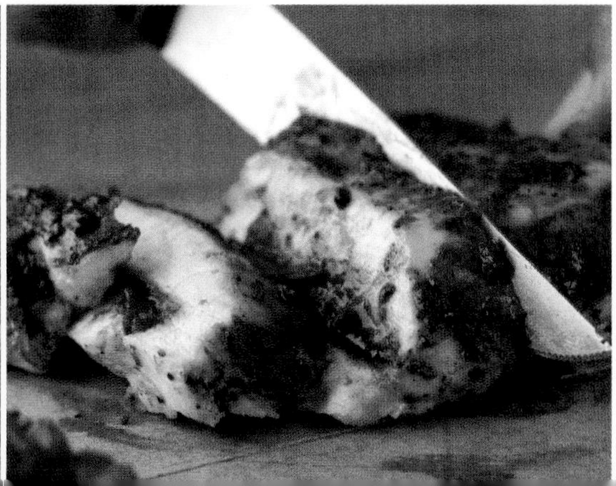

6. To assemble sandwiches, spread roll bottoms with avocado mixture. Top with romaine, chicken, tomato, and roll tops.

Fish Sandwiches with Red Pepper-Onion Relish

GRILLING THE ONION AND PEPPER FIRST IMBUES THE COLORFUL RELISH WITH WONDERFUL SMOKY SWEETNESS. ANY EXTRA WILL MAKE OTHER SANDWICHES SPECIAL AS WELL.

PREP: 25 MINUTES
GRILL: 8 MINUTES + 4 MINUTES
MAKES: 4 SANDWICHES

- 4 4- to 5-ounce fresh or frozen skinless catfish or white-flesh fish fillets, ½ inch thick
- 1 tablespoon lemon juice or lime juice
- 1 teaspoon lemon-pepper seasoning, Jamaican jerk seasoning, or Cajun seasoning
- 1 large onion, quartered
- 1 large red sweet pepper, quartered
- 1 tablespoon olive oil
- 3 tablespoons snipped fresh Italian parsley
- 2 tablespoons sugar
- 2 tablespoons cider vinegar
- 2 tablespoons balsamic vinegar
- ¼ teaspoon salt
- ¼ teaspoon black pepper
- 4 round hard rolls, hoagie buns, kaiser rolls, or other crusty rolls, split and toasted

1 Thaw fish, if frozen. Rinse fish; pat dry with paper towels. Brush fish with lemon juice. Sprinkle desired seasoning evenly over all sides of fish. Set aside.

2 For the relish, brush onion and sweet pepper with oil. For a charcoal grill, grill onion and sweet pepper on the rack of an uncovered grill directly over medium coals for 8 to 10 minutes or until tender, turning occasionally. Watch vegetables closely so they do not char. (For a gas grill, preheat grill. Reduce heat to medium. Place onion and sweet pepper on grill rack over heat. Cover and grill as directed.)

3 Transfer vegetables to a cutting board; let cool until easy to handle. Chop vegetables and place in a small bowl. Stir in parsley, sugar, vinegars, salt, and black pepper; toss to coat. Set aside.

4 For a charcoal grill, grill fish on the greased rack of an uncovered grill directly over medium coals for 4 to 6 minutes or until fish begins to flake when tested with a fork, turning once halfway through grilling. (For a gas grill, preheat grill. Reduce heat to medium. Place fish on greased grill rack over heat. Cover and grill as directed.)

5 Serve fish on buns. Using a slotted spoon, top fish with relish.

NOTE: The red pepper-onion relish can be covered and chilled up to 1 week.

PER SANDWICH: 473 cal., 17 g total fat (3 g sat. fat), 53 mg chol., 892 mg sodium, 55 g carbo., 4 g fiber, 25 g pro.

STEP-BY-STEP

1. Brush fish with lemon juice and sprinkle with the seasoning. Turn and repeat with second sides.

2. Place the pepper and onion quarters on the grill. Grill until tender, turning occasionally to cook evenly.

3. Place the fish in a greased fish basket. A fish basket makes it easy to turn the fish without breaking it and keeps the fish from sticking to the grill.

MAKE A COLORFUL, FRESH CHANGE FROM TARTAR SAUCE WITH THIS SIMPLE GRILLED RELISH.

STEP-BY-STEP

1. Sprinkle the meat with the rub and then use your fingers to press the rub into all surfaces of the meat.

2. Place the roasts in a disposable foil pan. Place the pan on the grill rack.

3. Scatter the onion over the meat. Pour the cola over the roasts. Add broth until the liquid in the bottom of the pan is ½ inch deep.

Pork Sandwiches with Roasted Tomatoes and Jalapeños

PORK SHOULDER PROVIDES TENDER, MELT-IN-YOUR-MOUTH MEAT. PAIRED WITH SOUTH-OF-THE-BORDER SEASONINGS, THE RESULTS ARE RADICALLY DELICIOUS.

PREP: 40 MINUTES **GRILL:** 4 HOURS
COOK: 19 MINUTES **MAKES:** 12 SANDWICHES

- 4 pounds boneless pork shoulder
- 5 teaspoons cumin seeds, toasted*
- 2 tablespoons packed brown sugar
- 1 teaspoon kosher salt or ¾ teaspoon salt
- ½ teaspoon cayenne pepper
- ½ teaspoon black pepper
- 3 cloves garlic, minced
- 1 medium onion, thinly sliced
- 1 12-ounce can cola
- 1 to 2 cups chicken broth
- 1 pound roma tomatoes, cored, seeded, and chopped
- ¼ cup vegetable oil
- 1 12- to 16-ounce jar pickled jalapeños or jalapeño slices
- ⅔ cup snipped fresh cilantro
- 1 teaspoon kosher salt or ¾ teaspoon salt
- ¼ teaspoon black pepper
- 12 hoagie buns, Mexican torta rolls, or other hard rolls, split and toasted
- 2 limes, cut into wedges

1 Remove netting from roast(s), if present. Trim fat from meat. Using a mortar and pestle or spice grinder, grind cumin seeds. For rub, in a small bowl stir together cumin, brown sugar, 1 teaspoon salt, cayenne pepper, and ½ teaspoon black pepper. Sprinkle evenly over meat; rub in with your fingers.

2 For a charcoal grill, arrange medium-hot coals around the edge of grill. Test for medium heat in center of grill. Place meat in a roasting pan on grill rack in center of grill. Add the onion and cola to pan with the meat. Add enough broth to make liquid ½ inch deep. Cover and grill about 4 hours or until meat is extremely tender, adding broth to roasting pan if necessary and adding fresh coals every 45 to 60 minutes. (For a gas grill, preheat grill. Reduce heat to medium. Adjust for indirect cooking. Place meat in roasting pan; place pan on grill rack over the burner that is turned off and add onion, cola, and broth. Grill as directed.)

3 Meanwhile, in a large skillet cook tomatoes in hot oil over medium heat for 4 minutes, stirring occasionally. Drain jalapeños, reserving ½ cup juice; set jalapeños aside. Add reserved juice, cilantro, 1 teaspoon salt, and ¼ teaspoon black pepper to skillet. Bring to boiling; reduce heat. Simmer, uncovered, for 15 to 20 minutes or until slightly thickened, stirring occasionally.

4 Using a slotted spoon, transfer onion in roasting pan to a large bowl; set aside. Using tongs, transfer pork to a cutting board; discard cooking liquid. Using 2 forks, gently pull the meat into long thin shreds. Add shredded pork to onion.

5 To serve, spoon meat mixture and tomato mixture evenly into split buns. Serve with jalapeños and lime wedges.

***NOTE:** To toast cumin seeds, place them in small dry skillet. Cook over medium heat about 2 minutes or until fragrant, shaking pan occasionally to toast seeds evenly.

PER SANDWICH: 683 cal., 22 g total fat (6 g sat. fat), 98 mg chol., 1,354 mg sodium, 80 g carbo., 5 g fiber, 42 g pro.

4. Cook the tomato mixture, uncovered, until most of the liquid evaporates and the mixture thickens.

5. To shred pork, first use a sharp knife to cut the roast in large pieces. Insert two forks into a piece of meat and pull in opposite directions to shred.

6. Divide the meat evenly among the roll bottoms. Spoon tomato mixture on meat.

Pork and Apple Sandwiches with Honey-Pecan Glaze

BUTTERFLIED PORK CHOPS GRILL TO PERFECTION IN LESS THAN 10 MINUTES. THESE HEARTY SANDWICHES ARE READY IN SHORT ORDER FOR THOSE BUSY WEEKNIGHTS.

PREP: 25 MINUTES **GRILL:** 7 MINUTES
MAKES: 4 SANDWICHES

- 2 tenderized butterflied pork chops, halved, or 4 tenderized boneless pork loin slices (1¼ pounds total)
- Salt and black pepper
- 1 large tart apple, cored and cut crosswise into 4 rings
- 1 recipe Honey-Pecan Glaze
- ⅓ cup dairy sour cream
- ⅓ cup mayonnaise
- 2 teaspoons prepared horseradish
- 4 kaiser rolls, split and toasted
- 4 1-ounce slices provolone cheese

1 Lightly sprinkle chops with salt and pepper. For a charcoal grill, grill chops and apple rings on the rack of an uncovered grill directly over medium coals for 7 to 9 minutes or until chops are slightly pink in center (160°F) and apples are just tender, turning once halfway through grilling and brushing with Honey-Pecan Glaze during the last 3 minutes of grilling. (For a gas grill, preheat grill. Reduce heat to medium. Place chops and apple rings on grill rack over heat. Cover and grill as directed.)

2 Meanwhile, in a small bowl stir together sour cream, mayonnaise, and horseradish; spread on cut sides of toasted rolls. Place a cheese slice, pork chop, and an apple slice on roll bottoms; add roll tops.

HONEY-PECAN GLAZE: In a small saucepan combine ¼ cup honey; ¼ cup chopped pecans, toasted; 2 tablespoons butter or margarine; and ½ teaspoon finely shredded lemon peel. Heat and stir until butter melts.

PER SANDWICH: 822 cal., 46 g total fat (16 g sat. fat), 126 mg chol., 936 mg sodium, 55 g carbo., 3 g fiber, 46 g pro.

Mix It Up!

PICK ONE FROM EACH COLUMN TO CUSTOMIZE THE SANDWICH TO YOUR TASTE.

SEASON IT

Instead of Honey-Pecan Glaze, use one of the following:

- ¼ cup maple syrup and ¼ cup melted butter
- ½ cup bottled Italian salad dressing
- ½ cup bottled honey Dijon salad dressing
- ½ cup bottled light cranberry walnut salad dressing
- ½ cup bottled roasted garlic salad dressing

MIX IT IN

Instead of horseradish, stir in one of the following:

- 1 teaspoon refrigerated basil pesto
- 2 teaspoons honey mustard
- 2 teaspoons Creole mustard
- 1 teaspoon wasabi paste
- 2 teaspoons sweet pickle relish
- 2 teaspoons salsa
- 1 teaspoon chopped chipotle in adobo sauce

TOP IT

Top sandwiches with one of the following:

- Arugula
- Baby spinach
- Crisp-cooked bacon
- Thinly sliced red onion
- Caramelized onions
- Crumbled blue cheese
- Shredded Gruyère cheese
- Semisoft cheese with garlic and herbs

STEP-BY-STEP

1. Place chops and apple rings on grill rack over medium heat.

2. During the last 3 minutes of grilling, brush the chops with the Honey-Pecan Glaze.

3. To assemble sandwiches, spread roll bottoms and tops with sour cream mixture. Layer cheese, pork, and grilled apple slices on roll bottoms. Add roll tops and serve.

STEP-BY-STEP

1. Using a long serrated knife, cut the top crust from the loaf of bread. Cut off the bottom crust, leaving a 1-inch-thick slice from the center of the loaf.

2. Holding the center slice on its side, cut in half from end to end, making two ½-inch thick slices.

3. Place one bread slice on a clean work surface. Arrange half the cheese slices on bread, overlapping slices as necessary. Carefully spread pesto mixture over cheese.

Grilled Italian Panini

MILAN'S FAMOUS GRAB-AND-GO SANDWICH ON THE GRILL? SURE! WEIGHTING THE SANDWICH WITH A BRICK OR A FEW POTATOES PRESSES AS WELL AS ANY EXPENSIVE PANINI PAN.

PREP: 20 MINUTES **GRILL:** 8 MINUTES
MAKES: 4 SERVINGS

- 1 16-ounce loaf unsliced ciabatta or Italian bread
- 6 ounces thinly sliced provolone cheese
- ¼ cup mayonnaise
- 1 tablespoon purchased basil pesto
- 4 ounces thinly sliced capocollo or cooked ham
- 4 ounces thinly sliced salami
- 1 recipe Red Onion Relish
- 1 cup arugula
- 1 tablespoon olive oil

1 Carefully trim off and discard the top crust of the bread to make a flat surface. Turn bread over; trim off and discard bottom crust. Cut remaining bread in half horizontally to form two ½-inch-thick slices.

2 Place half the provolone cheese on 1 slice of bread. In a small bowl stir together mayonnaise and pesto; spread over cheese. Top with capocollo, salami, Red Onion Relish, arugula, the remaining cheese, and the other slice of bread. Evenly brush both sides of sandwich with oil.

3 For a charcoal grill, place sandwich on the lightly greased grill rack of an uncovered grill directly over medium coals. Place a 13×9×2-inch baking pan on sandwich; weight pan down with a brick or several baking potatoes. Grill about 5 minutes or until sandwich is light brown. Use hot pads to remove baking pan. Use a spatula to carefully turn over sandwich. Place weighted pan back on sandwich; grill about 3 minutes more or until cheese melts. (For a gas grill, preheat grill. Reduce heat to medium. Place sandwich on lightly greased grill rack over heat. Grill as directed.)

4 To serve, cut sandwich into 4 pieces.

RED ONION RELISH: In a small bowl combine 1 medium red onion, halved and thinly sliced; 2 tablespoons olive oil; 1 tablespoon red wine vinegar; and 1 teaspoon snipped fresh oregano. Season to taste with salt and black pepper. Cover; let stand at room temperature up to 2 hours.

PER SERVING: 840 cal., 51 g total fat (15 g sat. fat), 77 mg chol., 2,118 mg sodium, 62 g carbo., 4 g fiber, 33 g pro.

4. Layer capocollo and salami on the cheese layer. Top with Red Onion Relish. Add arugula and another layer of cheese. Top with remaining bread slice.

5. Place panini on grill rack. Place a baking pan on the sandwich. Add a brick to weigh down the sandwich.

6. After 5 minutes, remove the baking pan and brick. With a large spatula, turn the sandwich over. Replace the baking pan and brick and grill until cheese melts.

Open-Face Veggie Melts

THIS SANDWICH IS PERFECT FARE FOR THOSE WHO DO NOT EAT MEAT—EVEN CARNIVORES MAY ASK FOR SECONDS.

PREP: 25 MINUTES **GRILL:** 8 MINUTES
MAKES: 6 SANDWICHES

- 6 slices eggplant (½ inch thick)
- 6 slices yellow summer squash (½ inch thick)
- 2 slices red onion (½ inch thick)
- 1 8-ounce package whole white mushrooms
- 1 large red sweet pepper, seeded and cut into ½-inch slices
- ¼ cup vegetable oil
- 1 tablespoon balsamic vinegar
- 1 clove garlic, finely chopped
- ⅛ teaspoon salt
- ⅛ teaspoon black pepper
- ½ teaspoon Dijon-style mustard
- 1½ teaspoons packed brown sugar
- ¼ cup olive oil
- 1 16-ounce round loaf crusty bread, cut into six 1-inch-thick slices
- Olive oil
- 1 large clove garlic, peeled
- 2 cups shredded fontina cheese (8 ounces)

1 On a large baking pan combine eggplant, squash, red onion, mushrooms, and red sweet pepper. Drizzle with vegetable oil. Sprinkle with ½ teaspoon *salt* and ¼ teaspoon *black pepper;* toss to coat.

2 For a charcoal grill, place eggplant, squash, and onion on the lightly greased rack of an uncovered grill directly over medium-hot coals. Grill for 6 to 8 minutes or until vegetables are crisp-tender, turning once halfway through grilling. Transfer to a large bowl; keep warm.

3 Place mushrooms and sweet peppers in a grill basket. Place grill basket on grill rack over coals. Grill for 6 to 8 minutes or until tender. Add to eggplant mixture.

4 For dressing, whisk together vinegar, garlic, ⅛ teaspoon salt, ⅛ teaspoon black pepper, mustard, and sugar. Gradually whisk in ¼ cup olive oil. Pour over vegetables; toss to coat.

5 Brush cut sides of bread with olive oil. Cut garlic clove in half; rub cut sides of bread with garlic. Place bread on the grill rack over coals. Grill for 2 to 3 minutes or until light brown, turning once halfway through grilling. (For a gas grill, preheat grill. Reduce heat to medium-high. Place vegetables, then bread on lightly greased grill rack over heat. Cover and grill as directed.)

6 Divide vegetable mixture evenly between bread slices. Top evenly with cheese. Serve warm.

PER SANDWICH: 520 cal., 30 g total fat (9 g sat. fat), 44 mg chol., 890 mg sodium, 47 g carbo., 7 g fiber, 18 g pro.

STEP-BY-STEP

1. Place the vegetables on a large baking pan. Sprinkle with salt and pepper. Drizzle vegetable oil over the vegetables.

2. Place the mushrooms and the sweet pepper slices in a grill basket.

3. To make the dressing, combine vinegar, garlic, salt, pepper, mustard, and sugar in a bowl. Add olive oil in a thin stream, whisking until combined.

4. Brush the cut sides of the bread with olive oil. Cut a garlic clove in half. Rub the cut sides of the garlic over the cut sides of the bread.

5. Grill the bread until toasted on both sides. If you like, rub the bread slices again with halved garlic cloves.

6. Divide the vegetable mixture evenly among the bread slices, arranging veggies as desired. Sprinkle with cheese and serve immediately.

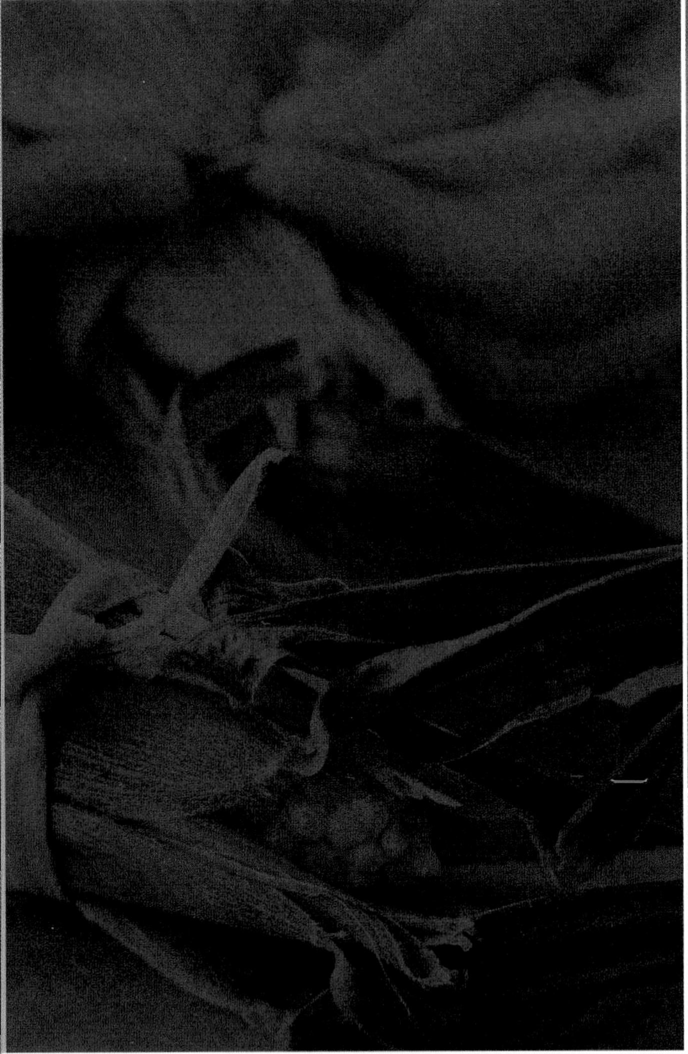

Vegetables

A KISS OF FLAME AND SMOKE IS THE PERFECT WAY TO HEIGHTEN THE FLAVOR OF THE ABUNDANCE FROM GARDENS, FARMERS' MARKETS, AND PRODUCE STANDS.

Grilled Eggplant Parmesan

THE PRETTY PURPLE SKIN OF YOUNG EGGPLANT IS DELICIOUSLY EDIBLE. WHEN EGGPLANT ARE EXTRA LARGE OR THE SKIN IS SLIGHTLY WRINKLED, PEEL THEM TO REMOVE BITTERNESS.

PREP: 8 MINUTES **GRILL:** 7 MINUTES
MAKES: 4 SERVINGS

- 8 slices eggplant, cut ¾ inch thick
- Salt and black pepper
- ¼ cup olive oil
- 2 cloves garlic, minced
- ⅔ cup finely shredded Parmesan cheese
- ⅔ cup finely shredded mozzarella cheese
- 4 medium roma tomatoes, thinly sliced
- ¼ cup finely shredded basil

1 Lightly sprinkle eggplant slices with salt and pepper. In a small bowl stir together olive oil and garlic; brush on both sides of eggplant slices. In another small bowl toss together Parmesan and mozzarella cheeses; set aside.

2 For a charcoal grill, grill eggplant slices on the rack of an uncovered grill directly over medium coals for 5 minutes. Turn eggplant slices and sprinkle with half of the cheese mixture. Top with tomato slices and the remaining cheese mixture. Cover and grill for 2 to 3 minutes more or until eggplant is tender and cheese melts. (For a gas grill, preheat grill. Reduce heat to medium. Place eggplant on grill rack over heat. Cover and grill as directed.) Before serving, top with shredded basil.

PER SERVING: 260 cal., 20 g total fat (6 g sat. fat), 22 mg chol., 494 mg sodium, 10 g carbo., 4 g fiber, 11 g pro.

Grilled Asparagus in Dill Butter

TENDER-SWEET ASPARAGUS WAS BORN TO BE BUTTERED.

PREP: 10 MINUTES **GRILL:** 7 MINUTES
MAKES: 4 TO 6 SERVINGS

- 1 pound asparagus spears
- 2 tablespoons butter, melted
- 1 tablespoon snipped fresh dill or 1 teaspoon dried dill
- 1 clove garlic, minced
- ¼ teaspoon cracked black pepper
- Finely shredded Parmesan cheese

1 Snap off and discard woody bases from asparagus. If desired, scrape off scales. Place asparagus in a large disposable foil pan. Drizzle with butter and sprinkle with dill, garlic, and pepper. Toss to combine.

2 For a charcoal grill, place foil pan on the rack of an uncovered grill directly over medium coals. Grill for 7 to 10 minutes or until asparagus is crisp-tender, stirring occasionally. (For a gas grill, preheat grill. Reduce heat to medium. Place foil pan on grill rack over heat. Cover and grill as directed.)

3 To serve, transfer asparagus to a serving dish. Sprinkle with Parmesan cheese.

PER SERVING: 142 cal., 11 g total fat (7 g sat. fat), 28 mg chol., 355 mg sodium, 2 g carbo., 1 g fiber, 8 g pro.

PREPARING GRILLED EGGPLANT PARMESAN, STEP-BY-STEP

1. Combine olive oil and minced garlic and brush onto both sides of the eggplant slices.

2. After turning the eggplant halfway through grilling, sprinkle with the mixture of Parmesan and mozzarella.

3. Top with tomato slices and the remaining cheese. Grill a few more minutes or until the eggplant is tender and cheese is melted.

WHEN CRISPY-FRESH BEANS STEAM TO PERFECTION WRAPPED IN A FOIL PACKET, CLEANUP IS A SNAP. THERE IS NO PAN TO WASH!

Green Beans Hobo Pack

WHEN CHOOSING GREEN OR WAX BEANS, LOOK FOR SLENDER PODS THAT SNAP WHEN BROKEN. BEANS WITH BUMPS ALONG THEIR LENGTHS ARE OVERLY RIPE AND MAY BE TOUGH.

PREP: 20 MINUTES **GRILL:** 25 MINUTES
MAKES: 4 SERVINGS

- 1 pound fresh green beans and/or wax beans
- 1 small shallot, thinly sliced
- 2 cloves garlic, thinly sliced
- ¼ teaspoon salt
- ¼ teaspoon black pepper
- 1 tablespoon olive oil

1 Remove stems and strings from beans. Fold a 36×18-inch piece of heavy foil in half to make an 18-inch square. Place beans, shallot, and garlic in center of foil. Sprinkle lightly with salt and pepper. Drizzle with olive oil. Bring up 2 opposite edges of foil; seal with a double fold. Fold remaining edges to completely enclose vegetables, leaving space for steam to build.

2 For a charcoal grill, grill packet on the rack of an uncovered grill directly over medium coals for 25 to 30 minutes or until vegetables are tender, turning packet occasionally. (For a gas grill, preheat grill. Reduce heat to medium. Place packet on a grill rack over heat. Cover and grill as directed.)

PER SERVING: 67 cal., 4 g total fat (0 g sat. fat), 0 mg chol., 152 mg sodium, 9 g carbo., 3 g fiber, 2 g pro.

Grilled Potato Salad

YELLOW-FLESH POTATOES ARE MEDIUM-STARCH VARIETIES THAT BOIL AND BAKE EQUALLY WELL. THE DELICATE SWEET YELLOW FLESH IS PERFECT IN SALADS.

PREP: 25 MINUTES **GRILL:** 50 MINUTES
MAKES: 8 TO 10 SERVINGS

- 6 medium Yukon gold or other yellow-flesh potatoes (about 2 pounds)
- 1 tablespoon olive oil
- ⅓ cup white balsamic vinegar
- ⅓ cup olive oil
- 1 tablespoon snipped fresh sage
- 1 tablespoon Dijon-style mustard
- 1 teaspoon maple syrup
- 1 clove garlic, minced
- ¼ teaspoon salt
- ⅛ teaspoon black pepper
- 2 cups fresh baby spinach
- 4 slices bacon, crisp-cooked, drained, and crumbled
- 2 hard-cooked eggs, coarsely chopped
- ¼ cup finely chopped red onion

1 Scrub potatoes thoroughly with a brush; pat dry. Prick potatoes with a fork. Rub potatoes evenly with the 1 tablespoon olive oil.

2 For a charcoal grill, arrange medium-hot coals around a drip pan. Test for medium heat above pan. Place potatoes on grill rack over pan. Cover and grill for 50 to 60 minutes or until potatoes are tender. (For a gas grill, preheat grill. Reduce heat to medium. Adjust for indirect cooking. Place potatoes on grill rack over the burner that is turned off. Grill as directed.)

3 Meanwhile, for vinaigrette, in a screw-top jar combine vinegar, the ⅓ cup olive oil, the sage, mustard, maple syrup, garlic, salt, and pepper. Cover and shake well. Set aside.

4 When potatoes are done, remove from grill and cool slightly. Coarsely chop potatoes. Transfer potatoes to an extra-large bowl. Add spinach, bacon, eggs, and red onion. Shake vinaigrette; pour over salad. Toss lightly to combine.

PER 1 CUP: 221 cal., 14 g total fat (3 g sat. fat), 56 mg chol., 209 mg sodium, 19 g carbo., 2 g fiber, 5 g pro.

Buttermilk Mashed Grilled Potatoes

BUTTERMILK ADDS WONDERFULLY RICH TANGINESS TO MASHED POTATOES. THEY TASTE LIKE FLAVORED WITH SOUR SOUR CREAM, BUT WITHOUT ALL THE FAT AND CALORIES.

PREP: 10 MINUTES **GRILL:** 50 MINUTES
MAKES: 6 SERVINGS

- 6 medium Yukon gold or other yellow-flesh potatoes (about 2 pounds total)
- 1 teaspoon vegetable oil
- ¾ cup buttermilk or milk
- 3 tablespoons butter or margarine
- ¼ teaspoon salt
- ¼ teaspoon ground white or black pepper

1 Scrub potatoes thoroughly with a brush; pat dry. Prick potatoes with a fork. Rub potatoes evenly with oil.

2 For a charcoal grill, arrange medium-hot coals around a drip pan. Test for medium heat above pan. Place potatoes on grill rack over pan. Cover and grill for 50 to 60 minutes or until potatoes are tender. (For a gas grill, preheat grill. Reduce heat to medium. Adjust for indirect cooking. Place potatoes on grill rack over the burner that is turned off. Grill as directed.)

3 Just before potatoes are done, in a small saucepan combine buttermilk, butter, salt, and pepper. Heat over low heat until warm, stirring frequently (do not boil).

4 When potatoes are done, remove from grill and cool slightly. If desired, peel potatoes. Transfer potatoes to a large mixing bowl; mash with a potato masher or beat with an electric mixer on low speed. Gradually add warm buttermilk mixture, mashing or beating until smooth.

PER ABOUT ¾ CUP: 157 cal., 7 g total fat (4 g sat. fat), 18 mg chol., 199 mg sodium, 20 g carbo., 2 g fiber, 4 g pro.

Grilled Vegetable and Orzo Salad

TINY, RICE-SHAPE ORZO COOKS MORE QUICKLY THAN MOST PASTAS—BE SURE TO LISTEN FOR YOUR KITCHEN TIMER.

PREP: 45 MINUTES **MARINATE:** 2 HOURS
GRILL: 10 MINUTES **MAKES:** 8 SERVINGS

- ⅔ cup balsamic vinegar
- ½ cup olive oil
- 2 tablespoons finely chopped shallot
- 4 teaspoons snipped fresh rosemary
- 4 teaspoons snipped fresh thyme
- 2 teaspoons coarse-grain Dijon-style mustard
- ½ teaspoon salt
- ½ teaspoon black pepper
- 1 large red onion, cut into ½-inch slices
- 1 medium zucchini, quartered lengthwise
- 1 medium yellow sweet pepper, quartered and seeded
- 4 medium roma tomatoes, halved lengthwise and seeded
- 12 ounces dried orzo (2 cups)
- ½ cup crumbled feta or goat cheese (chèvre) (2 ounces)

1 For vinaigrette, in a screw-top jar combine vinegar, olive oil, shallot, rosemary, thyme, mustard, salt, and black pepper. Cover and shake well.

2 To hold onion slices together during grilling, insert short wooden skewers* into onion slices from the sides. In a large resealable plastic bag set in a shallow dish combine onion, zucchini, sweet pepper, and tomatoes. Pour vinaigrette over vegetables in bag; seal bag. Marinate in the refrigerator 2 to 4 hours, turning bag occasionally.

3 Meanwhile, prepare orzo according to package directions; drain. Rinse with cold water; drain again. Place orzo in a large bowl; set aside.

4 Drain vegetables, reserving vinaigrette. For a charcoal grill, grill vegetables on the rack of an uncovered grill directly over medium coals until crisp-tender and lightly charred, turning once halfway through grilling. Allow 5 to 6 minutes for tomatoes, 7 to 8 minutes for zucchini and peppers, and about 10 minutes for the onion. (For a gas grill, preheat grill. Reduce heat to medium. Place vegetables on grill rack over heat. Cover and grill as directed.) Transfer vegetables to a cutting board; cool slightly. Coarsely chop the vegetables.

5 Add vegetables and reserved vinaigrette to orzo; toss to combine. Sprinkle with feta cheese. Serve at room temperature.

***NOTE.** To keep skewers from burning on the grill, before grilling soak them in enough water to cover for at least 30 minutes. Drain before using.

PER 1 CUP: 354 cal., 16 g total fat (3 g sat. fat), 6 mg chol., 265 mg sodium, 45 g carbo., 2 g fiber, 8 g pro.

PREPARING BUTTERMILK MASHED GRILLED POTATOES, STEP-BY-STEP

1. Prick each potato several times with a fork to allow steam to escape and prevent the potatoes from bursting.

2. Dip your fingers in vegetable oil and rub the oil on the potatoes.

3. Grill the potatoes until they are easily pierced with a fork and very tender.

4. Because the skins are tender, you don't need to peel the potatoes. Mash with a potato masher or electric mixer until almost smooth.

5. Slowly add the warm buttermilk mixture to the potatoes, continuing to mash or beat until smooth.

STEP-BY-STEP

1. Holding each half of zucchini, scoop out seeds and pulp, leaving ¼ to ½ inch of pulp on the bottoms and around the edges.

2. To keep the zucchini from falling into the coals, use a grilling tray. Turn the zucchini when the cut sides begin to turn brown.

3. Remove the tray from the grill and spoon the Bacon Gremolata into the zucchini shells. Return the zucchini to the grill and grill until zucchini is crisp-tender.

Zucchini Boats with Bacon Gremolata

PREPARE THESE SCRUMPTIOUS BOATS WHEN ZUCCHINI IS AT ITS PROLIFIC BEST. THE SMOKY GOODNESS OF BACON, RICH CHEESE, AND TANGY LEMON PEEL WILL WIN YOU OVER.

PREP: 35 MINUTES **GRILL:** 8 MINUTES
MAKES: 8 SERVINGS

- 4 medium-large zucchini (6 to 7 ounces each)
- 2 tablespoons lemon juice
- 4 teaspoons olive oil
- 3 large cloves garlic, minced
- ¼ teaspoon salt
- ¼ teaspoon black pepper
- 1 recipe Bacon Gremolata

1 Cut zucchini in half lengthwise. Using a spoon, scoop out centers to form ¼- to ½-inch-thick shells; set aside.

2 In a small bowl stir together lemon juice, oil, garlic, salt, and pepper. Brush insides of zucchini shells with lemon mixture. Place shells, cut sides down, on a lightly greased grilling tray.

3 For a charcoal grill, grill zucchini on grilling tray on the rack of an uncovered grill directly over medium coals for 5 to 7 minutes or until cut sides start to brown. Turn zucchini; grill for 1 minute more. (For a gas grill, preheat grill. Reduce heat to medium. Place zucchini on grilling tray on grill rack over heat. Cover and grill as directed.) Using hot pads, remove tray from grill.

4 Spoon Bacon Gremolata into zucchini shells, mounding slightly and pressing down lightly. Return to grill. Cover and grill for 2 to 4 minutes more or until zucchini is crisp-tender and cheese starts to melt.

BACON GREMOLATA: In a small bowl stir together 16 slices bacon, crisp-cooked, drained, and finely crumbled, or 1 cup finely chopped Canadian-style bacon; 1 cup finely shredded Parmesan and/or Romano cheese (4 ounces); ¼ cup snipped fresh basil; ¼ cup finely chopped pepperoncini salad pepper or fresh jalapeño chile pepper;* 4 teaspoons finely shredded lemon peel; 2 cloves garlic, minced; and ½ teaspoon black pepper.

***NOTE:** Because hot chile peppers contain volatile oils that can burn your skin and eyes, avoid direct contact with chiles as much as possible. When working with chile peppers, wear plastic or rubber gloves. If your bare hands do touch the chile peppers, wash your hands well with soap and water.

PER ½ ZUCCHINI: 168 cal., 12 g total fat (4 g sat. fat), 25 mg chol., 731 mg sodium, 5 g carbo., 1 g fiber, 11 g pro.

Mix It Up!

PICK ONE FROM EACH COLUMN TO CUSTOMIZE THE ZUCCHINI BOATS TO YOUR TASTE.

SEASON IT

To the lemon mixture, add one of the following:

- ⅛ teaspoon cayenne pepper
- ⅛ teaspoon crushed red pepper
- ½ teaspoon paprika
- 1 teaspoon chopped fresh dillweed or ½ teaspoon dried mint, crushed
- 1 teaspoon chopped fresh thyme or ½ teaspoon dried thyme, crushed
- 1 teaspoon chopped fresh mint or ½ teaspoon dried mint, crushed

MIX IT IN

Instead of Parmesan and/or Romano cheese, use one of the following:

- Monterey Jack cheese with jalapeño peppers
- Colby Jack cheese
- Smoked cheddar cheese
- Asiago cheese
- Crumbled blue cheese
- Gouda cheese
- Crumbled feta cheese

TOP IT

Sprinkle one of the following:

- Toasted pine nuts
- Toasted chopped walnuts
- Toasted chopped pecans
- Toasted sliced almonds
- Small fresh basil leaves
- Finely shredded lemon peel
- Chopped fresh chives
- Zucchini blossoms
- Finely shredded Parmesan cheese

Grilled Vegetable and Mozzarella Ensalada

WHEN SHOPPING FOR FRESH MOZZARELLA, SQUEEZE IT GENTLY. THE FRESHEST CHEESE WILL FEEL SUPER-SOFT AND YIELD TO GENTLE PRESSURE.

PREP: 35 MINUTES **MARINATE:** 30 MINUTES
GRILL: 7 MINUTES **MAKES:** 4 SERVINGS

- 4 medium roma tomatoes, halved lengthwise
- 2 small zucchini, halved lengthwise
- 1 medium yellow sweet pepper, seeded and quartered
- 1 medium red onion, cut into wedges
- 1 recipe Pear-Infused Balsamic Vinaigrette
- 8 slices baguette-style French bread, cut ½ inch thick
- 1 tablespoon olive oil
- 1 10-ounce package Italian mixed salad greens (romaine and radicchio)
- ¼ cup snipped fresh basil
- 4 ounces fresh mozzarella, cut into chunks

1 Place tomatoes, zucchini, sweet pepper, and onion in a large resealable plastic bag set in a shallow dish. Pour Pear-Infused Balsamic Vinaigrette over vegetables in bag; seal bag. Marinate at room temperature for 30 minutes, turning bag occasionally.

2 Drain vegetables, reserving vinaigrette. For a charcoal grill, grill vegetables on the rack of an uncovered grill directly over medium coals. Grill sweet pepper and onion for 7 to 10 minutes or until crisp-tender, turning once. Grill zucchini 5 to 7 minutes or until crisp-tender, turning once. Grill tomatoes, skin sides down, about 5 minutes or until soft and skins begin to char. (For a gas grill, preheat grill. Reduce heat to medium. Place vegetables on grill rack over heat. Cover and grill as directed.) Transfer vegetables to a cutting board; cool slightly.

3 Lightly brush baguette slices with oil. Grill directly over heat about 2 minutes or until light brown and crisp, turning once.

4 In an extra-large bowl combine salad greens and basil. Add reserved vinaigrette; toss to coat. Arrange greens on a large platter. Cut grilled zucchini and sweet peppers into bite-size pieces. Arrange grilled vegetables and mozzarella cheese on greens. Serve with grilled baguette slices.

PEAR-INFUSED BALSAMIC VINAIGRETTE: In a screw-top jar combine ¼ cup pear-infused white balsamic vinegar or other vinegar, 3 tablespoons olive oil, 1 tablespoon brown sugar, ½ teaspoon salt, and ½ teaspoon black pepper. Cover and shake well.

PER SERVING: 422 cal., 22 g total fat (6 g sat. fat), 22 mg chol., 720 mg sodium, 46 g carbo., 5 g fiber, 12 g pro.

Balsamic-Glazed Onion Hobo Pack

IT IS NOT NECESSARY TO USE EXPENSIVE, LONG-AGED BALSAMIC VINEGAR IN THIS RECIPE. ANY BOTTLE WILL DO MAGIC TO THE ONIONS IN THIS PACKET.

PREP: 15 MINUTES **GRILL:** 25 MINUTES
MAKES: 4 SERVINGS

- 1 pound assorted red or white sweet onions and/or spring onions, cut into ½-inch-thick wedges
- ¼ teaspoon salt
- ¼ teaspoon black pepper
- 2 tablespoons balsamic vinegar
- ½ teaspoon snipped fresh thyme

1 Fold a 36×18-inch piece of heavy foil in half to make an 18-inch square. Place onions in center of foil. Sprinkle with salt and pepper. Drizzle with balsamic vinegar. Bring up 2 opposite edges of foil; seal with a double fold. Fold remaining edges to completely enclose onions, leaving space for steam to build.

2 For a charcoal grill, grill packet on the rack of an uncovered grill directly over medium coals for 25 to 30 minutes or until onions are tender, turning packet occasionally. (For a gas grill, preheat grill. Reduce heat to medium. Place packet on a grill rack over heat. Cover and grill as directed.) Sprinkle onions with thyme before serving.

PER ABOUT ⅔ CUP: 44 cal., 0 g total fat, 0 mg chol., 156 mg sodium, 10 g carbo., 1 g fiber, 1 g pro.

PREPARING GRILLED VEGETABLE AND MOZZARELLA ENSALADA, STEP-BY-STEP

1. With a pastry brush, coat both sides of the bread slices with olive oil.

2. Grill the vegetables until they are charred on both sides. Tomatoes will be soft and other veggies crisp-tender.

3. Drizzle vinaigrette over the salad greens and basil. Toss with tongs to mix.

4. Using a large sharp knife, cut the tomatoes, zucchini, sweet pepper, and onion into bite-size pieces.

5. Toss all the cut-up vegetables together. Layer the vegetable mixture on top of the greens.

PREPARING GREEK HALOUMI LAYERED SALAD, STEP-BY-STEP

1. Cut the bottom off the pepper and pull out seeds and membrane. Slice pepper crosswise to make rings.

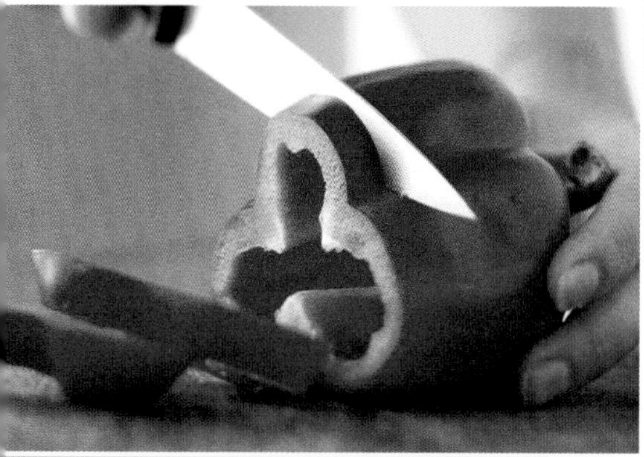

2. Choose a Haloumi cheese that is firm and will not crumble when sliced. Cut the cheese into ½-thick-slices.

3. Halve the peach, cutting around the pit. Separate the halves and remove the pit with your fingers.

4. Grill the onion and pepper until tender and the peaches and cheese until they are heated through, turning once.

5. Arrange the peach slices, onion slices, pepper rings, and cheese on a large platter. Drizzle with dressing and serve warm.

Greek Haloumi Layered Salad

HALOUMI—THE FAMOUS FIRM CHEESE FROM CYPRUS—HAS AN EXTREMELY HIGH MELTING POINT, WHICH MAKES THE SALTY GOAT'S AND SHEEP'S MILK CHEESE IDEAL FOR GRILLING. LEMON JUICE ACCENTUATES THE FLAVOR OF HALOUMI.

PREP: 20 MINUTES **GRILL:** 8 MINUTES
MAKES: 4 SERVINGS

- 2 tablespoons lemon juice
- 2 tablespoons olive oil
- ¼ teaspoon sugar
- ⅛ teaspoon salt
- 1 large red sweet pepper, seeded and cut into ½-inch-thick rings
- 1 large fresh peach, pitted, peeled (if desired), and cut into wedges
- 4 slices red onion, cut ½ inch thick
- 8 ounces Haloumi cheese,* cut into ½-inch slices
- Olive oil

1 For dressing, in a small screw-top jar combine lemon juice, the 2 tablespoons oil, sugar, and salt. Cover and shake well; set aside. Brush sweet pepper rings, peach wedges, onion slices, and cheese slices lightly with additional oil.

2 For a charcoal grill, grill sweet pepper, peach, onion, and cheese on the greased rack of an uncovered grill directly over medium coals until vegetables are tender and peach wedges and cheese slices are heated through, turning once halfway through grilling. Allow 8 to 10 minutes for cheese, 6 to 8 minutes for sweet pepper and onion, and 1 to 2 minutes for peach. (For a gas grill, preheat grill. Reduce heat to medium. Place sweet pepper, peach, onion, and cheese on greased grill rack over heat. Cover and grill as directed.)

3 On a serving platter arrange sweet pepper, onion, cheese, and peach wedges. Shake dressing; drizzle over salad.

***TIP:** When purchasing Haloumi cheese, be sure it is firm, not crumbly, and is free of cracks.

PER SERVING: 280 cal., 22 g total fat (10 g sat. fat), 50 mg chol., 708 mg sodium, 12 g carbo., 2 g fiber, 9 g pro.

Veggie Trio Salad

THIS FRESH-TASTING THREE-VEGGIE COMBO IS SENSATIONAL ALONGSIDE SIMPLY GRILLED FISH FILLETS.

PREP: 25 MINUTES **GRILL:** 8 MINUTES
MAKES: 6 SERVINGS

- 3 tablespoons snipped fresh basil, oregano, and/or parsley
- 3 tablespoons balsamic vinegar
- 3 tablespoons olive oil
- 2 cloves garlic, minced
- ¼ teaspoon salt
- ⅛ teaspoon cayenne pepper
- 1 medium eggplant (about 1 pound), cut lengthwise into ½-inch-thick slices
- 2 medium red sweet peppers, seeded and quartered lengthwise
- 2 medium sweet onions, cut into ½-inch slices

1 In a small bowl stir together herbs, vinegar, oil, garlic, salt, and cayenne pepper. Brush eggplant, sweet peppers, and onions with some of the herb mixture.

2 For a charcoal grill, grill vegetables on the rack of an uncovered grill directly over medium coals for 8 to 12 minutes or until crisp-tender, turning and brushing once with some of the herb mixture halfway through grilling. (For a gas grill, preheat grill. Reduce heat to medium. Place vegetables on grill rack over heat. Cover and grill as directed.)

3 Cut grilled vegetables into bite-size pieces. Transfer vegetables to a serving dish; toss with the remaining herb mixture. Serve warm or at room temperature.

PER ABOUT 1 CUP: 116 cal., 7 g total fat (1 g sat. fat), 0 mg chol., 103 mg sodium, 12 g carbo., 4 g fiber, 2 g pro.

Grilled Corn Salad

WHEN FARMER'S MARKET STANDS ARE PILED HIGH WITH GOLDEN EARS, BUY THEM BY THE BAGFUL TO MAKE THIS SALAD THE VERY SAME DAY—WHILE THE CORN IS AT ITS HEIGHT OF SWEETNESS.

PREP: 40 MINUTES **GRILL:** 25 MINUTES
COOL: 30 MINUTES **MAKES:** 6 TO 8 SERVINGS

- ⅓ cup olive oil
- ⅓ cup lemon juice
- 1 tablespoon Worcestershire-style marinade for chicken
- 3 cloves garlic, minced
- ½ teaspoon black pepper
- ¼ teaspoon salt
- Few dashes bottled hot pepper sauce
- 6 fresh ears corn (with husks)
- 2 tablespoons butter, softened
- 2 tablespoons snipped fresh rosemary or 2 teaspoons dried rosemary, crushed
- 1 teaspoon salt
- 1 teaspoon black pepper
- 20 miniature sweet peppers or 4 medium sweet peppers, seeded and halved
- ½ cup finely shredded Cotija or Parmesan cheese (2 ounces)
- Romaine leaves (optional)

1 For dressing, in a screw-top jar combine olive oil, lemon juice, Worcestershire sauce, garlic, the ½ teaspoon black pepper, ¼ teaspoon salt, and the hot pepper sauce. Cover and shake well; refrigerate until ready to serve.

2 Peel back cornhusks but do not remove. Gently rinse corn and scrub with a stiff brush to remove silks. Spread butter over corn. Sprinkle with rosemary, the 1 teaspoon salt, and 1 teaspoon black pepper. Fold husks back around corn and tie with 100%-cotton kitchen string or strips of husk.

3 For a charcoal grill, grill corn on the rack of an uncovered grill directly over medium coals for 25 to 30 minutes or until corn kernels are tender, turning and rearranging ears occasionally. Add sweet peppers to grill the last 8 to 10 minutes of grilling, turning often to brown evenly. (For a gas grill, preheat grill. Reduce heat to medium. Place corn and sweet peppers on grill rack over heat. Cover and grill as directed.) Cool ears for 30 minutes. Remove string; peel back husks. Cut kernels from cobs. Cut sweet peppers into bite-size pieces.

4 On a large baking pan or in a bowl combine corn, peppers, cheese, and dressing; toss lightly to combine. Serve warm or at room temperature. If desired, serve salad over a bed of romaine leaves.

SKILLET METHOD: Remove husks and silks from corn. Cut kernels from cobs. In a large skillet cook corn kernels in the 1 tablespoon oil over medium-high heat about 5 minutes or until corn is tender and golden brown, stirring often. Reduce heat as necessary to prevent corn from popping out of the skillet. Prepare salad as directed.

PER ABOUT 1 CUP: 260 cal., 19 g total fat (2 g sat. fat), 9 mg chol., 138 mg sodium, 24 g carbo., 4 g fiber, 7 g pro.

Lemon-Spiked Vegetables Hobo Pack

DO TRY BROCCOLI RABE IF YOU HAVEN'T ALREADY. ITS FLAVOR IS PUNGENT AND SLIGHTLY BITTER.

PREP: 15 MINUTES **GRILL:** 25 MINUTES
MAKES: 4 SERVINGS

- 1½ cups cauliflower florets
- 1½ cups broccoli rabe or broccoli florets
- 1 cup assorted baby carrots with tops, halved lengthwise
- 4 lemon slices
- ½ teaspoon lemon-pepper seasoning
- ¼ teaspoon salt
- 1 tablespoon water

1 Fold a 36×18-inch piece of heavy foil in half to make an 18-inch square. Place cauliflower, broccoli rabe, carrots, and lemon slices in center of foil. Sprinkle with lemon pepper and salt. Drizzle with the water. Bring up 2 opposite edges of foil; seal with a double fold. Fold remaining edges to completely enclose vegetables, leaving space for steam to build.

2 For a charcoal grill, grill packet on the rack of an uncovered grill directly over medium coals for 25 to 30 minutes or until vegetables are tender, turning packet occasionally. (For a gas grill, preheat grill. Reduce heat to medium. Place packet on a grill rack over heat. Cover and grill as directed.)

PER ¾ CUP: 28 cal., 0 g total fat, 0 mg chol., 314 mg sodium, 6 g carbo., 2 g fiber, 2 g pro.

PREPARING GRILLED-CORN SALAD, STEP-BY-STEP

1. Spread the butter on the corn. Sprinkle with the herb mixture, rotating the ear to cover all sides.

2. Fold the husks back in place to cover the corn. Tie a small piece of husk around the tip.

3. During grilling, turn the ears frequently so the corn cooks evenly.

4. Peel back the husks. Grasping the husk, hold an ear upright and cut the kernels from the cob with a sharp knife.

5. Combine the corn, peppers, and cheese. Add the dressing and mix well. Spoon the mixture into a serving bowl.

PREPARING MEXICAN-STYLE STREET CORN, STEP-BY-STEP

1. Turn the ears of corn and rearrange several times while grilling. To test for doneness, peel back a husk and insert a fork into the kernels.

2. When the corn is done, peel back the husks. Brush the corn with the mayonnaise mixture.

3. For easy cleanup, place the cheese in a pan. Hold the ears over the pan and sprinkle with cheese.

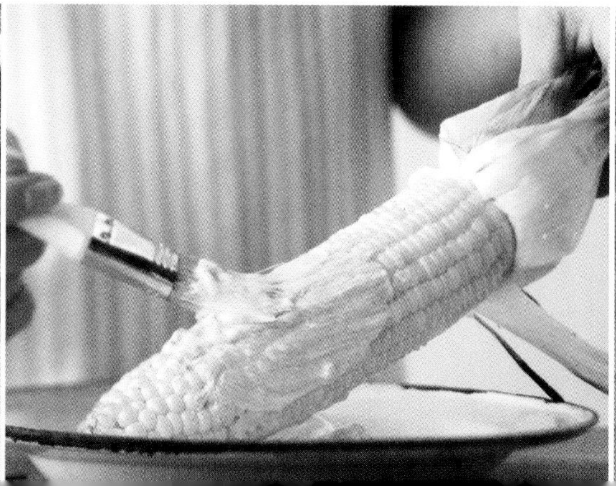

Mexican-Style Street Corn

STREET VENDORS IN MEXICAN CITIES LARGE AND SMALL SERVE THIS FRAGRANT TREAT FROM STANDS WHERE CHILDREN GATHER FOR AFTER-SCHOOL SNACKS.

PREP: 25 MINUTES **GRILL:** 25 MINUTES
MAKES: 4 SERVINGS

- 4 fresh ears corn (with husks)
- 1 tablespoon vegetable oil
- ½ cup mayonnaise
- 1 clove garlic, minced
- ¼ to ½ teaspoon paprika
- ¼ teaspoon bottled hot pepper sauce (optional)
- 4 ounces Cotija, Parmesan, or aged cheddar* cheese, grated
- Bottled hot pepper sauce (optional)

1 Peel back cornhusks but do not remove. Gently rinse corn and scrub with a stiff brush to remove silks. Brush corn with oil. Fold husks back around corn and tie with 100%-cotton kitchen string or strips of husk.

2 For a charcoal grill, grill corn on the rack of an uncovered grill directly over medium coals for 25 to 30 minutes or until corn kernels are tender, turning and rearranging ears occasionally. (For a gas grill, preheat grill. Reduce heat to medium. Place corn on grill rack over heat. Cover and grill as directed.)

3 Meanwhile, in a shallow dish stir together mayonnaise, garlic, paprika, and, if desired, the ¼ teaspoon hot pepper sauce. Place cheese in another shallow dish or pie plate.

4 To serve, peel back corn husks. Roll corn in mayonnaise mixture to coat; sprinkle evenly with cheese. If desired, serve with additional hot pepper sauce.

***NOTE:** If using cheddar cheese, choose an aged cheese that will be crumbly and dry when grated.

PER EAR: 396 cal., 36 g total fat (4 g sat. fat), 46 mg chol., 184 mg sodium, 17 g carbo., 2 g fiber, 11 g pro.

Grilled Vegetable Platter

THIS GORGEOUS PLATTER SERVES DOUBLE DUTY—AS A NUTRITIOUS SIDE DISH AND A STRIKINGLY COLORFUL CENTERPIECE.

PREP: 25 MINUTES **GRILL:** 30 MINUTES
MAKES: 8 TO 10 SERVINGS

- 1 pound baby pattypan squash (about 3 cups)
- 2 medium yellow, orange, and/or red sweet peppers, seeded and cut into strips or squares
- 12 ounces fresh green beans, trimmed (3 cups)
- 15 baby carrots with tops, trimmed
- 10 cherry sweet peppers
- 2 tablespoons olive oil or vegetable oil
- ½ teaspoon salt
- ¼ teaspoon black pepper
- 2 teaspoons finely shredded lemon peel
- 2 teaspoons lemon juice
- 2 cloves garlic, minced
- Nonstick cooking spray

1 In an extra-large bowl combine squash, sweet peppers, beans, carrots, cherry sweet peppers, oil, salt, and black pepper; toss to combine. In a small bowl stir together lemon peel, lemon juice, and garlic; set aside.

2 Lightly coat an unheated grill wok with nonstick cooking spray. Place the vegetables in the wok. For a charcoal grill, place the wok on the rack of an uncovered grill directly over medium coals. Grill for 30 to 35 minutes or until vegetables are crisp-tender and light brown, stirring occasionally. (For a gas grill, preheat grill. Reduce heat to medium. Place wok on grill rack over heat. Cover and grill as directed.)

3 Return cooked vegetables to the bowl. Add the lemon mixture; toss to coat. To serve, arrange vegetables on a large platter.

PER SERVING: 75 cal., 4 g total fat (1 g sat. fat), 0 mg chol., 289 mg sodium, 10 g carbo., 3 g fiber, 2 g pro.

Desserts

KEEP THOSE HOME FIRES BURNING. THESE DIVINE GRILLED DESSERTS END OUTDOOR DINNERS ON A SENSATIONALLY SWEET NOTE.

STEP-BY-STEP

1. Break pretzels into pieces and place in a plastic bag. Crush the pretzels by rolling a rolling pin over bag.

2. Cut butter in pieces and add to pretzels, brown sugar, and flour. Mix with your hands until crumbly.

3. Layer half of the peach mixture in pan. Drizzle with caramel topping and layer remaining peach mixture on top.

4. After 30 minutes, remove the foil. Evenly sprinkle the pretzel topping over peaches. Grill until peach mixture is bubbly.

5. To serve, spoon warm cobbler into bowls. Add a scoop of vanilla ice cream to each bowl and drizzle caramel topping over all.

Grilled Peach Cobbler

THE FRESH SWEETNESS OF COBBLER—A DESSERT ASSOCIATED WITH GRANDMA'S KITCHEN OVEN—BECOMES EVEN MORE WONDERFUL WHEN KISSED BY SMOKE AND GRILLED ALFRESCO.

PREP: 25 MINUTES **GRILL:** 40 MINUTES
COOL: 20 MINUTES **MAKES:** 6 SERVINGS

- ¾ cup coarsely crushed pretzels (about 3 ounces)
- ¾ cup packed brown sugar
- ⅓ cup all-purpose flour
- ⅓ cup butter
- 5 medium fresh peaches, peeled, pitted, and sliced, or 5 cups frozen unsweetened peach slices, thawed
- ½ cup granulated sugar
- 1 tablespoon lemon juice
- 1 tablespoon quick-cooking tapioca
- ½ teaspoon ground cinnamon
- ½ teaspoon ground ginger
- ¼ teaspoon salt
- ⅓ cup caramel ice cream topping
- Caramel ice cream topping (optional)
- Vanilla ice cream (optional)

1 For topping, in a medium bowl stir together crushed pretzels, brown sugar, and flour. Using your fingers, work in butter until mixture resembles coarse crumbs. Set aside.

2 In a large bowl combine peaches, granulated sugar, lemon juice, tapioca, cinnamon, ginger, and salt. Place half of the peach mixture in a 2-quart disposable foil pan. Drizzle the ⅓ cup caramel topping over the peaches in pan. Top with remaining peach mixture. Cover pan tightly with foil.

3 For a charcoal grill, arrange medium-hot coals around a drip pan. Test for medium heat above the pan. Place foil pan on grill rack over pan. Cover and grill for 30 minutes. Uncover pan. Sprinkle topping evenly over peach mixture in foil pan. Cover grill; cook for 10 to 15 minutes more or until mixture is bubbly and topping is light brown. (For a gas grill, preheat grill. Reduce heat to medium. Adjust for indirect cooking. Place foil pan on grill rack over the burner that is turned off. Grill as directed.)

4 Remove foil pan from grill. Cool on a wire rack for 20 minutes. If desired, drizzle cobbler with additional caramel ice cream topping and serve with ice cream.

PER ⅔ CUP: 441 cal., 11 g total fat (7 g sat. fat), 27 mg chol., 432 mg sodium, 86 g carbo., 3 g fiber, 4 g pro.

Mix It Up!

PICK ONE FROM EACH COLUMN TO CUSTOMIZE THE COBBLER TO YOUR TASTE.

SEASON IT

Instead of ginger, use one of the following:

- ¼ teaspoon ground cloves
- ½ teaspoon ground nutmeg
- ½ teaspoon finely shredded lemon peel
- ½ teaspoon ground mace
- ¼ teaspoon ground cardamom
- ¼ teaspoon ground allspice
- ¼ teaspoon ground chipotle chile pepper

MIX IT IN

Instead of the caramel topping, use one of the following:

- ½ cup fresh blueberries
- ½ cup fresh raspberries
- ½ cup fresh blackberries
- ¼ cup honey
- ⅓ cup white baking pieces
- ⅓ cup toffee pieces
- ⅓ cup crushed butterscotch candies

TOP IT

Instead of the pretzels, use ¾ cup of one of the following coarsely crushed:

- Graham crackers
- Vanilla wafers
- Shortbread cookies
- Granola
- Chopped mixed nuts
- Gingersnaps
- Amaretti

Dessert Polenta with Grilled Balsamic Plums

ITALIAN CUISINE IS FAMOUS FOR DESSERTS THAT FEATURE LOCAL FRUITS AT THEIR MOST FABULOUS, FRESH, AND FLAVORFUL PEAK. FOLLOW THE LEAD BY PICKING PLUMS AT THEIR FINEST IN LATE SUMMER.

PREP: 30 MINUTES **GRILL:** 8 MINUTES
CHILL: 4 HOURS **MAKES:** 8 SERVINGS

- 2¼ cups water
- ¾ cup yellow cornmeal
- ¾ cup cold water
- ¼ cup packed brown sugar
- ½ teaspoon salt
- ¼ teaspoon ground allspice or ground cardamom
- 1 teaspoon finely shredded orange peel
- 3 tablespoons butter, melted
- 8 small plums, halved lengthwise and pitted
- ¼ cup balsamic vinegar
- Powdered sugar
- Fresh thyme sprigs (optional)

1 In a medium saucepan bring the 2¼ cups water to boiling. Meanwhile, in a medium bowl stir together cornmeal, the ¾ cup cold water, the brown sugar, salt, and allspice. Slowly add cornmeal mixture to boiling water, stirring constantly. Cook and stir until mixture returns to boiling; reduce heat to low. Cover and cook for 10 to 15 minutes or until thick, stirring occasionally. Stir in orange peel. Pour hot cornmeal mixture into a buttered 8×8×2-inch baking pan; cool. Cover and chill for at least 4 hours or until polenta is firm.

2 Remove polenta from pan. Cut into 4-inch squares. Brush both sides of polenta squares with melted butter.

3 For a charcoal grill, grill polenta squares on the rack of an uncovered grill directly over medium coals for 8 to 10 minutes or until light brown, turning once halfway through grilling. Add plums, cut sides down, to the grill the last 4 to 5 minutes of grilling or until tender and heated through, turning once halfway through grilling. (For a gas grill, preheat grill. Reduce heat to medium. Place polenta squares, then plums on grill rack over heat. Cover and grill as directed.)

4 To serve, cut each polenta square in half diagonally, forming 8 triangles. Arrange a polenta triangle and 2 plum halves on each dessert plate. Drizzle plums evenly with balsamic vinegar. Sift powdered sugar over each serving and, if desired, garnish with thyme sprigs.

PER SERVING: 160 cal., 5 g total fat (2 g sat. fat), 12 mg chol., 184 mg sodium, 28 g carbo., 2 g fiber, 2 g pro.

STEP-BY-STEP

1. Scrape the hot cornmeal mixture into the generously buttered pan. Use the rubber spatula to spread the mixture evenly in the pan.

2. Invert the chilled pan of polenta onto a work surface to remove the polenta. Cut into quarters, making four 4-inch squares.

3. Grill the polenta squares until both sides are light brown, turning once. Grill the plums until they are tender, about 4 minutes.

DEEP, DARK, AND RICH BALSAMIC VINEGAR MARRIES AS HAPPILY WITH SUMMER-SWEET FRUITS AS IT DOES WITH SAVORY INGREDIENTS.

Cardamom Kulfi with Grilled Pineapple

UNLIKE OTHER FRUIT, PINEAPPLES DO NOT CONTINUE TO RIPEN AFTER THEY ARE HARVESTED. TO BE SURE THAT THE TROPICAL BEAUTY YOU CHOOSE IS FULL OF FLAVOR, LOOK FOR SLIGHTLY SOFT FRUITS WITH FULL, GOLDEN COLOR AND NO SIGNS OF GREEN.

PREP: 40 MINUTES **FREEZE:** 5 HOURS
GRILL: 8 MINUTES **STAND:** 15 MINUTES
MAKES: 6 SERVINGS

- 4 cups whole milk
- 1 slice white bread, crust removed, cut into ½-inch pieces
- 1 teaspoon cornstarch
- ¼ cup sugar
- ½ teaspoon freshly ground cardamom
- 1 medium fresh pineapple

1 For cardamom kulfi, in a food processor or blender combine ½ cup of the milk, the bread pieces, and cornstarch. Cover and process until smooth. Set aside.

2 In a large nonstick skillet bring the remaining 3½ cups milk just to boiling over medium-high heat; reduce heat. Simmer, uncovered, for about 12 minutes or until milk is reduced to 2½ cups, stirring frequently.

3 Stir bread mixture into the reduced milk. Return to boiling; reduce heat. Simmer, uncovered, for 4 minutes. Stir in sugar; simmer, uncovered, for 2 minutes. Stir in cardamom. Cool slightly.

4 Pour cooled milk mixture into a 2-quart square baking dish. Cover with plastic wrap touching the surface; freeze for 1 hour. Stir mixture. Cover and freeze about 4 hours more or until firm. Let kulfi stand at room temperature for 15 minutes before serving.

5 Meanwhile, peel and core pineapple; cut fruit into ¾-inch-thick wedges. Thread pineapple wedges onto wooden* or metal skewers.

6 For a charcoal grill, grill pineapple on the rack of an uncovered grill directly over medium coals for 8 to 10 minutes or until pineapple is warm and shows grill marks, turning once halfway through grilling. (For a gas grill, preheat grill. Reduce heat to medium. Place pineapple skewers on grill rack over heat. Cover and grill as directed.) Serve grilled pineapple topped with scoops of cardamom kulfi.

***NOTE:** If using wooden skewers, before grilling soak them in enough water to cover for at least 30 minutes. Drain before using.

PER ½ CUP + ⅙ PINEAPPLE: 183 cal., 6 g total fat (3 g sat. fat), 16 mg chol., 94 mg sodium, 29 g carbo., 1 g fiber, 6 g pro.

STEP-BY-STEP

1. Cut the top crown and bottom from the pineapple. Stand the pineapple on end and slice off the peel in strips from top to bottom.

2. With the peeled pineapple standing on end, cut in half from top to bottom. Cut each half into three or four wedges. Cut the core away from the fruit and throw the core pieces away.

3. Cut pineapple wedges into ¾-inch pieces. Thread the pineapple onto the skewers.

WARM, SPICY-SWEET CARDAMOM—A COUSIN OF GINGER— INFUSES INDIAN ICE CREAM WITH ITS UNIQUE FRAGRANCE. PAIRED WITH GRILL-CARAMELIZED PINEAPPLE, IT IS A HAPPY SPICE INDEED.

PREPARING LIMONCELLO SORBET WITH GRILLED STRAWBERRIES, STEP-BY-STEP

1. Once the sugar and water mixture boils and sugar has dissolved, add the lemon peel, lemon juice, and limoncello. Stir to mix well.

2. Sprinkle the powdered sugar in a shallow dish. Thread the berries onto skewers and roll in powdered sugar to coat well.

3. Position the skewers on the grill rack so each strawberry rests on two grill bars, or use a grill tray. Grill until berries are heated through, carefully turning to cook evenly.

Limoncello Sorbet with Grilled Strawberries

MEASURE LIMONCELLO—ITALY'S TANGY-SWEET LEMON LIQUEUR—PRECISELY. TOO MUCH ALCOHOL MAY PREVENT SORBET FROM FREEZING PROPERLY.

PREP: 30 MINUTES **CHILL:** 4 HOURS
FREEZE: 8 HOURS **GRILL:** 6 MINUTES
MAKES: 8 SERVINGS

- 2 cups granulated sugar
- 2 cups water
- 1 tablespoon finely shredded lemon peel
- 1½ cups lemon juice
- 2 tablespoons limoncello (Italian lemon liqueur)
- 1 cup powdered sugar
- 48 medium fresh strawberries

1 For sorbet, in a medium saucepan combine granulated sugar and the water. Bring to boiling, stirring until sugar dissolves. Stir in lemon peel, lemon juice, and limoncello. Cover and chill for at least 4 hours.

2 Transfer lemon mixture to a 2- to 4-quart ice cream freezer. Freeze according to the manufacturer's directions. Transfer sorbet to a nonmetallic freezer container with a tight-fitting lid. Cover and freeze for 8 to 24 hours or until firm.

3 Place powdered sugar in a small bowl. Halve strawberries. Thread strawberry halves on 4-inch skewers.* Dip skewered berries in powdered sugar, turning to coat. Place strawberries on a greased grill tray.

4 For a charcoal grill, grill strawberries on grill tray on the rack of an uncovered grill directly over medium-low coals about 6 minutes or until strawberries are heated through, turning frequently. (For a gas grill, preheat grill. Reduce heat to medium-low. Place strawberries on grill tray on grill rack over heat. Cover and grill as directed.)

5 Serve strawberries with sorbet.

***NOTE:** If using wooden skewers, before grilling, soak them in enough water to cover for 30 minutes. Drain before using.

PER ½ CUP SORBET + 6 BERRIES: 308 cal., 0 g total fat, 0 mg chol., 4 mg sodium, 78 g carbo., 2 g fiber, 1 g pro.

Grilled Gingered Melon Kabobs

TART CITRUS AND SPICY GINGER COAX FABULOUS FLAVOR FROM THE DEPTHS OF SUGARY-SWEET MELONS.

PREP: 25 MINUTES **MARINATE:** 30 MINUTES
GRILL: 6 MINUTES **MAKES:** 4 SERVINGS

- 2 cups cantaloupe, cut into 1½- to 2-inch cubes, balls, and/or triangles
- 2 cups honeydew melon, cut into 1½- to 2-inch cubes, balls, and/or triangles
- ½ teaspoon finely shredded lime peel
- ⅓ cup lime juice
- 1½ teaspoons grated fresh ginger or ½ teaspoon ground ginger
- 2 tablespoons honey

1 Place cantaloupe and honeydew melon in a large resealable plastic bag set in a shallow dish. For marinade, in a small bowl stir together lime peel, lime juice, and ginger. Pour marinade over melon in bag; seal bag. Turn to coat melon. Marinate at room temperature for 30 to 60 minutes, turning bag once or twice.

2 Drain melon, reserving marinade. On four long metal or wooden* skewers, alternately thread cantaloupe and honeydew melon.

3 For a charcoal grill, grill kabobs on the rack of an uncovered grill directly over medium coals for 6 to 8 minutes or until melon is warm and shows grill marks, turning occasionally. (For a gas grill, preheat grill. Reduce heat to medium. Place skewers on grill rack over heat. Cover and grill as directed.)

4 In a small bowl whisk together the reserved marinade and the honey. Drizzle over warm kabobs.

***NOTE:** If using wooden skewers, before grilling, soak them in enough water to cover for 30 minutes. Drain before using.

PER KABOB: 97 cal., 0 g total fat, 0 mg chol., 30 mg sodium, 25 g carbo., 2 g fiber, 1 g pro.

CLASSIC POUND CAKE RECIPES CALL FOR A POUND OF BUTTER, A POUND OF FLOUR, A POUND OF SUGAR, AND A POUND OF EGGS. PURCHASED AND GRILLED, AS IT IS HERE, IT CALLS FOR ONLY ONE OUNCE OF WORK.

Grilled Pound Cake with Espresso Chocolate Sauce

LOOK FOR ESPRESSO POWDER IN MOST SUPERMARKETS, SOMETIMES IN A GOURMET SECTION BUT OFTEN SHELVED WITH JARS OF INSTANT COFFEE.

PREP: 25 MINUTES **GRILL:** 2 MINUTES
MAKES: 8 SERVINGS

- 2 tablespoons boiling water
- 1 tablespoon instant espresso coffee powder
- ¾ cup whipping cream
- 1 tablespoon light-color corn syrup
- 8 ounces special dark baking chocolate or semisweet chocolate, finely chopped (about 1⅓ cups)
- 1 16-ounce loaf prepared or frozen pound cake,* thawed
- ¼ cup orange juice or 2 tablespoons orange juice with 2 tablespoons orange liqueur
- 1 cup whipping cream, whipped, or 2 cups frozen whipped dessert topping, thawed
- ½ cup pistachio nuts, chopped

1 In a very small bowl combine the boiling water and espresso powder; set aside.

2 For chocolate sauce, in a small heavy saucepan combine the ¾ cup whipping cream and the corn syrup. Bring to boiling; remove from heat. Stir in espresso mixture. Add chocolate all at once. Cover and let stand for 4 minutes. Whisk until chocolate melts and mixture is smooth. Cover to keep warm.

3 Cut pound cake into eight ¾-inch slices. Poke each slice several times with the tines of a fork. Drizzle orange juice evenly over cake slices.

4 For a charcoal grill, grill cake slices on the rack of an uncovered grill directly over medium-hot coals for 2 to 4 minutes or until toasted and heated through, turning once halfway through grilling. (For a gas grill, preheat grill. Reduce heat to medium-high. Place cake slices on grill rack over heat. Grill, uncovered, as directed.)

5 Serve grilled cake slices with whipped cream, pistachio nuts, and warm chocolate sauce.

***NOTE:** If the prepared pound cake is larger than 16 ounces, save the leftover cake for another use.

PER SERVING: 594 cal., 43 g total fat (25 g sat. fat), 199 mg chol., 249 mg sodium, 52 g carbo., 3 g fiber, 7 g pro.

STEP-BY-STEP

1. Place the pound cake slices on a tray. Pierce each slice several times with a fork.

2. Use a pastry brush to brush cake slices with orange juice. The holes made with the fork will allow the juice to soak through the cake slices.

3. Grill the cake slices until the bottoms are toasted. Turn carefully with a spatula and grill second sides.

Petite Fruit Tarts

DELICIOUS AND DAINTY, THESE LITTLE PIES BRING A BIT OF PASTRY-SHOP-SPECIAL TO OUTDOOR DINNERS.

PREP: ABOUT 1 HOUR **CHILL:** 1 HOUR
BAKE: 20 MINUTES **OVEN:** 375°F
MAKES: 8 TARTS

- 2 cups all-purpose flour
- ⅓ cup sugar
- ¾ cup cold butter
- 2 egg yolks, beaten
- ¼ cup sour cream
- 3 tablespoons ice water
- ⅔ cup sugar
- ¼ cup all-purpose flour
- 6 to 8 cups fresh fruit, such as blueberries, raspberries, blackberries, sliced nectarines, coarsely chopped apples, and/or sliced apricots
- ¼ to ⅓ cup sugar

1 In a medium bowl stir together the 2 cups flour and the ⅓ cup sugar. Using a pastry blender, cut butter into flour mixture until pieces are pea size. In a small bowl stir together egg yolks, sour cream, and ice water. Gradually stir egg yolk mixture into flour mixture. Using your fingers, gently knead the dough just until a ball forms. Cover dough with plastic wrap; chill for 1 hour or until dough is easy to handle.

2 Preheat oven to 375°F. Divide dough into 8 portions. Place on lightly floured pieces of parchment. Roll portions into 6- to 7-inch circles. Transfer, on parchment, to baking sheets.

3 In a small bowl stir together the ⅔ cup sugar and ¼ cup flour. Sprinkle a scant 2 tablespoons of the sugar mixture on each pastry shape to within ½ inch of the edges. In a large bowl combine fruit and the ¼ to ⅓ cup sugar; toss gently.

4 Spoon fruit evenly over pastry circles, using ¾ to 1 cup fruit for each tart. Fold pastry edges over edges of fruit. Bake for 20 to 25 minutes or until fruit is tender and pastry edges are golden brown.

PER TART: 467 cal., 21 g total fat (10 g sat. fat), 102 mg chol., 136 mg sodium, 66 g carbo., 3 g fiber, 5 g pro.

STEP-BY-STEP

1. Using a pastry blender, cut butter into the flour and sugar until the pieces in the mixture are about the size of peas.

2. Sprinkle 2 tablespoons of the sugar mixture over each pastry circle within a ½-inch border of edges. The border will be the portion of dough you will fold over the fruit.

3. Arrange the fruit mixture on the sugar mixture on the pastry circle. Fold up the pastry edge over the fruit, folding, pleating, and pinching pastry to stay in place.

Crunchy Caramel Apple Cake

USE YOUR FAVORITE APPLES WHEN PICKING FRUIT FOR THIS CINNAMON-SPICED CAKE. SWEET VARIETIES SUCH AS HONEYCRISP AND GOLDEN DELICIOUS WILL WORK AS WONDERFULLY AS THEIR TART COUSINS—RED ROMES AND JONATHANS.

PREP: 30 MINUTES **BAKE:** 45 MINUTES
OVEN: 325°F **MAKES:** 16 SERVINGS

- 1 cup plain granola, crushed
- 1 cup chopped walnuts or pecans
- ¼ cup butter, softened
- 3 cups all-purpose flour
- 1 teaspoon baking soda
- 1 teaspoon ground cinnamon
- ½ teaspoon salt
- 2 eggs
- 1½ cups vegetable oil
- 1 cup granulated sugar
- 1 cup packed brown sugar
- 3 cups finely chopped, peeled apples
- 1 recipe Caramel Sauce

1 Preheat oven to 325°F. Grease a 13×9×2-inch baking pan; set aside. In a medium bowl combine granola and ½ cup of the nuts. Using your fingers, work in butter until mixture resembles coarse crumbs. Set aside.

2 In a medium bowl stir together flour, baking soda, cinnamon, and salt; set aside. In a very large mixing bowl lightly beat eggs with a fork; stir in oil, granulated sugar, and brown sugar. Add flour mixture all at once; stir just until combined. Fold in apples and the remaining nuts (batter will be thick). Spread batter evenly in the prepared pan. Sprinkle evenly with granola mixture.

3 Bake for 45 to 55 minutes or until a wooden toothpick inserted near the center comes out clean. Transfer pan to a wire rack; cool completely. Serve with warm Caramel Sauce.

CARAMEL SAUCE: In a small saucepan melt ½ cup butter over medium heat. Stir in 1 cup packed brown sugar and ½ cup whipping cream. Bring to boiling, stirring constantly; reduce heat. Simmer, uncovered, about 5 minutes or until mixture is slightly thickened. Stir in 1 teaspoon vanilla. Cool about 10 minutes. Serve warm.

PER SERVING: 630 cal., 39 g total fat (10 g sat. fat), 61 mg chol., 240 mg sodium, 68 g carbo., 3 g fiber, 6 g pro.

STEP-BY-STEP

1. Spread nuts on the work surface. Use a chef's knife to cut into irregular about ¼-inch pieces.

2. To finely chop an apple, remove the peel and core and cut into thin slices. Cut the slices into thin strips. Line up the strips and cut crosswise into about ⅛-inch pieces.

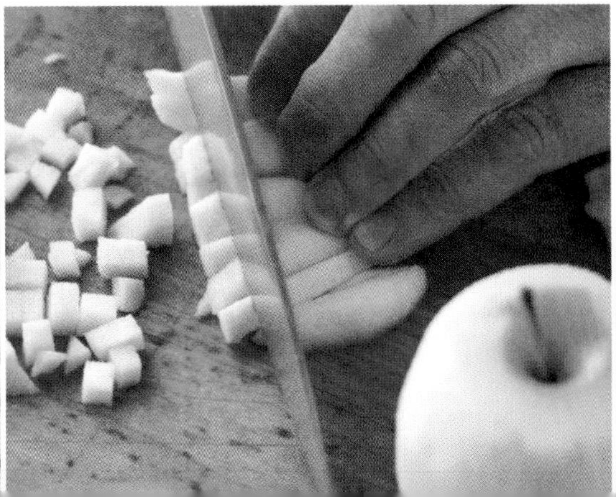

3. Pour the batter into the greased pan and quickly spread it to an even thickness.

STEP-BY-STEP

1. Break the graham crackers into squares. Place crackers in a food processor with almonds and sugar and process until fine crumbs form.

2. Spread the crumb mixture in the springform pan. Use the back of a spoon or your fingers to press the mixture over the bottom of the pan. Make sure the crust is an even thickness.

3. To soften ice cream, place it in a chilled glass bowl. Stir with a spoon until the ice cream is soft enough to spread but not melted.

Grown-Up S'mores Torte

IF SOME OF YOUR HAPPIEST MEMORIES INVOLVE SUMMER CAMP, CRISP AIR, CRACKLING FIRES, AND LICKING GOOEY MARSHMALLOWS FROM YOUR FINGERS, THIS DESSERT WILL BRING IT ALL BACK—SPECTACULARLY.

PREP: 30 MINUTES **BAKE:** 10 MINUTES
COOL: 1 HOUR **FREEZE:** 13 HOURS
BROIL: LESS THAN 1 MINUTE **OVEN:** 350°F
MAKES: 12 TO 16 SERVINGS

- 10 whole cinnamon graham cracker squares
- ⅔ cup sliced almonds, toasted
- 1 tablespoon sugar
- ¼ cup butter, melted
- 1 quart coffee ice cream, softened*
- 1 12-ounce jar fudge-flavor ice cream topping
- 1 quart dulce de leche ice cream, softened*
- 1 7-ounce jar marshmallow creme
- 2 cups tiny marshmallows
- 1 cup miniature semisweet chocolate pieces

1 Preheat oven to 350°F. In a food processor combine graham crackers, toasted almonds, and sugar. Cover and pulse with several on/off turns until crackers are finely crushed. Add butter; cover and pulse until moist crumbs form. Firmly press crumbs into the bottom of a 9-inch springform pan. Bake crust for 10 to 12 minutes or until edges begin to turn golden. Transfer pan to a wire rack; cool completely.

2 Using the back of a large spoon, spread softened coffee ice cream over cooled crust in pan. Spread fudge topping over coffee ice cream. Freeze about 1 hour or until topping sets.

3 Using the back of a large spoon, spread softened dulce de leche ice cream over fudge topping layer. Cover and freeze at least 12 hours or overnight.

4 Preheat broiler and arrange oven rack so top of torte will be about 4 inches from the heat. Place pan with torte on a baking sheet. Quickly spread marshmallow creme over top of torte. Sprinkle evenly with marshmallows and chocolate pieces.

5 Broil for 30 to 60 seconds or just until marshmallows turn golden brown. Run a warm knife around sides of pan to loosen. Remove pan sides. Cut torte into wedges. Serve immediately.

***NOTE:** To soften ice cream, place ice cream in a chilled bowl; stir with a wooden spoon until soft and smooth.

PER SERVING: 538 cal., 24 g total fat (12 g sat. fat), 37 mg chol., 255 mg sodium, 77 g carbo., 2 g fiber, 6 g pro.

4. Spoon the softened ice cream over the crust. Use the back of a spoon to spread it in an even layer.

5. Drizzle the fudge topping over the coffee ice cream layer. Use the back of a spoon to spread the topping to cover the ice cream.

6. Sprinkle marshmallows and chocolate pieces over the layer of marshmallow creme.

CASUAL COOKOUTS CALL FOR ALL-TIME FAVORITE SWEETS, SUCH AS BROWNIES. THE BUTTERY-RICH, CHOCOLATE-STUDDED SHORTBREAD FOUNDATION OF THESE BROWNIES MAKES THEM MAGNIFICENT—AND MEMORABLE.

Shortbread Brownies

TO PRESS SHORTBREAD EVENLY INTO THE BOTTOM OF THE BAKING PAN, RELY ON THE SLIPPERY SURFACE OF THE BACK OF A SPOON TO GLIDE AND PRESS AT THE SAME TIME.

PREP: 20 MINUTES **BAKE:** 48 MINUTES
OVEN: 350°F **MAKES:** 24 BROWNIES

- 1 cup all-purpose flour
- ¼ cup packed brown sugar
- ½ cup butter
- ¼ cup miniature semisweet chocolate pieces
- 1⅓ cups granulated sugar
- ¾ cup all-purpose flour
- ½ cup unsweetened cocoa powder
- 1½ teaspoons baking powder
- ½ teaspoon salt
- 3 eggs
- ⅓ cup butter, melted
- 1 tablespoon vanilla
- ½ cup miniature semisweet chocolate pieces

1 Preheat oven to 350°F. Line a 9×9×2-inch baking pan with foil, leaving about 1 inch of the foil extending over the edges of the pan. Grease foil; set pan aside.

2 In a medium bowl stir together the 1 cup flour and the brown sugar. Using a pastry blender, cut in the ½ cup butter until mixture resembles coarse crumbs. Stir in the ¼ cup chocolate pieces. Press into prepared pan. Bake for 8 minutes.

3 Meanwhile, in a large bowl stir together granulated sugar, the ¾ cup flour, the cocoa powder, baking powder, and salt. Add eggs, melted butter, and vanilla. Using a wooden spoon, beat until smooth. Stir in the ½ cup chocolate pieces. Carefully spread over baked crust in pan.

4 Bake for 40 minutes. Transfer pan to a wire rack; cool completely. Use foil to lift squares out of pan. Place on cutting board; cut into brownies.

PER BROWNIE: 180 cal., 9 g total fat (4 g sat. fat), 44 mg chol., 121 mg sodium, 23 g carbo., 1 g fiber, 3 g pro.

STEP-BY-STEP

1. Using a pastry blender, cut the buttter into the flour and brown sugar until the mixture looks like coarse crumbs.

2. Add the eggs, butter, and vanilla to the flour mixture. Using a wooden spoon, stir until all of the dry mixture is moistened and batter is smooth. The batter will be thick.

3. Grasp the foil at the edges of the pan and lift the brownies from the pan. Peel off the foil and place uncut brownies on cutting board. Cut into squares.

Smoking

EXPERIENCE THE CULTURE AND SAVOR THE SOUL OF AUTHENTIC BARBECUE, WHERE THE HAZE OF SWEET SMOKE PROVES THAT LOW AND SLOW IS THE WAY TO COOK.

Smoking

SUCCESSFUL SMOKING IS SIMPLE—ONCE YOU LEARN THESE BASIC TECHNIQUES.

Smokin' Tip!

KEEP A LID ON IT! WHEN FOOD SMELLS THIS GOOD, IT IS HARD NOT TO TAKE A PEEK. BUT RESIST THE TEMPTATION TO LIFT THE LID DURING COOKING. EVERY TIME THE LID IS REMOVED, IT WILL ADD 15 MINUTES TO COOKING TIME.

SET UP

Before striking your first match, make sure that your smoker sits on a level, heatproof, and noncombustible surface, such as a patio or driveway. Place the smoker in a spot where it is away from foot traffic. Determine the direction of the wind; position the smoker in an area where the breeze will not blow smoke into open windows.

Remove the lid and cooking chamber before lighting charcoal briquettes. Open all of the vents on the bottom of the bowl for good air flow. To achieve the best smoked flavor, use a chimney starter rather than lighter fluid.

Allow briquettes to preheat for about 20 minutes or until they are covered with fine gray ash. Spread the coals evenly over the charcoal grate using long-handled tongs. Toss a few chunks of natural wood on the coals.

GET SMOKING

Once the cooking chamber is placed on the bottom charcoal-containing section, place the empty water pan. Using a large pitcher or bucket, carefully fill the water pan with water, fill it three-fourths full, being very careful not to splatter water on the hot coals. Place food to be smoked on the grate. If your smoker has two layers of grates, fill both with food if desired. Place the lid on the smoker and fully open the lid vent.

FINE-TUNING HEAT A smoking temperature between 225°F and 250°F is best for most meats. To adjust heat, rely on the smoker's vents, located in the bottom chamber. Opening the vents will cause heat to increase and closing the vents will cause heat to decrease. Check smoker temperature often—every 15 minutes or so—and open or close the bottom vents as needed to increase or decrease the temperature. Once the smoker reaches the target temperature, check the smoker only every hour or so. Remember that the water in the smoker helps keep the temperature low, so check the water level every 3 or 4 hours, adding additional hot water as necessary.

Raw meat is porous and absorbs most wood smoke at the beginning of the cooking process. When little smoke is coming out of the top vent, it's time to add another chunk or two of wood through the door on the side. When smoking longer than 6 hours, add more charcoal ocasionally, depending upon the type of charcoal and how fast it burns. During long cooking times, replenish the water every few hours with warm water.

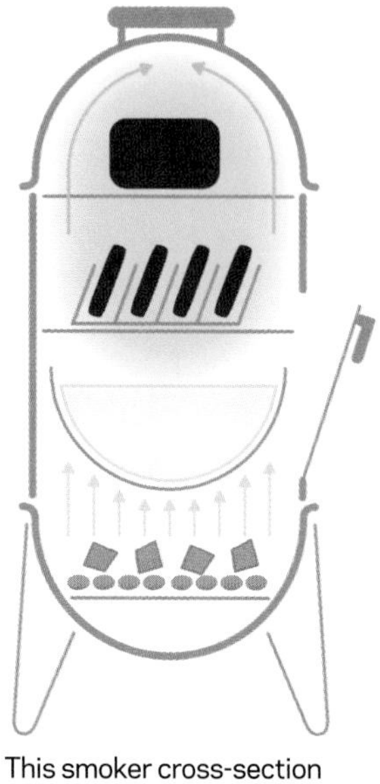

This smoker cross-section shows how the smoker works. Charcoal and wood chunks in the firebox heat water in the waterpan, which keeps heat low and meats moist. Food placed above the water pan is infused by circulating wood smoke.

CLEAN UP

When smoking is complete, extinguish coals by closing top and bottom vents tightly. When coals are extingushed and smoker is cool, remove water pan, discard water, and, if desired, wash pan with detergent and hot water. Brush grates vigorously with a grill brush or crumpled aluminum foil to remove all debris.

SETTING UP A WATER SMOKER, STEP-BY-STEP

1. Spread the preheated coals in the firebox. Add the wood chunks.

2. Place the cooking chamber over the firebox.

3. Set the water pan in place.

4. Add enough water to the tray to fill it three-fourths full.

5. Install the wire rack. Add the food and cover the smoker.

6. Let the food smoke cook as directed in the recipe. Depending on the length of smoking, you may need to add additional coals and wood chunks.

Smoke

WHERE THERE'S SMOKE, THERE'S FLAVOR. EACH VARIETY OF WOOD LENDS UNIQUE TASTE TO SMOKED SPECIALTIES.

WOOD TYPES

Available in chips, chunks, or planks, each variety of wood has unique attributes. The most popular woods for infusing foods with flavor:

MESQUITE Wood from this southwestern tree burns hot and slowly, and infuses foods with the most intense flavor of all wood. Described as sweet and earthy, mesquite smoke is the smoke of choice in the southwestern United States and necessary in cooking Texas-style brisket.

HICKORY The wood of choice for Southern barbecue, hickory adds its strong flavor to pork, beef, and lamb.

MAPLE, OAK, PECAN, AND WALNUT These hardwoods make beautiful furniture—and wonderful smoke. Milder than mesquite and hickory, they bring wonderful flavor to any meat.

FRUITWOODS From apple, cherry, peach, and plum to orange, lemon, and grapefruit, these mild woods infuse meats with just a hint of the fruits that their trees bear. Use fruitwoods for fish and chicken.

ALDER AND CEDAR These mild woods, native to the Pacific Northwest, are traditionally used to smoke salmon, yet also lend fantastic flavor to poultry and pork.

Smokin' Tip!

TO SOAK OR NOT TO SOAK? BARBECUE CHAMPIONS DISAGREE. SOME SAY THAT SPENDING AN HOUR OR SO SOAKING IN WATER EXTENDS THE SMOKE PRODUCTION. OTHERS SAY NOT TO BOTHER. TRY IT BOTH WAYS AND DECIDE FOR YOURSELF.

SMOKE COOKING CHART

At least 1 hour before smoking, soak wood chunks (for smoker) in enough water to cover. Drain before using. Trim fat from meat. Rinse fish; pat dry with paper towels. If smoking fish, lightly grease the rack of the smoker or coat it with nonstick cooking spray. Prepare smoker as directed. Place meat, poultry, or fish on the grill rack. For fish fillets, tuck under any thin edges. Cover and smoke for the time given below or until done. After smoking, cover roasts, turkeys, and large chickens with foil; let stand for 15 minutes before carving.

Cut	Thickness/Weight	Smoker Time*	Doneness
BEEF			
Boneless steak (ribeye or top loin)	1 inch	40 to 50 minutes 50 to 60 minutes	Medium rare Medium
Brisket (fresh)	3 to 4 pounds	5 to 6 hours	Tender
Ribeye roast	4 pounds	3 to 3½ hours	Medium rare
Ribs (back)	3 to 4 pounds	2½ to 3 hours	Tender
POULTRY			
Meaty chicken pieces	4 to 6 pounds	1¼ to 1¾ hours	180°F
Chicken, whole	3 to 3½ pounds 6 to 7 pounds	2½ to 3 hours 3¼ to 4 hours	145°F medium rare 160°F medium
Turkey, whole	8 to 10 pounds	4½ to 5 hours	180°F
Turkey breast, half	2 to 2½ pounds	2 to 2½ hours	170°F
Turkey drumstick	8 to 12 ounces	2½ to 3 hours	Juices run clear
Turkey tenderloin	8 to 10 ounces	1¼ to 1½ hours	Juices run clear
LAMB			
Boneless leg roast (rolled and tied)	3 pounds	2½ to 3 hours 3¼ to 3¾ hours	Medium rare Medium
Boneless sirloin roast	1½ to 2 pounds	1¾ to 2 hours 2¼ to 2½ hours	Medium rare Medium
Chop (loin or rib)	1¼ to 1½ inches	55 to 65 minutes 65 to 75 minutes	Medium rare Medium
PORK			
Boneless top loin roast (single loin)	2 to 3 pounds	1¾ to 2 hours	160°F
Chop	1¼ to 1½ inches	1¾ to 2¼ hours	Juices run clear
Ribs (loin back or spareribs)	2 to 4 pounds	3 to 4 hours	Tender

*All cooking times are based on meat removed directly from refrigerator.

Sweet 'n' Sticky Chicken

ON-THE-BONE POULTRY PARTS, SUCH AS LEGS AND THIGHS, BENEFIT MOST FROM WOOD SMOKING. LEAN CUTS, SUCH AS BONELESS CHICKEN BREASTS, COOK TOO QUICKLY TO ADEQUATELY ABSORB SMOKY FLAVOR.

PREP: 30 MINUTES **SMOKE:** 1½ HOURS
MAKES: 6 SERVINGS

- 6 whole chicken legs (drumstick and thigh)
- 1½ teaspoons dried oregano, crushed
- 1½ teaspoons dried thyme, crushed
- ½ teaspoon garlic salt
- ¼ teaspoon onion powder
- ¼ teaspoon black pepper
- 6 to 8 maple or hickory wood chunks*
- 1 recipe Sweet 'n' Sticky Barbecue Sauce

1 If desired, remove skin from chicken. For rub, in a small bowl stir together oregano, thyme, garlic salt, onion powder, and pepper. Sprinkle the rub evenly over chicken; rub in with your fingers.

2 In a smoker arrange preheated coals, wood chunks, and water pan according to the manufacturer's directions. Pour water into pan. Place chicken on the grill rack over water pan. Cover and smoke for 1½ to 2 hours or until juices run clear (180°F). Add additional coals and water as needed to maintain temperature and moisture.

3 Remove chicken from smoker. Generously brush some of the warm Sweet 'n' Sticky Barbecue Sauce over smoked chicken. Pass remaining sauce.

SWEET 'N' STICKY BARBECUE SAUCE: In a small saucepan cook ½ cup finely chopped onion (1 medium) and 2 cloves garlic, minced, in 1 tablespoon hot olive oil over medium heat until onion is tender. Stir in ¾ cup bottled chili sauce, ½ cup unsweetened pineapple juice, ¼ cup honey, 2 tablespoons Worcestershire sauce, and ½ teaspoon dry mustard. Bring to boiling; reduce heat. Simmer, uncovered, for 20 to 25 minutes or until sauce reaches desired consistency.

***NOTE:** For the most smoke production, soak wood chunks in enough water to cover for at least 1 hour before grilling. Drain wood chips before using.

PER 1 LEG + ABOUT 3 TABLESPOONS SAUCE: 535 cal., 29 g total fat (8 g sat. fat), 186 mg chol., 725 mg sodium, 25 g carbo., 2 g fiber, 43 g pro.

STEP BY STEP

1. To remove the skin from a chicken leg, start at the thigh end and separate the skin from the meat. Pull back gently until it comes off.

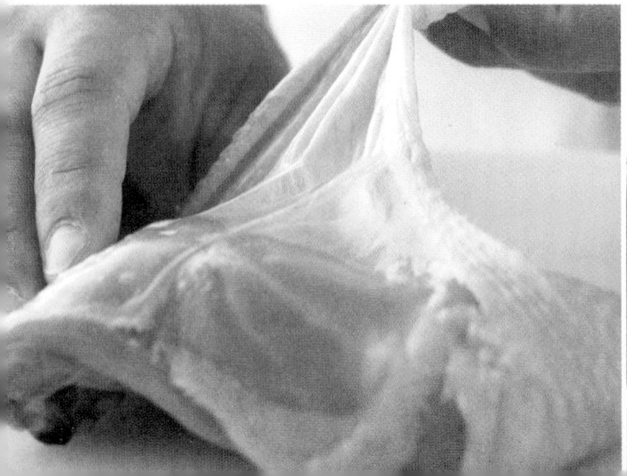

2. Cook the sauce until it's the desired consistency. It has to be thick enough to coat a spoon in order for it to cling to the chicken without dripping off.

3. After removing the chicken from the smoker, use a pastry brush to coat it with some of the warm barbecue sauce. Pass a bowl of the remaining sauce at the table.

THE SHEER DELICIOUSNESS OF THIS SMOKY CHICKEN IS WELL WORTH THE FINGER LICKING REQUIRED TO EAT IT. HOMEMADE BARBECUE SAUCE MAKES ALL THE DIFFERENCE.

Smoked Pineapple-Soy Chicken

IF A HAWAIIAN VACATION IS NOT ON THIS YEAR'S SCHEDULE, ENJOY THE SMOKY POLYNESIAN FLAVOR OF THIS BIRD IN YOUR OWN BACKYARD. PINEAPPLE JUICE SERVES AS TENDERIZER AS WELL AS FLAVOR ENHANCER. THIS DISH IS SUPER-SUCCULENT.

PREP: 15 MINUTES **MARINATE:** 4 HOURS
SMOKE: 1½ HOURS **MAKES:** 4 SERVINGS

- 1 3-pound whole broiler-fryer chicken, quartered
- ½ cup unsweetened pineapple juice
- ¼ cup vinegar
- 2 tablespoons vegetable oil
- 1 tablespoon soy sauce
- 1½ teaspoons sugar
- ¾ teaspoon salt
- ¾ teaspoon paprika
- ¾ teaspoon ground sage
- ¼ to ½ teaspoon black pepper
- ¼ teaspoon chili powder
- ⅛ teaspoon onion powder
- 6 to 8 apple or hickory wood chunks*

1 Place chicken in a large resealable plastic bag set in a shallow dish. For marinade, in a small bowl stir together pineapple juice, vinegar, oil, and soy sauce. Pour over chicken in bag; seal bag. Marinate in the refrigerator for 4 hours, turning bag occasionally.

2 For rub, in a small bowl stir together sugar, salt, paprika, sage, pepper, chili powder, and onion powder; set aside. Drain chicken, discarding marinade. Pat chicken dry with paper towels. Sprinkle rub evenly over chicken; rub in with your fingers.

3 In a smoker arrange preheated coals, wood chunks, and water pan according to manufacturer's directions. Pour water into pan. Place chicken, bone sides down, on the grill rack over water pan. Cover and smoke for 1½ to 2 hours or until juices run clear (170°F for breasts; 180°F for thighs and drumsticks). Add additional coals and water as needed to maintain temperature and moisture.

***NOTE:** For the most smoke production, soak wood chunks in enough water to cover for at least 1 hour before grilling. Drain wood chips before using.

PER ¼ CHICKEN: 548 cal., 38 g total fat (10 g sat. fat), 174 mg chol., 715 mg sodium, 5 g carbo., 0 g fiber, 43 g pro.

Mix It Up!

PICK ONE FROM EACH COLUMN TO CUSTOMIZE THE CHICKEN TO YOUR TASTE.

SEASON IT

Instead of pineapple juice, use one of the following:
- Apple juice
- Cola
- White grape juice
- Dry white wine
- Ginger ale
- Apricot nectar
- Peach nectar
- Prepared frozen limeade concentrate

MIX IT IN

Under the skin of the chicken, place one of the following:
- Whole fresh sage leaves
- Thin slices of lemon
- Thin slices of lime
- Softened butter
- Crushed red pepper
- Cracked black pepper
- Thinly sliced red onion
- Thinly sliced garlic

TOP IT

Instead of rub use 4 teaspoons of one of the following:
- Baja citrus marinade mix
- Chipotle pepper marinade mix
- Teriyaki marinade mix
- Zesty herb marinade mix
- Roasted garlic and herb grilling seasoning blend
- New Orleans pepper herb grilling seasoning blend

STEP-BY-STEP

1. To quarter a chicken, cut through the leg joint to remove the thigh and drumstick piece. Repeat with the remaining leg.

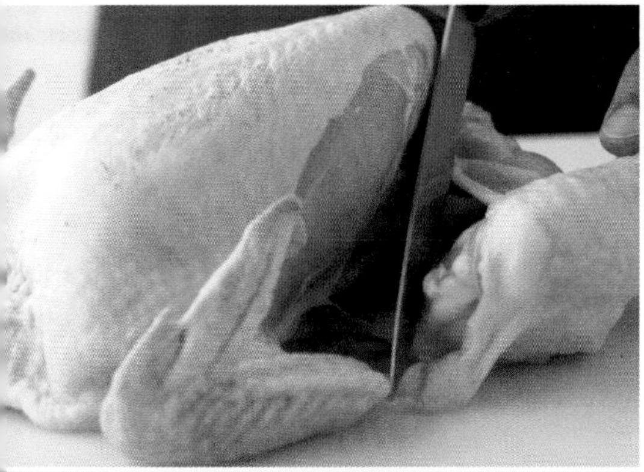

2. Using kitchen scissors, cut along both sides of the backbone and remove it. Throw the backbone away or save it to make broth.

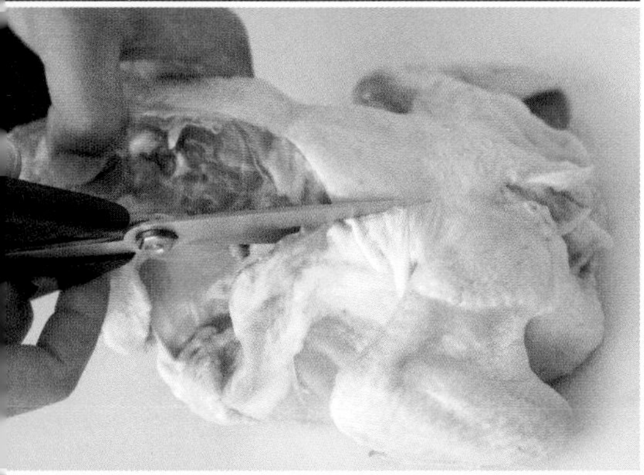

3. With the skin side down, cut the chicken breast in half starting at the top and cutting through the bone.

4. Put the chicken quarters in a large plastic bag. Place the bag in a shallow dish and add the marinade. Seal the bag and marinate in the refrigerator.

5. The chicken is done when an instant-read meat thermometer registers 180°F when inserted in a thigh and 170°F when inserted in a breast portion.

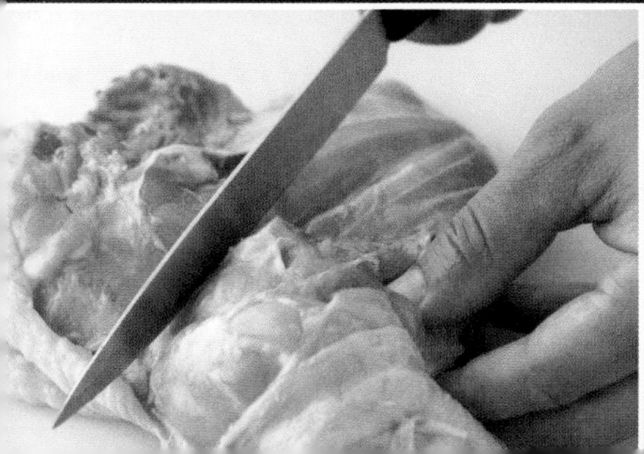

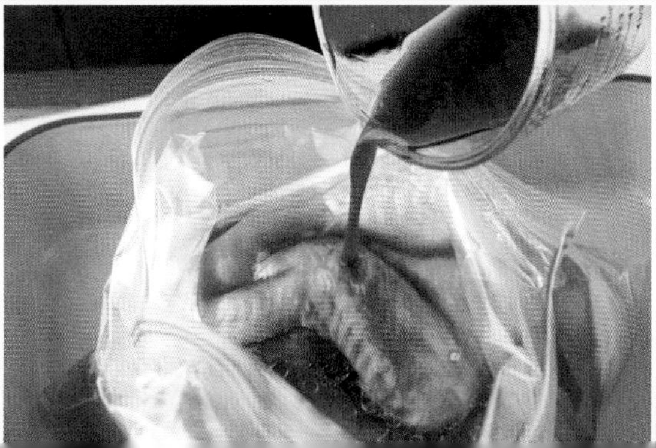

Jerk-Style Smoked Chicken

SPICY RASTAFARIAN FARE, SUCH AS CHICKEN RUBBED WITH INCENDIARY SEASONINGS, BRINGS THE SPIRIT OF JAMAICA TO YOUR SMOKER.

PREP: 15 MINUTES **MARINATE:** 1 HOUR
SMOKE: 1½ HOURS **MAKES:** 6 SERVINGS

- 3 pounds meaty chicken pieces (breast halves, thighs, and drumsticks)
- ½ cup tomato juice
- ⅓ cup finely chopped onion (1 small)
- 2 tablespoons lime juice
- 1 tablespoon vegetable oil
- 1 tablespoon Pickapeppa sauce* (optional)
- 4 cloves garlic, minced
- ½ teaspoon salt
- 1 to 2 tablespoons Jamaican jerk seasoning
- 6 to 8 fruit wood chunks**
- Lime wedges

1 If desired, remove skin from chicken. Place chicken in a large resealable plastic bag set in a deep dish. For marinade, in a small bowl stir together tomato juice, onion, lime juice, oil, Pickapeppa sauce (if desired), garlic, and salt. Pour over chicken in bag; seal bag. Turn to coat chicken. Marinate in the refrigerator for 1 to 4 hours, turning bag occasionally.

2 Drain chicken pieces, discarding marinade. Sprinkle jerk seasoning evenly over chicken; rub in with your fingers.

3 In a smoker arrange preheated coals, wood chunks, and water pan according to the manufacturer's directions. Pour water into pan. Place chicken, bone sides, down, on the grill rack over water pan. Cover and smoke for 1½ to 2 hours or until juices run clear (170°F for breasts; 180°F for thighs and drumsticks). Add additional coals and water as needed to maintain temperature and moisture. Serve chicken with lime wedges.

***NOTE:** If you can't find Pickapeppa sauce, substitute 1 tablespoon Worcestershire sauce mixed with a dash of bottled hot pepper sauce.

****NOTE:** For the most smoke production, soak wood chunks in enough water to cover for at least 1 hour before grilling. Drain wood chips before using.

PER ⅙ CHICKEN: 283 cal., 14 g total fat (4 g sat. fat), 104 mg chol., 331 mg sodium, 3 g carbo., 0 g fiber, 34 g pro.

Salt-and-Pepper Smoked Chickens

IF YOUR SMOKER HAS THE SPACE, CONSIDER SMOKING FOUR CHICKENS INSTEAD OF TWO. YOU'LL HAVE DINNER FOR EIGHT, PLUS A WEEK'S WORTH OF SENSATIONAL SMOKED CHICKEN SANDWICHES AND SALADS.

PREP: 20 MINUTES **CHILL:** 1 HOUR
SMOKE: 2½ HOURS **STAND:** 10 MINUTES
MAKES: 8 SERVINGS

- 2 3½- to 4-pound whole broiler-fryer chickens
- 1 teaspoon salt
- 1 teaspoon onion salt
- 1 teaspoon garlic salt
- 1 teaspoon seasoned salt
- 1 teaspoon paprika
- 1 teaspoon black pepper
- ¼ teaspoon cayenne pepper (optional)
- 6 to 8 hickory or mesquite wood chunks*

1 Rinse chicken body cavities; pat dry with paper towels. For rub, in a small bowl stir together salt, onion salt, garlic salt, seasoned salt, paprika, black pepper, and, if desired, cayenne pepper. Sprinkle the rub evenly over chickens; rub in with your fingers. Tie drumsticks to tails. Twist wing tips under backs. Place chickens in a shallow pan. Cover and chill for 1 hour.

2 Meanwhile, soak wood chunks in enough water to cover for at least 1 hour. Drain before using. Insert a meat thermometer into the center of each inside thigh muscle, making sure tip does not touch bone.

3 In a smoker arrange preheated coals, wood chunks, and water pan according to the manufacturer's directions. Pour water into pan. Place chickens, breast sides up, on the grill rack over water pan. Cover and smoke for 2½ to 3 hours or until drumsticks move easily in sockets and juices run clear (180°F). Add additional coals and water as needed to maintain temperature and moisture.

4 Remove chickens from smoker. Cover with foil; let stand for 10 minutes before carving.

***NOTE:** For the most smoke production, soak wood chunks in enough water to cover for at least 1 hour before grilling. Drain wood chips before using.

PER ¼ CHICKEN: 834 cal., 57 g total fat (16 g sat. fat), 296 mg chol., 1,023 mg sodium, 0 g carbo., 0 g fiber, 74 g pro.

PREPARING JERK-STYLE SMOKED CHICKEN, STEP-BY-STEP

1. To make the marinade, combine the tomato juice, onion, lime juice, Pickapeppa sauce, garlic, and salt.

2. Use tongs to remove the chicken from the marinade and place on a dish. Throw away the bag and marinade.

3. Mix the rub in a small bowl. Use your fingers to sprinkle the rub over the chicken. Pat it in with your fingers.

4. To ensure that the smoker maintains the proper temperature, add 8 to 10 briquettes every 45 to 60 minutes.

5. Smoke the chicken until the juices are clear when you prick the meat with a fork. Or check doneness with a meat thermometer.

Double-Smoked Salmon with Horseradish Cream

HEALTHFUL, DELICIOUS, AND COMPANY-SPECIAL—THIS ULTRA-ELEGANT STUFFED SALMON COVERS ALL THE BASES FLAVORFULLY.

PREP: 15 MINUTES **SMOKE:** 30 MINUTES
MAKES: 4 SERVINGS

- 4 6-ounce fresh or frozen salmon fillets (with skin), about 1 inch thick
- 4 slices smoked salmon (about 3 ounces)
- 4 teaspoons snipped fresh dill
- 1 tablespoon lemon juice
- Salt and black pepper
- 4 hickory or apple wood chunks*
- 1 recipe Horseradish Cream

1 Thaw salmon, if frozen. Rinse fish; pat dry with paper towels. Make a pocket in each fillet by cutting horizontally from 1 side almost to, but not through, the other side. Fill pockets evenly with smoked salmon slices and 2 teaspoons of the dill, folding salmon slices as necessary to fit. Evenly brush fish with lemon juice and top with the remaining 2 teaspoons of the dill. Sprinkle with salt and pepper.

2 In a smoker arrange preheated coals, wood chunks, and water pan according to the manufacturer's directions. Pour water into pan. Place salmon, skin sides down, on the grill rack over water pan. Cover and smoke about 30 minutes or until fish begins to flake when tested with a fork. Serve with Horseradish Cream.

HORSERADISH CREAM: In a small bowl stir together ½ cup dairy sour cream, 2 tablespoons thinly sliced green onion (1), 4 teaspoons prepared horseradish, and 2 teaspoons snipped fresh dill.

***NOTE:** For the most smoke production, soak wood chunks in enough water to cover for at least 1 hour before grilling. Drain wood chips before using.

PER FILLET + 2½ TABLESPOONS CREAM: 245 cal., 13 g total fat (5 g sat. fat), 48 mg chol., 337 mg sodium, 2 g carbo., 0 g fiber, 29 g pro.

STEP-BY-STEP

1. Cut a horizontal pocket in each fillet, cutting almost to the edges and almost to the opposite side.

2. Stuff the smoked salmon into the pockets, folding or cutting slices to fit. Add ½ teaspoon of fresh dill to each pocket.

3. Place fillets, skin sides down, on work surface. Brush tops of fillets with lemon juice and sprinkle with additional dill.

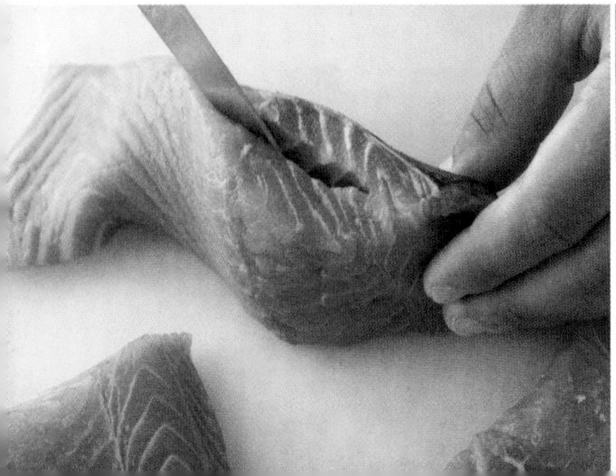

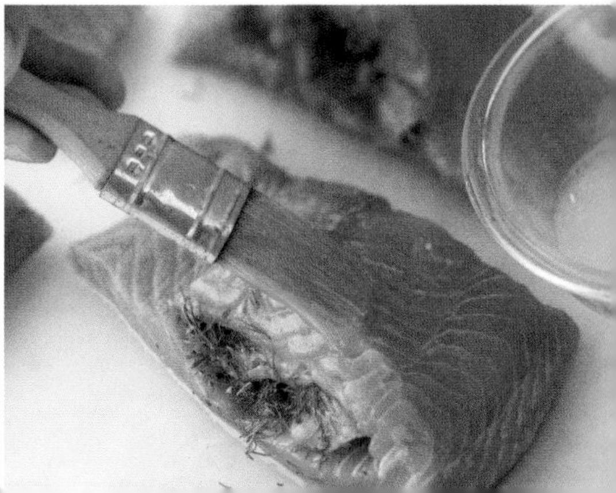

4. To make the sauce, stir together sour cream, green onion, horseradish, and dill. Cover and refrigerate until serving.

5. Arrange the preheated coals in the bottom of the smoker. Add wood chunks.

6. To see if the salmon is done, open the smoker and insert a fork into the fish and twist. Fish is done as soon as it begins to flake.

A MAGNIFICENT MOUNTAIN OF HOT PULLED PORK PILED ON A BUN DELICIOUSLY SUITS BOTH PICNICS AND RECEPTIONS.

Pulled Pork Shoulder

TANGY APPLE CIDER-BASED BBQ SAUCE IS THE HALLMARK OF TRADITIONAL SOUTH CAROLINIAN BARBECUE.

PREP: 15 MINUTES **SMOKE:** 4 HOURS
STAND: 15 MINUTES
MAKES: 14 TO 18 SANDWICHES

- 1 tablespoon paprika
- 1 tablespoon black pepper
- 2 teaspoons salt
- 2 teaspoons chili powder
- 2 teaspoons ground cumin
- 2 teaspoons packed brown sugar
- 1 teaspoon granulated sugar
- 1 teaspoon cayenne pepper
- 1 5- to 5½-pound boneless pork shoulder roast
- 6 to 8 hickory wood chunks or 3 cups hickory wood chips*
- 1 recipe Vinegar Barbecue Sauce
- 14 to 18 hamburger buns
- Bottled hot pepper sauce (optional)

1 For rub, in a small bowl stir together paprika, black pepper, salt, chili powder, cumin, brown sugar, granulated sugar, and cayenne pepper. Sprinkle rub evenly over meat; rub in with your fingers.

2 In a smoker arrange preheated coals, wood chunks, and water pan according to manufacturer's directions. Pour water into pan. Place meat on the grill rack over water pan. Cover and smoke for 4 to 5 hours or until meat is very tender. Add additional coals and water as needed to maintain temperature and moisture. Do not add wood after the first 2 hours of smoking. (Too much smoke can give a bitter taste to smoked meat.)

3 Remove meat from smoker. Cover meat with foil; let stand for 15 minutes. Cut meat into thick pieces. Using two forks, gently pull the meat into long, thin shreds. Place pulled pork in a large bowl. Add about 1½ cups of the Vinegar Barbecue Sauce. Stir until slightly moist, adding sauce if necessary.

4 To serve, pile meat mixture onto buns. If desired, sprinkle with hot pepper sauce. Serve with remaining sauce.

VINEGAR BARBECUE SAUCE: In a clean 1-quart jar with a screw-top lid combine 3 cups cider vinegar, ⅓ cup granulated sugar, 1 tablespoon dry mustard, 2 to 3 teaspoons crushed red pepper, 2 teaspoons bottled hot pepper sauce, 1½ teaspoons salt, and 1½ teaspoons black pepper. Cover and shake well.

***NOTE:** For the most smoke production, soak wood chunks in enough water to cover for at least 1 hour before grilling. Drain wood chips before using.

MAKE-AHEAD DIRECTIONS: To make ahead, prepare as directed through Step 3. Cover and chill up to 3 days. Reheat in a large pot over medium heat, stirring occasionally.

PER SANDWICH: 390 cal., 17 g total fat (6 g sat. fat), 76 mg chol., 875 mg sodium, 29 g carbo., 2 g fiber, 26 g pro.

STEP-BY-STEP

1. After removing the meat from the smoker, cover it with foil and let stand for 15 minutes. Cut the roast into large chunks.

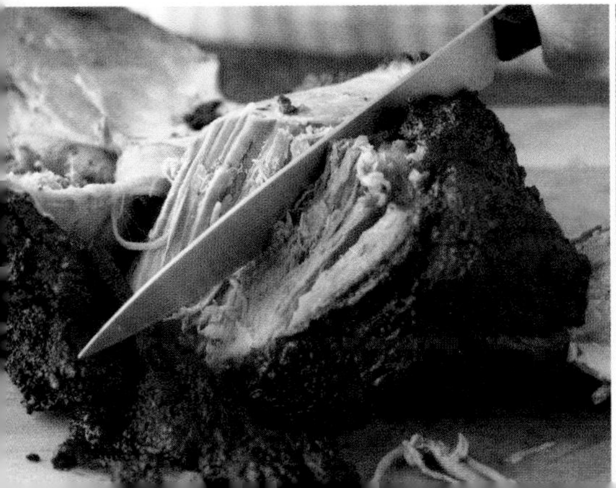

2. Place the meat chunks in a shallow pan. To shred the pork, insert two forks into a piece of meat and pull in opposite directions.

3. Pour Vinegar Barbecue Sauce over the shredded meat and stir until all the meat is moist. Add additional sauce, a little at a time, if needed.

Memphis-Style Smoked Pork with Bourbon Sauce

ONE DEEPLY FLAVORED BLEND OF SAUCE AND SEASONING SERVES TWO PURPOSES. FIRST, IT MARINATES THE PORK. SECOND, IT GOES ON AS A TOPPER. IT'S SUPER-SAUCY AND SASSY.

PREP: 40 MINUTES **MARINATE:** 24 HOURS
SMOKE: 4½ HOURS **STAND:** 15 MINUTES
MARINATE: 24 HOURS **MAKES:** 12 SERVINGS

- 1 cup finely chopped onion (1 large)
- 1 8-ounce can tomato sauce
- ¾ cup bourbon or beef broth
- ⅔ cup cider vinegar
- ¼ cup packed brown sugar
- ¼ cup Worcestershire sauce
- ¼ teaspoon salt
- ¼ teaspoon black pepper
- Dash bottled hot pepper sauce
- 1 4½- to 5-pound boneless pork shoulder roast
- 6 to 8 hickory wood chunks*

1 For sauce, in a medium saucepan stir together onion, tomato sauce, bourbon, ⅓ cup of the vinegar, the brown sugar, Worcestershire sauce, salt, black pepper, and hot pepper sauce. Bring to boiling; reduce heat. Simmer, covered, for 15 minutes. Cool. Reserve 1 cup of the sauce; cover and chill.

2 Place meat in a large resealable plastic bag set in a shallow dish. For marinade, stir the remaining ⅓ cup vinegar into the remaining sauce. Pour over meat in bag; seal bag. Turn to coat meat. Marinate in the refrigerator for 24 hours, turning bag occasionally.

3 Drain meat, reserving marinade. In a smoker arrange preheated coals, wood chunks, and water pan according to the manufacturer's directions. Pour water into pan. Place meat on the grill rack over water pan. Cover and smoke for 4½ to 5½ hours or until meat is very tender, basting occasionally with the reserved marinade during the first 3 hours of smoking. Add additional coals and water as needed to maintain temperature and moisture. Discard any remaining marinade.

4 Remove meat from smoker. Cover meat with foil; let stand for 15 minutes. Meanwhile, in a small saucepan cook and stir the reserved 1 cup sauce over low heat until heated through. Slice meat. Serve meat with sauce.

***NOTE:** For the most smoke production, soak wood chunks in enough water to cover for at least 1 hour before grilling. Drain wood chips before using.

PER 4 OUNCES PORK + ABOUT 1 TABLESPOON SAUCE:
354 cal., 17 g total fat (6 g sat. fat), 112 mg chol., 253 mg sodium, 6 g carbo., 0 g fiber, 30 g pro.

STEP-BY-STEP

1. Place the roast in a large resealable plastic bag and add the marinade. Seal the bag and place in a bowl or shallow dish.

2. Insert an oven-going meat thermometer into the thickest part of the roast. Check to be sure the thermometer isn't touching fat.

3. Save the marinade to baste the roast occasionally during smoking. After basting meat, quickly replace the smoker lid. Heat and smoke escape quickly when the lid is removed.

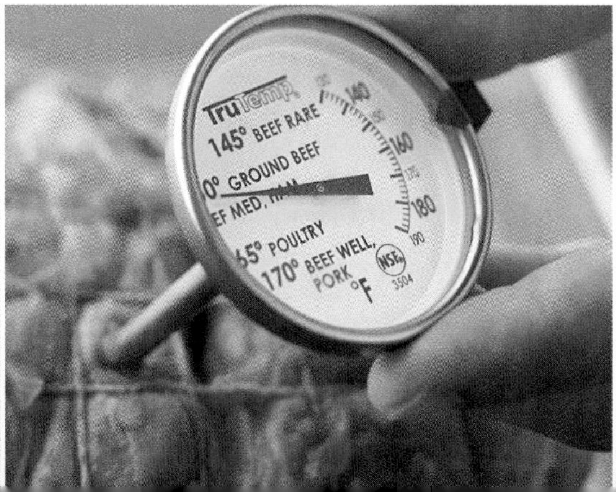

MEMPHIS TAKES GREAT PRIDE IN ITS BARBECUE, BELIEVING THAT IT IS THE BEST BARBECUE IN THE WORLD. WHEN TENNESSEE'S RENOWNED BOURBON IS INVOLVED—AS IT IS IN THIS RECIPE—THAT JUST MAY BE RIGHT.

STEP-BY-STEP

1. Place the ribs on a tray. Squeeze the lime halves over the the ribs. Rub the squeezed halves over the meat to use every drop of juice.

2. Sprinkle the rub evenly over the meat. Pat the rub into the meat with your fingers.

3. Place the ribs on the grill rack with the bone sides down. The bones make their own rack.

Spicy Hoisin-Honey Ribs

ALSO KNOWN AS PEKING SAUCE, SWEET, SPICY HOISIN SAUCE DRAPES RIBS WITH MAHOGANY COLOR AND CLINGS DELIGHTFULLY TO THE STICKY EXTERIOR.

PREP: 15 MINUTES **CHILL:** 1 HOUR
SMOKE: 3 HOURS **MAKES:** 4 SERVINGS

- 1 tablespoon paprika
- ½ teaspoon coarsely ground black pepper
- ¼ teaspoon onion salt
- 4 pounds pork loin back ribs
- 1 lime, halved
- 6 to 8 oak or hickory wood chunks*
- 2 dried chipotle peppers or 1 to 2 tablespoons finely chopped canned chipotle peppers in adobo sauce**
- ½ cup bottled hoisin sauce
- ¼ cup honey
- 2 tablespoons cider vinegar
- 2 tablespoons Dijon-style mustard
- 2 cloves garlic, minced

1 For rub, in a small bowl stir together paprika, black pepper, and onion salt. Trim fat from ribs. Place ribs in a shallow dish. Squeeze limes over ribs and rub the cut surfaces of the lime halves over ribs. Sprinkle the rub evenly over ribs; rub in with your fingers. Cover and chill for 1 to 4 hours.

2 In a smoker arrange preheated coals, wood chunks, and water pan according to the manufacturer's directions. Pour water into pan. Place ribs, bone sides down, on the grill rack over water pan. (Or place ribs in a rib rack; place on grill rack over pan.) Cover and smoke for 3 to 4 hours or until tender. Add additional coals and water as needed to maintain temperature and moisture.

3 Meanwhile, for sauce, if using dried chipotle peppers, soak them in warm water for 30 minutes; drain well and finely chop. In a small saucepan stir together the chipotle peppers, hoisin sauce, honey, vinegar, mustard, and garlic. Cook and stir over low heat until heated through. Before serving, brush ribs with some of the sauce. Pass the remaining sauce.

***NOTE:** For the most smoke production, soak wood chunks in enough water to cover for at least 1 hour before grilling. Drain wood chips before using.

****NOTE:** Because chile peppers contain volatile oils that can burn skin and eyes, avoid direct contact with them as much as possible. When working with chile peppers, wear plastic or rubber gloves. If your bare hands touch the peppers, wash your hands and nails well with soap and warm water.

PER ¼ RIBS + ¼ CUP SAUCE: 509 cal., 25 g total fat (8 g sat. fat), 110 mg chol., 898 mg sodium, 40 g carbo., 1 g fiber, 28 g pro.

4. Place the dried chipotle peppers in a bowl. Add enough warm water to the bowl to cover the peppers. Let stand on the counter for 30 minutes.

5. Drain the peppers and blot dry. Cut off and discard the stems. Chop peppers into tiny pieces. Combine chopped peppers, including the seeds, to the ingredients for sauce.

6. When the ribs are done, brush with sauce. Remove the ribs from the grill and cut between the bones into serving-size pieces.

THIS PIQUANT LATIN-INSPIRED SALSA HAS FLAVORS ASSERTIVE ENOUGH TO STAND UP TO HICKORY-SMOKED BRISKET.

Smoked Brisket with Black Bean and Corn Salsa

BEEF BRISKET IS AVAILABLE IN TWO CUTS. THE MORE EXPENSIVE "FLAT" CUT IS QUITE LEAN. THE "POINT" CUT CONTAINS MORE FAT AND IS THEREFORE MUCH MORE FLAVORFUL, MAKING IT THE BETTER CHOICE FOR SMOKING.

PREP: 20 MINUTES **MARINATE:** 6 HOURS
SMOKE: 5 HOURS **STAND:** 15 MINUTES
MAKES: 8 TO 10 SERVINGS

- 1 3- to 3½-pound fresh beef brisket
- 1 12-ounce can beer
- ¾ cup lime juice
- ½ cup chopped onion (1 medium)
- 3 tablespoons vegetable oil
- 3 tablespoons steak sauce
- 2 teaspoons chili powder
- 2 teaspoons ground cumin
- 4 cloves garlic, minced
- 1 recipe Black Bean and Corn Salsa
- 6 to 8 oak or hickory wood chunks*

1 Trim fat from meat. Place meat in a large resealable plastic bag set in a shallow dish. For marinade, in a medium bowl stir together beer, lime juice, onion, oil, steak sauce, chili powder, cumin, and garlic. Pour over meat in bag; seal bag. Turn to coat meat. Marinate in the refrigerator for 6 to 24 hours, turning bag occasionally.

2 Meanwhile, prepare Black Bean and Corn Salsa. Cover and chill.

3 Drain meat, discarding marinade.

4 In a smoker arrange preheated coals, wood chunks, and water pan according to the manufacturer's directions. Pour water into pan. Place meat on grill rack over water pan. Cover and smoke for 5 to 6 hours or until a fork can easily be inserted into meat. Add additional coals and water as needed to maintain temperature and moisture. Do not add wood after the first 2 hours of smoking. (Too much smoke can give a bitter taste to smoked meat.)

5 Remove brisket from smoker. Thinly slice meat across the grain. Serve meat with salsa.

BLACK BEAN AND CORN SALSA: In a large bowl stir together 3 cups seeded and chopped tomatoes; one 15-ounce can black beans, rinsed and drained; 1 cup frozen whole kernel corn, thawed; ¼ cup thinly sliced green onions (2); 3 tablespoons snipped fresh cilantro; 2 tablespoons vegetable oil; 2 tablespoons lime juice; 1 fresh jalapeño chile pepper, seeded and finely chopped;** ½ teaspoon salt; ¼ teaspoon ground cumin; and ¼ teaspoon black pepper.

***NOTE:** For the most smoke production, soak wood chunks in enough water to cover for at least 1 hour before grilling. Drain wood chips before using.

****NOTE:** Because chile peppers contain volatile oils that can burn skin and eyes, avoid direct contact with them as much as possible. When working with chile peppers, wear plastic or rubber gloves. If your bare hands touch the peppers, wash your hands and nails well with soap and warm water.

PER 5 OUNCES BRISKET + ¾ CUP SALSA: 381 cal., 17 g total fat (5 g sat. fat), 83 mg chol., 429 mg sodium, 17 g carbo., 4 g fiber, 40 g pro.

STEP-BY-STEP

1. Slice off the layer of fat on top of the brisket. Trim off any other bits of fat that you can.

2. For the marinade, mix the lime juice, onion, oil, steak sauce, chili powder, cumin, and garlic. Add the beer slowly to control foaming.

3. To slice the brisket across the grain, cut it on the diagonal. Start by cutting off a corner and continue cutting into thin slices.

STEP-BY-STEP

1. Slice off the layer of fat on the top of the brisket. Trim off any other bits of fat that you can.

2. Sprinkle the rub evenly over the meat. Pat the rub into the meat with your fingers.

3. Combine the ingredients for the Vinegar Mop Sauce in a bowl. Whisk to mix well. Use the mop sauce to brush over the meat during the last hour of smoking.

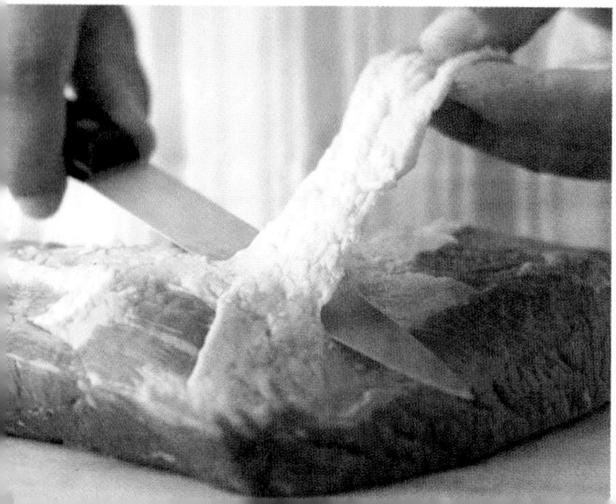

Texans' Beef Brisket

GIVE BEEF BRISKET A LEG UP INTO THE FLAVOR SADDLE BY BRUSHING THE BRISKET WITH VINEGAR MOP SAUCE AS IT SMOKES. OCCASIONAL BASTING WILL UP THE ANTE IN TENDERNESS AND TASTE.

PREP: 30 MINUTES **SMOKE:** 5 HOURS
MAKES: 12 SERVINGS

- 1 recipe Vinegar Mop Sauce
- 1 3- to 3½-pound fresh beef brisket
- 2 teaspoons seasoned salt
- 1 teaspoon paprika
- 1 teaspoon chili powder
- 1 teaspoon garlic pepper
- ½ teaspoon ground cumin
- 6 to 8 mesquite, hickory, or pecan wood chunks*
- 1 recipe Spicy Beer Sauce
- 12 kaiser rolls, split and toasted (optional)

1 Prepare Vinegar Mop Sauce; set aside. Trim fat from meat. For rub, in a small bowl stir together seasoned salt, paprika, chili powder, garlic pepper, and cumin. Sprinkle the rub evenly over meat; rub in with your fingers.

2 In a smoker arrange preheated coals, wood chunks, and water pan according to the manufacturer's directions. Pour water into pan. Place meat on the grill rack over water pan. Cover and smoke for 5 to 6 hours or until a fork can easily be inserted into meat, brushing occasionally with Vinegar Mop Sauce during the last hour of smoking. Add additional coals and water as needed to maintain temperature and moisture. Do not add wood after the first 2 hours of smoking. (Too much smoke can give a bitter taste to smoked meat.)

3 Remove brisket from smoker. Thinly slice meat across the grain. Serve with Spicy Beer Sauce. If desired, serve meat and sauce in kaiser rolls.

VINEGAR MOP SAUCE: In a small bowl stir together ¼ cup beer, 4 teaspoons Worcestershire sauce, 1 tablespoon vegetable oil, 1 tablespoon vinegar, ½ teaspoon jalapeño mustard or other hot-style mustard, and a few dashes bottled hot pepper sauce.

SPICY BEER SAUCE: In a medium saucepan cook ¾ cup chopped, seeded, peeled tomato (1 large); ½ cup chopped onion (1 medium); and ½ cup chopped green sweet pepper in 2 tablespoons hot butter over medium heat about 5 minutes or until onion is tender, stirring occasionally. Stir in 1 cup bottled chili sauce, ½ cup beer, ½ cup cider vinegar, 2 tablespoons packed brown sugar, 1 to 2 tablespoons chopped canned chipotle peppers in adobo sauce (see note, page 361), 1¼ teaspoons black pepper, and ½ teaspoon salt. Bring to boiling; reduce heat. Simmer, uncovered, about 10 minutes or until reduced to about 2¼ cups.

***NOTE:** For the most smoke production, soak wood chunks in enough water to cover for at least 1 hour before grilling. Drain wood chips before using.

PER 3 OUNCES MEAT + 3 TABLESPOONS SAUCE: 253 cal., 12 g total fat (4 g sat. fat), 77 mg chol., 770 mg sodium, 11 g carbo., 2 g fiber, 24 g pro.

4. Combine the ingredients for the Spicy Beer Sauce in a saucepan and simmer for 10 minutes, cooking the sauce down to 1¼ cups.

5. Add additional wood chunks to maintain the smoke during the first 2 hours. Adding wood chunks later may produce a bitter taste in the meat.

6. To slice the brisket across the grain, cut it on the diagonal. Start by cutting off a corner and continue cutting into thin slices.

Ginger-Orange Beef Ribs

A FEW SIMPLE STIR-INS BATHE BOTTLED BARBECUE SAUCE IN BRIGHT ASIAN FLAVORS—AND MAKE THIS CITRUSSY SAUCE A PERFECT PARTNER FOR ROBUST BEEF RIBS.

PREP: 10 MINUTES **SMOKE:** 2½ HOURS
MAKES: 4 SERVINGS

- 2 teaspoons paprika
- ½ to 1 teaspoon salt
- ½ teaspoon black pepper
- 3 to 4 pounds beef back ribs (about 8 ribs)
- ½ cup bottled barbecue sauce
- ¼ cup frozen orange juice concentrate, thawed
- 2 tablespoons soy sauce
- 1 tablespoon grated fresh ginger
- 6 to 8 hickory or oak wood chunks*

1 For rub, in a small bowl stir together paprika, salt, and pepper. Trim fat from ribs. Sprinkle the rub evenly over ribs; rub in with your fingers.

2 For sauce, in a small bowl stir together barbecue sauce, orange juice concentrate, soy sauce, and ginger. Set aside.

3 In a smoker arrange preheated coals, wood chunks, and water pan according to the manufacturer's directions. Pour water into pan. Place ribs, meaty sides down, on the grill rack over water pan. (Or place ribs in a rib rack; place on grill rack over pan.) Cover and smoke for 2½ to 3 hours or until ribs are tender, brushing once with sauce during the last 15 minutes of cooking. Add additional coals and water as needed to maintain temperature and moisture. Pass any remaining sauce with ribs.

***NOTE:** For the most smoke production, soak wood chunks in enough water to cover for at least 1 hour before grilling. Drain wood chips before using.

PER 2 RIBS + ¼ CUP SAUCE: 277 cal., 12 g total fat (5 g sat. fat), 79 mg chol., 897 mg sodium, 13 g carbo., 1 g fiber, 28 g pro.

STEP-BY-STEP

1. Using a sharp knife, cut away as much of the fat as you can.

2. To make the sauce, combine the barbecue sauce, orange juice concentrate, soy sauce, and fresh ginger. Stir to mix well.

3. To ensure that the smoker maintains the proper temperature, add 8 to 10 briquettes every 45 to 60 minutes.

4. Place the ribs on the grill rack with the bone sides down.

5. During the last 15 minutes of smoking, brush the meaty side of the ribs with the ginger-orange sauce.

6. Remove the ribs from the smoker and place on a cutting board. To serve, cut into individual ribs by slicing between the bones.

A

B

C

D

E-F

N-O

P

T

V-W

Y-Z

METRIC INFORMATION

PRODUCT DIFFERENCES

Most of the ingredients called for in the recipes in this book are available in most countries. However, some are known by different names. Here are some common American ingredients and their possible counterparts:

- Sugar (white) is granulated, fine granulated, or castor sugar.
- Powdered sugar is icing sugar.
- All-purpose flour is enriched, bleached or unbleached white household flour. When self-rising flour is used in place of all-purpose flour in a recipe that calls for leavening, omit the leavening agent (baking soda or baking powder) and salt.
- Light-color corn syrup is golden syrup.
- Cornstarch is cornflour.
- Baking soda is bicarbonate of soda.
- Vanilla or vanilla extract is vanilla essence.
- Green, red, or yellow sweet peppers are capsicums or bell peppers.
- Golden raisins are sultanas.

VOLUME AND WEIGHT

The United States traditionally uses cup measures for liquid and solid ingredients. The chart below shows the approximate imperial and metric equivalents. If you are accustomed to weighing solid ingredients, the following approximate equivalents will be helpful.

- 1 cup butter, castor sugar, or rice = 8 ounces = ½ pound = 250 grams
- 1 cup flour = 4 ounces = ¼ pound = 125 grams
- 1 cup icing sugar = 5 ounces = 150 grams
- Canadian and U.S. volume for a cup measure is 8 fluid ounces (237 ml), but the standard metric equivalent is 250 ml.
- 1 British imperial cup is 10 fluid ounces.
- In Australia, 1 tablespoon equals 20 ml, and there are 4 teaspoons in the Australian tablespoon.
- Spoon measures are used for smaller amounts of ingredients. Although the size of the tablespoon varies slightly in different countries, for practical purposes and for recipes in this book, a straight substitution is all that's necessary. Measurements made using cups or spoons always should be level unless stated otherwise.

COMMON WEIGHT RANGE REPLACEMENTS

Imperial / U.S.	Metric
½ ounce	15 g
1 ounce	25 g or 30 g
4 ounces (¼ pound)	115 g or 125 g
8 ounces (½ pound)	225 g or 250 g
16 ounces (1 pound)	450 g or 500 g
1¼ pounds	625 g
1½ pounds	750 g
2 pounds or 2¼ pounds	1,000 g or 1 Kg

OVEN TEMPERATURE EQUIVALENTS

Fahrenheit Setting	Celsius Setting	Gas Setting
300°F	150°C	Gas Mark 2 (very low)
325°F	160°C	Gas Mark 3 (low)
350°F	180°C	Gas Mark 4 (moderate)
375°F	190°C	Gas Mark 5 (moderate)
400°F	200°C	Gas Mark 6 (hot)
425°F	220°C	Gas Mark 7 (hot)
450°F	230°C	Gas Mark 8 (very hot)
475°F	240°C	Gas Mark 9 (very hot)
500°F	260°C	Gas Mark 10 (extremely hot)
Broil	Broil	Grill

*Electric and gas ovens may be calibrated using celsius. However, for an electric oven, increase celsius setting 10 to 20 degrees when cooking above 160°C. For convection or forced air ovens (gas or electric), lower the temperature setting 25°F/10°C when cooking at all heat levels.

BAKING PAN SIZES

Imperial / U.S.	Metric
9×1½-inch round cake pan	22- or 23×4-cm (1.5 L)
9×1½-inch pie plate	22- or 23×4-cm (1 L)
8×8×2-inch square cake pan	20×5-cm (2 L)
9×9×2-inch square cake pan	22- or 23×4.5-cm (2.5 L)
11×7×1½-inch baking pan	28×17×4-cm (2 L)
2-quart rectangular baking pan	30×19×4.5-cm (3 L)
13×9×2-inch baking pan	34×22×4.5-cm (3.5 L)
15×10×1-inch jelly roll pan	40×25×2-cm
9×5×3-inch loaf pan	23×13×8-cm (2 L)
2-quart casserole	2 L

U.S. / STANDARD METRIC EQUIVALENTS

⅛ teaspoon = 0.5 ml
¼ teaspoon = 1 ml
½ teaspoon = 2 ml
1 teaspoon = 5 ml
1 tablespoon = 15 ml
2 tablespoons = 25 ml
¼ cup = 2 fluid ounces = 50 ml
⅓ cup = 3 fluid ounces = 75 ml
½ cup = 4 fluid ounces = 125 ml
⅔ cup = 5 fluid ounces = 150 ml
¾ cup = 6 fluid ounces = 175 ml
1 cup = 8 fluid ounces = 250 ml
2 cups = 1 pint = 500 ml
1 quart = 1 litre